LONDON'S TEEMING STREETS 1830–1914

LONDON'S TEEMING STREETS 1830–1914

James Winter

London and New York

First published 1993
by Routledge
2 Park Square, Milton Park, Abingdon, Oxon, OX14 4RN

Simultaneously published in the USA and Canada
by Routledge Inc.
711 Third Avenue, New York, NY 10017

© 1993 James Winter

Phototypeset in 10 on 12 point Palatino by Intype, London

All rights reserved. No part of this book may be
reprinted or reproduced or utilized in any form or by
any electronic, mechanical, or other means, now known
or hereafter invented, including photocopying and
recording, or in any information storage or retrieval
system, wihtout permission in writing from the
publishers.

British Library Cataloguing in Publication Data
A catalogue record for this book is available from the British Library

Library of Congress Cataloging in Publication Data
Winter, James H.
London's teeming streets: 1830–1914/James Winter.
p. cm.
First published in London in 1993 and simultaneously published in
the USA and Canada.
Includes bibliographical references and index.
1. City traffic–England–London–History. I. Title.
HE363.G75L687 1993
388.4'09421'09034–dc20   92-37661

ISBN13: 978-0-415-03590-3 (hbk)
ISBN13: 978-0-415-51322-7 (pbk)

Front Jacket illustration: engraving by Gustave Doré
showing congested traffic by Ludgate Circus. From
G. Doré and B. Jerrold, *London: A Pilgrimage* (1872).

CONTENTS

List of plates   vii
Acknowledgements   viii
Introduction   ix

1 IMAGINING   1
2 STRAIGHTENING   16
3 SMOOTHING AND REGULATING   34
4 POLICING   50
5 ENJOYING   65
6 WORKING   100
7 CLEANING   118
8 RESCUING   135
9 BREATHING   153
10 INHABITING   173
11 PLANNING   190
CONCLUSION   207

Notes   217
Bibliography   238
Index   251

PLATES

(between pages 80 and 99)
1 Fleet Street in the 1890s
2 The Thames Embankment under construction (1867)
3 Holborn Viaduct nearing completion
4 London's first traffic signal (1868)
5 The organ in the court
6 German band on "Placid Place"
7 Olive Christian Malvery as flower girl
8 *Rus in Urbe*
9 A hard frost, February, 1865
10 Thaw after a snowstorm
11 Charles Cochrane reviewing his street orderlies
12 Meeting of the Health of Towns Association (1847)
13 A member of MacGregor's Shoe-Black Brigade
14 Salvation Army march (*c.* 1890)
15 Invitations to salvation
16 London's first people's park
17 George John Shaw-Lefevre, Lord Eversley (1831–1928)
18 Gender, class, and street use
19 Two generations in tandem (1913)
20 Confluence of traffic from Cannon Street and Queen Victoria Street
21 Kingsway in 1905

ACKNOWLEDGEMENTS

On the long journey from there to here, many friends and colleagues gave directions when I wandered, especially Judith Allen, Peter Bailey, Tom Blom, George Edgerton, Tina Loo, Richard Mackie, Harvey Mitchell, Fred Stockholder, John Norris, Peter Ward, and Robert Winter. Margerie Sinel warned about rough places and helped grind some of them down. Grants from the SSHRC and from the University of British Columbia supplied much of the fuel; seat C 6 in the Round Room of the British Library provided a fixed place; Brian Hurwitz gave me shelter and sustenance of every kind. My thanks to them all go far beyond the limits set by the conventions of formal acknowledgements. Even more scope would be required to convey the gratitude I feel toward Pierrette, my wife, constant companion, and well-disposed critic, and toward Ruth Richardson who lighted the way, from conception to completion: no traveller through nineteenth-century London could possibly find a better guide.

Thanks are also due to the following institutions for permission to reproduce illustrations from their collections: The British Library for the photograph of Olive Malvery from *The Soul Market*; the Bodleian Library, University of Oxford, for the postal card reproduction showing a Shoeblack and the cartoon of the German Band; the Greater London Photographic Library for the photographs of Kingsway in 1905, the LCC tramcar and trailer, Fleet Street in 1890, and Traffic on Queen Victoria Street; the Salvation Army, International Heritage Centre, for the photograph of the Army march on Whitechapel Road and the cartoon of "Happy Eliza" Haynes. In addition, I wish to thank *The London Journal* for permission to reproduce passages from my article, "The Agitator of the Metropolis," which appeared in vol. 14 (1989), 29–42.

INTRODUCTION

Since the time when, as a teenaged soldier, I negotiated my way through blackout and brown fog, the streets of London have been among my preoccupations; but always my view has been that of an outsider and not, in any true sense, of a direct participant. My home lies half a world away. The street where I live was once on the harborfront fringe of a small town that grew up around a lumber mill late in the nineteenth century. Now my street stands on the edge of one of those central city restoration projects that one finds in almost every North American city. Gold Rush era buildings have been stripped back to their handsome brickwork and the huge timber beams inside have been exposed; the main street has been paved with brick and stone; ornamental cast-iron lamp-posts are back again; in the summer months, two young ladies in flowery hats and long, old-fashioned dresses give directions to tourists who disembark from cruise ships to look in the shops that sell the things tourists seem willing to buy. So far, my part of the street has not been absorbed into that effusion of commercialized nostalgia but serves as the border area between fantasy and hard and not always sober reality. A block away is a shelter for the homeless; outside my door is an agency for assisting street people who have mental illnesses. The building which I share with other middle-class condominium owners was once a shelter for girls who had drifted into the city and found themselves alone and unprotected. A curiously shaped Anglican church not far away once ran the shelter and still continues to tend the sick, hungry, and dazed casualties of urban life. Just south of the church is one of the largest Chinese communities on the continent, and there the streets are jammed with shoppers making their way around stalls full of bak tsoi, gai tsoi, gow tsoi, bitter melons, hairy melons, winter melons, baskets of dried shrimp, squid, abalone, tanks of live fish and crabs, enormous frogs in wicker cages, beautiful pots filled with black-crusted duck eggs. The drama of that theatre makes the principal shopping streets and underground shopping malls

INTRODUCTION

a fifteen-minute-walk to the west seem, if possible, more banal and antiseptic than they already are.

In my city, traffic and transit become ever more pressing issues as two-income families discover they must go farther away from the centre where they work to escape the mounting ground rents. Bulldozers are constantly at work carving housing plots out of market gardens and out of the forests that used to give the city its reason for being. Not far away, but invisible behind another building on my street, the harbor narrows and a bridge connects a separate municipality on the North Shore with the major artery bringing vehicles into the city from the east. To unplug the stoppage that tends to occur there at rush hour, a new tunnel delivers the driver to the bridge and offers a sudden, stunning view of ocean and snow-capped peaks; nevertheless, concerned citizens are now asking how the bridge is to hold the heavier flow of traffic and how the receiving community, already chewing its way up the mountain side, will be affected. Not surprisingly there is a call for more planning and more co-operation between the various local authorities, as the once well-defined city transforms itself into a metropolitan region.

The setting is breathtaking, the climate is gentle, the pace of life is relaxed; otherwise this city is much like any other, the problems of growth and decay, movement and congestion, delight and fear not much different in quality from what other Western European and North American cities have been experiencing for a longer time than most modern urban dwellers are aware. Like most urbanites, we treat our problems and choices one by one. They become events which, when they are given any extension in time at all, are thought of as peculiar to the latter part of the twentieth century. We cannot think clearly about events which are presented to us episodically because we cannot see them clearly. Ferdinand Braudel writes:

> Take the word *event*: for myself I would limit it, and imprison it within the short time span: an event is explosive, a *"nouvelle sonnante"* ["a matter of moment"] as they said in the sixteenth century. Its delusive smoke fills the minds of its contemporaries, but it does not last, and its flame can scarcely ever be discerned.[1]

The aim of what follows is to take what Braudel calls the *longue durée*, to look back to the time when urbanites began to think systematically about the problems and opportunities of urban living and to come up with suggestions and projects for "improvement." The search is confined to London, partly because it was one of the first great Western cities to begin this process of analyzing the urban condition and of implementing reform programs and partly because, I must confess, it is the city I know and love best. The examination starts in the 1830s,

INTRODUCTION

that remarkable decade when so many were full of expectant enthusiasms about ways to make almost everything better, and ends in 1914, when the era of "horse-drawn London" was coming to an end and the era of speed, pollution, and parking had already begun.

The tone adopted will be appreciative, especially when the topic under discussion brings forward reformers who deserve to be remembered; yet there will also be the occasional touch of mild irony, since I cannot help feeling glad, as often as not, that the improvers hardly ever succeeded in making the streets of Victorian and Edwardian London as smooth, uncluttered, efficient, and orderly as they wished. A thread, which the first chapter discloses, is meant to run through all that follows: the perception of the public street as the emblem of individual freedom and the awareness that uncontrolled growth was creating a monster. Some reformers were aware of the tension between the wish to move without being obstructed and the wish to remove from the streets everything that obstructed movement. However, they were constrained in their search for an equilibrium between these two irreconcilables by the metaphors they drew from medicine and adapted to focus and explain their agendas for "improvement."

The language of medical diagnosis and pathology gave shape and force to all kinds of nineteenth-century reform programs, street reform being but one example. Straighteners, regulators, cleaners, purifiers, conservationists, and promoters of the municipal ideal, liberals most of them, tried to balance their vision of a London that was ordered, rational, efficient, healthy, and safe, in other words, "modern," with a sense that the freedom of the public thoroughfare disclosed what it meant to be English, a deep-seated feeling that they shared with most of their compatriots. In the first chapter I explore this difficulty of reconciling the metaphor of reform and a liberal devotion to individual self-determination. In the conclusion, I use Kingsway as an example of the consequence of failing to resolve that tension in a satisfactory way. The chapters between introduce qualifications, complicating factors, cross-currents between various kinds of reform programs and outlooks, and these are intended to subvert hopes that the secret of how to produce a "good" street can be easily unlocked or that the fabric and function of London's streets were shaped by one structural determinant or by one discourse. Attentive eyes will perceive that I have pirated conceptual tools from others and then gone on, perhaps without perfect consistency, to be skeptical about them when they tidy up, as they are meant to do, the messy leavings of past events.

The approach in what follows is topical, but the reformers, the willing or unwilling agents of reform, and in one case, that of Eva D'Angeley, the object of reform, appear in rough chronological order. It is difficult to say whether choice of person suggested context or the

INTRODUCTION

other way around. Desire to tell the story of Charles Cochrane led to the subject of keeping the streets clean, whereas a wish to examine the attempt to preserve some of the "natural" surroundings from the city's remorseless sprawl required that I pay attention to George John Shaw-Lefevre. The rich variety of reform approaches also needed exemplification. Thus MacGregor, the evangelical; Hill, the paternalist; Gomme, the municipal "socialist"; Babbage, the technocrat; and Mayne, the pragmatist, appeared along with a collection of nineteenth-century liberals, when, borrowing Lytton Strachey's net, I began to haul out characters from the rich and teeming pool of possibilities.

1

IMAGINING

Passageways and organic metaphors have natural affinities. From earliest times the human body has been thought of as a container made up of conduits for conveying blood and humors. Egyptian medicine understood the working of the body by means of the metaphor of the Nile's flooding and receding.[1] One branch of physiological studies in early eighteenth century Britain and on the Continent also defined the body as a structure of tubes and vessels and understood health to be the maintenance of a proper velocity of blood-flow through them.[2] This line of inquiry strongly impressed itself on medical amateurs and remained alive in metaphor after the main current of physiological studies was directed elsewhere.

Conversely, we have always read our built environments with our bodies.[3] Especially in the eighteenth century, when citizens of a number of European cities began to be conscious of an unprecedented expansion to areas outside the familiar margins, circulatory imagery, much in vogue since William Harvey's discoveries in the early seventeenth century, filled a need to express the anxieties aroused by such blurring of boundary lines.[4]

Centrifugal and centripetal movements seemed to characterize both the body physical and the body social. The tides of humanity that flowed in with the morning light and out again in the late afternoon seemed to be drawn into the city's heart, and then back out again, along crowded corridors. As this perception took hold in the eighteenth century, the notion of what a street was began to alter. Its definition tended to cast loose from the original meaning of "stratum" (any kind of artificial layer wherever constructed) and become something quintessentially urban: a passageway lined on one or both sides with a more or less regular and continuous row of buildings. Thus city dwellers among us may have for our addresses a Close, Crescent, Walk, or Way and do our shopping on an Avenue, Road, Terrace, or Place; but law and general usage will recognize them all as streets.[5] Furthermore, the streets we live on or frequent testify to our aspirations or to the way fate has dealt with them. They also supply us with lines of social demarcation inside an environment that is otherwise in constant flux. They are fixed points in our turning world and give definition to spaces lacking in margins.

That our cities are constantly tearing down boundary lines arouses anxiety in us, as it did in our predecessors. Thus we are able to bridge the years that separate us and respond in an immediate way to the dismay expressed by a mid-nineteenth-century Londoner at how his city seemed to be intent on devouring everything around it. It creeps, wrote W.J. Loftie, "like the tide of the sea, slowly but surely, year by year, and obliterates, as it goes, all the original features of the countryside." First to be eroded away are the green fields, then the villages with their old houses and historical memories, and finally the topography itself: "rivers and ravines are masked, hills are levelled, marshes are hidden. A flood of brick fills up the hollows. The brooks run far underground. The flats are elevated, and the heights depressed."[6] Perhaps we have lived inside this process so long that we no longer have quite the same sense of alarm, but we can still share the feeling, to use Loftie's word, of being "contaminated" by all this eating away, swallowing up, digesting, and excreting.

It would be in the London of the late eighteenth and early nineteenth centuries that Loftie's perception of chaos and the need to find ways to order it would have been first and most strongly felt. In that phenomenon among cities, confusion had a long history. During the Tudor period wheeled vehicles began to alter the circulatory system which had up to then been organized around the grand highway of the Thames, and this change caused people, but particularly visitors, to join their concept of the city with notions of disconnectedness and disarray. The phenomenal rate of population and spatial growth in the eighteenth century deepened the sense of those who jostled and threaded their way through swarms of strangers that each was "one atom in a drift of human dust,"[7] moving through the circulatory apparatus of some huge creature which was breathing, growing, and responding to forces beyond comprehension and control. Some people, unsettled by this perception, gave expression to their feelings in images of London as a parasite feeding off the countryside, Cobbett's "Infernal Wen" being one memorable variation on this theme.[8] Others, especially in the eighteenth century, observed this seemingly inexorable expansion with wonder. They used images of a hub, a giant market and entrepôt, of a vortex or spongelike invertebrate which drew vital and inert particles in and out. Men and women who were in tune with Dr Johnson's outlook took delight in the vast theatre and emporium of human variety and eccentricity. For them the London street was the epitome of life itself.

Subsequently, writers of poetry, fiction, and social reportage continued to make use of this profusion of imagery; and, as uneasiness about the blurring of margins increased, so did the use of illness analogies. Earlier it tended to be the irrepressible energy of the urban organism which fascinated or appalled; however, by the time Queen Victoria came to the throne, there appeared an overlay of concern about the possibility that something debilitating and self-destructive might be part of this growth process, fears that excessive strain was being placed on the delicate mechanism which determined how much should be drawn into the city's heart and how much vital fluid should be pumped out to the extremities. If that balance should be disrupted, then the circulatory system might cease to function properly, arteries might harden, and the body become sluggish or seriously ill. A journal article in 1866, entitled "How Our Millions Circulate," expressed it this way: "The great emporium of trade has been making blood too fast, and now its heart has become so over-burthened, that it can hardly perform its function."[9]

Now and then this kind of anxiety can be discovered in the eighteenth century. Early in Laurence Sterne's novel we learn that Tristram's father, Walter Shandy, when he had occasion to refer to the London he so despised, was prone to use the symbol of "distemper," a condition "where blood and spirits were driven up into the head faster than they could find their ways down. . . ." When this happened, he asserted (continuing the analogy between the human body and the body politic), "a stoppage of circulation must ensue, which was death in both cases."[10] This same idea, presented in a clinical rather than a satirical mode, can be found in a book published in 1766, about the bewildering changes taking place in the fabric of the city. The author was a noted architect and engraver, a friend of Dr Johnson's, John Glynn. He cautioned that "when the limbs extend themselves too fast, and grow out of proportion to the body which is to nourish and sustain them, it may very rationally be supposed that a consumption may be the consequence."[11]

The public at large was not likely to shrug off such a warning as this since "consumption" was a word freighted with anxiety and mystery.[12] Moreover, the equation of health with balance and proportion was deeply implanted in the culture. How that idea could be applied in the late eighteenth and early nineteenth centuries is demonstrated in William Buchan's popular manual of home diagnosis and remedy, *Domestic Medicine*, first published in 1770 and widely available in new editions into the mid-1820s. Again and again he returns the reader to the debilitating consequences of pumping into the system more than can be expelled by normal, natural means. If, Buchan warns, the body retains for too long that which it ought to expel or dissipate, the result is a "plethora, or too great fulness of the vessels," a condition which can cause "acrimony and putrescence." Fullness, he continues, is brought on by irregular eating, drinking, and elimination habits or by behavior which upsets "the animal economy." Blood-letting is, as might be expected, among his suggested remedies, but his emphasis is on prevention: more exercise; consumption of pure vegetables; and, whenever possible, filling the lungs with fresh, country air – escaping, in other words, the contagion, pollution, adulteration, excessive stimulation, and over-indulgence commonly associated with city environments.[13] This concept of plethora long outlasted in metaphor its value to medical science. Imagination reaches for what it needs to control anxiety, and that need was never greater than during the visitations of cholera in the 1830s and 1840s. It was at this time that cholera and fever came to be thought of as urban illnesses and a link formed between sanitary and urban reform, a connection which was bound to produce rich imagery,[14] especially since concern about density and epidemic coincided with a cluster of circumstances which, acting together, created a sense of emergency. Benthamite utilitarians joined with philanthropic enthusiasts to initiate reform legislation at a time when the ferment surrounding the parliamentary reform movement made the central government especially alert to the need to find ways to reduce popular discord. At the same time, an increase in the tempo of population growth and suburban expansion in London, facilitated by new forms of public transport, drew attention to the capital as a special problem. Out of this perception of crisis arose a consciousness that a new kind of human arrangement, the metropolis, was coming into being, the defining feature of which would be sustained growth and an ever-increasing complexity in the interaction of its separate functions.[15] In this atmosphere reformers were drawn to the possibility that if they could understand the structure of the metropolis, they might be able to control growth, find rational means to direct expansion, and treat the endemic "distempers," not by attending to one organ at a time, but by treating every component of this great body as part of one interacting whole.

Thus a sense of loss of control gave rise to an urge to control, to treat the urban illness. Body and contagion metaphors as well as purification rituals articulated the reform agenda and were the by-products of this age of improvement.[16] According to the anthropologist, Mary Douglas, the main function of these metaphors and rituals is to "impose system on an inherently untidy experience."[17] How untidy the margins of London must have seemed in the 1830s can be sensed if one imagines what it would have been like to walk them several decades earlier. A man of that time, if a sturdy walker, could make it around the built-up area north of the river in three or four hours. Edgware Road would have taken him north along the western limits;

at Marylebone he would have turned eastward and made his way to the City on the New Road, keeping on his left cultivated fields and a large nursery occupying the site where Euston Station would eventually be built. He would then have started on the leg taking him back to the river before reaching Hackney and Stepney, in the 1820s still mostly a patchwork of market gardens. Had our walker decided to visit Camden Town, Islington, Bayswater, Brompton, Chelsea, or Knightsbridge, he would have been aware that he was leaving the city and making an excursion across fields to communities which were still distinct entities.[18] Asked to define his city geographically, our Regency pedestrian could have done so, although not without difficulties; but by the time of Queen Victoria's Coronation he would probably have met the request with a shrug or perhaps have given an ironic smile and answered, "where the trees start turning black." If pressed, he might then have mentioned the various administrative districts which had been established in recent years, one for the Metropolitan Police, one for the Post Office, another for census purposes and so on, none of these coinciding. Such jurisdictions needed boundary lines, but these were drawn to fit administrative convenience and not the constantly changing city.

Reform also required conceptual and geographic limits. It could single out a specific evil as the root cause of urban sickness – overcrowded slums or defective sanitation facilities – and establish parameters. During the 1830s, however, reformers in greater numbers became aware that cutting a swath through the rookery of St Giles increased density elsewhere, that unplugging traffic stoppages by reconstructing Cannon Street aggravated the congestion around St Paul's Churchyard, and that better drains in Holborn contaminated water supplies taken from the Thames. Recognizing this, they wanted to treat the ever-evolving metropolis as if it were an entity. This difficulty in finding a conceptual framework for urban reform and the need to do so explains why so many early Victorians came to define the city as a circulatory system rather than a fixed place. That redefinition meant that attention was directed to the network of veins and arteries which had, in a sense, become what London was. Groups and individuals intent on "improvement" therefore tended to take up the already well-tried circulatory metaphor, to elaborate on it, and to adjust it to fit their purposes.

An article which appeared in an 1846 edition of the *Illustrated London News* provides an example of this technique. One passage deserves quoting at some length because it contains so many of the essential ingredients, rhetorical and figurative:

The intercourse and activity of an empire, and the commerce of half a world now run through streets and ways built nearly two centuries ago, and very badly even for the age that planned them, or rather built them without any plan at all. The result is that the streets of London are choked by their ordinary traffic, and the life blood of the huge giant is compelled to run through veins and arteries that have never expanded since the days and dimensions of its infancy. What wonder is it that the circulation is an unhealthy one? That the quantity carried to each part of the frame is insufficient for the demands of its bulk and strength, that there is dangerous pressure in the main channels and morbid disturbance of the current, in all causing daily stoppages of the vital functions, a kind of diurnal apoplexy which the ministrations of Mr. Daniel Whittle Harvey and his surgeons palliate slightly but can never prevent. No widening of these channels between point and point within the great fabric can remove the pressure, at best it will only redistribute it, leaving it on some points, to concentrate on another. The real remedy is the opening of entirely new routes through the whole mess.[19]

Here we notice the familiar image of a body ailing because its bulk exceeds the capacity of its circulatory system, only now the predicted consequence is not consumption, dropsy, or fullness of the blood vessels but cerebral haemorrhage, a stroke caused by an obstruction, a clot. The surgeons (Harvey was the City of London Police Commissioner) are advised to make a radical intervention and reroute the main arterial channels, to alter the arrangements of the entire system instead of simply applying local treatment to this or that "morbid disturbance" whenever it declares itself. Instead of recommending an abstemious diet and plenty of fresh country air, this prescription calls for surgery to correct by human art defects or sepsis that natural processes cannot be counted on to cure. Therefore such an approach was, for purposes of reform, an improvement over the plethora model. A methodical program for rebuilding the cardio-vascular system, thereby preventing clots from forming, gave more specific direction, supplied a more compelling rationale, and offered greater hope to an increasingly urbanized population than palliative regimes for removing groups or individuals as far as possible from the poisons which were thought to be intrinsic to city life. These palliatives and the notion of plethora did not lose their popularity until the late nineteenth century, but the threat of imminent apoplexy was a more powerful instrument in the hands of those improvers who believed the character and quality of a city could be measured by the condition of its streets.

Had the nineteenth century as much anxiety about heart disease as the twentieth, the metaphor might have had much greater force.

Although coronary thrombosis was identified as early as 1851, it was not until the 1920s that arteriosclerosis became a term that most people, including many doctors, were familiar with. Official statistics did not include heart attack as a cause of death for another decade.[20] Even so, Victorians were sufficiently aware of blood clots and their lethal effects to give considerable potency to rhetoric about stoppages and obstructions to the arteries. *Punch*, for example, included in an 1846 issue an article light-hearted in tone but not in purport, called "Aneurism in the City." The author admitted that there was a flaw in his comparison: if a human patient had a blocked artery, a surgeon could take it up and expect that its function as a conduit for blood would be taken over "by collateral or anastomosing Vessels," whereas a congestion in Fleet Street would never be compensated for in a similar fashion: "Chancery Lane becomes no wider."[21]

Arterial obstruction was not the only powerful diagnostic metaphor available to urban reformers; the language of respiratory illness could also be effectively employed to explain the cause of what an eminent late-Victorian surgeon, Sir John Cantlie, called "urbomorbis."[22] The consequences of breathing bad air had been a topic of discussion for many years before Sir John Evelyn published his *Fumifugium* in 1661;[23] therefore it is not surprising that Dr Buchan would explain at great length in his eighteenth-century home remedy book how fetid air "exalts the bile," giving rise to inflammation, fever, and cholera. So long as miasmal theories of contagion lingered in the minds of the lay public, as perhaps they still do, warnings of this kind were certain to be taken seriously. Although it is difficult to fix a date for the time when the cult of fresh air became almost a national obsession and a source of wonderment and discomfort to generations of visitors to the British Isles, it is certain that the danger of breathing in stale air and, with it, unwholesome effluvia was an idea that had been entrenched in the public consciousness long before the reform era of the 1830s; however, it was in that decade that the subject of air pollution (thought to be made up of a mixture of sulfurous smoke, putrid vapors from decaying matter, and gases exhaled from millions of lungs) took on a special urgency. For the rest of the century journalists and medical essayists cautioned that the sheer size of London accounted for respiratory problems since bad air drove out good, producing an absence of sufficient "ozone" in the city centre. Even in horse-drawn London lungs were thought to be at risk. Reflecting a particularly late-Victorian preoccupation, Dr Cantlie cautioned that the effects of this unhealthy situation might extend beyond the city itself. He predicted that those inner-city dwellers who were condemned by their poverty to inhale air deficient in condensed oxygen and mixed with noisome exhalations, would propagate "a puny and ill-developed race."[24]

Concern for such long-term consequences led many people to identify the lung as the organ most at risk in the social as well as the individual body and did so, not coincidentally, at a time when tuberculosis was the grimmest reaper of them all. Nevertheless, preoccupation with lungs and the respiratory system did not diminish the evocative power of the arterial image, since the remedy most recommended for pollution in slums was to drive wide, straight passages through the tangle of buildings so that fresh air (corridors running east-west were thought to be particularly efficacious) might enter and contaminated air escape. Lungs act to purify the blood, the symbol of life. Thus Victorian and Edwardian street reformers had to hand a set of complementary images which they employed to make their objectives comprehensible to the general public and to themselves. Used in tandem, the circulatory and the respiratory metaphors advanced the argument in favor of large-scale and systematic improvements designed to make the metropolitan environment, thought to be in itself injurious to health, into a wholesome place for humans to live and work.

Use of the two metaphors to justify programs for clearing passageways of obstructions and cleansing the spaces they occupied assumed that the public whose support was being sought would accept the premise that life on the unreformed street had few or no redeeming values, and to some extent at least that did seem to be the case. Used as a modifier for words like "walker," "woman," "language," "Arab," the term "street" lowered the value of the object by implying loss of innocence, accommodation to the seamy and vulgar, contact with, and perhaps enjoyment of, the unbridled, the mean, and the obscene. On the other hand, "street life" had more ambiguous connotations. One thinks of Dickens's word pictures of the London streets, cold and desolate in the hours of darkness but awakening with the dawn and by midday throbbing "with life and bustle," or of Charles Lamb's comment about the

> impossibility of being dull in Fleet Street; the crowds, the very dirt and mud . . . the pantomimes – London itself a pantomime and a masquerade – all these things work themselves into my mind, and feed me, without a power of satiating me.

He confessed to having "cried with fulness of joy at the multitudinous scenes of life in the crowded streets of ever dear London."[25] Less sentimental pedestrians might complain about noise, dirt, and dangerous traffic yet define themselves as Londoners by the arts they acquired to cope with these annoyances. And only the most hardened of the street rationalizers could be completely blind to the picturesque aspects of street culture. Victorian ladies and gentlemen might pray for the day when the German brass bands would be silenced, the importuning sweep removed, the intruding coffee stand taken out of the way; yet at other times and in other moods these same people might assume the role of the impartial and amused observer and revel in this untidy pantomime. Carried along by the eddies and flows, the Victorian Londoner might, depending on the occasion, compare the motion to that of a foul drain or experience exhilaration at being swept along in "the great stream of life."

In addition to sharing to some extent this ambivalence toward the communal, colorful, slow-moving, or stationary character of traditional street culture, the improver would also have a troubled conscience about seeming to interfere with the right of "free-born Englishmen" to come and go as they liked on a public thoroughfare. In law, symbol, custom, and rhetoric the highway had always been regarded as one place where any subject of the Crown or anyone else who was willing to accept its protection could pass freely. This sense received a concise statement in a protest by Lord Montagu, the leading champion of the private motor car in its early days, against a proposal to place, in the interest of public safety and amenity, more restrictions on drivers. "If I am right in my opinion," he wrote, "that the right to use the road, that wonderful emblem of liberty, is deeply ingrained in our history and character, such action will meet with the most stubborn opposition."[26] How correct Montagu was in this evocation of history can be shown in one example taken from the Putney Debates of 1648 (chosen because it began the train of thought which has resulted in this book). On that occasion Cromwell's son-in-law, General Ireton, disputing the Leveller claim that the franchise was a natural, not just a civil, right, argued that only those with "a permanent fixed interest in the kingdom" should be entitled to vote. Nevertheless he was willing to admit that there were a limited number of basic birthrights, among them, the right to have a place to stand on, the right to breathe, and, he added, shifting from the general to the specific, "the freedom of the highways." Considering that this concession did nothing to strengthen Ireton's position, its inclusion is evidence of how axiomatic he considered this particular liberty to be.

Fundamental to the liberal tradition, as Isaiah Berlin points out in *Two Concepts of Liberty*, is the notion that, if individuals are to be treated as autonomous, there must be an area where they can act as they choose and without interference. Furthermore, the frontiers of this area must be so clearly marked by tradition as to be automatically accepted and protected.[27] Thus the measure of how free a society is depends on the extent of this protected area, how many paths lead to, into, and through it, and on how solidly its boundary lines are constructed and maintained. Although Berlin is speaking about a conceptual space and not a physical one, in the case of the street the one can be transposed into the other without too much distortion. Wherever else English men or women might expect to make concessions to the needs of public safety, the general good, or some other value, they could expect support from tradition if they resisted those claims in the protected area of the street and clung tenaciously to the freedom to go their own way (see Plate 1).

Another aspect of this tradition about the freedom of the King's Highway was that all might claim the right to exercise it equally so long as the purpose be peaceful: foreigner as well as native born, women as well as men, young as well as old, poor as well as rich. It was generally acknowledged that much of the attraction of this public space was the opportunity it offered to leave one's private deportment behind, assume an appropriate public persona, and mix with those whom one could not or would not care to receive before the domestic hearth.[28] In theory at least, the street was a democratic island in a sea of privilege and stratified authority. As one Londoner observed in 1851, the cosmopolitan mix of passers-by takes place "on neutral and debatable ground, for all who consign themselves to the chances of the pavement are *equal*." Therefore, "Your Only true Republic / Is a crowded city street."[29]

Urban reformers, a high proportion of whom were committed liberals, had this tradition (as well as the mixed feelings mentioned above) to contend with whenever they gave orders or sponsored campaigns to move idlers and vagrants along, stop prostitutes from carrying on their form of free enterprise on the streets, remove costermongers' barrows from the pavement outside of shops, or restrict the right of brewery wagons from stopping to make deliveries during certain hours. They might justify such measures by appealing to other definitions of freedom such as the Hobbesian argument that while any obstruction to free movement constitutes a loss of natural liberty, some acts of intervention (a traffic policeman say) can greatly extend "practical" freedom, the ability actually to enjoy what liberties the authority permitted. By this logic, preventing an omnibus driver from picking up or depositing passengers wherever he chose would limit his freedom but promote the safety and the freedom of movement for the many. Obviously this second concept of freedom, the ability to move quickly, efficiently, and safely, unobstructed by stationary or slow-moving objects, was in harmony with the desire of the improver to rid the urban arteries of clots and thus to promote the health of the urban organism by allowing nutrients to flow along frictionless tubes from the heart to the continually lengthening extremities.

Convenient though this conceptual framework might have been for a street reform agenda, it was difficult to apply consistently and to reconcile easily with liberty, thought of as freedom from intervention.

Regulations aimed at ridding the streets of obstructions could never facilitate the movement of street users in an equal way. Some other theoretical ground had to be found for deciding why it should be that priority be given, for example, to speeding up the pace of wheeled vehicles if the result of doing so were to inhibit pedestrians in their use of all parts of the street. Was it unambiguously obvious that the freedom of the respectable gentleman to walk without needing to make his way around a costermonger's barrow was more valuable to the welfare of the city than the freedom of the street-seller to carry on his occupation?

Furthermore, intervention, it could be argued, distorted the free market. As we will see later, City merchants would be alarmed by proposals to allow police to decide when and where heavy freight haulers might operate. Restrictions on the movement of coal and lumber might increase costs to consumers and injure a long line of interest stretching from the Canadian lumberjack or the Welsh miner to the City bankers, shippers, and insurance underwriters who served those important sectors. One person's clot, it seemed, might be another person's life-blood.

Yet another difficulty for liberals was that the opportunity to exercise the freedom of the streets, however defined, was not really open to everyone on an equal basis. The London street of the nineteenth century was not a true democracy; it was, to use Susan Davis's definition, "a structure of contested terrain."[30]

As in the past, most streets of the city, or combination of streets, were more than just passageways: they were locales, with distinct organizations and, often, distinct cultures. As these organizations and cultures became more differentiated, as the tendency for class and status groups to separate continued during the century, and as police and other authorities made progress in their efforts to control access to certain areas and to protect them against intrusions from outside elements, freedom became increasingly conditional on who or what the user of the street might be. On the one hand, improvements in lighting and policing meant that the traveller from one locale to another could see danger or insult coming and take heart in the likelihood that a constable would be within earshot; but on the other hand, that constable could not be entirely an impartial outsider since he would be an essential part of the structure he patrolled, and his demeanour would depend, to a considerable extent, on the social complexion of the locale and how the entrant might or might not fit into it. Thus anyone who crossed a local border, and that could mean in some cases moving from one end of a street to another, would have been well advised to notice and to be able to read a complex set of signs. As we will see in a later chapter, a fashionably dressed, middle-class Victorian or Edwardian lady could spend a pleasant afternoon shopping on Regent Street and expect to be treated by the police and passers-by with courtesy (provided she knew not to linger too long in front of certain shop windows), but if she remained on that fashionable street, unescorted, after the lamps were lit, she risked insult and loss of reputation. Similarly, a top hat might command deference in one place and a short distance away invite attack. Law and tradition might decree that any peaceful user of the streets should have the right to go anywhere at any time and to expect to be protected in doing so, but the ability to exercise that right depended on who had control over the terrain and how power was distributed locally.

Here was a fact of life few reformers were willing to acknowledge openly, for, according to the paradigm, the trouble with most streets, especially in the poorer neighborhoods, was that they were structureless and that the evils to be found there were the consequence of disorder – hence the need to impose structure from outside. As a result of this misconception, street reformers frequently could not foresee what complications their interventions might encounter. Almost every time municipal engineers proposed what seemed to be perfectly straightforward plans to ease the grade for struggling horses along a particular stretch, or lovers of peace and quiet campaigned to have street musicians evicted, these reformers discovered that they had stirred up a hornet's nest of interests and loyalties. Horrified by some public display of shamelessness and obscenity, purity crusaders might press for suppression and then find that respectable persons, the sort they expected to have as allies, would rise up in indignant opposition. Almost always the improver would be surprised and puzzled, even though the drama kept repeating itself. The fact was that hardly any street in London was exclusively or even predominantly a passageway – a truism that so many of those bent on straightening, cleansing, policing, and quieting were unwilling, or found it inconvenient, to accept. Freeing the streets of Victorian and Edwardian London was, therefore, a concept riddled with ambiguities. It will be argued in some of the subsequent chapters that this difficultly with conceptualization, along with the lack of insistent economic or political imperatives for reform, explains why the more things changed the more they remained the same.

Street rationalizers, purifiers, and rescuers did lay claim to solid accomplishments. It was generally assumed by those who expressed the views of the establishment that, for example, the Metropolitan Police had succeeded by mid-century in their primary goal: gaining control of the streets. Nevertheless a longer perspective suggests that the taming process was so complex and the effects so ambiguous that it is difficult to make so simple a discovery of agency. It is unlikely that the decrease in riot and individual acts of criminal violence came about simply because Col Charles Rowan and Sir Richard Mayne carried out their duties as joint Commissioners of Police so sensibly and effectively. The most that can be said is that these men and the force they commanded were part of a progressive development. The engineers did not have even that consolation. They could point to impressive works. Experts timed and measured the volume of traffic, located bottlenecks, and performed prodigies of tunneling, bridging, and widening; yet Londoners at the end of the century moved no faster on the surfaces of their streets than their early-Victorian predecessors had done. Increasingly professional doctors had taken up diseased veins and arteries and had removed numerous clots but had not been allowed to attempt a systematic cure for the capital's traffic snarl or for other kinds of ailments.

Thus it seems fair to say that, viewed from a distance, nineteenth-century street reform was, despite these accomplishments, a conspicuous failure. This was certainly the conclusion of a great many Edwardians who had occasion to express their opinion on the subject. One of them, Harold Clunn, published a book in 1932 about the physical transformations that had taken place during his lifetime. He included the quotation from the *Illustrated London News*, noted earlier, and then made the comment that every word written in 1846 about London's "diurnal apoplexy" might have been written yesterday.[31] He agreed that from the 1880s to the Great War important advances had been made in underground and surface rail transport: the Metropolis gained an electric tramway system and the electrified tube; improved suburban rail service and cheap working-class fares had both expanded and expedited commuterism; petrol-powered buses and taxis, after 1905, had rapidly put an end to the horse omnibus and cab. Perhaps for the briefest of interludes, the pace of street movement had quickened slightly. But soon the time-tested equation asserted itself: improvements in urban transit encouraged people to travel more. Thus Charing Cross Road, Shaftesbury Avenue, and Kingsway improved access north and south but without relieving the pressure of traffic in any significant way. Boundary lines kept on blurring at an accelerated rate as speculative builders leap-frogged each other along the new suburban lines. The result was yet another wave of anxiety couched in language closely resembling that of the 1830s and 1840s.

Still, the rhetoric of crisis did change somewhat over the course of Queen Victoria's reign and the interval between 1901 and 1914. While respiratory and circulatory metaphors remained in fashion, disease imagery became less prominent, perhaps reflecting a widening acceptance of the germ theory of contagion and some softening of anxiety about premature death. Psychological reactions to the sense of boundlessness tended more frequently to be expressed in the imagery of explosion and fragmentation. This can be observed in an essay called *Anticipations* which H.G. Wells published in 1905 about the future consequences to city life of electricity and petrol motor technology. He remarked that through most of the previous century London had inflated the way "a puffball swells"; the rate of growth had been astounding, yet the metropolis had managed to retain its "rounded contours." But a new wave of immigration and the shock of the new transportation technology had shattered the containing walls: London had burst its "intolerable envelope and splashed."[32] That same year Ford Maddox Hueffer (Ford Maddox Ford after 1919) used another robust metaphor to suggest formlessness and the process of disintegration. From the end of the Dickens era onward, he wrote, the city had become a "ragout of tidbits," a dish so fluid that not even that runny abstraction seemed to fit. He concluded that about all that could be said by way of definition was that London had become a background for a host of disparate urban activities: a "permanent world's fair" for some, for others, a "central conduit, more or less long," or a "postal district," or a "great slip-shod, easy-going, good-humoured magnet."[33]

Clunn, musing on this failure to impose shape on the shapeless, to do for London what Baron Haussmann did for Paris or the architects of the Ringstrasse did for Vienna, blamed "our English habit of doing things by halves."[34] A writer for *The Saturday Review* also attempted to explain this neglect by referring to traits in the national character. Noting the beauty and ambience of the newly-built Parisian boulevards, he predicted that Britain would never pay good money to make streets into places of leisure because Londoners assume, "with good reason," that a second of hesitation in one's passage from one place to another is "a second wasted."[35] Others offered economic and administrative explanations; they pointed to the seeming inability to put together a municipal government sufficiently powerful and well-funded to carry out a large-scale transformation. Ancillary to that was the difficulty in raising tax revenues for civic projects,[36] the irrationality with which the city's fabric had been formed, and the long romance with the steam railway – all of these working together to prejudice the cause of street improvement. Also frequently mentioned was lack of civic pride, the intransigence of ancient corporations, and the jealousy of the central government in Westminster.

Whether London lacked the will because it lacked the means or the other way around is not a question likely to find an answer. That the Metropolitan Board of Works did, with assistance from Parliament, manage to construct Sir Joseph Bazalgette's great sewer system does suggest that administrative barriers were not completely insuperable; in that case however, immediate fear of epidemic gave the push, and not, at least initially, an urge to perform an act of civic munificence. Moreover, will has to do with more than desire and determination; it also depends on having a conceptual framework attractive and comprehensive enough to awaken desire and focus determination. Not only was the liberal street reform idea full of serious contradictions, it predisposed those who used its metaphors of illness and fragmentation to adopt a negative approach to street life and function; therefore, when improvers found themselves in positions to influence or to carry out improvements, they tended to conceive of them as cures for ailments and not as opportunities to grace the Imperial Capital or to bring pride and delight to its inhabitants. The construction of the Embankment may be seen as an exception to this generalization, but even there the interest of moving sewage below the surface and tramcars and other vehicles above predominated. On the outlook for clots, prone to associate the straight and the wide with modernity, ready to look for medicinal remedies when local surgery seemed counterproductive, convinced that evil and infection walked the city streets, and insensitive to the complicated structures to be found in even the meanest of streets, they had difficulty in responding to the idea that a "good" street might be one with a multiplicity of uses, that it was often the stationary or slow-moving object or activity which gave a street vitality, or that the quality of a city might depend on the beauty and amenity to be found on its streets. Because their ends were constricted, their accomplishments won few hearts and their ministrations worked few cures.

2

STRAIGHTENING

In 1990 the transport editor of the *Guardian* issued this warning: "The capital is in the grip of an environmental catastrophe which would have seemed inconceivable to the nineteenth century planners who mapped out its arterial roads."[1] Two of the premises here are faulty: first, the Victorians had considerably more imagination and far less scope as planners than the statement implies. Second, journalists, engineers, social investigators, and writers of letters to the newspapers were talking about "a congestion crisis" and predicting imminent strangulation a century and a half ago. For example, *Punch* in 1846 recommended that Fleet Street omnibuses carry elastic ladders to give passengers a way of escaping, when blockages threatened to become permanent, to upper-story windows.[2] A year earlier Mr Punch passed on the information that a small brandy bottle had been picked out of a "dangerous channel of Fleet Street." Inside was a note reading, "The Celerity omnibus stranded off Temple Bar. Every passenger lost; great distress."[3]

Near the end of the Victorian period, in 1898, the same distress signals, sounded this time in a rather more sober mode, were the text of an address that Sir John Wolfe Barry, one of the leading civil engineers of the time and son of the architect of the new Houses of Parliament, gave to the Society of Arts. Year by year, he said, "the pressure on the streets" was "becoming more and more unmanageable"; the Strand was in "monstrous condition," the "confusion at the Mansion House" had been even "worse compounded" by the construction of the would-be improvement, Queen Victoria Street, and converging streams of traffic near the Elephant and Castle threatened any moment to become hopelessly dammed up.[4] He went on to point out that Colonel William Haywood had sounded the same warning about impending paralysis fully thirty years earlier, attempting to alert the public to the danger traffic congestion posed to the economy of a great commercial centre and also making a forceful case for co-ordinated, large-scale planning and reconstruction – to no apparent effect.[5] How right Haywood had been, Wolfe Barry added, to predict that parsimony and *ad hoc*-ery would make the well-nigh unbearable inconveniences of his own day completely intolerable in the future.

Although somewhat less pessimistic than we in the late twentieth century about finding a solution to the problem of urban traffic congestion, Wolfe Barry at the end and Haywood in the middle of the nineteenth century were already troubled by this Victorian liberal conundrum: how could London, the symbol of freedom, find the authority it needed to revitalize itself without surrendering its vital principle? At every point in the Victorian and Edwardian periods one encounters liberal reformers expressing frustration at not being able to come up with an adequate response to this problem. For example, during a debate in 1860 on the advisability of using central government assistance to embank the Thames, the eminent builder, Sir Morton Peto, spoke in the House of Commons about how "he could not help regretting, when he observed what was happening in Paris, the puny, haphazard spirit with which our Government shrinks from dealing with great questions." Yet Peto, impatient as he obviously was with the impedimenta cluttering the path of any English "Haussmannizer" (large-scale planner), nevertheless felt it necessary to preface his remarks by disclaiming any "wish to introduce an Imperial regime into this country."[6] Would, then, some smaller entity be able to act with anything like the sweep and magnificence that was evident in the changes under way across the Channel? Only the most enthusiastic among the champions of the municipal idea thought so. One such optimist was Arthur Cawston, an architect and an admirer of Joseph Chamberlain's gas and water socialism. He felt that "redemption" lay in abandoning individual effort and finding some communal focus, a municipal authority with the dedication, energy, and pride to make what was narrow broad, what was crooked straight, what was old new. He agreed with Albert Shaw, an American expert on comparative local government, that London was perfectly capable of following the example of Paris and transforming itself ("the brilliant nineteenth century task") from a "labyrinthine tangle" into an exemplar of modernity, providing it surrendered its stubborn insistence on "uncontrolled freedom of individual action."[7] Cawston also believed that municipal reformers needed to cast aside their sentimental attachments to the picturesque qualities of past ways and things, so that they might clear the way for broad, continuous, limited-access throughways with segregated traffic, designed to bring commuters from the spreading rings of suburban residences to workplaces in the central city. Only by consciously embracing modern concepts of rationality and utility could London begin to "evolve out of chaos." Such an effort was well within her powers, wrote Cawston in 1893, now that the creation of the London County Council had at last given the city "a real municipality."[8]

George John Shaw-Lefevre, a Gladstonian faithful who, late in life, was elected to the London County Council (LCC) and headed its Improvements Committee from 1897 to 1901, recognized that transformationism of this bold kind was probably not compatible with his own brand of bourgeois liberalism. He thought it might be possible to get permission to tax ground rents as well as the unearned increments which accrued to property owners as the result of street improvements, allowing planners then to proceed with some sense of realism and work out a general design for the city's future growth. He agreed with Wolfe Barry that it would be necessary to include in such a plan broad parkways containing multiple tramlines, circular belts around the center, and boulevards linking large urban spaces, making them accessible to residents of densely populated regions. Engineering solutions would, he thought, have the added advantage of making it less necessary for outside authorities to put restrictions on rights of passage. However he cautioned reformers, inside the LCC and elsewhere, about the folly of ignoring large property interests or trying the patience of ratepayers by moving too rapidly.[9] Hindsight suggests that it was Lefevre's old liberalism and not Cawston's new liberalism which came closer to defining the real nineteenth-century parameters.

What the two liberals had in common was the conviction that London must modernize, that failure to do so posed grave dangers not only for the city's future but for nation and empire, that efficient communication was the essence of modernity, and that progress along these lines had been so slow and had been carried out in so haphazard a fashion as to constitute an emergency. What alarmed them and many others was the realization that, from the late eighteenth century until the mid-nineteenth century, much of the world had looked upon London as the epitome of modernity, the place where the most extensive and most imaginative civic improvements, especially street improvements, were being carried out.[10] In no other European city of the early nineteenth century did reconstruction projects match the scale and elegance of Nash's Regent Street, a broad avenue from the Haymarket running north to his newly constructed Regent's Park with its "garden city." It was modern in the Victorian sense of the word in that it carried a main sewer pipe underneath its surface, provided a badly needed access north for traffic moving along the already heavily travelled Strand, and cleared a path through an overcrowded region; but "Utility to the Public" was only one of Nash's stated aims, "Beauty of the Metropolis" being another, and by "beauty" he meant "magnificence."[11] That James Pennethorne was directed in 1848 by his employer, The Commissioners of Her Majesty's Woods and Forests, to tear down the street's splendid colonnades and auction them off – they went at £7 10s. apiece – demonstrated that the time of such magnificence had passed.

What Pennethorne's feelings may have been on receiving that particular assignment may be wondered at, for he was Nash's protégé and had learned his trade on the Regent's Park works. He moved into his mentor's place as official architect for developments having to do with Crown lands and properties and in that capacity acted as the designer of New Oxford Street, another major undertaking and one which demonstrated officialdom's growing concern about the traffic problem. An added incentive was the opportunity the new street would create to drive, as the architect, Sydney Smirke, put it, "the plow of civic improvement" through the notorious St Giles rookery, (a plow which displaced five thousand people and sent them to other dense areas like Drury Lane and Whitechapel).[12] The street project, an impressive civic improvement in the context of the 1830s, was intended to take some of the strain off what seemed a disastrous situation in Fleet Street and the Strand by allowing east-west traffic to move directly from High Holborn to Oxford Street and the west. Though Pennethorne was not authorized to make the "Beauty of the Metropolis" a priority in his design, foreign visitors were impressed by this evidence that Londoners were determined to adjust the fabric of their city to a world of progressive movement where time, as street engineers were wont to point out, was money.

There were additional reasons to conclude in the 1830s that London was a model reformers everywhere might do well to emulate, for it was then that local authorities and MPs for London ridings began to overhaul existing street regulations and send investigators to strategic corners to count traffic volumes and types of vehicles with an eye to discovering patterns of movement and to learn why blockages happened. Parliamentary Select Committees concerned with traffic issues (and there were many of them in the 1830s and 1840s) as well as parish vestries and the City of London Corporation were inundated with statistical material.[13] The conclusions that followed from the figures were clear: what seemed bad was bound to get worse; and in this mood Parliament was inclined to permit local authorities to raise rates and to use duties on coal and other commodities to construct not only New Oxford Street but to improve and to lengthen Cannon Street in order to draw vehicles away from Cheapside and the Poultry and to give Blackfriars Bridge a new surface and London Bridge, the most clogged artery of them all, new approaches.

Because of these and other accomplishments London could confidently present itself to the world in 1851 as the exemplar of modern improvements, a theme of the Crystal Palace Exhibition; but by the middle of the decade the mood had changed dramatically: Paris,

Vienna, Berlin, and New York quickly replaced London as the standard against which other cities measured their own progress. Londoners began asking, if they can why cannot we?

English visitors returning from the Paris Exhibition of 1867 could not help but be struck by the contrast between the French capital, "in the high noon of glitter and sparkle," and the dowdiness and disorder of their own. Editorialists wondered why it should be that their own great city, the centre of a huge empire and a place so rich in interior spaces, should have become so inferior in externals (see Plate 2). "A Frenchman," noted a writer for the *Saturday Review*, not only moves about more pleasantly and rapidly than his London counterpart but also "lives in his streets and boulevards, is proud of them, loves them, and will spend his money on their beauty and decoration."[14]

Such comments were partly apologetic, partly boastful. The Londoner, another article explained, lives his real life indoors; for him streets "are simply and solely a means of transit from one point to another."[15] The implication here is that the streets of Paris or London were bound to reflect their respective municipal or national characters. It could be made to follow, then, that love of externals indicated a certain frivolity; neglect of these and preference for inner values might then be taken as a sign of moral superiority. Take for example several long letters to *The Times* in 1867 from a self-educated mechanic named Randal who had traveled to the Paris Exhibition with a group of skilled English workers. He remarked that commuters in the omnibuses and on the Seine steamboats smiled and behaved as though on holiday and confessed that it had been a revelation to him to discover that city streets might be used for innocent recreation. How different was the mood in London, he noted. There people on their way to work wore only their destinations on their faces. But he did not mean necessarily to fault his fellow countrymen. It was obvious from the tone that, much as he might enjoy the seductive graces of the French capital, Randal wanted London to be itself: purposeful, serious, responsible.[16] Some of his contemporaries agreed. An observation not infrequently heard was that while the Frenchman cleans his footways, the Englishman cleans his feet. Few, however, would have wanted to go so far as to suggest that the comparative sluggishness of street reform on the English side of the Channel and the failure to produce a Ringstrasse or a Champs Elysées should actually be a source of civic pride.

A somewhat more convincing explanation for why London lost its reputation as a model of modern improvements is that no effective metropolitan government existed to promote, initiate, and guide a transformation process. Nash's impressive accomplishments were a case in point. His square, street, and park could be built as a co-ordinated whole because they were built, for the most part, on Crown land at a time when the king happened to be a man of taste and style. Thus there was no need to appease powerful interests or to place a burden on the national treasury; but when, by contrast, the same George IV gave his enthusiastic endorsement to Nash's proposal to drive a grand boulevard straight from St Paul's Cathedral to Kensington Palace through some of the most valuable properties in the West End, no political entity took up the cause.

But the absence of an effective administrative apparatus is not a sufficient explanation. As we have seen in the case of New Oxford Street and in large projects carried out in the 1860s like the Thames Embankment and Bazalgette's great sewer complex, when there were alarms about epidemics of cholera and fever or fears about the consequences for health or public order of continuing to allow slum areas to be cut off from outside inspection, ways could be found to overcome governmental inertia and appease recalcitrant interest groups; but such stimulants to reform as these were too localized or transitory to rally support for any large-scale or systematic street reconstruction plan. That required some pressing necessity. It might have been widely accepted that time was indeed money: traffic blockages certainly were great time-wasters but throughout the nineteenth century, despite frustrating snarls, coal continued to be delivered promptly and public houses usually received their barrels when they required them. Dock companies did eventually suffer from slowdowns in transhipments to railway termini and dealers in perishable items like fish were undoubtedly discomfited. Nonetheless, clerks usually managed to get to their offices on time and City businessmen continued to arrive early and stay late. People like William Haywood expended huge amounts of effort in calculating to the last shilling what a major slowdown cost, but there is no evidence that many banks or insurance companies contemplated leaving the central city because communication slowdowns interfered with profit-making. Also, despite its evil reputation for hubbub, congestion, and pollution, perhaps because of it, revenues from tourism became an increasingly important part of the city's economy. On the one hand, "National efficiency" became an important concern in the latter part of the century and had political manifestations at the national and metropolitan levels; renewal of urban infrastructures was part of its agenda. On the other, what astonished so many observers was how well, not how badly, suppliers gave Londoners what they needed and could afford, when and where they required it. The point to be made here is not that the condition of the streets had no important economic or social consequences but that, despite all the rhetoric about arteriosclerosis and the value of time, no major economic interests in this city of commerce, finance, and services really took seriously the warning that traffic chaos would lead to economic catastrophe. Thus major "improvements" to the existing structure could be made and even some embellishments might be permitted, providing the political climate was just right and influential persons were ready to push hard and not shirk from lobbying and maneuvering; but reformers who called for systematic reconstruction and large-scale, co-ordinated planning were not responding to any strong economic imperative.

Examination of the improvement aims of two outstanding engineers, William Haywood and Sir Joseph Paxton, and the two projects with which they were closely involved, the Holborn Viaduct and the Thames Embankment, gives us a chance to see these possibilities and limitations at closer range.

Of the two, the Holborn Viaduct is the more obvious example of a purely utilitarian undertaking, the purpose of which was to carry out local surgery on one major defect in the system. The need for the viaduct was obvious. In the 1850s, many more people, traveling more often on longer journeys, requiring a larger provision for public transport, and being able in larger numbers to pay for it, were being carried by the new railways and a multiplying fleet of omnibuses and cabs. Nowhere were the effects more apparent than on Fleet Street and the Strand, the main route for east-west travel. There was an alternative: if a gentleman hailed a cab at the Bank in the heart of the City and asked to be driven to his West End house in Mayfair and if the driver was not in a mood to enter the inevitable scrum of turning carts at what is now Ludgate Circus, before trying to squeeze through the twenty-three-foot-wide bottleneck at Temple Bar, he could take his chances on an alternative route down Cheapside and then on to Holborn and New Oxford Street. This required gambling on the chance that no drovers had filled the area around the small Newgate Street slaughter houses with cattle and trusting that the horse still had enough strength to manage the steep grade into and out of the Holborn Valley, that "heavy hill."[17]

The idea of raising that valley had been discussed for well over a century, but John Glynn, in 1766, was the first to suggest building a viaduct from Hatton Garden across to the top of the steep-sided Snow Hill.[18] Detailed designs for carrying out this project began reaching various improvement bodies from the 1830s on, and finally in 1862 the Corporation of the City of London decided to act. Not only had the reasons for doing so become more compelling, but the Government, headed by Lord Palmerston (who had been sensitized to London's health and communication problems during his spell at the Home Office in the 1850s), agreed in 1861 to earmark the proceeds from the coal duty (4d. on every ton that entered the docks, producing some £100,000 a year) for public improvements. The viaduct, as well as Haywood's Queen Victoria Street, the renovations on Ludgate Hill,

Farringdon Street, and Cannon Street, the reconstruction of Blackfriars Bridge and of the Smithfield Market, and the purchase of Epping Forest, were some of the results of this incentive.[19] Access to the coal duty revenue does not in itself explain why the extensive (over 4000 buildings had to be demolished) and expensive (approximately £2,500,000) Holborn construction was undertaken and carried to completion so expeditiously. A considerable degree of credit for this and so many other accomplishments carried out by the City of London in the 1850-70 period, including a highly successful street paving and cleaning programme, was, according to David Owen, an expert on Victorian administrative history, "due largely to the energy and competence . . . of William Haywood."[20]

Like most of the other master builders of the century, Haywood had acquired this competence through apprenticeship. Son of a City businessman, who died young and left his family in straitened circumstances, he had gone from a local grammar school into the offices of the architect and engineer George Aitchison. When barely 20, he had built a mansion in Berkshire for the Marquis of Downshire. Soon after, in 1846, he accepted an appointment with the Commissioners of Sewers, a semi-autonomous body established under the Tudors and appointed by the City Corporation. The following year he became its chief architect and surveyor, an office he held for forty-eight years.[21] He was handsome, a man of the world, and mixed well at literary gatherings and fashionable garden parties. He was also, in a century rich in dedicated civil servants, a paragon. Only a few weeks before his death in 1894, when he attempted to retire, the Commissioners urged him to stay on as a consultant at full salary.[22] It is not difficult to understand why: he had collaborated with John Simon in a campaign to remove cess-pools and connect the dwellings of the City with drains. In the 1850s he contributed in a major way to plans for diverting sewage from the Thames by means of a main drainage system; when Joseph Bazalgette was finally able to undertake that Herculean enterprise, he incorporated features of Haywood's designs. Although Haywood irritated Simon by acting as what we would now call a public relations flack for his employers,[23] no one did more to make the old City a comparatively clean and healthy place. Between 1879 and 1883 he laid down a system of fire hydrants; about the same time, he carried out a resurfacing project to replace granite or wooden blocks and macadam with asphalt in order to facilitate the removal of dung and slush. He was one of the century's master cleansers.[24]

The Corporation recognized his value and probably assumed from the start that he would be in charge of the Holborn Valley project, although its Improvements Committee did hold a public contest and considered eighty-five submissions before announcing that Haywood, who had acted as an advisor to the committee, was the winner. There were raised eyebrows, but procedural nicety was never one of the Corporation's salient features; criticism was also muffled by the rapid progress on the work of arranging for demolitions (see Plate 3), negotiating compensation settlements, moving 12,000 bodies from a churchyard to a cemetery Haywood had designed at Ilford, dumping twelve million bricks into the disgusting Fleet River ooze, raising existing approach streets, constructing several new ones, and putting up the ornate cast-iron bridge over Farringdon Street. The digging began in 1863 and the opening ceremonies took place in November, 1869. On that occasion Haywood declared that "nothing so large and comprehensive in its range" had been attempted so far in the century, an exaggeration but an understandable one.[25] *The Builder* thought the project "so grand and yet so simple."[26] The Victorian diarist, Sir William Hardman, predicted that it would become a symbol of modernity, of "a future in which London would be transformed out of recognition."[27]

Considering the almost universal approval that greeted Haywood's great undertaking, it is curious that he received so little recognition for it. An early twentieth-century expert on the history of London streets and buildings, Harold Clunn, gave a full description in his *The Face of London* of how the viaduct was constructed. The book seems to have been widely read, for it went through a number of revisions and reprintings in its first year, 1932. Nowhere in it can Haywood's name be found, the credit for the viaduct going to a "Mr. Marrable," one of the unsuccessful contestants in 1862.[28] A letter Frederick Marrable wrote to *The Builder* in 1869 may explain Clunn's obviously deliberate slight. Haywood's speech at the Lord Mayor's dinner following the formal opening by the Queen of both the viaduct and the reconstructed Blackfriars Bridge was, Marrable wrote, "a flourish of self-blown trumpets," an act of hubris, Marrable thought, considering that Haywood had been the Improvement Committee's own advisor and had apparently recommended that the first prize go to himself for a design which, Marrable claimed, bore suspicious resemblances to his own.[29] Haywood issued a strong denial, claiming that his submission had been unsigned and that the deliberations had been fair and honorable; and there the matter might have rested, since such post-competition recriminations were almost always part of the process, had it not been discovered, only days after the gala opening, that cracks were appearing in the granite seatings for the bridge support columns. For several weeks the press printed alarming predictions, and what a professional engineering journal called "a large body of amateur casuals of the engineering and architectural professions" were to be seen at the site, digging around the shafts, and probing the cracks with sharp instruments.[30] Eventually a committee of engineers assured the public that the structure was "perfectly safe," placed most of the blame on the masons for faulty workmanship, and expressed regret that a work of "such magnitude and public importance" should have "sustained any blemish."[31] Even so, the cracks spoiled Haywood's triumph and may explain why someone so deserving of a knighthood never received one.

Privately he expressed his bitterness; the decision to give up practice as a private architect, he said on several occasions, was "the great mistake of my career."[32] Nevertheless he was circumspect in public and a loyal team player, with a considerable capacity for detachment even from his own creations. While the Holborn work was still in its early stages he made an official report on traffic improvements carried on inside the City and included recommendations about what steps might be needed in the future. The main point of this analysis, which so impressed Wolfe Barry thirty years later, was that a program for relieving blockages was certain to be self-defeating. Furthermore, he used his own great improvement as an example. When finished, he pointed out, horses would be able to pull their wagons comfortably between Hatton Garden and Snow Hill; but as a result, more drivers would choose this route. Thus most of the time and effort saved by not having to climb in and out of the valley would be lost in the increased congestion at the west end of Newgate Street. The moral he drew was that the "facility of locomotion stimulates traffic of itself"; thus the more successful the improvement, the greater the need for more improvements, an insight that anticipates by many decades experience gained in the age of mass motor transportation.[33] His "solution" also sounds familiar to our ears: the construction of "a new arterial line of thoroughfare" through the City from the eastern end of the viaduct to Whitechapel High Street, a route followed in part after the Second World War, when the dismal London Wall drive was pushed through bomb damage left by the Blitz.

For a technical work, studded with statistics, this report seems to have been widely read or at least commented upon. It reminds the modern reader of how different the engineering "cast of mind" was then. Victorian engineers worked inside a culture that encouraged them to look for long-term ramifications, to show how a device or a project might not only meet the problem at hand but how it might contribute to a more general progress toward a more efficient, hence a more productive, civilization and perhaps a higher morality. Thus Haywood and Wolfe Barry felt obliged to show that to build their wide and straight throughways would not just expedite traffic flow but require and help generate agencies capable of comprehensive planning. These agencies would, in turn, develop a sense of civic pride which would revitalize London and allow it to continue into the future as the "world city." Invigorated as they were by such bold, consequential reasoning, they were not inclined to be pessimistic even when their own reasoning suggested that a "more bold and comprehensive system" might, like the piecemeal improvements they cautioned against, increase the number of travellers by improving the felicity of travel. If Paris was the exemplar of the benefits of comprehensiveness, then one might have thought these engineers would have investigated the traffic problem there to see whether or not Haussmanization had solved it. If the answer was still unclear in the 1860s and 1870s, it was obvious by the time Haywood retired and before Wolfe Barry began to concern himself with street reform: the widening and straightening in the French capital had not increased its pace of travel. When a specialist in street architecture went there at the turn of the century, he found blockages as severe as any he had experienced in New York and complained of being totally immobilized for fifteen minutes during rush hour in the Rue de la Paix.[34]

Haywood was able, however, to apply his paradox to the other great street engineering project which was under way at the same time as the viaduct, the Thames Embankment. He agreed that it would, like his own construction, be a way of avoiding some of the congestion on the Strand and Fleet Street, but would only add to the snarl created by intersecting and turning vehicles in front of the Bank and would further clog the passageway east along Cornhill. Once again London would have acquired a magnificent "improvement" which, because unco-ordinated by any overall plan, was bound to become part of the problem.[35]

What London did acquire was a magnificent riverfront. Because the Embankment, for strategic reasons, was promoted mainly on grounds of utility (it would serve as a conduit for a low-level sewer pipe, gas line, and underground railway tube below the surface and be a traffic diversion above), citizens reacted to the finished work with a kind of delighted surprise. How had it come to pass, some of them wondered, that a Gradgrind-spirited Metropolitan Board of Works and a government which, especially after Gladstone took over its leadership in 1867, seemed ferociously determined to cut public spending, had managed to produce anything so splendid: a wide, tree-lined boulevard, furnished with handsome cast-iron benches and lamp fixtures and faced with granite so lovingly cut that it fitted like cabinet work?[36]

Why the Thames was embanked at all is a somewhat easier question. *The Times*, in 1864, when the project was finally under way, gave a plausible account of the chain of circumstances, the first link being the Great Stink of 1858 when a long spell of hot weather brought miasmas from the festering river palpably before the noses of the Members of Parliament, a pungent reminder of the consequences of using the river as the Cloaca Maxima. According to this version of events, Parliament then passed legislation enabling the Metropolitan Board of Works to proceed with the construction of a high, middle, and low-level sewer system and that meant finding a route for pipes along the north side of the river, the Strand and Fleet Street being the logical one. With the Holborn Valley in a state of demolition and reconstruction, the idea of turning the major east-west artery, even temporarily, into a deep ditch was unthinkable; therefore, a multiple-use Embankment seemed the only possible course. Faced with this dilemma, Parliament could hardly refuse to allow a rate on the whole metropolis and grant permission to use revenues from coal and wine duties, thus allowing Joseph Bazalgette, assisted by Sir William Tite, architect of the new Royal Exchange and a man of refined tastes, to begin the work in 1864.[37]

The timing was fortunate. Palmerston was still Prime Minister, and he had been a warm and consistent supporter of the Embankment idea since 1824, the year an eccentric Irishman, Colonel Fredrick William Trench, MP, rented a Thames barge, gathered some dignitaries, including among others his patroness, the ravishing Dutchess of Rutland, her gallant, the Duke of York, the Lord Mayor, and Palmerston, to describe plans for a quay which the brothers Wyatt, assisted by the eminent engineer John Rennie, had drawn up for him. The work was conceived in true Regency style: a "healthful and beautiful" gas-lighted, tree-lined promenade, jets of ornamental water to be sent fifty or sixty feet into the air by tide mills, and a large equestrian statue of George IV. It would, Trench enthused, combine "profit with amusement"; while fulfilling its main function, easing the flow of vital fluids, it would also be for London a thing of beauty.[38]

When Trench presented the scheme to Parliament, Palmerston remarked that, if the bill were to go through, it would be said of Trench that "he found the banks of the Thames covered with mud, and left them protected and embellished with granite."[39] But the bill was allowed to die, perhaps not so much dead as "gone before." On the Tory side, Trench's vision was kept alive by the Duchess's son, Lord John Manners, who served in Lord Derby's cabinet as First Commissioner of Works from 1858 to 1859, when serious discussion about reviving the project began. Of those who carried on Trench's generous vision of what the Embankment should be, the most active and persistent was the great botanist and engineer, Joseph Paxton.

Having caught the imagination of the nation in 1851 with his immensely successful Crystal Palace, Paxton's reputation was nearly inviolable and therefore did not suffer when, four years later, he presented what was called at the time a "visionary" plan to solve the traffic by ringing the central city with a crystal girdle almost eleven miles long. Shortly before, he had entered the House of Commons on the Liberal side where he was to sit until his death in 1865. Readers of *Hansard* might conclude that he was one of those backbenchers who spoke sparingly and on a narrow range of subjects, when in fact his influence was far wider; he was almost constantly appearing as an expert witness before dozens of parliamentary committees, sitting on them, or chairing them; therefore, when he testified before the Select Committee on Metropolitan Communications in 1855, he was on familiar ground.

The appendix of evidence presented with this committee's report makes unusually interesting reading because it dealt with a wide range of urban conditions and was a cornucopia filled with bold and fanciful schemes. Although Paxton's Great Victoria Way was only one of them, it was the most comprehensive and the one the Committee considered most carefully and favorably.[40] Had the report been acted upon, Londoners wishing to move between the dozen or so railway termini ringing the central area would have been able to walk or drive along a glass arcade as wide as the transept of the Crystal Palace or could have chosen to be whisked to their destinations by atmospheric engines in a gallery some twenty-five feet above. In defending this daring concept Paxton indicated that he wanted his silver girdle to be as the ancient London Bridge had been, a place to live and to work, to stroll along and to enjoy, not simply a passageway. Asked if he thought that those who had destroyed medieval bridges had not done so in the modern spirit of improvement, Paxton answered, "I daresay they thought it would be an improvement to pull them down, as it was thought an improvement originally to put them up."[41] Although he did not neglect to defend the huge cost of his elevated corridor on the grounds that it would, like the bold concepts of Wren and Nash in the past, be a reconstruction "of the whole of the communications of London,"[42] he did not disguise the fact that he had Haussmann-like intentions: he would give every part of London "a beautiful promenade." "It would," he said, "make London the grandest city in the world."[43] The reception was generally favorable. The Committee was, as his granddaughter put it, "prepared to soar into the air on a raised Causeway," and so was the Prince Consort; nevertheless, those who controlled the purse strings decided to take "the more practical course of burrowing below the earth."[44]

Disappointed in his grand design, Paxton turned his mind in the late 1850s to the Thames and became the leader and the co-ordinator of a renewed campaign to build a boulevard along its banks. He was, as he claimed in 1862, "the originator of the scheme" which finally set the piledrivers and the stone masons in motion,[45] a circumstance which goes a long way toward explaining why the project was carried through in such a generous spirit.[46] However, more aware than he had been earlier that grandeur and amenity would not be accepted by officialdom as a good reason for spending many millions of pounds, he decided to make the traffic situation the point of emphasis in public statements. His theme would be, "the more free you make your communication throughout the country the better it must really be for everybody."[47]

The first step was to organize the support of government officials, a task made easier by the fact that the Chairman of the Board of Works in May, 1860, the Prime Minister's step-son, William Francis Cowper, was well-disposed and willing to second Paxton's motion for a Select Committee. On the floor of the House the motion also got a strong endorsement from Palmerston. There was little opposition and Paxton got his committee, picked its members, and made sure it produced a favorable report. At this point, however, lessees of Crown lands on the north side of the river between Westminster and Blackfriars Bridges, particularly the Duke of Buccleugh, rallied opposition forces (Pennethorne acted as one of their spokesmen), but a second committee, in which Paxton played a leading role, managed to fend them off. Parliament passed the enabling bill, and after two years of complicated negotiations about who would administer what, dignitaries laid the foundation stone for the North Bank section late in 1864. By 1869 the walks and drives on both sides were open to the public.

During these and other ceremonies, thanks were liberally bestowed on Bazalgette, Tite, and the various local and national politicians involved, but Paxton's crucial role was not mentioned. The probable reason for such a large oversight was that he became ill at about the time the way was cleared for the operation to begin, and although he continued to take part in committee work having to do with another of his preoccupations, how sewage might be used to further plant growth, he ceased to be involved in the project which had absorbed so much energy for at least four years. In 1866 a writer for *Once a Week* gave notice that out of the muck and scaffolding along the river's edges, "beauty is beginning to appear."[48] One of the principal authors of that beauty did not live to see it. On June 9, 1865, the great builder, gardener, and public servant died. Mournful music played in the Crystal Palace at Sydenham all that afternoon.[49]

Ironically, had he lived to contemplate what the Embankment soon became, he might have been distressed. It is true that few European cities provide so long and continuous a river prospect; yet, for all of its many blessings, the Embankment never became a Nevskii Prospekt, a place where people of fashion went to be seen or where "ordinary respectables" took the air and enjoyed the shade. Some of the riverbank reclaimed from the Thames became parkland but most of it went to developers of expensive dwelling blocks, hotels, and office buildings. Thus strollers had few window displays to look at or places to take refreshment and enjoy the entertainment and sense of belonging provided by a successful public place. Instead, this splendid river way became a haven for what the Edwardian Secretary of the Howard Association, Thomas Holmes, called "the miserables of London." He described the midnight scene in front of Cleopatra's Needle: two long lines, three deep, one for men and one for women, waiting to climb up and down the steps to receive a small bread roll and a cup of soup before dossing down for the night and waiting for the ritual to repeat itself at dawn. These "nomads," this "mass of diseased and unclean humanity," Holmes claimed, had come to "monopolize" what had been intended as a public space.[50] No doubt Holmes exaggerated, but it does seem that the Embankment did become associated in the public mind not just with destitution but also with suicide. Desperate heroes, and especially heroines, of Edwardian drama tended to go there to experience the depths or to immerse themselves in them.[51]

However, the Embankment did not fail as a promenade because desperate people took it over but because wide pavements, lines of trees, ornamental lights and benches, monuments, patches of shrubbery and flower bedding, even the stirring and ever-changing river prospect, were not enough to draw people from their homes. Strollers want to be with other strollers, to view the passing parade and be part of it. Density breeds density. Also, users need to feel comfortably in touch with people not radically different from themselves, and neither the West End rich nor the City and East End poor lived close enough to make the Embankment an integral part of their daily or even weekly routine.[52]

Paxton seems to have had a feeling for these basic requirements and Nash, when he laid out Regent Street, certainly did. It is impossible to learn about the long history of the project for building a Thames estuary or indeed even to glance at the flights of fancy in Barker and Hyde's *London As It Might Have Been* and suppose that all Victorian engineers, architects, and city planners lacked imagination and breadth of vision. Sometimes, as in the case of Paxton's Crystal Palace, vision was allowed to prevail over convention. Unfortunately Bazalgette was no Paxton and no Royal patronage opened the way. The architect of the great sewer project was a consummate engineer with a politician's sense of the possible. He was the Victorian "improver" at its best. When an opportunity, unique to his period, arose to build a spendid passageway, he responded with energy and panache. But it was a beautifully-crafted passageway that he gave London, not a splendid public space.

There can hardly be any doubt about what response would have greeted a plan for turning the reclaimed river bank into an integrated development which included high-density housing and clusters of cafés, restaurants, small shops, and informal entertainment facilities; those who wished to preserve as much as possible for public recreation would have asserted the need for greenery and "breathing space" while the Office of Woods and Forest would have objected on the grounds that planned building would interfere with the object of raising as much income as possible out of any development. Given what David Owen described as "the chronic, cheese-paring, tax-cutting compulsion of Victorian Liberals,"[53] the surprising thing is not how restricted but how generous the finished result turned out to be.

Post-Palmerstonian governments and the Metropolitan Board of Works from the 1870s were not inclined toward heroic engineering projects, whether of the monumental Thames Embankment variety or of the more utilitarian Holborn Viaduct one. The only major new street constructions to be carried through subsequently by the MBW were the north-south traffic diversions, Shaftesbury Avenue and Charing Cross, built in the 1880s – "the story," writes Clunn, "of a wasted opportunity."[54]

Although bold and generous, compared with what came after, in their utilitarian objectives, neither the Embankment nor the viaduct did much to relieve traffic congestion. Writing in the early years of the twentieth century and looking back over his experience as an observer of the changes that had taken place in the fabric of London since 1830, George Augustus Sala, journalist, novelist, and writer of travel books, gave an admiring account of the engineering works which had made the city of his youth, those "bad old days," almost unrecognizable. But had they, he asked, improved traffic conditions? Here is his answer:

> Alas! I am constrained to admit – and the greater number of thinking Londoners must, I fear, agree with me – that our position in regard to locomotion is a very dismal one indeed, and that the obstructions to traffic appear rather to have been increased than diminished. We are daily confronted by a perplexity and well-nigh inexplicable fact: that, albeit facilities for going to and fro, on wheels or on foot, have enormously multiplied, the crowd of passengers and the crush of vehicles in the streets are more hopelessly dense than ever.[55]

Sala's language is different from that used by the editor of the *Guardian* whose statement began the chapter, but the message is similar and so is the sense of puzzlement. At least the history of how the Viaduct and the Embankment got built should dispel the idea that Victorian planners were unable to conceive of the possibility of "environmental catastrophe." The discontinuity between the nineteenth and twentieth centuries lies more in the attitude toward the proper role of the state in street reform, although disputes about jurisdiction between municipal and central authority certainly have not disappeared. But underlying changes in administrative policies are related to fluctuations in how the general public and officialdom define street reform and conceive of its purposes. At no time have these attitudes been monolithic (Paxton's respect for the medieval street as a place where things happen as well as his awareness that "improvement" is a relative concept should be kept in mind), but it is probably fair to say that most mid-Victorian liberals equated "reform" with "modern" and "modern" with "rational." Few of these reformers had serious reservations about removing reminders of the past from the path of their planned highways. Progress for them meant making the irregular straight, the cluttered orderly, the unbridled controlled, the communal impersonal, the narrow wide, the dark light. In taking this attitude they put themselves in direct conflict with powerful currents in the prevailing culture which resisted the "tyranny of the straight line."[56] Max Beerbohm articulated this resistance in a charming piece for the *Pall Mall Magazine* in 1902, in which he expressed pity for the "humble old houses" which were being "duly punished for their timidity" and for

> the little old streets, so narrow and exclusive . . . we lose our way in them, do we? – we whose time is money. Our omnibuses can't trundle through them, can't they? Very well, then. Down with them! We have no use for them. This is the age of "noble arteries."

Then, dropping his ironical pose, he asked Londoners why they bothered to out-Americanize the Americans, since "after all, our past is our *point d'appui.*"[57]

Admiration for noble arteries was not merely the product of structural changes in productive forces, it also had roots in the neoclassical tastes of the eighteenth century and the Regency years and in the romantic rebellion against formalism, the contest continuing to the present. But the grid arrangements of by-law streets had few admirers; suburban estate development for the well-off, particularly in the last quarter of the nineteenth century, tended deliberately to avoid the corridor street and attempted to recapture the naturalness of the winding village lane.[58] Just how numerous were the forces on either side of the contest is difficult to say but the voices of resistance were often the more impassioned and articulate. Illustrative of this romantic opposition is a survey conducted by *The Strand Magazine* in 1907 into what some of the best-known London cultural spokesmen of the day thought was the most interesting street. The favourite by a respectable margin was the much-maligned combination of Fleet Street and the Strand. Lawrence Gomme, municipal civil servant and antiquarian, spoke of the "kindly bustling humanity" to be found there; Percy Ames, Secretary of the Royal Society of Literature, liked the "gay pageant"; another writer, Tom Gallon, found its old buildings, many of them surrounded with literary associations, comforting; and a visiting historian from Canada, Beckles Willson, gave his vote to the Strand because it was so characteristically English. Bond Street, Cheapside, St James's, Piccadilly, even the Ratcliff Highway, received mention and were chosen for their theatrical values or for their connotations. The noted painter, Sir Lawrence Alma-Tadema, for example, was drawn to Whitehall because it always evoked emotion – he could almost see the pageantry that had happened there in days gone by. Only one writer, Tighe Hopkins, stood out against this wash of nostalgia and even his resistance was qualified. He said he never groaned for the past: the newer, the more "delectable," as far as he was concerned. He liked Piccadilly's fresh air, clean pavement, bright lamplight, its policemen, shops, hotels, restaurants, its "good looking women." But even though his preference was for the present and not the past, his measure of a street was the quality of urban delights it offered and not its comfort or efficiency as a passageway.[59]

The record of street reform aimed at freeing clogged veins and arteries was, as Sala remarked, "a dismal one" because only a group of specialists shared the conviction of Haywood, Cawston, Wolfe Barry, and so many other Victorian and Edwardian engineers and urban planners (even Paxton in certain situations), that facility of communication was the key to modern urban progress. It is, therefore, a difference in priorities, and not a perception that the traffic problem may prove to be intractable, which separates "horse-drawn London" (which for most people was still, after all, a "walking city") from the London of the motor car.

3

SMOOTHING AND REGULATING

John Burns, fiery socialist fallen among Liberals, told a group of civil engineers in 1919 that it had become their paramount duty "to make crooked roads straight and rough places smooth."[1] By that time the more sophisticated among the street reformers had come to recognize the truth in Haywood's insight that straightening did not in itself constitute a panacea. What then of the other half of Burns's pronouncement; might it be possible to leave the irregular web of London's streets more or less intact and ease the flow along it by introducing new paving surfaces and experimenting with regulating mechanisms? Particularly from the 1860s onwards, when it became obvious even to the congenitally optimistic that Shaw-Lefevre had probably been correct in predicting that a comprehensive restructuring of surface communication was not a practical expectation, this alternative gained in appeal, and a number of engineers and others concerned with traffic problems came up with a variety of suggestions. One of these engineers was a railway manager named John Peake Knight. He proposed in 1865 that semaphore signals be placed in every major intersection. Because his idea that drivers and pedestrians could be disciplined into becoming more orderly street users by means of an impersonal, mechanical monitor has such a range of metaphorical possibilities, it can serve as a template against which a variety of engineering and regulatory devices for smoothing the public way can be measured.

Although Knight was an active member of the Institution of Civil Engineers, his chief contribution to the profession was an ability to apply inventions made by others to the railways he helped manage. This career started in 1841, when a second wave of rail expansion was about to begin. At the age of 12 he dropped out of a Nottingham grammar school to join two of his brothers in the parcel room of the Midland Railway. An official there noticed that he was quick and literate; on moving to a new position with the Brighton Line, he took the boy along and found him a position in the audit office. The timing was right for upward mobility; by his twenty-fifth birthday, Knight had become Superintendent of the South Eastern Railway and by his fortieth, he was back at the Brighton Line as Traffic Manager, then General Manager, a post he held until an apoplectic stroke ended a life of continual work and attention to detail at the age of 59.[2]

Obituary notices emphasized his concern about passenger safety: he was first to adopt the improved Westinghouse brake system, to light carriages with electricity, and among the first to introduce a bell-pull which would allow passengers, particularly women who were being molested, to alert guards and to stop trains.[3] This concern with safety extended beyond his business interests and seems to have been the incentive for bringing his semaphore recommendation to the attention of the Commissioner of the Metropolitan Police, Sir Richard Mayne, who passed it on with a warm endorsement to a Parliamentary Select Committee in 1866. Knight's idea was to treat the main arteries and their feeder streets as though they were main and branch lines on the railways. For thirty seconds in every five minutes an arm of his proposed semaphore device would rise to horizontal and stop traffic and then lower to indicate that traffic should proceed with caution, the same directions to be indicated at night by red and green lights, fuelled by a gas pipe running up the middle of the signal post. A lever would allow a constable to work the mechanism when he thought it advisable to allow vehicles to turn or to enter the main stream (see Plate 4).[4]

Mayne took the proposal to an official at the Home Office who liked the idea and arranged for Messrs Saxby and Farmer, engineers for a company which manufactured railway signals, to design an experimental model. They turned one out with high Victorian exuberance: Gothic paneling at the base supporting a hollow cast-iron pillar, painted green and relieved with gilding, which then evolved into a thick metal coil, encompassed at the top by acanthus leaves which appeared to be growing out of an octagonal box containing the lamps, itself finished off by a pineapple finial. Just below the lamps were three sets of four-foot-long semaphore arms, painted crimson with gilt borders. The designer, as one critic aptly remarked, "does not seem to have restrained himself by any rigid rules of any particular order."[5]

To prepare the public for this "chromatic glory," Mayne had 10,000 leaflets posted on lamp-posts, cab stands and omnibus stops before the signal was placed on an island in the middle of the junction where traffic coming off Westminster Bridge met the flow from Great George Street and where vehicles going east in front of Parliament met those going west on Whitehall, an even more lethal intersection then than it is now. That such an innovation, placed in front of Palace Yard, happened to coincide in December, 1868, with the formation of Gladstone's First Ministry invited jests about there being new means of direction outside as well as inside Parliament. In the case of the signal, the public seems to have adjusted quickly and with little fuss, if reports from Mayne's office can be believed. A letter-writer to *The Engineer* did leave some room for doubt by suggesting that compliance would be improved were the attending constable placed on a high stand so that all could be aware that the "eye of the governor" was upon them.[6]

Knight, delighted with this apparent success, was soon predicting that his signal would be appearing at the bottom of Fleet Street and other important junctions,[7] but this was not to be. In January, 1869, a leaky main underneath the pavement filled the hollow shaft with gas, causing several explosions, one of them seriously burning a constable's face.[8] An editorial in *The Engineer* praised the experiment and regretted that in addition to the "inherent nature" of the opposition to this restraining mechanism there should have been an extraneous one as well.[9]

Whether the cause was inherent or extraneous, the project died that January, not to be revived until the first electric signals appeared in the London streets in 1929.[10] That the demise coincided fairly closely with Mayne's retirement was probably not a coincidence; moreover, resistance from drivers had probably been greater than optimistic reports indicated. Given the sensitivity of the public to direct intervention even if it came in the form of a mechanical arm or a red light, those who wanted to exert more control over the street environment were constrained to find indirect and less obtrusive means to that end. Just as prison, school, workhouse, asylum, and housing reformers sought to discipline and to rationalize by means of architecture rather than by less predictable human agency, so street engineers and their employers were attracted, especially from the 1860s on, to the idea that alterations in street shapes and surfaces might have the same effect.

Thus paving was, and was known to be, political. Texture, contour and relative hardness, and permeability did determine to a considerable extent access and use. Before Thomas Telford and John Loudon MacAdam introduced their revolutionary techniques in the late eighteenth century, most London roads were made of packed earth into which rounded stones and rubble had been rammed or were surfaced with granite blocks bonded together with gravel. The first type gave advantages of a sort to walkers and pack horses in wet weather; the second allowed heavy wagons to pass over surfaces which would jolt a lighter cart or carriage. Similarly, footpaths were commonly on the same level as the rest of the street, marked off by posts and sometimes paved with egg-shaped stones. This meant that male pedestrians wearing heavy boots could use this pavement with some degree of comfort while others wearing light footwear or none found it difficult going.[11]

Freedom of movement for the pedestrian and the horseback rider was narrowed when vestries, paving boards, and turnpike trusts, during the late Regency period, gave most of the major streets new surfaces, made either of granite sets or macadam. It has been remarked that the use of these paving techniques, particularly MacAdam's, marked a shift from the attempt to adapt the wheeled vehicle to the existing roads in favour of the opposite strategy, thus expediting the process, long under way, by which the wheel gained dominance over foot and hoof on the public way.[12] One consequence was that the carriageway, all through the nineteenth century, took up an increasing proportion of the street, this despite the fact that 75 percent of street users were pedestrians and that their absolute numbers kept growing.[13] Thus the colonization of foot space by the wheel long antedates the arrival of the motor car and the motor bus.

The way a macadam road was constructed helps to explain why the carriageway expanded and tended to differentiate between the various street components. The method was to create a nearly impermeable crust by spreading small pieces of sharp-edged granite of uniform size (some stone-breakers used their mouths as the gauge)[14] in a layer from eight to ten inches deep on top of a carefully prepared base, usually, in the Metropolitan area, made of concrete. Under the pressure of wheels, or occasionally a horse or steam-rolling mechanism, the edges would break off and fuse together around the stones. Because it was almost water-tight, the surface could be shaped to allow water to drain off on either side rather than through a kennel down the middle, as had been common earlier.[15] This pronounced camber and side drainage made essential the construction of curbs and raised footways or pavements ("sidewalks" in North America) – although the decision by the City Commissioners of Sewers to substitute Purbeck paving blocks for Guernsey pebbles in 1765 had already begun to eliminate the chains, posts, or wooden railings which had previously defined the footways.[16] As a consequence, the carriageway part of the street not only became proportionally larger but more sharply differentiated from the other parts (increasing the amount of legal ambiguity about what the term "street" was meant to convey).[17] Between the late eighteenth century and the beginning of Queen Victoria's reign, vestries and paving authorities of various kinds had gained the powers and revenue sources to apply this technology to a large proportion of the city's streets.[18]

In some respects, everyone was the gainer; horses had better footing than before and could pull heavier loads with less risk of injury, and walkers were spared some of the ordeals described so graphically by John Gay in his early eighteenth-century poem, "Trivia, or the Art of Walking the Streets of London." Keeping to the wall to avoid being splashed ceased to be the strategic aim of pavement maneuvers. Nevertheless, macadam did have drawbacks, one being that it was expensive to clean and to maintain in good repair on heavily-traveled city roads. At mid-century some of the seventy-seven parishes having that responsibility took advantage of legislation allowing them to amalgamate into district boards of works but, even so, a welter of vestrymen, trustees, commissioners, and board members collected tolls and raised rates (about a million pounds' worth in 1870) to bring in over 600,000 tons of high-grade granite a year and to hire labor, directly or contracted-out, to cart, break, and ram it.[19] As might be expected, some authorities did their duty well and some miserably, but it seemed to be the general consensus about 1870 that London roads were well-made but "barbarously maintained."[20]

An important cause of this unevenness in administration was that some parishes resented having to repair the damage done in their local districts by heavy vehicles belonging to breweries, railways, coal suppliers, lumberyards, and omnibus companies, usually with head offices located outside district borders. With, for example, a capacity load of twenty-six persons, an omnibus weighed over three tons. A civil engineer employed by the Metropolitan Board of Works determined that on a wet day the rim of its wheel would sink a half inch into a macadam surface, making it the "most destructive vehicle on the road."[21] The cost of filling in the rut would fall on the local ratepayers and not the omnibus company. If authorities, under these circumstances, were slow to act, then traffic slowed down; even if they acted quickly, the carriageway would need to be blocked and traffic held up. Therefore, the challenge facing the engineer was to find a paving material or technique which would give a surface smoother than granite blocks and more durable than macadam. Perhaps technology could succeed where administration seemed destined to fall short.

Parish and corporation engineers had been experimenting with other surfaces since the 1830s, and by the 1870s there were at least a dozen to choose from: tar, wood, concrete blocks, artificial stone, several kinds of asphalt, and Carey's Cast Iron Channels (hollow iron blocks filled with concrete) being among them.[22] Since each alternative served different interests, each had its champions and detractors. The wealthy carriage-owning class and the merchants who served them favored pine blocks, six or seven inches square, grouted with sand and soaked in coal tar or creosote, because they muffled traffic noise. Haulage companies and cabbies disliked them, complaining that, during light rains, wooden paving was treacherous for horses, especially when brooms or sweeping machines had spread a light film of brown ooze over the surface. This faction preferred macadam or granite blocks, providing they were not so large as to lose their edges and turn into "petrified puddings." On the other hand, those whose main concern was sanitation, economy, and traffic control campaigned for asphalt. As we have already seen, William Haywood was the leading representative of this interest. He and others who were like-minded pointed out that it was the surface which best served the combined interests of the general public.[23] Thus parts of the social hierarchy and the conflicting interests within it were reflected in the surfaces upon which Londoners walked and rode.

By the mid-1880s pine blocks imported from the Baltic replaced macadam on fifty-three miles of streets, mainly in the West End. In at least one neglected back lane in Bloomsbury, one can still see patches of them. But, thanks to Haywood, asphalt prevailed in the City and parts of the East End used by omnibuses and heavy wagons. Initially there were high expectations that a street with the seamless, non-absorbent surface which asphalt provided could be made flatter, thus encouraging users to keep to the curb lane.[24] Had that been the effect, one of the leading causes of traffic blockages might have been eliminated without the need for direct human intervention. For example, every omnibus driver knew from experience that if he found himself behind a brewery dray in the curb lane, he ran the risk of a lengthy wait, immobilized, should the driver ahead need to stop for a delivery. Driver and assistant would need to secure the horses, summon the publican to open the cellar doors, fix ropes from the wagon across the footway to help ease the heavy barrels into the basement and pull up the empty ones (forcing passers-by to negotiate a perilous detour into the stream of traffic.) Some banter and possibly a drink would be part of a ritual that could go on for half an hour. Considering how long it took for a heavy wagon to overcome inertia, especially if compelled to pull up a pronounced incline, chances of passing might be remote. Unless he wished to lose his job, the omnibus driver would, therefore, do everything he could to command the center of the road even if that meant stopping in mid-stream to load and unload his passengers.[25] It did make some sense to assume that this chaos might be reduced by lowering the camber and by building refuges in the streets which would force vehicles to keep in line. These things were done in the last quarter of the century; nevertheless, the results proved disappointing. Advances in the systematic analysis of how traffic functioned had led engineers to make logical conclusions and authorities to act on them and yet the problem grew worse. Complaints about the habits of cabbies and of omnibus and wagon drivers continued unabated.

The same disappointment followed attempts to find some engineering solution to another impediment to the smooth flow on the carriageway: the seemingly continual ripping up of street surfaces to lay pipes and cables. During the first three decades of the century, legislative authorities gave a large number of water and gas companies permission to lay their pipes under the streets and did so in such a way as to make those companies virtually autonomous.[26] There were attempts later in the nineteenth century to limit their freedom to tear up streets whenever they chose, but these measures had little effect. Aware of this, Haywood and Bazalgette concluded that the best procedure would be to incorporate underground installation and repair facilities into their designs. A beautifully executed wood engraving in *The Builder* for 1860 seems intended to illustrate Hollingshead's comment that "the bed of a London thoroughfare may be compared to a human body – for it is full of veins and arteries which it would be death to cut."[27] The engraving shows a cross-section of Bazalgette's plan for Garrick Street, intended as a short connector into Covent Garden. There is a continuous passageway, tall enough for workmen to stand in and to push a hand truck through, giving access to the underground pipes. Even more complex was the substructure of Haywood's Holborn Valley project. One commentator spoke of it as a "species of elongated honeycomb," at the same time "an aqueduct, a viaduct, a gas tube, a line of telegraph, a sewer and a pneumatic railway" (for carrying letters and packages from the Post Office). He found it full of meaning: an emblem for "the compressed energies of London life, representing its civilization, its artificiality and its exigencies."[28] As a response to one particular exigency, finding a permanent way that was also amenable to continual change, this example was effective, but, as a general rule, it was far too expensive to be widely employed.

Not only did reform through technology have its limitations, some technological innovations could work against the objective of making streets into unobstructed conduits. One of these was the development of new types of cast iron which could be made cheaply and used lavishly for street furniture.[29] Ornate urinals, drinking troughs for animals, fountains, lamp-posts, pillars, railings – orderable from catalogues – tempted improvements boards and charitable organizations to fill the streets with the kind of profusion we usually associate with the Victorian front parlor. Similarly, the horse tramway, which reached the Metropolitan area in the 1870s, made the streets less smooth: usually the tracks ran down the centre of the streets, which was, as we have seen, hotly contested territory. Also, carts, other light vehicles, and bicycles, when they began to appear in large numbers in the 1890s, found the tracks perilous to cross. No other conveyance was capable of moving so large a volume of passengers as the tram, yet no other was more capable of tying up traffic for such long periods when there was a breakdown. Progress through technology, it seemed, marched in different directions.

Was direct intervention by means of legislation and law enforcement therefore inevitable? Proponents of *laissez-faire* liberalism (and the majority of engineers were prominent among them) gradually found themselves forced to conclude that it was, but trusted that their technological innovations would work to keep such intervention to a minimum. Promoters of Knight's traffic signal, for example, pointed out that, although the semaphore arms and red and green lights gave "the timorous" (meaning, of course, women, children, and the aged) freedom to cross at intersections in safety, they did not prevent hardy individualists from dodging their way to the other side whenever they saw fit.[30] In the same spirit, free-traders could argue that omnibus companies be allowed to form conglomerates on the pattern of the railways and agree that police should be allowed to inspect and to license vehicles and drivers but maintain that it was unnecessary to dictate which streets they might use and where they should load and unload, the argument here being that the instinct for self-preservation and the desire for gain would induce the omnibus managers to be rational in their choice of routes and innovative in their methods of coping with traffic conditions. Self-interest and the war of all against all in the streets, it could be and was argued, would lead omnibus companies to adopt the best possible disciplines and strategies for moving their product through the congestion with the least possible delay, wear on horses, and cost to the consumer.

A difficulty with this optimistic, compromise position was that, however wonderfully this process of natural selection might concentrate the minds of the directors of the London General Omnibus Company, it was producing slow-motion anarchy on the major thoroughfares of the nation's capital. The unseen hand seemed capable of keeping the omnibus competitive with the horse tram but incapable of unlocking jammed vehicles at 9:00 a.m. on Ludgate Hill or helping old ladies and gentlemen across Park Lane at 4:30 p.m. Perturbed by this difficulty, *The Times* devoted several leading articles in 1867 to the possibility that exercise of an unrestricted right to come and go as one liked or dared might actually decrease the sum of individual liberty. When the city's "great arteries are overcharged to bursting," it pointed out, free circulation ceases to have much practical value.[31] "Prisoners in a street block, chained to the wheels of a coal wagon," the article continued, have been compelled to submit to brute force and, thereby, have lost all claims to dominion over "the material creation and lower intelligence of every kind."[32] Readers were asked to reflect on the paradox that this regression had come about as the result of the progress of civilization. The old, picturesque, leisurely, untrammeled way of doing things would no longer "suit Fleet Street or Cheapside." "Progress," *The Times* regretfully concluded, "has its drawbacks, and in nothing so much as traffic and locomotion."[33] Thus, it would appear, the time had come when free-born Englishmen should accept the fact that regulation was the price to be paid for becoming modern, a conclusion Haywood and other traffic experts arrived at as well. Haywood's 1866 report on traffic, after showing what engineering might do to reduce the need for more and more enforcement, nevertheless ended with a plea for "more stringent police regulations."[34]

In its editorials of 1867, *The Times* made the point that kings, parliaments, and local governments had not been greatly concerned in earlier centuries about controlling movement because the public way in medieval and early modern times was as much a place to work and worship in, to demonstrate, shop, and display oneself as it was to move through,[35] an acceptable generalization so long as one does not conclude that the history of street legislation began in the nineteenth century.[36] What did begin in the early years of that century was the attempt to make a comprehensive law designed specifically for the Metropolitan area which had as its object clarification of where responsibilities lay for getting rid of all manner of street nuisances. This Act of 1817, called Michael Angelo Taylor's Act, aimed at making streets cleaner, quieter and safer; it also stipulated who was to be responsible for enforcement. Penalties were assigned for such things as sweeping rubbish into sewers, beating carpets over footways, allowing vehicles or animals to block the right of way, slaughtering pigs, slacking lime, piling up bricks or timbers, and depositing wares. It permitted an eyewitness to arrest without warrant any vehicle driver who failed to place flash-boards around a load of night soil or noxious chemicals, thus allowing the contents to slop over on to the road.[37] Most of these provisions were incorporated in subsequent legislation; nevertheless, this measure looked more to the past than to the future in that it made no reference to traffic speed or to the rules of the road and did not give any agency the authority to restrict or to direct traffic. The concern of the Act's sponsors was to improve the condition of the streets; the need to accelerate movement through them or to control reckless or obstructive driving was not yet understood to be a pressing issue. Londoners were instructed in how not to behave while in a street but were left to decide for themselves how to move through it.

Even had legislators wished in 1817 to regulate traffic, they would have lacked an enforcement agency. Their tactic of assigning to individual citizens or vestries responsibility for seeing that footways be swept and the dumping of rubbish be prevented meant that the Act had little effect on the actual condition of the streets. It was in 1829 that Sir Robert Peel supplied that agency, although traffic supervision was no part of the agenda for the Metropolitan Police which he established that year. Ten years were to pass before that responsibility was added to the tasks assigned the joint Commissioners. The 1839 Police Act formed the legal base for police intervention into non-criminal street activities during the remainder of the century. Most of its provisions were borrowed from the Highways Act of 1835 which had specifically exempted London, both City and Metropolitan Police District. Both the 1839 and the 1835 Acts gave official recognition to the seriousness of the traffic problem by making the observance of the rules of the road a legal obligation, trying to define "excessive speed," and spelling out (or attempting to do so) how legal language about negligence should be applied to drivers and owners of vehicles used for public hire. Further, the 1839 Act stipulated that the Metropolitan Police, under the supervision of the Home Office, should "from time to time and as occasion shall require . . . make regulations for the route to be observed by all Carts, Carriages, Horses and Persons, and for preventing the obstruction of the Streets and Thoroughfares. . . ."[38]

At first glance this last provision appears to give the police sweeping discretionary powers, but in fact it expected police regulation of movement to be occasional, not routine. "Time to time" meant "public Processions, public Rejoicings, or Illuminations"; the places where legislators wanted the police to direct traffic were streets near royal palaces, public offices, the Houses of Parliament, courts, theaters, "and other Places of public Resort," and not all the time but only when throngs of people were likely to cause obstructions. Where police constables were not restricted in their authority, for example, was when they observed someone driving so "carelessly" or "furiously" as to endanger a person or persons or someone who was "willfully" obstructing traffic at street crossings. On the other hand, vagueness about what "careless," "furious," and "willful" actually were limited the ability to exercise those powers.[39]

Rowan and Mayne had no great enthusiasm for this new role but endeavored to do their duty. This was made more difficult by constant resistance from magistrates who were sensitive about the incursion of the central state into an area where individual rights to free movement had been so long established. Sometimes juries would be even more recalcitrant, as in the case of a young widow who, in 1865, sued for damages for loss of her husband. He had been struck by an omnibus while making his way (not at a regular crossing) from one side of Borough Road, one of the feeder streets to London Bridge, to the other. The omnibus driver claimed to have been proceeding at a walking pace down an incline and, because intent on watching his horses, had not seen the victim in time. Justice Cockburn, in his charge to the jury, gave the opinion that there was evidence of negligence on the part of the driver: he was going six miles per hour, too fast to control his horses properly, particularly since the paving was wet and the vehicle lacked a "skid" or brake. The Judge agreed that the victim had been unwise to venture out into heavy traffic when the surface of the road was slippery but dismissed the argument of contributory negligence, saying that a pedestrian "had, of course, a right to pass where he pleased." "Besides," he added, "men are not to be recklessly or carelessly run over merely because they are themselves careless." Presented with this reasoning, the jury had little choice but to find for the widow; nevertheless, they awarded her and the children only forty shillings. Such a derisory sum, jury members wanted to make clear, reflected no want of sympathy for the plaintiff; what they wanted to convey was a conviction that adult individuals had a responsibility to look after themselves and if they chose to take risks, should accept the consequences, even though, as in this case, some innocent parties suffered also.[40]

Also worthy of note is Cockburn's comment that "of course" the pedestrian could act as he pleased, assuming that there could be no question about the matter: the accident victim had more right than the omnibus to be on the Borough Road carriageway; the right of the walker was unconditional, the right of the driver and his vehicle was not. Alkar Tripp, head of the Traffic Branch at Scotland Yard in the early decades of the twentieth century, recalled the public concern when his department introduced studded pedestrian crossings lest a prior right for the foot traveler in one part of the street might jeopardize that right in all the rest. Tripp said that his force did all it could to reassure this public, although police knew only too well the consequences of pedestrians acting as "virtually free agents," especially now that the motor vehicle had taken command of the road. He went on to predict that the conflict between the duty of a traffic policeman, on the one hand, to prevent accidents and regulate the movement of vehicles moving and, on the other, to maintain "cordial relations with the public," was certain to be the source of increasing tension.[41]

From 1839 on, nothing contributed more to this tension than the duty the police were assigned to enforce the rules of the road, the principal one being the ancient usage of keeping to the left. Theories abound about the origins of this peculiarly English convention, one of the more convincing being that the right-handed majority finds it convenient to hold the reins in the left hand and, with a leftward twist of the wrist, turn the horse to the margin of the road, while keeping the right hand free to use the whip.[42] Quite possibly this explanation has something to do with a wish to show that the English way is the natural one. Language, however, has some difficulty in making this adjustment, although making the left, right does have amusing possibilities, as in this old jingle:

A rule of the road is a paradox quite;
For if you go right you go wrong,
And if you go left you go right.

In any case, the antiquity of this convention made it no easier to turn it into a legal obligation since doing so directly challenged the right of individuals to use the highway as they liked, providing the purpose be peaceful. Thus enforcement turned out to be by no means a straightforward matter, for the courts determined that drivers, providing they were not being overtaken or were not being met on a narrow road by an oncoming vehicle, were entitled to use any part of the carriageway they found convenient, so long as they recognized that to use the middle or the right-hand side called for extra caution. That meant negligence could not be found against them simply because they chose not to stay in line.[43] Therefore, it is not surprising that until the 1870s, it was rare to encounter a London bobby standing on a raised island directing traffic, whereas the Parisian traffic conductor had become a feature of the street scene across the Channel many years before. Noting this English peculiarity, an article in Dickens's *All The Year Round*, entitled "The Dangers of the Streets," concluded, "In England, we are so very much afraid of interfering with the liberty of the subject, that sooner than put coercion upon one ill-conditioned rascal, we permit a hundred good men to be inconvenienced and endangered."[44]

Given these impediments in the path of regulation, it is not surprising that many insular men and women of property were apprehensive about the possible threat the influx of tourists in 1851 to view the Great Exhibition might pose for the maintenance of public order. Initially there were complaints that constables frightened horses when they held out their arms to direct traffic near Hyde Park.[45] But these apprehensions rapidly subsided. To almost everyone's surprise, the Metropolitan Police performed admirably, gained considerable experience in traffic control, and also secured Mayne a knighthood. One of the reasons his police could perform so effectively was that they could take advantage of the clause in the 1839 Act which allowed them to intervene on special occasions, even though Mayne was not at all sure whether the Exhibition really qualified.[46] Nevertheless, visitors from abroad before the late 1860s must have been struck by how unregulated the streets were. They might have had the same impression later on as well, although Traffic Acts, in 1867, one for the City and another for the Metropolitan Police District, increased police regulatory powers to a degree disturbing to many Londoners, including supporters of the measures. The journalist, John Hollingshead, was one of these ambivalent supporters. "Martial law," he wrote, "is not a thing to look forward to with rapture." He assumed, correctly, that the City police would be as apprehensive as he was, since so much of their time was already deflected from crime prevention and given over to "the daily struggle with traffic."[47]

The Act of 1867 was the response to one of those seismic eruptions of concern that took place at fifteen to twenty-year intervals throughout the nineteenth and early twentieth centuries about the possibility of a complete traffic congealment. In 1866, Haywood had estimated that vehicular traffic had increased by 25 percent between 1850 and 1860.[48] Two Select Committees met to receive expert opinion on the possible effects of the various clauses. Mayne was a prominent witness at their deliberations. His testimony is a valuable source for finding out what it was like to experience mid-Victorian traffic conditions and also for understanding police attitudes toward regulation in general. Responding to questions, Mayne agreed that congestion had reached the stage of intolerability and that considerably more police intervention was probably inevitable; nevertheless, he was firm in his position that the police should be given no more additional responsibilities than were absolutely necessary. He was concerned that, having once decided virtually to hand over control over street movement to his men, Parliament would grant them discretion so wide that it would seriously interfere with crime prevention and antagonize those ordinary citizens whom he had been trying assiduously to win over for thirty-five years. Did he think it wise to insist that wagon drivers be at least 16 years of age? That would be "unreasonable." Should there be a speed limit? People "would not stand for it." Was he in favor of a clause in one of the bills which would allow his men to arrest without warrant anyone who willfully disregarded their directions? He thought not. "I am sure," he added, "I should have a great many complaints if I were to stop riders going into the parks, and compel them to obey the policeman on duty." The riders he had in mind would, presumably, have lived near Hyde Park and would have been on their way to take exercise and to display themselves on Rotten Row, not the sort of people accustomed to taking orders on the public way from social inferiors with coarse accents. He was willing, he said, to stop traffic in order to let women and children cross into the park; indeed his men were doing so already, even though they had no legal authorization; and for years his men, also without authorization, had been separating fast and slow traffic on London Bridge into lanes; but beyond that he was not eager to go. What steps might legislators then take to make the police task easier? He mentioned a few. Parliament could define "furious driving" in such a way that his unsophisticated constables would know for certain what that misdemeanor actually was; it could make enforceable existing laws restricting the driving of cattle and sheep to the one thousand or so inner-city slaughter houses (the daily sight of sheep being pushed down the steps into basement abattoirs close to St James's Church, Piccadilly, Mayne thought "quite a barbarism"); it could give him the power to restrict the access of wagons pulled by multiple teams of horses and of scavengers and their carts into some streets from 9:00 a.m. until evening; and finally, it could control the increasing number of stray, and sometimes vicious and rabid dogs by having them rounded up, sending the well-behaved to a private shelter in Holloway and killing the others. (Hollingshead remarked that, as usual, the Commissioner wished to separate the deserving from the dangerous classes.)[49] But with these exceptions he demonstrated with consistency his reluctance to intrude the state into the ordinary activities of life, even when people of refinement found those activities ugly, vulgar, disrespectful, sacrilegious, or irregular – and irregular traffic was no exception. It is ironic that he had to weather a storm of abuse in the last year of his long career for supposedly becoming obsessed with muzzling dogs and arresting boys who threw snowballs and rolled heavy iron hoops on the pavements when, in fact, he heartily disliked involving his men in such assignments. To one irate dog-lover he wrote in 1868, "the Duty is extremely disagreeable." He said it had been made clear to superintendents that he "had no interest whatever to make them unduly enforce the Law on the subject".[50] Controlling the streets was his first priority, and it was his conviction that police should not be deflected from that task by being asked to get rid of every possible nuisance, vexing though it might be. Preferring prevention to detection, he was however willing to have police expand the licensing functions they had acquired since 1839. He thought it a good idea to compel owners of commercial vehicles to display their names on the sides and to attach number boards behind, for such publicity would act as a deterrent to carelessness and involve the public in the control process.

This preference for minimalism suited the mood of the time: Mayne got more or less the kind of legislation he wanted in the Metropolitan Traffic Act of 1867. What opposition there was in Parliament came from representatives of the City Corporation. Alderman Lawrence (leader of the "Dirty Party" in its opposition to Haywood and Simon's sanitary reforms) complained that Sir Richard Mayne now controlled what goods could enter the City. London was no Paris, he said; it was not a "city of pleasure" where "elegant trifles form the staple of its products"; instead, his city was a robust free-trader in rough, indelicate, masculine commodities.[51] Gladstone's Home Secretary agreed with the premise that the Act had handed over to the police the regulation of traffic.[52] Subject to Home Office approval and, if appropriate, that of the Lord Mayor and City Aldermen, the Metropolitan and the City Police Commissioners could, when they saw fit, close off streets to certain types of conveyances and direct traffic into lanes. Policemen could order cab-drivers to attach lamps at night (a regulation which caused a one-afternoon strike later in the year) and to display license boards at all times. Carriers of unusually bulky loads or haulers of freight requiring more than four horses to pull it had first to secure police permission. Furthermore, these and other new or augmented powers were discretionary and stated in such general terms that they almost invited the police authorities to extend the range of their activities.

That was an invitation Mayne, of course, was disinclined to accept; but Col Edmund Henderson, who succeeded him in 1868, was somewhat more flexible. In 1869 the first traffic constables appeared in the streets, and by 1872 there were 176 on full-time duty, assisted by another 230 at rush hours. They stood on platforms in the middle of the traffic stream and, like Parisian *sergents de ville*, directed traffic by hand signals; however, they were distinguished from their counterparts on the Continent by being under strict orders not to move their bodies or to gesticulate.[53] Whether the flow became faster or smoother as a result of their presence is not certain; it can be established, however, that this direct form of regulation did nothing to reduce the accident rate, although it might have kept that rate from increasing more rapidly than it did. Between 1869 and 1872 the number of fatalities remained the same, but the number of people injured rose alarmingly, from 1,706 a year to 2,677.[54] By the end of the century the annual injury count was up to 7,730, and in 1912, 537 were killed and 20,166 injured. Considering that in 1990, 100 motorists and 250 pedestrians died as the result of accidents, it is clear that Londoners paid a heavy price for their relative freedom from regulation.[55]

The Traffic Branch had better success in training London drivers to obey hand directions than they did in training them to stay in line or control their speed. Foreign visitors later in the years ahead often remarked on how coolly and skillfully traffic police orchestrated movement at major intersections. Lawrence Gomme, in 1898, recalled how the American writer, James Fenimore Cooper, on a visit to London in the early 1830s, had witnessed a rescue on Regent Street where a large crowd prevented constables from taking several hackney drivers to a station house. A considerable revolution in manners and attitude had taken place over the intervening years. "It says much for the modern police system," Gomme observed, "that traffic can be directed by the lift of a policeman's finger."[56] The effect Mayne had wished to achieve by means of Knight's mechanical monitor had been achieved, after all, by the direct intervention of men in uniform – but trained to become automatons.

Perhaps it is a paradox that this progress in disciplining the London cabby (and even that scourge of traffic, the boy behind the reins of the butcher cart) did not, as supporters of regulation had hoped, make the streets less congested. *Laissez-faire* still prevailed. Men with shovels from the gas and water companies continued to block up lanes during rush hours, despite attempts to regulate their timing; cab-drivers, who were supposed to pick up fares at fixed stands, continued to "crawl" along the most traveled streets; omnibuses continued to keep to the centre because loading and unloading wagons continued to make curb lanes into potential traps. If anything, it was more harrowing in 1905 than it had been in 1865 for a passenger to alight from an omnibus or for a mother with small children in tow to negotiate the crossing of most streets.[57] Londoners could reflect on the irony that at a time when technological advances were constantly improving the means by which passengers, goods, and information were carried from London out to the four corners of the globe, movement inside this world city had, during the thirty years after 1876 and despite the devices of the engineers and the efforts of the regulators, slowed down by approximately 25 percent.[58]

4

POLICING

In 1834 a group of distinguished politicians was appointed to assess the results of Robert Peel's experiment in turning the control of London's streets over to a professional police force. Their conclusion was that it had been a success beyond almost everyone's expectations, although they acknowledged that in the five years since Parliament had agreed to create the Metropolitan Police, mistakes had been made under the pressure of severe trials. Liberal-minded critics had been sensitive to incidents in which individual freedom had been unnecessarily curbed, radicals had reacted vigorously when the police appeared to be acting to suppress dissent, and conservatives had resisted the intrusion of centralized bureaucracy into traditional and communal ways of controlling crime and violence. Yet, the Committee remarked, nothing had been done which was "not entirely consistent with the fullest practical exercise of every civil privilege, and with the most unrestrained intercourse of private society." They expressed satisfaction that the exercise of this new kind of authority in public spaces so closely associated with the very essence of English liberties could take place without sacrificing "that perfect freedom of action and exemption from interference which are the great privileges and blessings of society in this country."[1]

It is especially remarkable that so bountiful a claim should have been made at a time when the tension between liberty and order was particularly intense. Two different Select Committees in the previous year had been set up to investigate charges that police had behaved brutally in breaking up gatherings, had sent spies to infiltrate political groups hostile to the regime in power, and had countenanced entrapment techniques. During the spring of 1833 the Home Office had been receiving reports, forwarded by the police, that elements of the National Union of the Working Classes were planning to turn a demonstration, scheduled for May 13 at Cold Bath Fields, into an armed confrontation. Reacting pugnaciously, as he usually did when faced with civil insubordination, Melbourne, the Home Secretary, issued a proclamation declaring the event illegal and instructed the police to arrest the leaders as soon as any of them began to speak. (Afterward, the joint Police Commissioners, Charles Rowan and Richard Mayne, insisted that Melbourne had also ordered them to disperse the crowd, a claim which he, pointing out that no written record had been made, half-denied and then, when pressed, half-admitted.)[2] Some 4000 demonstrators and onlookers ignored the warning, the speeches began, and Rowan, who with most of the police reserves had kept out of sight, ordered the attack. The formation of baton-wielding constables headed not just for the speakers' stand but for clusters of demonstrators gathered around banners and flags, including a tricolor and the Stars and Stripes. In a twenty-minute battle the police drew some blood but inflicted no serious injuries; however, two constables received stab wounds, one dying instantly.[3]

The man who killed the policeman was arrested and tried, but the jury, after listening to accounts of police brutality and deliberate Home Office provocation, brought in a verdict of justifiable homicide. This expression of popular hostility caused a stir which the Whig Government could not ignore. Furthermore, questions were raised in Parliament about charges that a plain-clothes constable, William Popay, had acted not only as a police spy but as an *agent provocateur*. The result was the appointment of not one but two Select Committees to inquire into the truth of the allegations. As one might expect, Rowan and Mayne, appearing together, were the most prominent witnesses. While they seem to have convinced the first Committee that the initiative for the strategy adopted for suppressing the demonstration had originated with Melbourne and his undersecretary, charges that some of the constables had followed retreating stragglers and beaten them did stick.

The spy scandal also put the Commissioners on the defensive. Sergeant Popay, a 35-year-old former schoolteacher from Norfolk, who had joined the Metropolitan Police in 1831, had in the following year been ordered by his Division Superintendent to attend meetings of the Political Union, wearing his ordinary clothes, and to make regular reports on what he heard. Popay did far more than that. With what the Select Committee who examined him called "misjudging zeal," he insinuated himself into the private lives of some of the members, altered resolutions to make them more inflammatory, purchased a pistol from one Unionist (probably on Melbourne's orders), suggested that target practice and exercise with the broadsword might be useful, and offered to give instruction.[4] One day, however, he was spotted entering his station house and denounced. Members of the Union sent a protest petition to Parliament. Promptly calling the sergeant in, Mayne told him that his denial about spying on the private life of citizens was unconvincing and warned him that he could expect no support from police headquarters.[5]

After some close questioning, Committee members were satisfied, once again, with the Commissioners' emphatic insistence that the idea of sending Popay to Union meetings had originated in the Home Office. During the questioning, the Commissioners were asked about evidence that plain-clothes policemen had been sent to report on a meeting where a radical MP, Henry Hunt, had addressed a peaceful gathering (Cobbett was on the Committee and could have been the questioner). Was police surveillance to be extended everywhere, the Committee-men asked; was it police duty to be an information-gathering body for the Government; had it become policy "to employ spies to pry into people's private actions?" It was with evident emotion that Rowan answered: "there are no two men in the town that would more abhor such an action." Mayne joined in: even "the imputation that we could have sanctioned or allowed any such practices has been painful to us in the highest degree." Before accepting such a duty, Mayne declared, he would resign.[6]

This Select Committee, like the one investigating the Cold Bath Fields incident, exonerated the Police Commissioners and expressed confidence in their intentions. Their earnestness and command of detail, the explicit way they answered questions about policy, reassured people of property and influence that the police were a far better instrument for controlling civil unrest than soldiers or mounted yeomen. The result was that when called on to explain their policies the following year, the Commissioners were not subject this time to hostile or embarrassing questions. However, they did not forget the ordeal of 1833. It confirmed Mayne and Rowan in their conviction that the general policies they had worked out, following guidelines Peel had set down for them in 1829, were wise ones, and it taught them to be even more strict in seeing to it that they were implemented.

Peel had gained from his experiences in Ireland a grasp of what a professional constabulary could accomplish in a state with responsible government and a tradition of respect for civil liberties. He recognized that, in an open society where the desire for order and the desire for personal freedom must be in permanent tension, a police force must seek to find an equilibrium, one which those most likely to come into contact with law-enforcement on a day-to-day basis would be likely to accept. Thus from the start, his two Commissioners had clear-cut guidelines: they would be magistrates overseeing a force of constables, officers traditionally responsible for organizing a locality to maintain the King's peace, servants of the community, and answerable, in the same way as other civilians, to the law of the land. At the same time, they would be placed under the supervision of the Home Office to insure that they remained detached from local interests, the pressures of political faction, and the vagaries of personality. Keeping the peace, in the sense of preventing crime from happening, would be the first priority; the older tactic of waiting for a crime or act of civil disorder to take place before responding would be replaced by more systematic ways of controlling behaviour, especially in the streets. From the start this concept of a depersonalized, non-military, virtually unarmed, impartial force, answerable not just to the Home Office but to the same laws that the rest of the community must obey, gave the Metropolitan Police its defining characteristic and explains why it did in fact become, as *The Times* wrote in its obituary article on Mayne, part of the "natural order of things."[7]

As one experienced policeman commented, but for Peel, Rowan, and Mayne, "it might not have been so."[8] That the Commissioners were able to arrive at their own personal equilibrium and maintain it until Rowan retired in 1850 was a stroke of good fortune that Peel could hardly have anticipated. Differences between the two, if there were any, got settled in private. Committees who listened to their testimony heard one voice. The fact of their co-operation goes a long way toward explaining why, within five years of taking office in 1829, their force had either won over or mollified the most formidable of their opponents. Therefore it does seem odd that so little is known about the lives and connections of these two men other than what one finds in general histories of the Metropolitan Police. This is particularly puzzling in the case of Mayne who, after 1850 and until 1868, ruled Scotland Yard as "King Mayne." Perhaps the most obvious explanation is that the two Commissioners succeeded so well in practicing what they constantly preached to their men: the need to bury one's subjective self in the office and to do one's duty in the most self-effacing way possible, although the failure of inquirers to unearth private papers may be partly responsible for the impression that they had practically no private lives. George Dilnot, who had a long career at Scotland Yard and wrote its history in the 1920s, especially regretted the neglect of Mayne: "he had the qualities of a great man," yet, he commented, "lesser men have lingered longer in public memory."[9]

We do know a few details: he was born in Dublin in 1796, the youngest of four sons. His father, Edward Mayne, a judge of the Court of the King's Bench, sent Richard to Trinity College, Dublin, after that to Cambridge, and then to Lincoln's Inn. While serving on the northern circuit the young barrister fell in love with Georgiana Carvick and seemed destined to begin one of those long nineteenth century vigils wherein struggling younger son waits for the "competency" which will secure the young lady's hand and her father's permission. But then, like a contrivance from a popular novel, a letter suddenly arrived from Robert Peel, with an offer of a joint Commissionership and £800 a year. The Home Secretary and the 33-year-old Mayne had never met. Peel was a careful man, so the choice was not likely to have been entirely whimsical; he had already secured an experienced military man in Rowan, who had served with Wellington during the Peninsular Campaign and at Waterloo. Peel wished to balance this appointment with someone with legal training, a barrister who knew something about the Irish constabulary system (perhaps Peel was not aware that Mayne had left Ireland when he was 18) and who was sufficiently junior in the profession to be willing to accept the less than magnificent salary. A younger cousin of Peel's on the northern circuit put Mayne's name forward, and Henry Brougham, William Gregson, and Justice Park agreed to act as sponsors. Mayne accepted the offer with alacrity. The marriage that could now take place produced children. One son, Robert, became Chief Magistrate of Logos; another, Captain (later, Rear Admiral) Richard Mayne, became a cartographer for the Royal Navy and helped to chart and to explore Puget Sound in what is now the American Pacific North-west and also the Gulf Islands of British Columbia, one of which now bears his name.[10]

What Richard Mayne was like as a father, husband, or friend we may never know, but two illustrations of Mayne's style as Commissioner will help to give us a sense of his public persona. Timothy Cavanagh, finding himself out of work in 1855, joined the force, put on the blue, swallow-tailed coat, leather top hat (reinforced with iron and cane), heavy Wellington boots, and wide belt with heavy brass buckle, and began walking his beat in Southwark. His superiors, noting that the recruit was sober and literate, recommended that he be promoted to the Whitehall Division despite his being several inches under the height requirement for that elite branch. The final step was an appearance before the Commissioner, a duty never undertaken lightly by any policeman no matter what the rank or how long the service. Cavanagh entered, stood at attention, and waited for the white-headed and whiskered man of 63 to look up from whatever he was writing. It was an exasperatingly long wait. Then suddenly Mayne fixed him with "an eye like that of a hawk," noted that the man before him had maintained his surface composure, and then approved the promotion, concluding the episode with a curt dismissal. "There never was a stricter disciplinarian," Cavanagh said; the Commissioner was "respected but feared by all the service." How even-handed that discipline could be, Cavanagh indicates by recalling how on one occasion, just before Christmas, Mayne sent out a directive saying that anyone reported for drunkenness during the festive season would be summarily dismissed. On Boxing Day sixty from all ranks, several having spent more than twenty years as policemen, appeared before him and, without receiving a chance to explain or appeal, were turned out on the spot.[11]

The ordeal by committee that the Commissioners had undergone in 1833 convinced them that this kind of inflexibility was essential and that there must be no let-up in their efforts to instill self-control. Orders continued to stream from Mayne's pen instructing his men to be impassive when insulted, to avoid if possible seizing people by the collar, and to use minimum force at all times. Constables were not to sit or to lean during their tours of duty and were to step aside for other passengers on the pavement; they were never to use the term "cabby," but were to say "cab-driver," and should address even the most bedraggled or vicious citizen respectfully. There was to be no relenting on the strict code of sobriety; one infraction would bring a warning and the second, a dismissal. Of the nearly 3,000 suspensions in the first three years, Mayne testified, four out of five were for being drunk while in uniform;[12] one should keep in mind that constables were required during this period to wear their uniforms in public, unless ordered otherwise, on duty or off.

Strict orders, however, did not guarantee strict observance. Some of Mayne's constables continued to send in to pubs for free beer, retaliate forcefully when abused, use rough language, and intimidate prisoners during interrogations. Some continued to cuff the rebellious, swing the belt buckle at cheeky youths, and take bribes from touts, madams, and prostitutes. According to two reliable sources, Mayne, on one occasion, had to remove the entire contingent responsible for the vice-ridden area around Regent Street. Wrote a former Commissioner of the City Police: "No man stood higher in the estimation of the public as a fearless disciplinarian than Sir Richard Mayne, yet, in his reign, the whole C Division was corrupt to the very core."[13] That reputation was, however, of greater long-term consequence than the many lapses. From the start, Rowan and Mayne recognized that to safeguard an area which by 1839 had grown to 688 square miles and contained nearly two and a half million people with a force made up of only 3,444 men, two-thirds of them deployed during the night hours, it was essential to win the co-operation of working people. They also were aware that success would depend not merely on how well the police performed but on how they were perceived. That the police did achieve a "grumbling working-class acquiescence" by mid-century can be traced to that insight.[14] Cold Bath Fields and the Popay affair provided a forceful confirmation of what Mayne had known from the start.

So well had the events of 1833 impressed upon Mayne the danger of using non-uniformed constables that there was no chance that the detective arm of the police would receive more than the most guarded encouragement until after 1868, when a new Commissioner came to

Scotland Yard. Mayne did tell the Committee in 1834 that he believed it necessary to send a few of the more experienced constables to legal and non-threatening meetings, and to marches and public gatherings, not to spy but to catch thieves and pickpockets, something uniformed police could do only if they were present in large numbers. Furthermore, given the widespread hostility among some elements of the populace, he thought uniforms would be, on occasion, more of a provocation than a protection. Without permission to use non-uniformed constables, on an occasional basis, there would be no way to control street robberies except to rely on professional informers, a practice, the Commissioners pointed out, the Metropolitan Police had been, in part, established to eradicate.[15] They explained that it had been Peel (also a Committee member) who had convinced them that a uniform with an identifying number would give law-abiding citizens confidence, enlist their aid in making sure crimes did not happen, and also restrain the wearer and make him accountable for his actions. Experience, they added, had shown how efficient this preventative policy had been.[16] Any departure from it would be exceptional and closely monitored, they reassured the Committee. There can be little doubt that they were also sending the Home Office a message to back off. The result was that from 1833 to 1842, Scotland Yard had no regular detective department and when one was formed, it was limited, so long as Mayne was in charge, to a handful of experienced men. Furthermore, policemen apparently were not used to spy on meetings during the Chartist days; indeed in 1850 a directive went out forbidding police to attend Chartist meetings out of uniform.[17]

Another theme that ran through the Commissioners' testimony in 1834 was the importance of maintaining a distance between the police and whatever government happened to be in power at any given moment. One way to accomplish this, Mayne suggested, was to cut off all direct contact between subordinate policemen and the Home Office. He recognized that being answerable to the Home Secretary made it difficult to preserve the political neutrality which was an essential aspect of their policy. Early on they managed to resolve that ambiguity in a way most favorable to themselves. They got tacit agreement from successive governments that they could have it both ways: if obliged to take some unpopular action, they would be able to claim that they were merely carrying out orders; and if pressed to do something unpopular, they could drag their feet without needing to fear criticism from Whitehall. It also came to be understood that ministers would restrain their impulse to interfere directly in the administration of the police force. It can be assumed that the policy, implemented at the start, of requiring everyone to enter the force at the lowest rank and basing all promotions on merit, was partly designed to prevent the

Home Secretary from asking for favors (Lord Melbourne, apparently, having been an offender).[18] During nearly four decades of service, Mayne was able to avoid identifying himself with any particular party or political ideology; therefore his reputation as incorruptible served as much as anything to fix the notion of police autonomy in the official mind.

As time passed and the Commissioners gained a reputation for integrity, Home Secretaries recognized that confrontation between themselves and Scotland Yard would be impolitic. Even when Mayne, his powers obviously failing, came under intense criticism for his handling of the Hyde Park Riot in 1866, Derby's government did not put any pressure on him to retire. One reason why ministries, especially during Mayne's regime, showed restraint was because they recognized that there were advantages in this arrangement. It was useful to have a buffer between the authority of the central state and the citizenry, especially as the police learned techniques of crowd control and became increasingly efficient at preventing and suppressing riots. It is generally recognized that the main reason why Chartists were never able to make London a center for demonstrations, up to and including 1848, was that the police were so effectively in control of the streets.[19]

That effectiveness was not, however, simply a matter of technique; it depended also on the willingness of the general public to co-operate, and that willingness, in turn, depended upon a perception that the policeman enforced the law and not the will of the ruling class. Mayne, in particular, had a deep understanding of the importance of image. There was a reason, for example, why he seemed to be so fanatically assiduous in responding to complaints. He took every occasion to advertise the fact that his office was open night and day to receive complaints and communications; replies, stating what action was being taken, were sent out within twenty-four hours (written, as likely as not, by Mayne himself). Because it would guard against suspicions of bias, Mayne said, he would welcome the suggestion that complaints be directed not to the Commissioners but to magistrates; citizens already had that recourse if they thought a constable had broken a law. If so charged, the policeman could not escape by claiming that he was merely obeying orders.[20]

Behind this attention to image was the conviction that most ordinary Londoners would welcome safer and more orderly streets, that, given some support, they would act co-operatively to prevent and to punish crime. In other words, he did not assume that poor Londoners were potentially criminal unless restrained by fear of punishment, and he did assume that neighborhoods retained some sense of community, despite the corrosive effects of overcrowding and the city's uncontrolled growth. The object was to demonstrate to artisans, small shopkeepers, and others who were close to street life and had a personal interest in making sure that it was safe and orderly, that they would be backed up whenever they acted against disturbers of the peace.

A memoir, published anonymously in 1858 by a silkweaver, provides a rare chance to see what kind of person and situation Mayne had in mind. The author, who called himself "A Working Man," said the region of the city he lived in while learning his craft in the 1820s was a real community with a structure and a cultural life that went back to the seventeenth century when Huguenot refugees had established a silk industry in Spitalfields. Nevertheless, it had become, even before hard times set in after the mid-1830s, "a bad neighbourhood." Two rival youth gangs virtually ruled the surrounding streets. One of their diversions was to select a bullock from the herd regularly driven through the streets on Sunday to slaughter houses near Smithfield, keep the animal hidden, and let it loose on Monday for a tumultuous chase down the streets of Spitalfields, Whitechapel, Stepney, and Bethnal Green. "Idlers by the hundreds" would take part, some to chase and be chased and others to assault and rob citizens who had retreated into doorways. Parish officials felt powerless to interfere with this Monday tumult, although occasionally they would swear in some local tradesmen as special constables and arrest a few stragglers.[21] Obviously a stronger hand was needed, and in 1829, the author announced, with a dramatic flourish, "Sir Robert Peel stretched out that hand." According to his account, the effect was immediate. The Peelers brought peace to streets once ruled by violence and intimidation. "No Arcadia now," the memoir-writer concluded; at least gangs of bullies no longer robbed people in broad daylight, and abused citizens had the courage to press charges.[22]

The weaver was no ordinary working man, and Spitalfields was, as he said himself, "distinctive" in its culture and organization. However, it is clear from the tone of the memoir that its writer wanted readers to appreciate that many working people did in fact welcome attempts to bring more order to the streets. He thought he was speaking for respectables in general when he expressed his detestation of gang terrorism and his contempt for the culture that seemed to condone it. While many others of the artisan class must have shared these feelings, outside that circle dislike of the police was nearly axiomatic. Mayne accepted that, but believed he could appeal to the need for protection that all but a minority felt. The point was not to be liked, but to be needed. It is true that most street workers regarded the "Blue Locusts," or "Peel's Bloody Gang," as the natural enemy. Until the mid-1850s, when attacks on police began to decrease, constables had to accept, almost as part of the terms of employment, that they would be assaulted and injured. At the same time, those most likely to be in conflict with the constable on the beat were the ones who were the most likely to seek his protection. That was certainly true of costermongers who laid claim to some favored spot in a street market, of street sweeps, shoeblacks, cab-drivers, and, in some cases, of prostitutes and betting touts. Studies from the nineteenth and early twentieth centuries have shown that it was the most *lumpen* of the proletariat who were the most dependent on the police for protection or help in settling disputes.[23]

When the review committee in 1834 asked the Commissioners for recommendations they took the opportunity to point out that the main source of tension was not police intervention into street behavior but failure to intervene. They wanted new legislation to clarify whether or not a constable was entitled to make an arrest on the spot for an assault he had not witnessed. As matters stood, the Commissioners explained, the police could not win. When, as so often happened, a victim sought assistance in apprehending the assailant, the only thing the policeman could do was accompany the injured party to the station house to obtain a warrant; in the meantime the person responsible for the injury could disappear. If that happened, Scotland Yard could expect to hear loud complaints. But if, instead, the constable laid hands on the culprit, magistrates would dismiss the case and the constable himself could be charged.[24] The Commissioners emphatically stated that they sought no additional powers but did wish to be able to respond to demands for assistance when those demands came from the community itself. That way, order could be advanced without diminishing the scope of individual liberty. Therefore, police policy should follow, or at least appear to follow, rather than lead opinion. For example, any interference with a working man's right to consume beer was certain to stir the most violent reaction; on the other hand, nothing gave the police more trouble on a day-to-day basis. The compromise worked out was to arrest for drink-related offenses but not press charges. Figures about the number apprehended for being drunk and disorderly are completely unreliable since it was police practice to keep most offenders in a cell overnight and release them before the Magistrate's Court opened in the morning.[25] Zeal about enforcing laws governing other kinds of offenses for which there was widespread public tolerance was also not encouraged. Eventually this approach helped to achieve what has been called a "fragile toleration" among working-class Londoners. This was a considerable accomplishment, but more significant was the rapidity with which people came to turn to the policeman as the arbiter of disputes and the agency for deciding what was and what was not acceptable street behavior.

The policeman was, therefore, both inside and outside the neighborhood community; he was, at the same time, the symbol of state authority, a disciplined, uniformed unit in an impersonal bureaucracy and someone who knew almost everyone who passed by sight or name and, more often than not, who participated in the informal methods used in communities to punish and restrain. That this adjustment did not simply evolve but was carefully thought out and meticulously scripted testifies to the quality of the men Peel chose to conduct his experiment.[26] It was their deliberate policy to assign police recruits to localities where they lived so that they would be familiar to the community and be able to recognize who belonged in it and who did not. Therefore, as far as possible, constables would spend all their careers in the same place so that they could learn every face and connect that face with a reputation. That was why, Mayne told the Committee, the men who walked beats were taken, once a week, to visit the jails so that they might recognize offenders about to be released.[27]

That this situation of being both in and above the community placed a constable in a kind of limbo, Rowan and Mayne understood. They were willing to accept the large turnover such alienation was bound to cause and believed the benefits to be worth the large administrative headaches brought on by constant resignations. Mayne went so far as to predict that after this constabulary method had a chance to work for a while, it might be possible to make yearly cuts in the size of the establishment.[28] He seems to have had no worries about how communities might react to individuals who were, and at the same time were not, insiders. He was sure that artisans, shopkeepers, and people with a bit of property or steady wages would quickly come to appreciate the protection such a system could give. And there is every reason to believe he was right. Mayne's strategy was not to protect the rich from the poor but to protect the settled members of a neighborhood from those who, for one reason or another, had no strong ties there. The positive reaction of the Spitalfields silkweaver was not an isolated one. We have the testimony of a, presumably, far less well-disposed workman, a chimney sweep named James Brown, who was clubbed on the head by a policeman while trying to flee the charge at Cold Bath Fields. He said he was surprised by the brutality. The men of G Division where he lived would have recognized him and known he was not a trouble-maker. The error, Brown thought, was to have brought in police from the outside. Asked if the local police were liked, he replied, "Yes, most of the G Division are."[29]

That was overdoing it; it sounds as though Brown was tempering his replies to suit the atmosphere of the Committee Room. Rowan and Mayne may have welcomed his remark, but they could not have wanted their men quite that comfortable in the regions they patrolled. The Commissioners recognized that there was a paradox in wanting policing to be both "mechanical" and "social" but they had no intention of trying to resolve it. Balancing the tension between the two, finding an equilibrium: that was their object and their accomplishment.

The optimism which lay behind this conception of what role the Metropolitan Police should play was based, at least in Mayne's case, on a conviction that criminality was neither widespread nor endemic to the city and its street environment. He did not believe that those who fell into the hands of the police were victims of hunger, discrimination, wretched housing, or careless upbringing, although he was willing to grant that those conditions allowed weak characters easily to be led astray; therefore, he never responded with enthusiasm to pressures to remove from the streets the temptations of drink and sex. He felt no call to the social mission. What did stir this austere man was the prospect of removing from the city a reasonably small group of hardened professionals, the so-called "criminal class": excise that source of contagion and the police could then simply be there to allow the generally peaceful instincts of the rest of the citizenry to come forward freely; "when," he said, "the present race of thieves, who may be called the schoolmaster, are sent abroad, as we hope they will soon be, and the rising generation will become better."[30]

There seems to be a consensus that this notion of a criminal subculture or "race" was largely mythical, that it obscured the fact that most Victorians who went to jail were poor people who ran afoul of the system because they were more desperate or unlucky than their fellows, and that it also served as a rationale for suppressing any behavior which seemed to threaten the existing power structure.[31] Mayne was prominent among the myth-makers and known to be so, as evidenced by Hollingshead's joke, noted earlier, about the Commissioner and the "dangerous class" of street dogs.

The Garotting Panic of 1862 demonstrated the uses and abuses of this idea that the greatest danger to communal order came, in a sense, from outside. On July 17 two men "put the hug on" Sir Hugh Pilkington, MP, while he was strolling down Pall Mall. One attacker approached from behind and twisted a cord around Pilkington's neck and the second robbed him and pushed him, gasping, into the gutter. Because street robbery with violence was perceived to have decreased since mid-century, the shock was more intense than it otherwise might have been. Eighteen arrests had been made in the Metropolitan Police District in 1860 and twenty-one in 1861; during the six months before the Pilkington attack the rate remained about the same, but from then on to the end of the year the figure rose to eighty-two. The press reaction was shrill: danger walked even the daylight streets; London had become "as unsafe as Naples."[32] West End gentlemen armed themselves with canes and truncheons and demanded better police protection. Members of Parliament called for, and got, a Royal Commission. Upon its report, Parliament passed a Garotting Act in 1863 which stiffened the punishment for second offenders and gave judges the option of making whipping part of the sentence, a sure indicator of the extent and depth of the fear which had been generated.

Mayne, of course, was called before the Commission as a witness and asked to explain how it was that his figures could show that while 10,000 fewer people had been taken into custody for all crimes in 1862 than in 1857, this particular form of street violence had gone so shockingly against the trend. Those who, with the benefit of hindsight, have given the question careful attention generally agree that the panic was largely what we would now describe as "media-generated." Jennifer Davis uses the term "moral panic" to describe the state of mind from the summer of 1862 to the summer of 1863. By that she means an episode contrived by the press and by moral crusaders and politicians who wished to be identified with the cause of law and order. This panic was used by them to "amplify deviance" in order to build public support for suppressive measures, in this case, harsher punishments, stricter treatment of convicts, and additional powers and resources for the police. A by-product would also be a sharpening of the distinction between the respectable and law-abiding working poor and a "dangerous class." Thus magistrates, in the excitement of the moment, often inflated crimes like purse-snatching into garotting assaults, and the police seized the opportunity to bring known troublemakers before them on charges which, in a normal atmosphere, would have been thrown out. Moreover, excited victims of lesser assaults would have been prone to inflate them into the crime that they read about every day. Hence the sudden increase in reports of garotting and hence the harsh legislation of 1863.[33]

One wonders what Mayne might have thought of this "moral panic" theory had it been explained to him. Unfortunately, we have only his highly public testimony to go on, and he would never have admitted in public to opportunism even if he had been conscious of it. About all one can say is that his answers and recommendations are consistent with similar public expressions he made during his long career. As to the cause of the surge in violent street crime he could only speculate that fashion in crime resembled mysterious fluctuations in dress. Perhaps the attention given to the Pilkington case attracted the attention of professional criminals, and others simply imitated them; he recalled that a similar wave of garotting had taken place in 1853.[34] This was a clever way of avoiding the implication that poor police work could have been a cause and introducing the subject he wanted to fix in the minds of the Committee, the pressing necessity of finding ways to drive professional criminals from the city. The press had fastened onto some decidedly shaky evidence which seemed to indicate that the perpetrators were mostly convicts, out of prison on tickets-of-leave. Now that transportation had been abolished and criminals no longer exercised their freedom in far-off Australia, they were, supposedly, flocking to the criminal haunts of London. This interpretation of events Mayne supported either for strategic reasons or because he believed it to be true or, most likely, a combination of the two.[35] He complained that it was precisely this "schoolmaster" element which had been allowed to escape his surveillance system. Since 1856 he had been under orders, he said, not to question or harass convicts free on license. Those orders, he had to admit under questioning, originated in his own office, but he claimed that he had issued them when criticisms reached the Home Office that constant police attention was making it impossible for the released men to find jobs. He had, he implied, been told to leave them alone. Therefore, there is every reason to believe, as Davis does, that Mayne was using the occasion to embarrass the "sentimentalist."[36] He argued that habitual criminals were unredeemable. He favored long sentences for repeat offenders, the denial of early release, and the right to keep a permanent watch on anyone who had been in prison for a serious offence. Did it make sense, he asked, that his men should do everything they could to expose suspected villains but then assist in concealing those who had already been imprisoned for actually carrying out their villainous intentions?[37]

This was a decidedly limited understanding of what caused "Street Outrages." Another outbreak of attacks on passers-by took place in 1867 and 1868, during the last two years of his career. This time the culprits bore no resemblance to professionals but were juveniles, moving in large packs. They followed parades of volunteer militia and preyed on those who were watching the bands and marching men, much as the Spitalfields gangs had done under less modern circumstances in the 1820s, except that the place where the attacks occurred was more likely to be Cavendish Square than Hackney Road.[38] Again the press attacked the police for first being pusillanimous and then over-reacting. However the search for causes in this later period concentrated on the debilitating and fragmenting effects of urban density and instability. By the troubled 1880s, hardly anyone shared Mayne's optimism that the streets might be made well simply by removing from them a relatively small number of alien contaminating agents.

There is irony in reflecting that because Mayne believed most urban contamination to have originated in back rooms of criminal pubs and not in the streets themselves, he did much to instill in the Metropolitan Police an attitude of *laissez-faire* toward so many of those aspects of street life that moral crusaders and efficiency enthusiasts found intolerable. Many unfortunate people suffered as a result of those attempts to isolate the "dangerous classes" from the working poor and treat these "deviants" as if they were moral degenerates. Nevertheless, it was, to some degree at least, also due to this outlook, as well as to the traditions Mayne and Rowan had established, that London never really became a "policed society" during the Victorian and Edwardian periods and that a rough sort of balance could be struck between order and freedom, an accomplishment which stirs a considerable amount of justifiable nostalgia in late twentieth-century observers.

5

ENJOYING

A late Victorian cosmopolite, Michael Henry Dziewicki, wrote an article about how beauty reveals itself in London by night. "Life is in movement," he wrote, "and here, what movement, what life!" The kind of motion that attracted him, however, was not the traffic's rush or the flowing in and out of a great tide of humanity but the gestures of children dancing, the turning arm of the organ-grinder under the flaring gas lamp, the rippling effect of light from windows reflected in the Thames, the passing of shadowy figures in the curling, shifting mist. In the harsh reality of day, he believed London to be in no way superior to many other great European cities. When skies were bright and clear, street life was about freedom – to carry on the enterprise of everyday life. But when the fog, "this dingy yellowish monster," descends, the imagination is set free and London becomes, he thought, "the most beautiful city in the world."[1]

Had the century's straighteners, wideners, purifiers, controllers, moralists, and rationalists been impervious to this kind of romantic sensibility, their confidence in the reform agenda might have been greater than it was. If the temptations and moral contaminants were to be removed from the streets, then obstacles to free movement needed to be swept away and that meant that the Italian organ-grinder who turned his crank under the street lamp and the girls who danced to his tune would have to be moved along. Evident in the tone of Edwardian commentators on London life is the sense that modern efficiency, often associated with Americanization, must inevitably rob the London streets of the very quality that made them unique. One of them, Thomas Burke, made Queen Victoria's funeral procession through the streets of London into the symbol of the passing of a culture. After that great ritual there might, he thought, have been other parades and popular festivals, but the spirit had departed from them. "With the increase of population and of traffic, and with the coming of the American gospel of 'the strenuous life,' the people's own pageants came to an end."[2]

In one form or another that end had been proclaimed, usually by elderly men, for at least two centuries, the proclamation often marking a shift in the character of street life rather than any real demise. Much of the recent discussion of the popular culture of the past agrees that the campaigns mounted by the rich, powerful, or pious to suppress the spontaneous, cruel, and orgiastic aspects of traditional leisure began in the seventeenth century. Thus agitation against blood sports, gambling, and public displays of obscenity, as well as the rougher kinds of street games and festivals which we tend to associate with the period of social discord between the French Revolution and the decline of Chartism, were continuations of a much longer process. Like so many reform causes, this one took on a more systematic character in the 1830s. In this decade politicians and reformers began to formulate theories connecting the rapid shrinkage of urban space available for recreation with what was perceived to be a deterioration in health and morals. According to this view, the poor slum dwellers were forced to live and play in the only places left, the streets outside their cramped and cheerless dwellings.

A consequence of this perception was a sustained drive to provide alternatives, "rational recreations," activities which would not simply amuse but enlarge the mind and empower the participant. Until the third quarter of the century, these rational recreationists did not, beyond the provision of a number of People's Parks, have much to show for their efforts; nevertheless, there was a growing awareness, during the time when the New Police were being used to suppress fairs and put a stop to bear-baiting, cock-fighting, bullock-hunting, boisterous street games, and the public singing of lewd songs, that it was short-sighted, when the time available for leisure was increasing, to destroy old amusements without providing new ones to take their places.[3]

Although binary divisions of this kind between old and new, irrational and rational, traditional or communal, and modern or individualistic were commonly employed by Victorian reformers to explain to themselves and others what they were about, they give a distorted, because overly simple, description of the changes actually taking place, or not taking place, in street culture. It is true that reform had its successes, particularly in suppressing obscene entertainments and cruel sports. It forced the pornography industry to shift from London to Paris and Brussels, causing the sale of its products to move indoors and be concentrated in shops along Holywell Street, just off the Strand. As a youth in the late eighteenth century, Francis Place frequently listened to bawdy street songs. He remembered two women in particular who used to stand in an open space between Holywell Street and Wych Street and sing a song, with gestures, about a man who complained that his wife's lecherousness had reduced him to a skeleton. Place said the crowd always joined in to shout the refrain: "And for which I'm sure she'll go to Hell / For she makes me fuck her in Church Time." But such sights and sounds, he noted, were, by the late 1820s, things of the past.[4] Animal-baiting, cock-fighting, bull-running, and what John Gay called "the furies of the football war" were also suppressed or driven indoors during the second quarter of the century. It is highly questionable, however, that the virtual disappearance of these activities weakened communal ties or that the initiative came entirely from above. The Monday morning bullock chase described in *Scenes from My Life* was not a community-affirming ritual, not a pre-Victorian Pamplona; working-class self-improvers like the Spitalfields weaver, as well as artisans, small shopkeepers, secularist radicals, and chapel-goers, welcomed police intervention whenever the sport was disruptive to normal neighborhood life and work. Boisterousness and lewdness had been toned down by the time Henry Mayhew made his investigations of street life in the late 1850s, yet much that was raw and bawdy remained. Saturday-night repartee between market sellers and their customers, perhaps the most ubiquitous of London's street entertainments, depended for its zest on sexual innuendo; violent street games like "Knock Down Ginger" continued to be popular into the twentieth century. In that one, gangs of older boys would run down a street knocking on doors and upsetting anything movable.[5] When viewed from the perspective of Place's youth in the 1820s, these survivals of gaminess and rough play would have seemed tame, nipped in as they were by police surveillance and "decent inhibitions." If the point of view shifts to the late twentieth century, however, Edwardian streets seem to be fairly bursting with activities. Girls' skipping games and boys' ball and marble games adjusted to traffic by shifting to the pavement, and in the process, reached unprecedented heights of invention. The capacity of this part of popular culture to withstand changes is remarkable. One Londoner, living at present in Notting Hill, can identify almost every activity taking place in Bruegel's sixteenth-century painting, *Children Playing Games*, and give the names he knew them by in Acton, where he grew up in the 1920s and 1930s.

Not all Edwardian streets were constantly filled with children playing hopscotch or "Nicks and Spans" or with acrobats, dancing bears, penny profile-cutters, or youths, arm-in-arm, singing Marie Lloyd's latest music-hall hit. Robert Roberts, in his memories of Salford life, spoke movingly about "the dumb accidie of the back streets . . . silent figures leaning against door jambs, staring into vacancy waiting for bedtime." "In general," he wrote, "slum life was far from being the jolly hive of communal activity that some romantics have claimed."[6] (See Plate 5.) Memorable too is Hippolyte Taine's complaint in the early 1870s that "after an hour's walk on the Strand," on a foggy Sunday morning, when the rain is "small, compact, pitiless, the spleen rises and one meditates suicide."[7] Foreign visitors before and after Taine frequently spoke about how sadly Londoners took their pleasures, particularly on the day of rest. But most visitors agreed that there were diversions even on Sunday: a visit to Petticoat Lane, window-shopping on Regent Street, watching the mechanical orchestra set up just off Northumberland Avenue, perhaps following Gladstone's recommendation and going for a long ride on the top of an omnibus or observing the summer evening Monkey Walk on Fleet Street when separate parades of swaggering boys and girls in feather hats went through, with "little shoves and nudges," their courtship rituals.[8]

Searching for just that point where the streets lost their *joie de vivre* is probably a futile exercise, although people whose memories stretched from the mid-Victorian period to the 1920s or 1930s tended to blame the motor car, or the kind of municipal Puritanism which closed the notorious Alhambra, or the triumph of the commercial entertainment industry.[9] Important though these developments were in producing what M.J. Daunton has labelled the "socially neutral 'waste' spaces" that so many urban streets were to become,[10] there was no chance that the streets could have been sterilized so long as increasing density in the inner city forced people to use these streets as playgrounds and extensions of their sitting rooms. Furthermore, there was a limit to the amount of tidying up that could be done so long as there were so many casual laborers who needed to make their purchases close to home and in small quantities, a service street vendors provided. Under these circumstances, the urban poor showed a talent for adjusting changes to their needs, and not the other way around. The argument can be made that the proliferation of music halls, gymnasia, popular theaters, drill and assembly halls, fenced parks, walled sporting grounds, and the success of the popular press competed with the attractions of the street for the increasing amount of leisure time available to most workers from the 1870s on; but it seems more likely that those enclosed and regulated institutions taught skills and tastes which were then carried outdoors – street singing and marching being two examples. Therefore, well into the twentieth century, street life not only managed to survive its competition but to retain its exuberance and its variety.

That the culture of the streets had such vitality was a source of concern to reformers. Alexander Patterson, an Edwardian boys-club leader in South London, spoke feelingly about the formative influence of the streets and how the "succession of inconsequent episodes" to be found there were "calculated to produce smart, resourceful, but unreliable men at the age of fourteen."[11] About the same time, a Fabian social investigator named Arnold Freeman argued in his *Boy Life and Labour* that the variety of experiences to be found in the street was dangerous, not so much because it was degrading or demoralizing but because it was so compelling. The working-class boy, he noted, prefers to spend his spare time on the street "loafing about" or "playing games, singing, exchanging witticisms, and generally making himself obnoxious to the police and the public."[12] For Patterson and Freeman, as for so many of their nineteenth-century predecessors, the free spirit and quick wits of the Cockney were admirable traits and worth preserving, yet the path to responsible citizenship and the higher life led away from the streets where those traits were acquired. If a cultural consensus were to be built, it would have to be done indoors and in a quiet, ordered environment.

A possible point of contact for all classes was thought to be music. It was the hope of many positive-minded reformers that harmony might beget harmony. An especially articulate and respected representative of this type was the noted economist and logician, William Stanley Jevons, who, in 1878, wrote a much-discussed article in *The Contemporary Review* about the need for Sunday concerts. His theme was the absurdity of using police to discourage working-class festivals and street amusements, forbidding band concerts in the parks on Sunday, the one opportunity for most city families to enjoy leisure together, and then pretending to be shocked when any "unusual elevation of spirits which the fresh air occasions" finds expression among these people in beer or in "horse-play and senseless vulgarity."[13] "Pure music," he maintained, was the ideal corrective to vulgar tastes, jangled nerves, discordant lives. He thought that provision of theaters, galleries, museums, libraries, parks, and science lectures assumed the prior existence of a demand for rational recreations, experiences which were "removed from the concrete and sensuous ideas of ordinary life"; but how, he asked, can we expect the "rich, rowdy, drunken artisans of England" to feel such needs, cut off as they are from rural peace or any remnant of folk culture? The obvious place to start, he said, was to attract them to something "above the trifling affairs of life." Copenhagen's Tivoli supplied the model; there all classes joined together under the trees to listen to a fine orchestra play a program of semi-classical music. There amusement and recreation merged in an atmosphere of "good taste and decency." He thought it a sad comment that London's educated classes should find delight in foreign pleasure gardens like this one, while at home, they ape the aristocracy, adopt its cultural aloofness, "fly the *profanum vulgiis*" and leave places like Ranelagh or Vauxhall to be "invaded by the *demi-monde.*" One part of society goes to the opera, endows symphony orchestras and at the same time, tells the other half that amusement is sin. No wonder,

Jevons concluded, popular taste finds what it seeks in "our inane music halls."[14]

The Revd Hugh Reginald Haweis, whose parish was in Bethnal Green, also gave voice in the 1870s to this hope that music might be the means to draw the whole nation together in a bond of sympathy. His *Music and Morals* continued to be reprinted for the next thirty years.[15] The refrain of the book was: "Teach the people to sing and you will make them happy; teach them to listen to sweet sounds, and you will go far to render them harmless to themselves, if not a blessing to their fellows."[16] John Ruskin also took up this theme but gave it a more weighty treatment. In lectures and published letters during the 1860s and 1870s he maintained that music was "the most effective instrument of moral instruction" but warned that it could also be "the subtlest aid of moral degradation."[17] He believed good music to be that which calms and orders the soul. Unique among all creatures, human beings are conscious, he said, of the rules of harmony; in a truly virtuous society, musical creativity takes place within those cultural bounds and has for its purpose the "expression of a lofty passion for a right cause."[18] He concluded that the musical expression of his time bore sad testament to the disharmony of cultural life. The modern city, he noted, gives out discordant sounds; its dance melodies are often "frantic," its march music "blatant," the songs its populace sings "reckless, sensual, sickly, slovenly, forgetful even of the foolish words it effaces with foolish noise." He thought the love of novelty, the disconcerting pace of urban life, and excessive stimulation broke the connection between music and virtue and led to as well as reflected a growing anarchy both in the body politic and the individual soul.[19]

Advice and dark foreboding of the kind served up by Jevons and Ruskin moved some reformers to action. A Congregational minister named John Curwen publicized the Tonic Solfa method, developed by Sarah Ann Glover, as a way to teach choral singing to those working-class people who did not have sufficient time or energy to learn the conventional rules of reading music. Factories, schools, mines, clubs, regional associations, as well as Sunday Schools and Mechanics Institutes, used this method, and by the 1880s contests between choral societies had, like brass-band competitions, become an established feature of working-class culture.[20] The repertoire, especially of the vocal groups, was largely classical. Thus the promoters of cultural consensus could point to some solid victories, even though those choruses and bands were largely working class and despite the fact that, in most other areas, the gap between "high" and "low" culture continued to grow wider.

As in the early part of the century, most working-class Londoners in the 1880s and afterwards sang, played, and listened to music in the pubs and streets, the main difference being that from the 1860s a new opportunity for musical entertainment and participation opened up with the dramatic expansion of the music hall. It had been the expectation of the rational recreationists that once a young working-class man or woman became accustomed to singing Handel or listening to Beethoven, he or she would lose all taste for "The Old Woman of Rumford," chanted in the street by the broadsheet busker, and find George Leybourn's rendition of "Champagne Charlie" at the Canterbury Arms distinctly vulgar. But that proved decidedly not to be the case.

In fact, to judge by the mounting complaints in journals and the press, the decibel count on the streets seems to have increased from mid-century on, despite laws aimed at depriving hawkers and entertainers of their whistles, bells, and trumpets. A component of that sound, one that caught the most attention, was the increase after the Continental upheavals of 1848, in the number of Italian organ-grinders and German street bands. To many Londoners it seemed as though the foreigner had all but displaced the native-born busker on the streets of the capital. Reform-minded Londoners, whether of the positive variety, those who wanted to promote music as a cultural bridge, or the negative kind, those who wished to rid the streets of obstructive and irrational behavior, responded uncertainly to this alteration in street culture.

One prominent Londoner, however, knew his own mind and saw no ambiguities. Charles Babbage's vision of the good society had no room in it for sentiment, disorder or, especially, noise. Ironically, there was little harmony in his own life or career. That life started at Walworth, Surrey, in 1792. His father, a wealthy banker, provided tutors for this precocious and rather odd only son before sending him up to Trinity College, Cambridge, in 1810. Making no effort to hide his contempt for the backwardness of mathematical studies he found there, young Babbage turned for intellectual stimulation to fellow students, John Herschel, son of the famous astronomer, William Herschel, and George Peacock, later to become one of the country's leading theoretical mathematicians. Gregarious and good company though Babbage was, he was self-obsessed to quite an extraordinary degree, so much so that he transferred to Peterhouse because the competition would be so much less formidable. This need to be recognized as "The Philosopher," the title he gave himself, only partly in jest, never left him and assured that no success could bring much satisfaction. Successes there certainly were. In 1828, Cambridge acknowledged his contribution to algebraic studies by electing him to the Professorship once held by Newton, the Lucasian Chair of Mathematics. Wellington, convinced by advisors that Babbage's project for building a calculating machine, "the Difference Engine," might have revolutionary practical applications, secured public financing to build a workshop next to the inventor's home on Dorset Street, Manchester Square, and to contribute £17,000 toward the project's completion. Between 1820 and 1834 Babbage was instrumental in founding the Astronomical Society, the British Association for the Advancement of Science, and the Statistical Society of London. Laplace, Humbolt, Erasmus and Charles Darwin, Fourier, Malthus, and Brunel sought his company and respected his work. Byron's gifted daughter, Lady Ada Lovelace, found him "one of the most *impracticable, selfish, intemperate*, persons one can have to do with," but went on to become his protégée and later on his "High Priestess."[21] Preoccupations which earned him a reputation among the general public for being a crackpot were taken seriously by some of the best minds of the time. These preoccupations make an impressive list: oscillating lights and telegraph signals, a ship-to-shore communication system, submarine technology, and rocket propulsion. He recounted in his memoirs how he almost drowned in a youthful experiment with a device for walking on water. More prescient than any of these, perhaps, and his permanent claim on history, was the never-quite-finished Analytical Engine, an automatic digital computer. Although it was not the stored program instrument we are familiar with today, it establishes his position as the father of a technology which was to transform almost every aspect of civilization a century after his death in 1871. He would not have been surprised by this belated fame, for he understood what the consequences of, as he called it, the "Thinking Machine" might be; but this made it harder to bear that his contemporaries withheld from him the credit he believed was his due. Harriet Martineau wrote that he "spent all his days gloating and grumbling over what people said of him."[22] In 1861 he told some visitors that he had never had a happy day in his life. He spoke "as though he hated mankind in general, Englishmen in particular and the English government and organ-grinders most of all."[23]

Babbage's near mania about what he called "Street Nuisances" has more than mere anecdotal interest because it demonstrates, in a heightened form, the mental set of one type of urban reformer, one that was characteristically Victorian but that survived, in a more muted form, to later days. What filled his imagination was the possibility of reducing all human activity to components, assigning numerical values to each, and, with the help of analytical devices, rearranging them so as to eliminate waste and irrationalities. He passionately believed that social conditions as well as commerce and industry could be made infinitely more efficient and productive if scientific inquiry were to be released from the confines of academe and other realms of pure inquiry and applied in a systematic way to industry. In 1832 he put these convictions into print with the publication of his *On the Economy of Machinery and Manufacture*.[24] So extensive and important is the "economy of time," he wrote, that "all other advantages might be subsumed under its head."[25] Karl Marx was particularly impressed with the section of the book which showed that as industry rationalizes in the sense of applying time and motion studies, refining mass-production techniques, and using applied science to advance the specialization of labor, it would be the largest commercial and industrial units, the ones able to afford long-term investment in technological research and human engineering, that would inevitably come out on top in the competitive struggle.[26] Time was for Babbage literally of the essence.

It followed that any process or behavior, no matter how trivial it might seem to the ordinary person, was for Babbage worthy of the most exacting investigation. His unguarded, unself-conscious autobiography is full of examples. He tells us that it was on first coming to London that he encountered street beggars. His response was to ask for particulars and then investigate. One mendicant, he recalled, said he was a watch-maker and gave an address in Clerkenwell. Babbage paid a visit and discovered that no person answering to the name given had ever lodged there. On meeting the man again he confronted him with this information and was told that the person answering the door bore a grudge and had deliberately given false information. So back Babbage went to Clerkenwell, reinterviewed the lodgers, and then, to make sure, checked all of the watch-makers' shops in the vicinity. The beggar, he determined, was not only an imposter but a liar.[27] After many such episodes, each described in detail, he came to the conclusion that indiscriminate charity was an evil, that hunger was the result of folly, and that poverty was best addressed by increasing the productivity of labor through the application of new technology and systematic procedures for increasing worker incentive, profit-sharing being one possibility.[28] How these busy, dedicated workers were to spend their leisure was not a subject that interested him. We can be sure, however, that listening to street bands or dancing to the sound of the hurdy-gurdy was the last thing he thought they should be doing. Distraction had no place in his technocratic utopia, especially noisy distraction which destroyed "the time and energies of all the intellectual classes of society by its continual interruptions of their pursuits."[29]

Many from London's intellectual classes smiled at Babbage's monomania but had some sympathy for his cause. Had the German and Italian entertainers confined themselves to the East End and brought a touch of lightness into grey areas there, it is unlikely that such illustrious figures as Carlyle, Dickens,[30] Mill, Tennyson, Millais, Wilkie Collins, and Holman Hunt would have put their names to a petition, as they did in 1864, asking Parliament to give the intellectuals and creative artists some relief. Their charge was that these foreigners came to London because of the city's reputation for generosity to street buskers. Blackmail, not entertainment, was their object. According to this version, they would seek out the residences of wealthy people, especially those who were known to be sensitive to outside noises, and tootle or grind away until the victim sent a servant out with a shilling bribe. This had long been a traditional busker's gambit. What seemed to make the situation intolerable was that these performances had become louder, more frequent, and better organized. Worse, it was carried on by what many inhabitants of Belgravia thought to be riff-raff from Berlin and, as *The Saturday Review* sniffed, "filthy Italian refugees," who have left "the Abruzzi for Saffron Hill for the musical instruction of our foggy land."[31]

Householders had been given some legal recourse against such invasions of their privacy in the Police Act of 1839. It authorized constables to remove musicians if asked to do so by the head of the house, either directly or by means of a servant, providing that the grounds given were the illness of a resident or some "other reasonable cause." To learn that Sir Richard Mayne chose not to exercise in an aggressive way the considerable discretionary powers this language provided will come as no surprise. In 1859 he gave instructions that his men were to refuse requests to move musicians on unless there was no reason to doubt that a resident of the house was actually ill. Otherwise, the constable on the beat was to report the complaint and wait for instructions. The householder could request the musicians to leave and could obtain (and pay for) a warrant if the request were ignored, but the constable was not authorized to make a summary arrest unless the offense had taken place within his view.[32]

Under these circumstances it would take an unusually determined as well as exasperated man to put the law into motion, and Babbage was that man (see Plate 6). A letter he wrote to Mayne in 1859 shows how far he was prepared to go. Distracted, he said, at 10:30 in the morning from his labors on improvements to a device for communicating with ships in stormy weather, he asked a brass band playing under his window several times to desist and then went in search of a policeman, but to no avail. On returning home he found his persecutors being invited into a neighbor's house. Undeterred he searched a second time for the constable, returning with him just as the four-man band was emerging from its visit next door. At the station house, Babbage seems to have insisted on his right to make a citizen's arrest and demanded the group be brought before Mr Broughton, the magistrate. Broughton listened to the case and immediately dismissed the defendants. They emerged from the station to the cheers of a throng which had gathered. At 4:00 p.m. that afternoon, Babbage wrote, two horn players appeared near his office window and four hours later two more men showed up to serenade him with pipe and tin whistle beneath the library window. And if that were not enough, the group leader had the cheek to threaten action for false arrest and demand £5 in compensation.[33]

When Mayne's answer gave no satisfaction, Babbage, some months later, fired off another detailed complaint. In this one he included a list of the nuisances that had made his life miserable during the interim. Included were "Organs, Brass-bands, Fiddlers, Harps, Monkeys, Punch . . . athletes, males and females walking on stilts, Fantoccini [Marionettes], Hindu and Mohammedan impostors beating monotonous drums and shamming insanity, troops of Scotch impostors, dancing with bag-pipes."[34] And now the organ-grinders were back again. On their latest visit, he told Mayne, he had been followed by about a hundred "men, women, children and idlers shouting and hooting" when he set off on yet another search for the suspiciously elusive local constable. In a draft of the letter he noted that, even as he wrote, twenty children were assembled in front of his house, "singing, dancing, shouting and beating sticks." He concluded by asking the Commissioner: since your men have discretionary powers, why don't they use them?[35]

Mayne, in his answer, tried to persuade Babbage to desist. He said that it was obvious the neighborhood wanted the entertainment the musicians provided; indeed, there seemed to be, he added, "a very strong feeling by many persons against the enforcement of the law even in cases to which it is applicable, and I have received many angry remonstrances against the interference by the police." He ended with the advice that, since the law was not effective, it might be wise for Babbage to give up his attempt to enforce it himself.[36]

Needless to say, that advice was wasted. Not only did Babbage continue to brave taunts and occasional missiles but he found a confederate in Michael Bass, the head of the famous brewery and a Liberal Member of Parliament, someone who was as annoyed as he was and able to get the ear of Palmerston's ministry. Neither the Prime Minister nor his Chancellor of the Exchequer, William Gladstone, had any enthusiasm for the cause and stalled Bass in 1863 when he raised the question of street music in the Commons. But Bass was determined. He organized the petition mentioned earlier, got *The Times* and a number of influential journals on side, wrote a short book on the subject (*Street Music in the Metropolis*), and finally managed to steer an amending bill through Parliament in 1864. Speaking before the House the previous year, he recounted having "had the occasion to call on his neighbour, Sir Richard Mayne, and found a band on his doorstep." On the south side of Eaton Square a second band had gathered and was in action, and on the north side, a third. Finally, in yet another part of Eaton Square, stood a fourth, in front of the house of the Home Secretary, "shrieking, blasting, counter-blasting, and creating the most horrible discord." Can these gentlemen deny, he asked, that these "unfortunate foreigners who were blowing their wind away" are not a "hindrance to the serious business of life"?[37]

An Irish MP, Baron Fermoy, could not pass up the opportunity to wonder whether Bass's dislike of noise in the streets included the racket made by drays and beer barrels in comparison to which sounds of the bands and organs were melodious and sweet. He advised the wealthy and powerful who were annoyed to reflect that street music was about the only innocent recreation the poor and powerless had left to them; besides, he said, it was a generally accepted fact "that the streets must be free for all legitimate occupations." A colleague, Sir John Shelley, agreed: if men, women, and children of the working classes lost their street music, "there would be no life, no pleasure, no amusement."[38]

The bill that passed the next year did not go that far, but it did remove the "reasonable cause" phrase and direct the police to act upon being requested to do so by any householder. Gladstone spoke against the principle of giving a single individual a "purely arbitrary veto," doubting whether opera and concert-goers could be good judges of what amused the people. John Francis Maguire, Irish journalist turned nationalist politician, thought the proposed legislation reflected the "spirit of Professor Babbage." But it was the Liberal Member for the Tower Hamlets, Acton Smee Ayrton, who managed to undercut Bass's strategy by amending the bill so that a complainant would need to accompany the entertainers and the policeman to the station house and lay charges, an effective deterrent, it proved, in the great majority of cases.[39]

Babbage, of course, carried on, literally until the day he died, what one defender of street music called "the German Crusade."[40] In 1868 we find the sad, bitter old man complaining to the Home Secretary that a neighbor, seeing him remonstrating with "an Italian," came out and gave money for the music to continue. A crowd gathered and shouted curses. Babbage jumped into a cab followed by cries of "Turn it over!" The cabby managed to escape and to find a policeman. Although invited to ride, the constable refused and instead walked slowly back toward the still-angry crowd while the 76-year-old Babbage, believing himself now safe, descended from the cab. He was immediately surrounded by a pack of children who, crying "Old Babbage," showered him with filth from the street. The magistrate would not hear the case against the neighbor, and Mayne refused to take any action against the constable. Babbage informed the Home Secretary that he had been forced to bar his windows and that friends had warned him against walking alone even in streets remote from Manchester Square.[41]

The reaction of many of the retail merchants on Oxford Street when Babbage did manage, on one occasion, to get a number of convictions, confirms this impression that the opposition to removing the bands and hurdy-gurdies was not simply a local incident provoked by a particularly cantankerous and eccentric individual. Store-owners all the way from Edgware to Tottenham Court Road placed large placards in their windows (the language was abusive, some of it in rhyme), denouncing the campaign by Babbage and his supporters.[42] One assumes that the merchants of Oxford Street believed that street entertainments were good for business.

However, it is not because street music suited some commercial interests that Edwardian as well as Victorian London was filled with melody. Parliament was never indifferent to the wishes of shopkeepers, but that does not explain why it responded only half-heartedly to pressure from influential people who had genuine grievances, nor does it explain why police chose to exercise their discretionary powers so sluggishly and why magistrates sided, more often than not, with the ragged, immigrant buskers who appeared before them. Far more important was the fact that street music provided a cultural meeting ground for almost every segment of the social structure. Michael Dziewicki, Ford Maddox Ford, Augustus Hare, Clarence Rook, Walter Besant, George Gissing, Emily Cook, Thomas Holmes, Charles Booth, Thomas Burke, Robert Roberts, indeed almost everyone we turn to in order to sense the flavor of street life in the period, confirms the impression that street music was one of the few aspects of urban life that just about everyone could enjoy, including, probably, many of those philosophers, artists, composers, scientists, and men of letters who signed Bass's petition. The American writer James Fenimore Cooper visiting London at the beginning of Victoria's reign, enthused about the street music he heard: "positively the best in the world," better even, he claimed, than that of Venice or Naples. Instrumentalists who would in most large cities, he thought, be engaged by orchestras walked the London streets and played Mozart, Beethoven, Mayerbeer, and Weber beneath one's window. Just the other evening, on his way to dinner, he had encountered a kind of wheelbarrow containing a "grand piano on which someone was playing an overture of Rossini, accompanied by a flageolet."[43] A story went the rounds in the 1860s that Bellini once said to Rossini, "My songs are sung in the streets of Paris and London." "Ah," Rossini was supposed to have retorted, "but mine *grind!*"[44]

We can be sure that selections from Italian opera were not the only musical fare served up by griddlers (glee singers), street-corner violinists, brass bands, or barrel-organs. Nevertheless, it was not just in concerts or choir rehearsals that the working class came in contact with "high culture"; for every working man or woman who sang the *Messiah* at a local concert hall, there were many more who heard music from the classical tradition on the street. Mayhew interviewed the owner of a flute harmonicon organ who said that of the eight tunes his instrument played, one was "I Lombardi," by Verdi ("All of the organs play that piece"), and another was from "Il Trovatore." That the third and fourth items were the "Liverpool Hornpipe" and "The Ratcatcher's Daughter"[45] illustrates the point that, unlike the programs offered in almost every other kind of milieu, the repertoire presented in the streets was seldom an expression of one or several identifiable class cultures but a promiscuous jumble of tastes. This jumble continued up to and a little beyond the Great War.

Furthermore, there is abundant evidence that middle-class and aristocratic Londoners not only enjoyed street music but frequently invited its performers into their homes and gardens to entertain at wedding receptions, birthday parties, and other domestic celebrations; indeed this patronage was the cause of some of Babbage's most intemperate outbursts. It seems safe to assume that on these occasions arias from Verdi and Rossini would not have been the only pieces requested, since the likelihood of hearing something bawdy or politically tendentious from professional street musicians, especially after the 1850s, was surprisingly remote. Therefore, there was at least this exception to the increasing tendency for working-class and middle-class leisure activities to draw apart, physically and in every other way, a process clearly evident in most recreational activities well before mid-century.[46]

People interested in social reform, providing they were not at the Babbage end of the spectrum, recognized the value of retaining this cultural bridge; they wished for cultural consensus and sought ways to bring it about. At the same time they valued privacy, which they thought of as control by individuals over who and what entered their personal space. The diarist Sir William Hardman recorded in February, 1863, that barrel-organs were "licensed nuisances."

> I, for example, am sitting, writing or reading, in my castle, for all our houses are castles! (save the mark!) comfortable, with slippers on feet, and spectacles on nose; and I must, forsooth, find a Peeler before I can rid myself of my nuisance.[47]

It would be the rare middle-class heart that would not have resonated to that sentiment. To complicate matters further, it is likely that tolerant and kindly liberals like Hardman would have agreed in a general way with the view of a writer in the *Examiner* that "the streets are for traffic and communication . . . not for orchestras, or stages, and to turn them to such usages is an abuse permitted in no capital in Europe but unhappy London."[48] But it is doubtful if these same moderate reformers would have been entirely comfortable with a sentiment expressed by Lord Stanley in a mollifying letter to Babbage, wishing him success in driving "The Organ Pest" out of the city. "But," Stanley continued, "the idea that this is a free country, and that therefore every man has a right to annoy his neighbour, is deeply rooted in a certain class of mind."[49] In fact those roots extended more widely. The idea, confused and overlaid with contradictions though it might be, that individuals should have the right to do as they chose on the highway had long ago been firmly planted in almost every class of mind and helped to give English men and women a sense of who they were. Middle-class reformers wanted to defend their castles and rationalize street use yet, at the same time, make cultural contact with the urban poor and not surrender a peculiarly English liberty, the right to use the streets with a minimum of interference. One consequence of the tension among these various goals and values, every one in conflict, was that London continued to provide the safest haven in Northern Europe for street entertainers even though they could often be intolerable nuisances and did sometimes obstruct the free flow of traffic and communication.

Figure 1 Fleet Street in the 1890s. This shows how ill-defined the boundary was between pedestrians and vehicles in the pre-motor era. Although the law set limits on pedestrian use of the public street, Londoners were not easily intimidated. Note the one bright feminine face and hat in a sea of male blackness. Before and after the tide of commuters slackened, women shoppers would appear; on warm Sunday evenings, girls and boys would turn Fleet Street into a "monkey walk," a place to conduct courtship rituals.

Figure 2 The Thames Embankment under construction (1867). Londoners were frequently reminded that while London's "improvements" might lack the superficial impressiveness of Parisian counterparts, they were more "substantial." This engraving from the *Illustrated London News* was meant to disclose the Embankment's interior in all its rationality and complexity – sewage and trains would run below and a "new channel of oxygen" would run above. Like the Holborn Viaduct, the Embankment was much more than met the eye.

Figure 3 Holborn Viaduct nearing completion. Traffic moving slowly behind a one-horse lumber cart up Farringdon Street, itself built over what was once the Fleet River, now little more than a sewer. William Haywood, the project's engineer, remarked that his task was not just the bridging of Holborn Valley but the "demolition and reconstruction of a whole district." Four thousand dwellings were knocked down and the inhabitants forced into the margin – slum clearance, Victorian style.

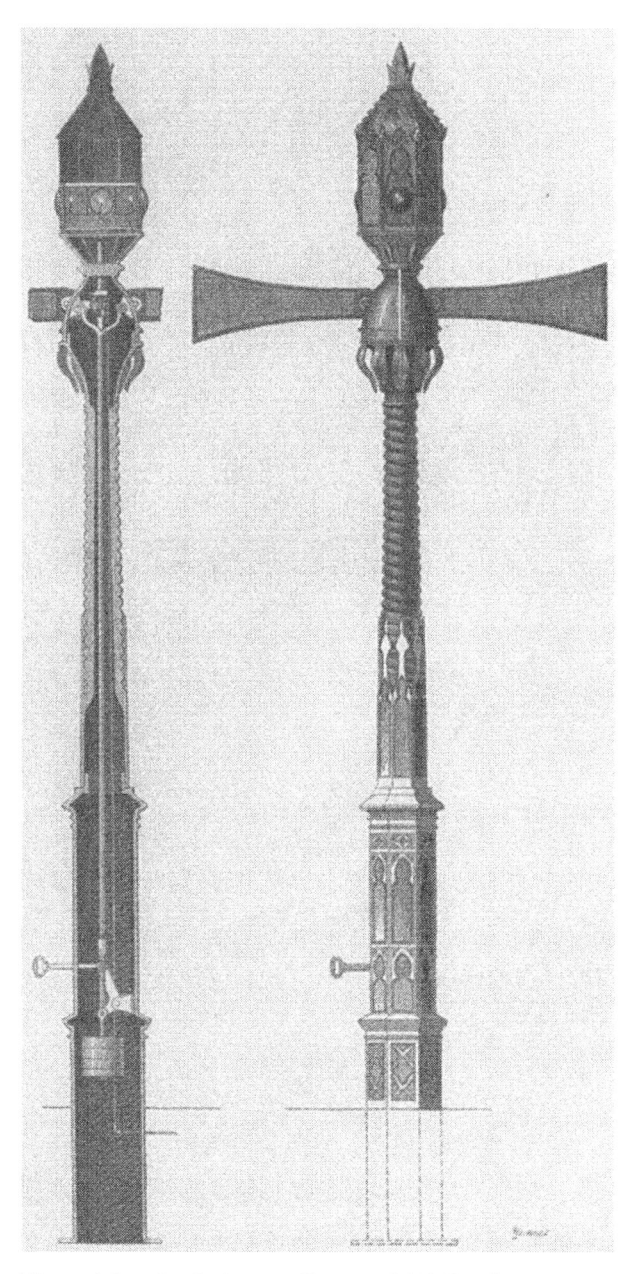

Figure 4 London's first traffic signal (1868). Commenting on this gas-lit device for directing traffic at the junction of Parliament and Bridge Streets, *Engineering* praised the "ingenious arrangement," by means of which a balanced lever near the base of the column actuated the semaphore arms and gave "a rotating motion to the drum within the lantern." A gas explosion caused this "chromatic glory" to be removed after a short trial. Fifty years went by before the experiment was tried again.

Figure 5 The organ in the court. Gustave Doré's bleak comment on popular recreation in the late 1860s. Blanchard Jerrold, who wrote the accompanying text, remembered walking up "a woe-begone alley" to the sound of a barrel-organ and noticing the faces of listeners, "pleasurably stirred, for an instant, in the long disease, their life." Doré hardly allows even that instant of joy. Images like these helped to fix the association of the city street with decay and lurking menace.

Figure 6 German band on "Placid Place." This cover for a musical score engages with the commotion stirred up by Charles Babbage in the mid-1860s. The players stand back to back, form an "English Square," and produce cacophonous sound, quadrophonically. Contemporaries would recognize "The Philosopher" as the irate householder exhorting the obviously reluctant bobby to do his duty – that duty being by no means straightforward. Cabbies needed to learn how to perform delicate balancing acts to maintain trim in emergencies like the one depicted here.

Figure 7 Olive Christian Malvery as flower girl. Although she assumes here a theatrical pose for her book, *The Soul Market*, Malvery's articles on women's street occupations were never sentimentalized. She was struck by the contrast between the crudity surrounding the lives of flower girls and the delicacy of what they sold. Malvery would have been in her mid-twenties when this photograph was taken.

Figure 8 Rus in Urbe. Two decades after the live meat market was moved from Smithfield north to the Caledonian Market, traffic could still be snarled, pedestrians frightened, and the streets of central London fouled by cattle and sheep being driven to basement slaughterhouses. Drawn for *The Graphic* in 1877 at what used to be the junction of New Oxford Street and Hart Street, only minutes from the British Museum, the engraving shows that English belief in unrestricted movement extended to include the animal kingdom.

Figure 9 A hard frost, February, 1865. Icy roads were particularly hazardous for horses. Since killing horses required a licence, drivers could not put their stricken animals out of their misery but had to wait for men from Harrison and Barber Ltd, who dispatched some 26,000 horses annually. For many slum dwellers, frost often cut off water supplies, as this group gathered around the standpipe illustrates.

Figure 10 Thaw after a snowstorm. Victorian Londoners were notorious for throwing oyster shells and other rubbish into gutters. This meant that during a run-off, crossings often turned into ponds. Street sweepers earned their ha'pennies in these conditions, especially those with mats to lay in front of pedestrians. A century and a half after they were written, Jonathan Swift's lines still applied: "Now from all parts the swelling kennels flow, / And bear their trophies with them as they go."

Figure 11 Charles Cochrane reviewing his street orderlies. Early morning parades, prayers, and inspirational talks were part of the routine at the National Philanthropic Society hostel near Great Windmill Street. The drill and naval-style uniform were intended to give dignity to what was, according to Mayhew, the "most unpopular work among the poor." A broadsheet song of the late 1840s has an orderly say, "Look at me and speak true on, / I'm better off than in a Union" (in a workhouse).

Figure 12 Meeting of the Health of Towns Association (1847). The *Illustrated London News* artist places Charles Cochrane (third from left in second row) close to Lord Ashley (Lord Shaftesbury) and shades his figure almost as darkly even though this enthusiast for clean streets was not invited to sit on the platform and had stalked out of the meeting – a reminder that visual evidence can be as misleading as any other kind.

Figure 13 A member of MacGregor's Shoe-Black Brigade. The original shows the bright red of the uniform worn by the first recruits from the Field Lane Ragged School. As new brigades formed, they adopted distinctive colours, much enlivening the generally monochromatic tone of the Victorian street. The boy's friendly but enigmatic gesture is an attempt by the artist to present an image of polite cheerfulness and self-respecting independence. The notice on the wall invites the public to a meeting of the Ragged School Union, with Lord Shaftesbury in the chair.

Figure 14 Salvation Army march (c. 1890). The procession is heading down Whitechapel Road toward an open space in front of a pub called the Blind Beggar, the destination of William and Catherine Booth's first march after forming their Christian Mission in East London in 1865. By the 1890s, the need for police escort had greatly diminished.

Figure 15 Invitations to salvation. "Happy Eliza" Haynes, one of the Salvation Army's first women officers in the 1880s, demonstrates her famous promotional skills, inviting street people in Marylebone to a hall where she will lead in singing "Shout aloud Salvation, boys!" to the tune of "Marching through Georgia."

Figure 16 London's first people's park. It took a visit by the Queen in 1873 to draw the attention of fashionable London to Victoria Park, "The Hyde Park of the East End." Note that the images in this *Illustrated London News* engraving descend, like the social hierarchy, from the aristocratic picturesque at the top to the "rational" leisure activities of the middle class to (by means of a bridge) the coarser tastes of the multitude – the three layers unified by a "rustic" border.

Figure 17 George John Shaw-Lefevre, Lord Eversley (1831–1928). Arguably the nineteenth century's leading British environmentalist. In the 1890s, when he sat for this photograph, his labors to secure public ownership of tramways, to save the commons around London, and, perhaps paradoxically, to relieve motor vehicles from crippling legal restrictions had ended and his labors for the London County Council's Improvements Committee were about to begin.

PROTECTOR AND PROTECTEE.

Miss Gulpin, belated at a Friend's House, in Bloomsbury, till after Sunset, borrows her Friend's Maid to protect her from Insult on her way back to Belgravia. This is all very well; but who's to Protect the Protector back to Bloomsbury again?

Figure 18 Gender, class, and street use. It was a convention in literature and genre painting that professional seducers and "rich sensualists" constituted the greatest threat to unprotected women. By contrast, this *Punch* cartoon of the mid-1860s locates danger in the knot of shabby men gathered around the pub door. This attempt at "realism" is offset by the romantic treatment of the servant girl. Meant to amuse, material like this served to heighten anxieties as well as to prick consciences.

Figure 19 Two generations in tandem (1913). A shiny electric tram pulling a converted horse car, both proudly displaying their London County Council provenance. While electrification did increase carrying capacity, the most dramatic gain in public transit efficiency had occurred thirty years earlier when the horse tram was introduced. On much of the system, power was transmitted by means of a slotted middle rail – one reason why trackless trollies, which required overhead wires, were slow to catch on.

Figure 20 Confluence of traffic from Cannon Street and Queen Victoria Street. An Edwardian mixture of vehicles. By 1912 the motor taxi had displaced the four-wheeled "growler" but not the two-wheeled hansom. Although steam, electric, and petrol-driven lorries were available, most freight and delivery vehicles remained horse-drawn until the late 1920s and early 1930s. Note that private carriages and automobiles are conspicuous by their absence and that the two constables by the lamp-post are there to assist pedestrians and not, except in an emergency, to direct traffic flow.

Figure 21 Kingsway in 1905. This view, looking north, was made only weeks before the official opening, the shallow tunnel for the tramline still exposed. Most former residents of the six hundred dwellings demolished in a fourteen-acre area were moved to five blocks of flats and consoled with provision for private water closets and with sculleries containing boiling coppers (for doing the washing) and sinks.

6

WORKING

Defining what a street was became more complicated from the seventeenth century on. The process of differentiation was at work on the highway as it was in so many other aspects of life. The entry of more and more vehicles pushed other traffic to the margins. Pedestrians retained their right of access to every part of this carriageway but received, by way of compensation for the effective loss of the centre, exclusive use of the footways which were raised up from the vehicle level and given a special surface. These different spaces developed distinctive rules and procedures. On the passageway for wheel and hoof, for example, tradition and then law kept users to the left, while on the part reserved for foot passengers anarchy prevailed, moderated slightly by a vague sense that keeping to the right was preferable. In the competition for space, the carriageway tended to have the advantage, although pedestrian interests began to receive the support of by-laws by the 1840s in their efforts to resist the erosion of their sovereignty.

Between the two contending passages a border territory gradually became delineated. It began at the edge of the footway nearest the carriageway and extended to the first line of wheeled traffic. Inside this area was the verge where costermongers most commonly parked their barrows and set up their stalls, the curb where vehicles paused to load and unload, and the gutter where rainwater or melted snow, mixed with refuse, was carried away. As with most border areas, proprietary and jurisdictional rights were much more confused and open to dispute there than in the passageways on either side.

With this differentiation of parts came the assignment to them of distinct values and social meanings. Riders had, speaking generally, higher prestige and social standing than walkers. The passage they rode through was an artery along which the life-blood of the urban organism flowed. Thus a "good" carriageway was one which allowed for free (unobstructed) movement between one place and another. The pavement, used by those who could not afford to keep a carriage or could not spare the cost of a cab, omnibus, or tramcar was of course a passageway too, but never simply that. The vital signs of the city did not depend on keeping the foot traveler moving. Congested or obstructed pavements never slowed by much the tide of pedestrian traffic or caused clots to form. Moreover, the pavement had to be, especially for the poor, a place as well as a path. For them and, in differing degrees, for everyone, the "good" footway contained provision for entertainment, sociability, and commerce. As for the border area, there could hardly be a "good," since one of its components, the "verge," connoted the problematical and another, the "curb," suggested restraint on unwanted impulse while a third, the "gutter," brought to mind everything that is vile. Down that foul runnel corruption flowed. Around Smithfield, until the live meat trade was moved to the Caledonian Market, and in parts of Southwark, blood from dead animals used to coagulate in the gutters.[1] Until the end of the horse-drawn era, men customarily urinated against the curb wheels of standing carts and wagons. Women with their long skirts risked defilement every time they made the transition from pavement to carriageway. After the 1830s, sandwich-board advertisers, recruited from the old and destitute, were required to walk in the gutter, and drivers thought it amusing now and then to give one of these poor creatures a lash of the whip. Vagabonds, prostitutes, drunks, gambling touts, and beggars sought their livelihood on the pavements but, according to convention, were continually teetering on the verge of a descent into that part of the street where, according to tradition, all immorality and corruption finally end.

This marginal ground, constantly bordering on corruption, a stationary place between the two areas of movement, was the special province of a marginal group, the costermongers. Ambivalent in every possible way, they were workers yet penny capitalists, recognized by law but never securely on legal ground, free yet harassed by policemen and constrained by the claims of poverty, envied for their freedom and sense of community yet despised for their anarchistic ways, at the same time fascinating, amusing, useful, pitiful, reprehensible, and dangerous.

We seem to know them better than any other part of the London working class because Henry Mayhew interviewed so many of them during the late 1840s and the 1850s and published their stories in the *Morning Chronicle* and later in his *London Labour and the London Poor*. A number of historians who have examined these rich sources with a critical eye have remarked on an ambivalence, not only in what Mayhew reveals about street workers, but in his own response to them. One of his severest critics, Gertrude Himmelfarb, makes the point that while claiming to be disclosing the plight and character of all the poor and the laboring people of London, what he actually describes is a subculture within these larger categories. Marx called the members of this subculture the *lumpenproletariat*, and John Bright gave them the equally evocative label "the residuum," referring to the residue which collects at the bottom as a result of the stresses and conflicts endemic to the struggle for existence. Himmelfarb points out that Mayhew's social reportage had a shock effect because the mixture of compassion and repugnance with which he treated his characters tapped the extensive storehouse of guilt his middle-class readers carried around with them. In doing so, she argues, he helped to fix the impression that the people who chose or had to be exposed to such a precarious, unregulated, depraved way of life must be defective human beings. Himmelfarb goes on to suggest that what repelled Mayhew's respectable readers also attracted them, particularly the freedom from conventional restraints, sexual and otherwise, which was supposed to be the essence of street culture. Not only does Himmelfarb object to Mayhew's habit of confusing a subculture of the working poor with the whole, but she wonders whether that special group was really as cohesive, anarchical, and dangerous as he believed or wanted his readers to believe.[2]

Richard Maxwell accepts much of this criticism but wants to preserve Mayhew's reputation as a social analyst. He points out that Mayhew had a "distinctive vision of city life," one that understood the quality of the urban experience to be discontinuity. It followed, then, that the urban mentality was a product of the need to adapt to unrelated stimuli, to constant exposure to strangers, to a multiplicity of forms. That conception drew Mayhew to the street as the epitome of discontinuity and to street people as that part of the population which had most completely adjusted to that urban fact, thus anticipating an important school of urban sociology which was to develop later. At the same time, says Maxwell, the great social reporter was unable to resolve the ambivalence he felt toward this quintessentially urban type; he admired the freedom, toughness, wit, and spontaneity and recoiled from the seeming purposelessness, restlessness, and heedlessness.[3] Two other commentators, Peter Stallybrass and Allen White, carry on this theme of Mayhew's ambivalence: in the slum street, "the bourgeois spectator surveyed and classified *his own antithesis*," and was both drawn toward and repelled by it.[4]

One of the greatest of the early photographers, John Thomson, teamed up in 1876 with a journalist named Adolphe Smith to capture in images the subjects Mayhew had described. They called their book *Street-Life in London*. Its first item is entitled "London Nomads"; it shows a group of gypsies gathered around their caravan. One notices at second glance that the setting is not a field or common but a vacant lot surrounded by grim terraces and smoking chimneys; we are meant to see his subjects as traditional, nomadic people who have adapted to but have not been truly integrated into an ordered urban world. The gypsy, Thomson commented, is the prototype of the street sellers whose portraits will follow. He went on to say:

> In his savage state, whether inhabiting the marshes of Equatorial Africa, or the mountain ranges of Formosa, man is fain to wander, seeking his sustenance in the fruits of the earth or products of the chase. On the other hand, in the most civilized communities, the wanderers become distributors of food and of industrial products to those who spend their days in the ceaseless toil of city life.[5]

For Thomson, therefore, the transitory people who sell, gather, and scavenge in the city streets were not fully urban creatures but survivals from an earlier stage of human development, pre-modern men and women, living unchartered lives in chartered streets. Nevertheless, though a "race apart," they serve the civilization they are in, but not of, by performing necessary tasks which more evolved workers are no longer equipped to do.

Photography, the authors claimed, had allowed them a precision, an "unquestionable accuracy" which not even Mayhew could achieve with words. The fact is, of course, that every picture in the collection was artfully composed to express the thesis stated above. Thomson's eyes were as keen as Mayhew's ears, but both did far more than record and both were outsiders looking and listening in.

A young East Indian woman, Olive Christian Malvery, carried on this tradition of social reportage at the beginning of the twentieth century, when Charles Booth was making his survey of the London poor. The difference was that she made a heroic effort to close the distance between herself and the street workers by sharing, for a brief time, their food, shelter, and work lives. As she put it, "one sees things . . . with altogether different eyes when one lives among people as one of themselves."[6]

In 1906 she described in a book called *The Soul Market* an account of what she had seen and done as, among many other things, a flower girl (see Plate 7), a street singer, a member of a busker troop, a costermonger selling tomatoes, a licensed hawker, and a "hokey-pokey" (ice cream) pedlar. As the title indicates, she made no claim to hard-edged objectivity; rather than attempting to gather evidence for a systematic theory about the nature of the urban dynamic, her aim was to awaken sympathy and to call attention to the need for Christian mission, literally at London's doorstep. Looking back to the time when she was collecting her material, she remembered "burning with a sort of mad enthusiasm."[7] She wrote in *The Soul Market*:

My heart was sore with much contact with poverty and misery, and I was burning, not only to touch "the heart of things," but to see some way out of the awful slough of crime and misery for the miserable creatures I have been travelling among.[8]

What brought her to this burning passion not just to see but to touch misery must be a matter of inference since she made only a few glancing references to her background, for example, that her grandmother ran a school in India and that "a friend who loved her" paid for her passage to England in 1900, when she would have been about 16, so that she could receive vocal training at the Royal College of Music. Photographs show her to have been lovely, soft-eyed, and unmistakably Indian. A devoted Anglican, she collected money, while still a girl in India, for Dr Barnardo's orphanages. Through her family or her connections with Christian endeavor movements she was noticed by important members of the Anglo-Indian establishment, given an English education and probably sponsored not only because she was talented but because she might be useful to charitable and temperance organizations in London. If so, she turned out to be an excellent investment. She was to bring to her careers as a singer, reciter, journalist, social worker, and crusader against the "White Slave Traffic" that burning Christian zeal and relentless inspirational hopefulness which was evident in everything she did or wrote.

One senses, however, a note of defensiveness when she relates the chain of circumstances which involved her in the working lives of poor women in London. The reason may be that her stories had first appeared in *Pearson's Magazine*, and, since Arthur Pearson, the founder had, in 1900, created the *Daily Express*, she may have been concerned that her determination to expose misery had a slight whiff of commercialism about it. Obviously, she wanted to distance herself from those who made professional careers out of giving charity performances. At the same time, she was a skilled self-promoter. It should be added, however, that her adult life was so filled with philanthropy that one is inclined to believe her claim that the sight of vagabonds sleeping at night on Embankment benches and a chance meeting with a flower girl had given her the idea of living with street workers and writing about her experiences, and that this had happened even before a friend had advised her to contact Pearson, who, in addition to his other enterprises, had published a set of readings and recitations to be used by the Band of Hope, a temperance youth organization.[9] Before becoming a journalist, Malvery, in need of money to pay for Royal College expenses, had attracted attention by reciting, to music, some of her own poems, called "Indian Pictures," and had begun a career as a professional reciter. A melodious voice, an attractive accent, her good looks, the shimmering sari she wore on stage, and her loyalty to King and Empire quickly established her reputation and secured her bookings in England, several European capitals, and North America. On a tour for the Women's Temperance Union of America and Canada, she met Jane Adams and toured her Chicago settlement house. Teddy Roosevelt invited her to the White House and impressed her with his "straight-forward wholesomeness." She fell in love with a rich American, Archibald MacKirdy, who shared her interest in opening refuges for homeless girls and boys and seems to have been closely involved with the Salvation Army in America and England. For twenty-five years he had been the American consul to "Muscat Arabia," although apparently not overburdened with that rather dubious responsibility. When the two married, MacKirdy accompanied his bride to London and occupied himself with Olive's projects: a girl's club at Hoxton Hall, on Hackney High Road, a social club for coster girls and lads in Battersea, and a Salvation Army hostel on Great Tichbourne Street. The couple had two children before MacKirdy died in 1911. Sadly, Olive only survived him by three years, dying, apparently of cancer, shortly after the war started.

That she managed to fit a particularly arduous form of journalism into such a short and eventful adult life is an indication of how energetic she was. Her description of a month or so spent as a coster girl also gives an idea of her dedication. She met and teamed up with a cabbage seller named Sal, who found her a room with a cousin in a lodging house up a narrow alley. Made queasy by the customary diet but not wanting to offend, Malvery said that she lived mainly on meat lozenges and biscuits which she carried around in her pocket. She then decided to have the experience of setting up for herself, asking a Covent Garden woman who hired out barrows at one shilling a week for advice. She was told that a pitch might be had on the Fulham Road. The next day at 4:00 a.m. she hired a barrow and, giving a few coppers to someone who made a living minding empty barrows, she bought tomatoes and plums and paid a porter to carry her purchases to the barrow. Unable to push the heavy load, she had to hire a man to help her. By this time, she had already gained experience at a great many different street occupations but found this one the most exhausting. At best, after a fifteen or sixteen-hour day, she could occasionally make ten shillings, though four shillings was more common, and this before paying for rent and services. Everything depended on the location, she discovered. A good one on the New Cut or on Lambeth Road could bring in as much as £15 on a lucky weekend, but such "informal freeholds" usually had to be paid for. Malvery said that one pitch for a haddock stall supposedly went for £80. Interlopers who did not recognize these illegitimate property rights to verge areas of the public streets could expect trouble from the local costermonger community and, it is interesting to note, from the neighborhood bobbies.[10]

To some extent this observation supports Mayhew's contention that street sellers recognized themselves to be a group apart and had worked out systematic ways to adapt to the precariousness of their life on the verge. For example, Malvery attended a benefit (called a "friendly lead") for "Boss 'Ooker," a costermonger whose wife had just died. A Chairman and "Vice" presided over the singing and drinking, and at the end of the gala, participants left silver coins on the table. "I never understood charity till I lived with the poor," Malvery wrote.[11] She explained that she was allowed into this community only because she was young, foreign-looking, and had learned to keep her mouth shut. In addition, she was shadowed by a man from the magazine (probably Stuart Cumberland, a managing editor) who, she said, could speak in a convincing Cockney accent and had an actor's sensitivity to nuances of dress and manner. If necessary, she could pass him off as her "bloke."

In one important respect, however, Malvery's description of the way street workers organized themselves differed from that of Mayhew, who tended to generalize from the behavior of costermongers to the whole undermass. Malvery was struck by how many gradations there were and how little one segment shared with another. Costermongers at the top of the hierarchy had their own language and characteristic dress;[12] they also had a corporate sense, but it was not, as Mayhew thought, given its main focus by hatred of a common enemy, the police, but by a shared need to control entry into a relatively unskilled livelihood, one that required only a small amount of capital to enter. And within that category there was, as Malvery learned by experience, a distinction between the "haves," those who could afford to go to the Caledonian Market and buy or rent a "moke" (a donkey) to pull their barrows, and the "have-nots," who had to do that strenuous labor themselves.[13] But even the poorest barrow-seller looked down on the hawker, who sold merchandise from a basket or a pack. It would be about as likely for a coster girl, who might herself be homeless, to associate with a woman street pedlar, Malvery declared, as for a squire's wife to mix socially with the village postmistress.[14] By way of compensation, Malvery pointed out, the pedlar felt superior to the street musician. Between them there was "no intercourse"; they would scarcely speak to each other.[15] Then there was the distinction between the professional entertainers and those whose performance was merely a slightly disguised form of begging. Even at the bottom rungs, the beggars and the scavengers had their complex pecking orders. Therefore, although Malvery does not say so explicitly, she leaves us with the impression that the people among whom she worked on the streets were not a sufficiently coherent segment of society to be made into exemplars of the urban mentality or specimens of an earlier evolutionary stage. Neither were they Thomson's "nomadic tribes" nor even "the poor," the "residuum," or the *lumpenproletariat*.

Malvery wanted to stir pity in audiences for the many exploited and oppressed workers within the wide spectrum of street occupations and to persuade women readers to boycott goods made by employers of sweated female labor. She also wanted people to support her program for providing shelters where women buskers, pedlars, and costermongers could find protection from male predators. Beyond that, she seems to have had no political agenda, not even a feminist one, nor did she have any urge to hold up the wounds or eccentricities of poor people to public gaze. She supplies the inquirer with little in the way of conceptual framework, but, perhaps as a consequence, brings us closer in touch with the untidiness of actual experience than do many of the other social investigations being carried on during her time.

Although Malvery does not make a particular point of it, ethnic differences and hostilities also segmented street traders. The potato famine sent waves of Irish immigrants into the streets. By 1861, street selling had become their most important source of employment.[16] After the Irish came the Italians. English and Irish costers complained that these new immigrants worked impossible hours, lived on nothing, huddled together, and ignored the informal rules of the trade. Complained one coster in 1903, "they have no regard for an Englishman's stand."[17] The large influx of Jewish refugees from East European persecution brought similar complaints, along with charges that they monopolized certain trades and excluded outsiders.[18] Two English sellers, examined by an Edwardian Royal Commission on Alien Immigration, said that southern and eastern Europeans now outnumbered English and Irish two to one. A hawker of china and glass articles remarked that native Britons would not sleep under the same roof with their donkeys the way these aliens did.[19]

As a result of these cross-currents and the ambiguities nearly everyone recognized when it came to determining the nature, worth, function, and territory of street sellers, reformers had difficulty deciding how, whom, and what to regulate. This confusion of intent is clearly evident in the making and amending of the Metropolitan Streets Act of 1867, a measure noticed earlier in the discussion about traffic regulation. The framers of this legislation blundered into and upset a compromise worked out between small shopkeepers and the upper division of the costermongers (what might be called the "Sixpence" as distinct from the "Penny Capitalists"). In some respects compromise between law and practice had always been necessary since, as Mayhew said, street selling existed by "sufferance"; neither common law nor statute bestowed the right to set up a stall or put down a basket on the public way. Vestries received explicit powers to remove barrows and stalls from street markets in the Regency period, and the Police Act of 1839 had shifted some of the responsibility over to the New Police by giving them discretionary powers to confiscate goods obstructing the carriageway or other parts of the street. So long as vendors kept moving, they stayed within the law, but not if they stopped for longer than was necessary to make a sale or if they put their burdens down. Mayhew asked one young woman whose loaded basket was strapped around her waist and neck if the work tired her. She answered, "After eight hours of it, it swaggers me like drink."[20]

Applied strictly, the 1867 Act could have greatly curtailed street selling in the Metropolitan area, but, of course, Rowan and Mayne had no intention of allowing their force to be put in that position and tended to act only when under pressure to do so.[21] While shopkeepers would almost always be the ones to take the initiative, their mood would depend on local circumstances. Especially where street markets were long established, inside and outside merchants often had a symbiotic relationship. The housewife who came to the stall to buy potatoes would be inclined to step into the nearest shop for her loaf or Sunday joint. Even in the case where both shop and stall sold the same things, the quality of the commodity might differ and be intended for different classes of customers. Because many working-class people preferred to patronize street sellers out of habit or as an expression of class solidarity, a shopkeeping family might divide their labors, the husband often outside, selling the less attractive goods, while his wife dealt with the "quality" inside.[22] Therefore, when pressures mounted on the police in the 1860s to act more vigorously to relieve worsening traffic conditions, Mayne turned *ad hoc* practice into policy: the proprietor of a building would be considered to have a kind of *de facto* right over those parts of the street in front of the premises not used for foot and wheeled passage. If shopkeeper or householder lodged a complaint against sellers who used that territory, the police would move them on. This meant that individual street traders and shopkeepers could work out an agreement whereby the one would have some security in the no-man's-land he or she occupied and the other would be able to control competition. Itinerant sellers were left out of this arrangement and had to work constantly with one eye out for the constable on the beat, but the costermonger "aristocracy" did benefit – it was this working compromise between shopkeeper and street seller that the 1867 Act upset.

The drafters of the bill, with traffic problems in mind, thought it might be well to put an end to the confusion about whether the border territory between footway and carriagepath was or was not part of the street. The Act declared that it was. A clause tightened the language forbidding the placing of goods anywhere on the street for purposes other than loading and unloading. Few who supported the bill noticed that they had just given the police direction to end all street commerce and had to be reminded by vigorous protests and demonstrations organized by both the inside and outside sellers. The threat even caused the better-off costermongers to form a union in order to protect themselves.[23] Mayne had no intention of using this opportunity to clear streets of obstructions and made sure that the *status quo* prevailed. But Gathorne Hardy, Disraeli's Home Secretary, hurried to rectify the mistake. His Amendment Bill exempted from the previous Act's penalties all costermongers (defined as those traders in fish, fruit, and other victuals, as well as goods of home manufacture, who had been, traditionally, immune from licensing requirements), hawkers (licensed sellers who cried their wares), and itinerant dealers. These specific kinds of street workers, but no others, received as a result, legal protection for their goods, stalls, and barrows. Police could still move on street traders (almost always the casual ones) on the grounds that they were obstructing traffic, but now a magistrate had to be convinced that a nuisance or an act of obstruction had actually taken place. It was partly because police and street reformers were forced to act under these restraints that street selling continued for the next half century to distribute goods and services to people with low incomes, to obstruct the public way, and to insure that the streets remained places as well as passages.

That improvers were thus constrained in their desire to move street commerce inside does not, however, explain why the proportion of street traders to central city population increased by something like 25 percent between 1851 and 1911, despite the rapid development of large-scale retailing operations in the last quarter of the century.[24] The reason was that street selling supplied a real social need. So long as a large proportion of the population lived by casual labor and had highly unreliable family incomes there would be a demand for the services street sellers were particularly equipped to offer: the breaking up of bulk shipments into small quantities and distributing half-pint measures of periwinkles or a single cabbage to customers who needed to shop frequently without leaving their neighborhoods. In addition, competition offered by sellers who were forced to labor long hours for tiny profits forced shops that catered to a working-class clientele to keep their prices in line. Thus, until the war-time employment opportunities improved family incomes and made them more regular, street vending remained an "economically efficient use of the economy's real resources."[25]

A somewhat different kind of utility was often claimed at the time for allowing street trading to continue. George Dodd, for example, began his book *The Food of London* (1856) on a note of wonder that, seemingly without conscious human agency, the intricate and responsive mechanism of the city draws in the provender needed to satisfy every taste and delivers it in the precise quantity desired. A shipload of French apples lands at Southampton or several tons of gherkins pull into King's Cross at night, and well before they reach their destinations at Covent Garden or Monument Yard, the electric telegraph has arranged for transhipments, and other markets outside the city are preparing to receive their share. Even more remarkable, another and more mysterious telegraph has alerted the street sellers, so that, in the early morning hours they can plot their strategies for the day ahead. Passing over items that bring shops most of their profit, they will load barrows that might have carried melons the day before with cheap pickles and apples and distribute them at low cost to customers who must watch every penny. Thus, Dodd marvels, do the poorest and often despised workers serve the interests of all.[26]

Defenders of costermongers' interests used still another rationale. They pointed out that the obstruction and disorder itinerant pedlars and street markets caused was a small price to pay for a system which gave useful and self-supporting work to marginal people who would otherwise become paupers. During the debate on Hardy's amendment bill, supporters estimated that something like 50,000 Londoners, counting dependents, might go on the rates if their livelihoods were taken away. Even an inferior kind of labor on the borderline of mendicancy was better than that. So compelling was this argument, especially when supported by all the others, that even some sanitationists, traffic engineers, philanthropists, and advocates of national efficiency must have had the occasional second thoughts whenever the costermonger question resurfaced, as it continued to do.

Decidedly less compelling would be arguments in favor of tolerating the open sale of sex. The great mechanism of London might harness the street gypsies and put them to use, but not many Victorians would claim that it could turn vice into virtue. Nearly every visitor to nineteenth-century London recorded shock at seeing so many prostitutes in the open and carrying on their trade in such an aggressive fashion. Why that should have been so was the subject of speculation then as it continues to be to the present. A post-Freudian analysis points to middle-class sexual repression and the cult of respectability. As in the case of the street worker, so this argument goes, what repels also fascinates. That "prostitutes exist so that our wives might be chaste" was another, more functional, explanation put forward at the time. But there is no convincing evidence to show that politicians, policemen, and significant sections of the general public resisted campaigns to rid the streets of "The Social Evil" for either of these reasons. We do observe, however, that every time the police responded to pressure and tried to find ways efficiently to convey the "riotous and disorderly" street walker to the magistrate's court, they met stiff opposition. Havelock Ellis thought this reluctance to give police the power to repress or forcibly regulate stemmed from a deep-seated respect for individual liberty and a reluctance officially to establish sin. "English love of freedom and English love of God combine to protect the prostitute" was his way of putting it.[27] To that list might be added the belief that free trade and *laissez-faire* should apply to what was, according to law, a commercial, not a criminal, enterprise. According to this point of view, any intrusion by the state would simply distort and relocate the market, encourage monopolistic tendencies, and make supervision more costly and difficult.

Until the campaign against the Contagious Diseases Acts, culminating in their repeal in 1886, removed regulation from the list of options, the Metropolitan Police would have preferred that method of containment. Mayne made that clear in 1866 when he was examined by a Parliamentary Committee inquiring into charges that theaters, music halls, and penny gaffs had become dens of iniquity. In answer to questions, he admitted that the task of controlling the streets would be far easier had he the authority to forbid prostitutes entry into certain streets and premises, as the Paris *police des moeurs* were able to do. Nevertheless, he knew that if his police were to become involved in licensing and supervising they would need to have laws which clearly defined their authority, magistrates who would co-operate, a public which would acquiesce, and a considerable augmentation of resources; he also knew that the chances of receiving any of these requirements were remote. Therefore, firm pragmatist that he was, he told the Committee, in effect, that he favored *laissez-faire*. He said that hounding prostitutes whenever and wherever they appeared conspicuously in public would cause them to carry on their trade in ways his men would find difficult to control. It was his personal opinion that open parading on some of the major streets of London was offensive and ought to be discouraged but not to the extent that street walkers would be obliged to rely on pimps to bring in clients. His position was that too much active intervention would turn informal exchanges between buyer and seller into institutionalized ones; middle-men were more "odious" by far than the private retailers of sex, so much so that, "with all the evils of our system, I think the other [strict regulation or outright suppression] must be called the greater evil."[28]

Colonel Henderson, Mayne's successor, had fewer reservations about extending police powers, disagreeing with the conclusion that applying the Contagious Diseases Acts to London was impractical. He thought it was worth trying the practice, under those Acts, of sending special vice police into the streets to identify women thought to be prostitutes and compelling these women to register and to submit to inspection for venereal diseases. "The threat of detection," Henderson noted in an official report in 1873, "is very salutary." As proof of this, he added, in areas where the Acts already apply, "young women in the position of domestic servants and others, after nightfall, leave their male acquaintances directly the police employed under the acts appear in sight."[29] Given this attitude, it was not surprising that there was, during the early years of Henderson's regime, some increase in police harassment of prostitutes, although the experiment with regulation was never attempted. Sir Charles Warren, who replaced Henderson, was disturbed by the effects on police morale of being caught between the moral purity crusaders and the civil libertarians and reverted to Mayne's more prudent strategy – respond to pressures when necessary but refuse to take the initiative – a policy followed by Commissioners up to the 1914–18 War.

A number of scholars have noticed that several decades after Mayne had given his warning about the possibility that a more active policy of suppression might institutionalize the sex industry, that change was beginning to happen.[30] By late in the century a system was in place, complete with specialized procurers, a domestic and international distribution system, a professional cadre of pimps and a formal system of brothel management. Abraham Flexner, an American who made investigations into European prostitution just before the outbreak of war, noticed that a consequence of this industrial development was that public opinion, lethargic for the most part before, became easy to arouse once third parties entered in on a large scale.[31] As the police in particular were to discover, the press and its readers could be expected to pounce upon a blunder in an arrest if the person in question were a single woman but be indifferent to blunders or excesses in the case of a suspected pimp or white slaver.[32]

Another result of the institutionalisation of vice, one that worried Mayne especially, was that the police might find themselves adapting to this change and becoming part of what they were supposed to control. As we have already seen, this had been a major problem even while street prostitution was still in its individual free enterprise stage. One of the reasons why magistrates were so reluctant to convict women under the Vagrancy Act of 1824 or the Police Act of 1839 on police evidence alone was concern that constables might use such discretionary powers to exact bribes. Whether in fact more formal organization of prostitution led to more or less police corruption is difficult to determine. A Royal Commission in 1908 did make some hesitant inquiries among police officials and, not unexpectedly, received categorical denials.[33] They examined several street missionaries and rescue workers who generally supported police claims to the strictest probity. Only Catherine Matson, supervisor of a refuge in Paddington, had some reservations, and not about the present but the recent past. She said that her girls, mostly Piccadilly street walkers, told her that they used to bribe the police to escape arrest but no longer needed to do so. That was as close to communicating with the prostitutes themselves as the Commissioners cared to get. Perhaps, since there is so little hard evidence to go by, the most that can be said is that there were remarkably few bribery scandals involving the police and their control of the vice industry during the Victorian and Edwardian periods. Whether that was due to police probity or Home Office vigilance or the skill of both in covering up is uncertain; probably it was a combination of all three.

Studies of street networks in modern cities indicate that police and prostitutes can work out symbiotic relationships, the police receiving information about the underlife and the prostitute receiving protection.[34] It is more than likely that this was true of nineteenth and early twentieth-century London also. We have abundant testimony from people involved in street rescue that police often tried to discourage newcomers from entering a stable area, sometimes directing them to the nearest hostel and occasionally supplying the omnibus fare to get there.[35] Like other street workers, prostitutes had reason to fear the police and resent being harassed by them, but it is as much an exaggeration to say that the policeman was the street walker's nemesis as it would be to claim that he was her ally.

That generalization can also apply to male prostitution. Curiously, this form of prostitution seems never to have been of great concern to the police. Even during the period of intense homophobia in the latter part of the century, Scotland Yard never attempted to drive male prostitutes off the streets. That could not have been because that particular branch of the vice trade was inconsequential. Anyone seeking the services of a male prostitute would know what streets and parks to go to and could be assured of an "ample" supply.[36] The police also knew where to go: the open spaces and streets in the neighborhood of what is now Oxford Circus, the south side of St James' Park, the environs of the Albany Street Barracks, the Alhambra Theatre, and the Empire Music Hall.[37] Had they been determined to harass and arrest, they would have known which faces to look for.

Admittedly, to do that, the law would have needed some stretching. It was clearly the understanding of the framers of the 1824 Vagrancy Act, as it was to all compilers of criminal statistics before that date and after, that "common prostitute" applied exclusively to females.

However, had the will been there, ways might have been found around this difficulty, although the lack of vocabulary to speak about male prostitution was certainly an obstacle. Finally in 1898 an Act did clear up some of these difficulties with language and definition. It stretched the definition of "rogue and vagabond" to include a male who "in any place persistently solicits or importunes for immoral purposes." A further refining of terms occurred in 1912 when a revival of concern about White Slavery caused the Home Secretary, Reginald McKenna (who was responsible for the sadistic Cat and Mouse Act against Suffragette hunger-strikers), to push for a more flexible definition of pimping and for a provision to whip male second offenders. It was clear during the heated debate that members had either forgotten or found it convenient not to notice that, because of the way the 1898 Amendment Bill was drafted, the penalties assigned to the pimp applied to the male prostitute as well.[38]

Reports from the Metropolitan Police show that arrests under the Vagrancy Act did increase significantly in the Edwardian period, doubling in 1903 and rising from 836 at that date to a peak of 1,325 three years later.[39] Statistics disclose that the 1912 legislation resulted in the arrest of 320 pimps in 1913, an increase of 82 over the previous year. However, these figures conceal the number of male prostitutes included under the wide category of offenses called "other." That catch-all figure stood at 85 male arrests in 1911 and then, curiously, shrank to 78 in 1913.[40] Thus it seems safe to assume that, despite the mood which produced the notorious Labouchere Amendment in 1885, making crimes of all sexual acts between consenting adult males, and despite the hysteria following the sentencing in 1895 of Oscar Wilde under that Labouchere Amendment, only a few male street prostitutes were arrested, sentenced, and whipped. That any were treated in this way is a matter of deep regret, but the fact remains that while the police could have harassed them with impunity, they chose not to do so, at least as part of a concerted policy.

Obscurity in the legal language, therefore, cannot explain why the male street prostitute was just short of tolerated. Preservation of health and order on the streets was what Scotland Yard cared about, and this form of deviant behavior threatened neither of these objectives. Persons concerned with the health and preservation of the Empire did not associate male-to-male sexual practices with the spread of venereal disease among the armed services, and because male prostitutes and their customers were a territorially circumscribed group and a distinct subculture, reformers felt no need to find means, as they did with female prostitutes, to segregate them from the main body of the poor.[41] Finally, males who solicited males did so discreetly, using coded signals, and created almost no disorder.

Like most of the other forms of street commerce, the selling of vice did not diminish in quantity and quality during a century of reform, evangelical mission, and charitable endeavor. There were some changes: tourists stopped being attracted to the nightly Bacchanalia on the Haymarket after the Home Office finally decided to find a way to close its brothels in the 1870s, and Piccadilly eventually surrendered its reputation as the most notorious thoroughfare in Europe to Berlin's Friedrichstrasse. By the end of Victoria's reign a number of veteran street rescue workers concluded that conditions had at last begun to improve in the sense that the selling of sex had become somewhat less conspicuous. Compared to the streets he had known in the 1870s and 1880s, said the Vigilance Society's busy gadfly, William Coote, the area around the Haymarket and Piccadilly in 1908 was "an open-air Cathedral."[42] William Taylor, a colleague with an equally long memory, thought that the moral state of the West End was "vastly better now."[43] The Recorder of London believed that the chances of a man being solicited had diminished and attributed the improvement to an "enormous reduction in public drunkenness." "It is quite a different thing to what it was when I came to London forty years ago."[44] Sir Mackenzie Chalmers, Permanent Undersecretary at the Home Office, agreed. He said that thirty years back, in the 1870s, he could not walk at night to his club without being constantly caught hold of; now he could do so with a minimum of annoyance.[45]

But was this optimism fully justified; had prostitution really declined or had it simply changed some of its marketing techniques and become more dispersed? Was Piccadilly's improvement Tottenham Court Road's degeneration, and was the path from Whitehall to Sir Mackenzie's club less taxing to a respectable man's sensibilities because the paths around Whitechapel were more so? These questions did trouble Edwardian rescue workers. Soloman Cohen, agent for the Gentleman's Committee of the Jewish Association for the Protection of Girls and Women, was sure that the West End's gain was the East End's loss. He said that Bishopsgate in 1906 was "in a terrible state every night," and the corner at Aldgate, "as bad as it can be." On both sides of the city, he said, the incidents of men harassing women were on the increase.[46]

Another modification within this general pattern of continuity was the constant increase in the power of the police to set the rules for street commerce and to govern the spaces where it might be carried on. It is inevitable therefore that a discussion of street workers should involve the constable on the beat as much as the prostitute, the hawker, or the costermonger. In the seventy or so years after the uniformed bobby appeared on the pavements, he became increasingly the centre of street networks. An old sandwichman walking in the gutter, a barrow woman setting up her stall on the verge, the prostitute approaching a potential customer on the pavement, came more and more to govern their behavior in relationship to authority figures who were, in some respects at least, also street workers.[47] Like other people who made their living on the street, the policeman played a role that was ambivalent in almost every respect: he was personally and intimately involved with people whose names and reputations he knew, sharing their tastes, living nearby in similar housing, receiving much the same wages, yet trained not to show emotion and restrained by regulation and community feeling from drinking in the local pub or taking part as an equal in street-corner banter. Indeed, he was often the object of that banter. Juvenile sellers on the streets where he walked his beat called him, among other things, "Bull's Head," "Bandy Shanks," "Old Cherry Legs, "Black Diamond." If hired to help keep order at the local music hall, he would almost certainly watch a skit where "Old Bill" was the butt of jokes. But when some disaster struck a household, he was usually the first to be summoned. He, as much as the pastor or priest, presided at the crucial rites of passage in the lives of poor, and not so poor, people.

Since few urban dwellers today have this experience of having direct personal contact on a regular basis with someone whose relationship to us is so full of ambivalences, one illustration, selected from a copious storehouse in the police records, might be worth giving. In the summer of 1859, thirty people, calling themselves residents of Gray's Inn Lane, complained to the Holborn Board of Works about shocking scenes, disgusting language, and riotous behavior in nearby Charlotte Court. Crowds of costermongers and their families lived there, a mixture, claimed the petitioners, of thieves, prostitutes, and low characters. They lounged against the walls of Gray's Inn just opposite and threw stones and filth at passers-by. They blocked the Court and part of the Lane with barrows and filled the whole neighborhood with the stench of rotting straw, shavings, and over-ripe fruits and vegetables.[48]

The Board passed this complaint on to Scotland Yard, and the Commissioner's Office asked C Division for a report. The reply was that there did not seem to be any reason for police to become involved. Charlotte Court had only one entrance, was extremely narrow, and only forty yards long. It was not a thoroughfare but part of the residential space. The Irish costers who lived there sat outside on warm days and evenings, the air of the court being anything but fresh; but, the Superintendent of C Division believed, this practice constituted neither a nuisance nor an obstruction. Every ten minutes a constable passed by; he seldom or never had problems to report. Upon being questioned, that constable did agree that the Court was full of barrows and litter left over from preparing loads for the day's selling, but no one he was aware of found this a nuisance since it was obvious that this clutter was necessary to the communal livelihood. The Superintendent went on to report that Mr Carroll, the organizer of the petition, kept a low public house on the corner and that, as a consequence of a dispute, had been boycotted by the residents of the Court. Having checked the residences of all the petitioners and finding that all of them lived at least a mile away, the Superintendent could assure his superiors that none of them could possibly have been overcome by the odor of rotting cabbage leaves.[49] Mayne passed on this assessment to Holborn authorities, and there the matter seems to have rested.

What must strike the modern Londoner in this incident is the thoroughness of the investigation and the physical closeness of the constable who passed Charlotte Court so frequently. For many of us who live in large cities, the most tangible reminder of a police presence in our midst is not a uniformed person whose name and habits we know but a patrol car, with an official insignia. Even if we see the face of the driver, we are not likely to recognize it. A survey carried out in the 1980s showed that only 5 percent of London's police live where they are assigned.[50] Increasingly since the Second World War the policeman or woman looks out on the pavement and its life through a window and communicates to the outside world by means of electronic equipment. For most citizens direct interaction is more likely to be with a traffic warden than with any other law enforcer. One Victorian policeman commented that he was always a specter at the feast,[51] but at least he attended the feast in person and on foot.

Perhaps "feast" is the appropriate metaphor to describe the street selling and consuming that went on undiminished well into the early period of the motor vehicle revolution, although "dinner" might come a little closer to the reality. The fare was not elaborate, but it was varied and plentiful. It is true that those who sat down to it were usually ragged and unkempt and the leavings were often messy. But, looking back, one regrets never having been able to attend.

7

CLEANING

Lord Palmerston struck a deep chord when he defined "dirt" as "the right thing in the wrong place." Disorder was clearly what concerned the framers of the Michael Angelo Taylor's Act of 1817; they forbade the dumping into the street of "Slop, Mud, Dirt, Dust, Rubbish, Ashes, Filth" or "Offal, Dung, Soil, Blood," and warned carters not to cast out "any Soap Lees, Night Soil, Ammoniacal Liquor" while hauling their loads.[1] Thirty years later another current of street reform began to run strongly, directing attention to the street as a major source of contagion. To a large extent this alteration in direction was a result of the sanitary movement which began after the 1832 visitation of cholera, then gathered momentum with the typhus epidemic of 1837–8, to become a major political force when it became obvious by 1846 that another cholera attack, the one that finally arrived in 1848, was on its way. A less dramatic reason for concern about dirty streets was the accumulation from the 1830s onward of muck, as the number of vehicles and horses greatly multiplied. Early Victorian Londoners grew to fear dirt at the same time that they and the animals they used were producing it in ever larger quantities. As F.M.L. Thompson has observed, "the horse struck her blow at the quality of urban life long before the waste products of modern technology began to cause trouble."[2]

How many horses there were on the streets at any given time could only be roughly estimated. Mayhew's figure of approximately 25,000 at mid-century is almost certainly too low.[3] When he was conducting his investigations in the 1840s, the number of vehicles was increasing at a considerably higher rate than the population. In the 1830s there was one cab for every 1,000 people, and by the end of the century there was one for every 350.[4] In 1834 there were 376 omnibuses; by 1850 the number of these vehicles, each needing a stud of 10–12 horses, had risen to 1,000.[5] Thus more and more wheels churned up more and more muck. Each horse, Mayhew estimated, dropped about forty-five pounds of dung in a day; and, of course, horses had to share the streets with the cattle, sheep, and swine brought to inner-city slaughter houses on foot in huge numbers before the Caledonian Market in Holloway was built to receive them in the mid-1850s (see Plate 8). By that time, according to Mayhew, the streets were receiving 39,592 tons of animal dung annually.[6] Added to this mixture of animal manure and urine was "human guano," especially before the overflow from cess-pits began to be diverted into sewers after 1847. Mixing all this excrement with grit produced when iron wheels passed over macadam or granite block surfaces, moistening it with what Mayhew referred to as "more or less water," and, finally, churning it over and over, produced a "highly agglutinative compound," with properties so adhesive that, according to William Farr, when attached to heavy wagon wheels, it could pull paving stones up from their settings.[7] Still more dangerous to animals and to traffic than its stickiness was the slipperiness of this compound when lightly mixed with rain. William Haywood discovered that over a fifty-day period the daily average of accidents to horses on the asphalt surface of Cheapside was 18.64.[8] Thus it is possible to understand why so few horses used for commercial purposes died natural deaths. Several companies which were licensed to despatch horses, Jack Alcheler's in the period before 1860 and Harrison Barber Ltd after that, had carts constantly ready to go to the scene of a fall, equipped with experts at pole-axing the stricken animal and carting it away. Through the second half of the century a special slaughter house in Wandsworth worked night and day producing cats' meat. One estimate reports that 156,000 horses a year ended their service this way in the last part of the century.[9]

Scooping, shoveling, and washing away this "peculiar gruel" was a gigantic task, the details of which endlessly fascinated readers of newspapers and official documents. Haywood complained in the 1850s that householders were dumping increasing quantities of ashes and house refuse into the gullies at the edges of streets and that scavengers, instead of carting away wet, heavy "slop," were pushing it into the gutters, hoping the street sewers, designed only to drain rain water into the Thames, would carry it away. In 1853, Haywood reported, men under his direction had removed 1,098 yards of hard deposit from stopped-up sewer pipes in the City. This practice of dumping waste into the street, long illegal, was especially troublesome during frosts and snow storms, when the ooze would harden and block the run-off (see Plate 9). A particularly heavy snow-fall on January 3, 1867, paralyzed much of the central part of the city, but everyone agreed that the thaw of January 5 was even worse. That was because workers had cleared the centre by piling the snow in the gutters, thus turning the carriageways into brown, slush-filled rivers (see Plate 10).[10] This seasonal "disaster,"[11] in addition to the frequent accidents to horses and the slowing effect of the muck (called "mac" if concocted on a macadamized surface), were serious impediments to free movement, fully as frustrating to the aims of street reform as any of the other obstructions.

The cause and cure, almost everyone agreed, had much to do with the way the cleaning of the streets was administered. A ten-mile walk at mid-century from Hammersmith to St Mary-le-Bow took the traveler through ten different administrative districts made up of parishes, sewer commissions, paving boards, and corporations. Technically, until 1899 individual householders and shop-owners had the responsibility for clearing the pavement, verge, and carriageway in front of their premises, but in fact the job was done, up to 1855, by a bewildering tangle of authorities and paid for out of rates. While the Metropolitan Management Act of 1855, which established the Metropolitan Board of Works, introduced some uniformity by putting parish vestries in charge of local services, travel only improved where vestries were conscientious and adequately funded. Crossing a parish border often meant going from cleanliness into filth or from dry surfaces into snow banks. The City was exempted from the Act and constituted yet another jurisdiction; there the Commissioners of Sewers were able to carry out policies which, by the third quarter of the century, produced impressive results. But, speaking generally, street dirt remained a vexing problem until the motor vehicle began to bring relief after about 1910.[12]

One pre-1855 vestryman, Charles Cochrane, instead of being daunted by the state of London's streets, became inspired with the possibility that filth could be turned into an instrument for social regeneration. Because his devotion to the cause of street-cleaning started with a concern about dirt as an impediment to movement, quickly developed into a concern about dirt as a cause of contagion, and went on from there to a concern about the whole welfare structure of the nation, his career as a reformer demonstrates how easily one conception came to overlay another. The vehemence of his attack on administrative stubbornness and inertia in the 1840s and early 1850s can also allow us to sense the peculiar flavor of street and sanitary reform at a critical period in its history.

It was a romantic path that led Cochrane to his position as, to use the title he chose for himself, "The Agitator of the Metropolis." Those (and there were many) who considered him nearly as great a nuisance as the ones he so boisterously set out to remove, spoke of him as an upstart who had clawed his way into public notice out of "nowhere." Since he was the cousin of the 10th Earl of Dundonald, an admiral who had spectacular careers in the British and then the Peruvian, Chilean, Brazilian, and Greek navies, this slur only makes sense when understood to be a code for "illegitimate." The natural son of a nabob, Basil Cochrane of Portland Place, he was well connected but not well born. According to his own, not altogether reliable account, Lady Dundonald promised to take him to South America so that he could begin a naval career under the tutelage of his famous relative and assist new nations in their struggles for freedom. To prepare himself, he studied navigation and learned Spanish, only to see another, legitimate, Cochrane go out in his place. Several years later he claimed to have been cheated by the Battle of Navarino and the destruction of the Egyptian and Turkish fleets of another possibility to serve in a romantic cause, this time for Greek independence.[13] Blocked twice from fulfilling his dreams of Byronic adventure, he set out, at age 19, on one closer to home. Disguising himself as Don Juan de Vega, a Spanish minstrel, and pretending to speak no English, he toured Great Britain and Ireland for almost a year in 1828 and 1829, singing patriotic Spanish songs and, supposedly, raising funds to aid Spanish *émigrés* fleeing from oppression in their homeland. An account of his adventures, including his amorous ones, called *Journal of a Tour*, appeared soon after.[14] It caused a small stir. Henry Mayhew used the situation for the plot of a one-act farce, "The Wandering Minstrel," which opened at the Royal Fitzroy Theatre in 1834. Years later, when Cochrane was forced to admit that he had, in fact, been the author, he claimed that justice, not titillation, had been his only object. The money he raised, £54, had gone, he claimed, to the *émigrés*. Furthermore, the journey had taught him a lesson, he said, one that shaped the course of his future life: that the ordinary man is good and generous "whenever his nature is not stifled with the selfish customs of art."[15]

Despite all the posturing and bravado with which he customarily conducted his affairs, this sentiment does, in fact, give coherence to his later career as a reformer. That career began soon after the troubadour adventure was over, when his father died leaving him a small fortune, part of which he immediately spent on raising a contingent of 240 volunteers to aid Dom Pedro, claimant to the throne of Portugal, during the siege of Oporto. He and his troops seem actually to have got to Oporto only to have been sent packing, "for powerful reasons," by the man whose cause he tried to serve.[16] Frustrated, once again, in his hopes of becoming a hero, he turned instead to local politics and got himself elected in 1839 to the St Marylebone parish vestry. There, in his own neighborhood, he finally found his vocation.

The process began in 1841 when he proposed, probably at the instigation of local merchants, who expected to benefit from the amenity, to pave the whole of Oxford Street with wooden blocks. He tried to persuade his fellow vestrymen that, compared to macadam or granite sets, this type of pavement was easy to clean, tended to muffle the noise of traffic, and also provided excellent traction for horses' hooves in all conditions except light rain, when a greasy film of liquid dung made wooden surfaces especially slippery. But a majority of the vestry voted against the proposal on the grounds that the initial costs and the expense of keeping a wooden surface clean would be burdensome to ratepayers. However, as many parish officials were to learn over the next few years, Cochrane's enthusiasms were not to be easily contained. He drew up a memorial, got up a delegation, and set out to stir up support. In a series of speeches he demonstrated how practical in the long run such expenditures might be. These tactics worked, at least to the extent that at a later meeting the vestry authorized the paving of a section of Oxford Street on an experimental basis.[17]

Cochrane's plan expanded as he struggled to get it adopted. He wanted to pave the streets of the whole city with wood. To make sure that dung and urine never had a chance to impregnate the blocks, seep into the edges, or grease the surface, he would place street sweepers at intervals, depending on traffic volumes, provide them with scoops and short-handled brooms or brushes, and train them to dart out and remove animal excrement almost as soon as it plopped onto the carriageway. His idea was to recruit sweepers from boys and single, able-bodied men on the Poor Law lists and form them into Street Orderly Brigades. They would wear uniforms, be paid regular wages, live in barracks, and receive moral and spiritual guidance. It was true, he acknowledged, that ratepayers would see their payments for street cleaning double, but they could expect substantial benefits in return: poor rates would be reduced and there would be less crime because paupers would become productive, self-respecting workers and, as auxiliaries to the police, would turn into instruments for "preserving public order and safety." Shopkeepers could expect more sales, considering that ladies often began their recreational shopping promenades at about 4:00 p.m., the time of day under the existing system or non-system when the streets, and consequently, the pavements, were at their foulest. Dirt, he explained to merchants, cost them about a quarter of a million pounds a year. For example, shops on filthy Chandos Street let for half the price commanded by premises on clean Cavendish Square nearby. Savings, he thought, would also accrue to ordinary householders who could cut their bills for soap, soda, flannels, brushes, and furniture restoration. Finally, the Metropolitan parishes and the City Corporation could expect to make a profit of exactly £17,706 9s. by selling farmers 188,043 one-ton loads of prime manure, unadulterated with grit. He was convinced that by supporting his bold experiment, the citizens of London could turn waste, including cast-off humanity, into wealth (see Plate 11).[18]

Ambitious though this scheme obviously was, it appealed to some substantial interests and to many experienced reformers and philanthropists. Liberal reformists like Henry Mayhew praised Cochrane's scheme for reclaiming the destitute rather than subsidizing or patronizing them; it was, he wrote, "the only rational and efficacious mode of street cleaning."[19] Moreover, in offering an example of how a great city could make something useful out of its own detritus, Cochrane touched on something that resonated in the early Victorian psyche. Many people, among them Dickens, Henry Cole (the force behind the creation of the South Kensington museums), Mayhew, and, of course, Chadwick, had what has been called an "excremental vision." Charles Babbage pointed out in his writings that the positive side of gathering together large agglomerations of people was that, in the scramble to survive, everything that could be repaired, cannibalized, or reclaimed would find hands willing to do the work and outlets to receive the product. He marveled, as did the photographer John Thomson, that through the agency of dustmen, sorters, pickers, finders, and scavengers, most commodities moved in stages down and up the ecological system. A woolen coat, for example, might evolve from an item of high fashion into a great variety of forms before finding a final resting place on a compost heap, and, on an upward swing, a worn horseshoe might be promoted eventually to the dignity of a well-tempered gun barrel.[20] New life out of decomposition, a powerful image at any time, was a particularly compelling one in the troubled 1840s. And this was what Cochrane had to offer.

How this labor-intensive recycling could be reconciled with a faith in progress through technology, Babbage did not explain. In 1842 the noted machine-tool and cannon maker, Joseph Whitworth, had conducted successful trials in Manchester of his horse-drawn street-sweeping machine.[21] He demonstrated there and in Birmingham that four of his machines could do the work of seventy or eighty hand-sweepers. Recognizing that arguments would be raised about displacing pauper labor, he argued that savings to ratepayers would increase the total demand for services. Besides, scavenging was humiliating work. Take labor out of the gutter, he urged, and employ it, if need be, in cleaning the footpaths. Do that, he said, lift workers up out of the street, "and the degradation vanishes."[22]

Chadwick, who acted on this occasion as a commentator, agreed: "Machinery itself is progressive and tends to ameliorate its own inconveniences."[23] Cochrane, by contrast, consistently argued the case that employment served the end of social justice and should always be preferred over what he considered to be short-term efficiency. Therefore he rejected the premise that technological advances always served the general good, although he did take the point that scavenging, as it had always been carried on, degraded the worker. However, he believed he had found a way around that problem. He would dress his orderlies in naval-like uniforms and subject them to "the most exact discipline and order." "Military time" would regulate their hours of work, rest, and refreshment. Self-control and the uniform would separate the worker from other street people and, more important, from the task he was performing. Dirty work would be done by individuals who were, themselves, impeccably clean because laundry and bathing facilities would be essential features of the barrack environment.[24] Thus paupers could learn the dignity of labor while carrying on work that had always born a particular stigma. With self-respect thus gained, the former pauper could be expected to take advantage of the labor-exchange which would be an essential part of the plan. Street cleaning need not be, Cochrane pointed out, a dead-end occupation.

That Cochrane had the model of the Metropolitan Police before him is obvious. With a regular beat to supervise, the orderly would be as familiar with the neighborhood as the constable and be able to assist him in watching for suspicious characters and behavior; he would also be there when accidents happened or when passers-by needed assistance. As a maintainer of order he would be regarded, and regard himself, not as a scavenger, not as a "Metropolitan Pariah," but as an auxiliary policeman. Also like the bobby on the beat, he would always be conscious of wearing a badge with a number on it and be restrained, accordingly, in the way he related to the public.[25] Thus could the sweeper of dung be assisted to reclaim himself.

Well-schooled by his three years at the Marylebone Vestry Hall in the difficulties of moving the rickety machinery of parish government, Cochrane decided in 1842 to proceed with his project on his own and to win support by actual demonstrations. Out of his own pocket he rented a building on Great Windmill Street, recruited and equipped over a hundred orderlies, and offered their services to any group willing to try the experiment. The first to respond was a group of Oxford Street and Regent Street shopkeepers who agreed to pay part of the expense of keeping Oxford Circus and a stretch between Vere Street and Charles Street "perpetually clean," and fifty men and boys went to work during the winter months of 1843-4. During that time, Cochrane boasted, a lady could walk the length of the experimental area in the worst weather without soiling her shoes.[26] Over the next eight years several streets behind Westminster Abbey, Hanover Square, Covent Garden, Church Lane in St Giles ("notorious for its filth"), stretches of Bloomsbury, and an area around St Martin-in-the-Fields remained briefly free from muck. St Pancras, for a short period, set up its own brigade and purchased a large property on the Caledonian Road to house it.[27] The press gave support, Mayhew printed a lengthy endorsement, merchants applied pressure on local government authorities to continue the orderly system, and the public appears to have been well pleased. But, as a general rule, paving commissioners and vestry committees were glad to see the back of Cochrane. One reason was that scavenging contracts were a form of vestry patronage. In St James', Westminster, for example, the contractor, Mr Tame, refused to remove the sweepings that the orderlies collected, complaining that the amount they swept up was excessive. He demanded an extra £22 10s. Cochrane complained loudly and hinted at corruption, then paid up out of his own pocket. The parish gladly took the opportunity to cancel the experiment.[28] In another Westminster parish, the vestrymen, after listening to a National Philanthropic Association (NPA) offer to cleanse one of their worst areas and refund the difference in cost if the ratepayers were dissatisfied, replied that the lowest possible element lived there and, like very poor people in general, "preferred dirt."[29]

Where the method did catch on was in the City. Haywood, its surveyor, authorized a trial demonstration in Cornhill, Cheapside. The NPA mounted another experiment in the neighborhood of the Bank and the Royal Exchange, after several large meetings at the Guildhall, supported by leading bankers and merchants, produced a petition signed by 8,000 of the 12,000 ratepayers in the area affected. Six months of work by a hundred orderlies on that project cost the NPA £1,000, well over the estimate. Haywood refused to pay and recommended cancellation, but, when large financial houses objected, the Sewer Commissioners were forced to carry on.[30] Shortly afterward the City took over direct management and eventually worked out a compromise whereby the streets would be swept or flushed once a day by both machine and hand labor after which a smaller number of orderlies than Cochrane envisioned would remove most of the manure as it accumulated. The results were impressive. In his memoirs about growing up, partly in a flat above a police station in the City, C.H. Rolph marveled at how spotless the "street orderly boys" kept neighborhood streets, "cleaner than I have seen in any part of the world. . . ." At dawn, he recalled, "the air was cleaner and sweeter than anyone could have supposed possible in any built-up area."[31]

While this campaign to establish the street orderly system was underway, Cochrane became closely involved in the sanitary movement of the 1840s and made a substantial contribution to it. Like Southwood Smith, Edwin Chadwick, Hector Gavin, and many others in the movement, Cochrane was a miasmatist, that is, instead of assuming as contagionists did that cholera and most fevers were spread by physical contact or ingested by drinking water contaminated with infected excrement, he believed that the disease originated in putrefying matter which was carried in tiny particles by the air, entering the body through the respiratory system – a belief which gave the strongest possible theoretical support to his street-cleaning program. Cochrane did not use medical or scientific language, leaving that to confederates like Dr Hector Gavin, but he could assume that the message was well planted in the consciousness of all classes of Londoners by 1847. Stinks from foul drains, overflowing cess-pools, blocked gully holes, and vacant lot refuse piles could, to some extent, be avoided by moving to the suburbs, but less easy to avoid would be the "effete organic matter rising up" from the "highly agglutinative compound" called "London mud," described in 1865 by William Farr as a "grimy, muddy paste of decomposing animal and vegetable matters and inorganic substances." Looking back over the preceding two decades, Farr noted that the city had managed to get rid of most of the filth which had accumulated underground, beneath courts, yards, and houses; yet, he commented, "we still surround ourselves with a slough of despond in our higher regions."[32]

Not unexpectedly, this was Cochrane's line from the beginning. Particularly from 1847 on, when he was smarting from what he felt to be insulting neglect from the leaders of the Health of Towns Association, Cochrane became openly critical, to put it mildly, of people like Edwin Chadwick, with his obsession about flushing away human wastes, or William Haywood, with his concentration on abolishing cess-pits, building sewers, and finding simple, engineering solutions to the problem of how to keep streets clean. The personal hygiene of the poor, Cochrane maintained, was not the real problem. For one thing, the human contribution to the miasmatic fog was relatively small; furthermore, working people needed no instruction in cleanliness. *"Poor people are not absolutely fond of wallowing in filth,"* he wrote; "no sooner do they begin to taste the sweets of cleanliness, than they begin to ascend the ladder of social improvement."[33] Baths, laundry facilities, decent public toilets, and clean outside surroundings would do more, he thought, to build self-respect and develop habits of cleanliness than any amount of drains or patronizing moralizing.

Partly to that end, he sold his home (or so he claimed) to raise money to buy premises on Leicester Square to serve as headquarters for his National Philanthropic Association, a blanket organization to house and to promote what came to be a complex of related services and propaganda activities. One of the NPA's accomplishments was to construct free lavatories, with soap, clean towels, urinals, and water closets at the St Bernard Hospice in Ham-Yard, where a contingent of his orderlies were housed. No doubt he chose that place because the NPA had done battle with the Paving Board of St James's Parish when it designated a nearby wall as a suitable urinal. Cochrane had organized a group of women who petitioned the Board about the urine and excrement on the street and the embarrassment of having in full view, men attending to "the calls of Nature in the Public Street."[34] Cochrane's concern was not only for women's sensibilities but also for their convenience, he being one of the first to do something about a major impediment to women's freedom, the scarcity of public toilet facilities. In this area, however, his efforts to embarrass local authorities produced few results. Thirty years later the Ladies' Sanitary Association was still trying to get them to respond.[35] At its request, Dr James Stevenson, a Medical Health Officer for Paddington, published a tract on the subject. He felt it necessary to point out that it was false to suppose that women suffered less than men from being deprived of public facilities; on the contrary, pregnancy and menses made their need greater. Few parishes had responded to an enabling law in 1855 allowing them to spend rates on building public urinals and water closets, and it was time something was done about the situation, considering that stricter sanitation laws had abolished most of the urinating walls for men outside of pubs and that women in ever greater numbers were participating actively in the world outside the home.[36] Messages such as these had some effect, especially since many of the technological difficulties of Cochrane's day had been overcome with the inventions of George Jennings and others. Underground conveniences and cast-iron street urinals were installed here and there from the 1880s on, although Victorian and Edwardian London never became as well-equipped as Paris. The architect, William Woodward, writing in the mid-1880s, complained that the only public convenience equipped with water closets was in Covent Garden, near St Paul's Church, and it had no provision for women. By that time the number of public bath houses and laundries had expanded considerably, but they were not, as a rule, free. Woodward recounted how he had seen crowds of poor people gathered around drinking fountains in Endell Street and Gray's Inn Road, washing themselves without soap or towels.[37]

Cochrane would not have been surprised to learn that sanitary reform, one of the success stories of the Victorian era, had not made it much easier for women to relieve themselves while away from home or for poor people to take baths or wash their clothes. Experience had convinced him that bumbledom would not yield to persuasion but could be moved by noisy demonstrations, inflammatory language, mass meetings, petitions, news-making events; and at these techniques, Cochrane was one of the outstanding practitioners of his day. Because he was willing to do outrageous things in such good causes, the distinguished figures who were involved in the sanitary movement, or who recognized the practical value of his various cleaning projects and wanted to support his large soup kitchen in Leicester Square, made contributions, often agreed to sit on platforms at the meetings he was constantly arranging, and sometimes paid tribute, if wanly and nervously, to his generosity. The semi-retired proprietor of *The Times*, the elder John Walter, pleased to discover an ally in his anti-Poor Law activities, accepted the presidency of Cochrane's Poor Man's Guardian Society; Charles Dickens agreed to be a vice-president and made some modest subscriptions.[38] He was joined by John Fielden, a leader of the 10-Hours movement; the former Young Englander, Lord John Manners; Thomas Wakley, editor of the *Lancet*; and Benjamin Bond Cabell, an important art collector and open-handed philanthropist. Lord Ashley (later Lord Shaftesbury), the Dukes of Grafton, Bedford, Buccleuch, and Devonshire, the Bishop of Durham, Lord Robert Grosvenor, James Silk Buckingham, the Solicitor General, and Sir Fitzroy Kelly lent their names, gave money, or participated directly in one or another of Cochrane's causes. Even Lord John Russell, the object of some of Cochrane's most intemperate hyperbole, found it expedient to make several contributions. Nevertheless, these distinguished people, many of them the most public-spirited reformers and philanthropists in the land, never dreamt of including the noisy and self-advertising agitator in any of their inner circles.

The formation and activities of the Health of London Association show this ambivalence about having Cochrane on their side. The occasion for the Association's formation was a letter published in *The Times* early in 1846 from the City Corporation's Chief Clerk to the Lord Mayor, warning that cholera had entered the city. Seeing a chance to draw attention to his street orderly plan, Cochrane called a meeting of members of the Health of Towns Association, which drew up a resolution asking that the City Corporation protect the public by embarking on a clean-up campaign. When a delegation waited on the Corporation and asked to present their resolution, the Lord Mayor is reported to have blurted out, "Cholera, Cholera; no such thing!" and closed the meeting, remarking that "the sanitary condition of the City ... was perfect."[39] Cochrane's response was to offer Dr Hector Gavin funds for starting the London branch of the Health of Towns Association and for sending out, under its auspices, a questionnaire to 3,000 professionals: surgeons, surveyors, clergymen, architects, and parochial officers. Gavin made effective propaganda use of the responses in a published summary. Perhaps in deference to the special interest of the sponsor, the document pointed out the connection between dirty habits and filthy streets and the need to attend to the second before any progress with the first could be expected.[40]

Gavin's report gave Cochrane full credit for his contribution, but the parent organization, the Health of Towns Association, nevertheless snubbed him. At one large meeting, held to hear addresses by Lord Ashley and Lord Normanby, all of the notables of the movement were gathered on the platform, but Cochrane was not among them. Not to be deterred, he turned up anyway and, from his seat in the audience, interrupted the proceedings to ask why he, who had so "much information to offer," had not been invited. The secretary tried to mollify him, but without success, and he retired, "apparently in a huff" (see Plate 12).[41]

Why he was not summoned to the feast after such heavy labor in the vineyard is, in the circumstance of the moment, not difficult to explain. A fringe group in the radically inclined Westminster riding association had asked Cochrane to stand for Parliament against the nominated candidate, Charles Lushington. Cochrane eagerly accepted, pointing out that his cousin, the Admiral, had once been a radical representative of the borough. The campaign that followed was a colorful one, conducted on the level of personalities, since both candidates agreed about issues. The *Sun* newspaper asked if Juan de Vega, the trickster who first kissed then told, and Charles Cochrane had ever been one and the same.[42] Flustered, Cochrane denied it and threatened libel suits but then called his supporters together and confessed. It was, he agreed, a silly book, written when he was young and foolish. Even so, he said, it showed signs of a good heart. Besides, what did the charge amount to, after all, but that "when I was a youth of 19 or 20 years of age I was fond of girls."[43]

Probably this publicity helped him since he lost to Lushington by only twelve votes – claiming that he had been beaten by a horde of "plumpers."[44] Considering the odds, it was not a bad showing, and, even with his claims to respectability somewhat tarnished, his bid for recognition might not have been lost. However, he soon involved himself in the Chartist demonstrations of 1848 in such a way that he damaged his reputation irreparably not only among the people who had sponsored his soup kitchen and his orderlies but also among the leaders of London radicalism.

Encouraged by a renewal of support in the city during the difficult winter of 1847–8 and by the February Revolution in France, Chartist leaders made overtures to prominent London radicals and joined with them in demonstrations against the indifference of the government to the plight of the unemployed and against a proposal to raise the income tax. Cochrane saw an opportunity to become a serious player; to show his leadership abilities, he announced, without consulting his allies, that a giant rally would be held in the still-unfinished Trafalgar Square. The Home Office and police were edgy. With ugly confrontations in Glasgow and the events of Paris fresh in their minds, they forbade the meeting, and Cochrane reluctantly agreed to back off. He had placards put up announcing that he would not appear in the Square and advising followers to stay at home. Some 10,000–15,000 East Enders ignored this advice; assembling at 1:00 p.m. and presided over by the republican journalist, George Reynolds, they listened peacefully to speeches. As the formal part of the meeting ended, a scuffle broke out, a nervous police contingent charged, and skirmishes between hundreds of police and determined groups of stone-throwers, referred to by the press as "The Cochrane Mob," lasted into the night and resumed the next day.[45]

Small shopkeepers who might have been sympathetic to the joint Chartist and radical messages were alienated, and everyone blamed Cochrane: Ernest Jones blamed him for not having consulted with Chartist Headquarters, middle-class radicals blamed him for his defective timing, the press blamed him for having frightened the city at a sensitive moment and then having run for cover. When the excitement was over, Mr Punch took credit for having "put down" the leading humbug of 1848:

> Who settled Cochrane?
> I, answered Punch,
> With my staff and hump
> I settled Cochrane.[46]

There was some substance to this boast, since the magazine went after him mercilessly, calling him "Cockroach," the "Shy Cock-rane of Westminster," and "Mr. Odillon Barrot Cochrane." One piece recommended the setting up of an "Institution for the Early Shutting-up of Mr. Cochrane."[47]

Cochrane was disgraced but not shut up. With little now to lose, he threw himself into the role of, as one newspaper put it, "a political busy-body," and "an awfully heavy joke."[48] He seems to have had no family or private life. Mornings and afternoons he spent in committee rooms and vestry halls. Early in the morning he could be found inspecting his orderlies or checking conditions at his free lavatories and public conveniences. Evenings found him speaking in tavern meeting rooms or exploring slum alleys to gather information for his *Poor Man's Guardian*. His attacks on local bureaucracies quickened. Much of the damage was sustained by the newly formed Metropolitan Commissioners of Sewers. For example, he managed to have published in *The Times* a letter signed by fifty-four residents of Carrier Street and Church Lane, a particularly noisome part of St Giles where the street orderlies had carried out one of their demonstrations. How much Cochrane had to do with the picturesque text of the letter is not certain, but, one suspects, it was quite a lot. The first paragraph began:

> Sur, – May we beg and beseach your proteckshion and power. we are Sur, as it may be, livin in a Wilderness, as far as the rest of London knows anything of us, or as the rich and great

people care about. We live in muck and filthe. We aint got no priviz, no dust bins, no drains or suer in the hole place. The Suer Company, in Greek St., Soho Squre, all great, rich and pourfool [surely a Cochranean touch] men, take no notice whatsomediver of our complaints. The Stench of a Gully-hole is disgustin. We all suffer, and numbers are ill; if the Cholera comes Lord help us.

It ended: "Preaye Sur come and see us, for we are livin like piggs, and it aint faire we soulde be so ill-treated."[49]

For several days all of the London press commented on the stir of conscience the letter caused. *The Times* answered the prayer by sending a reporter, accompanied by a police sergeant, to examine the dwellings of the correspondents court by court and room by room. In his report he gave the readers all the shocking details while on the leader page the editor thundered against slum landlords, vested interests, and bureaucratic negligence. In the next NPA report Cochrane laid on generous helpings of irony. Until *The Times* joined the chorus, he wrote, "that redoubtable body of Do-nothing Philosophers, the Metropolitan Commissioners of Sewers," "these Deodorising Doctors and Sewage Manure Manufacturers" (the target was Chadwick) were able to tolerate "within *scent* of their own Court-house" these dreadful conditions and "took no heed of St. Giles Rookery, – this Pandora's Box of pollution, plague, and pestilence!" But let the newspaper of the rich and powerful get their attention and "Lo and behold," these *"repudiators of respectable and really practicable Street Cleansing* prepare for a *grand field day."* All at once they appear with a report promising that the area will have new drains, public urinals, new paving, water-pipes, dustbins, and prompt action against slum landlords who allow cesspools to build up and fester. Such promises, he concluded, are as questionable as their consciences.[50]

This was gentle treatment compared to what he did to his old vestry in Marylebone. Poor Law Guardians there, feeling the effects of the immigration of hungry Irishmen in the autumn of 1847, decided to cut relief costs by reducing wages paid to paupers for hammering granite blocks into the walnut-sized pieces used in making macadam paving. Cochrane got twenty-five of these paupers to sign a letter to the *Poor Man's Guardian*, describing the misery and danger of their work. Parish stinginess meant that they must work with worn tools, the result being that hardly any of the stones produced were broken properly; and much worse than that, the letter continued, five of their mates had each lost an eye due to the narrow confines of the pens where the hammering went on. Cochrane promptly gathered about a thousand people in Portman Square, put ten of the stonebreakers on the platform to tell their stories, and got a petition approved. When he took it to the vestry meeting, he used the occasion to harangue the chairman, Sir James Hamilton, a man who had prior experience with Cochrane's tactics. When Hamilton asked to see proof that five eyes had been lost, Cochrane, as a parting shot, asked if the vestry and the Marylebone ratepayers might not want to hear the detail directly from the paupers, a suggestion that seems to have convulsed the meeting with laughter.[51]

Immediately the NPA organized another, even larger, gathering where there were excited words and some dark threats. Back went Cochrane with a second resolution, this time taking with him six pauper workers, four friendly ratepayers, and two packages of carelessly broken stones to present as evidence. The vestrymen ordered the paupers to remain in the vestibule. There were shouts of anger when Cochrane dumped the stones on the floor and pandemonium when he tried to read the fire-breathing resolution. Summarily dismissed, the furious Cochrane stormed into the vestibule where he discovered a reporter from the *Observer* interviewing the stonebreakers. There was shouting, shoving, insults – the scene ending in a highly newsworthy uproar.[52]

Local board members and commissioners all over London were subjected to these confrontational tactics between 1846 and 1853. In the midst of one donnybrook, a participant shouted that Cochrane was a "common disturber of public meetings," and, of course, he was right.[53] When one rattled chairman refused to put a particularly outrageous motion, Cochrane shouted:

> Won't you put it through, by Jove? Won't you! Then if you don't, mark, – we'll keep possession of this place till you do. I tell you we insist on that being put. You tell us to go to the Poor Law Board. What the devil have we to do with the Poor Law Board? We pay our rates, my good fellow, and this is our place.

Sniffed *The Times* on its leader page in July 1852, "the Kossuth of the soup-kitchens is at his old work again – in other words, making such noise and doing as much mischief as he can conveniently accomplish in a given space of time."[54]

A year later the harassment had stopped, at least on the English side of the Channel. The reason was that Cochrane decided to expand his soup kitchen, contracting for furnishings and giving his personal surety for them, only to discover, when the expected subscriptions failed to come in, that he must face imprisonment or flee to France since all of his fortune had been used up – whereupon the port of Boulogne began to experience the effects of this 44-year-old Englishman's irrepressible energy. Perhaps a connection he had made with Louis Napoleon in London explains why the Mayor of Boulogne immediately agreed to accept Cochrane's offer to set up an orderly brigade and keep the Grande Rue permanently clean.[55] Cochrane went on from Boulogne to organize a drive to close all the cafés and shops along Paris's Rue Vivienne on Sunday. Supposedly seeking the help of the Lord's Day Observance Society in this eccentric endeavor, he decided to return to London.[56]

Not long after, in June, 1855, he died, alone and with his affairs in hopeless confusion. The cause of death was recorded as "brain fever." The Revd Joseph Brown preached the funeral sermon on the exactly appropriate text: "Whatsoever thy hand findeth to do, do it with all thy might." He recalled seeing the departed kneeling in the New Cut Market among the costers' barrows, praying for grace. It had been Cochrane's custom, said the vicar, to put on Sunday morning breakfasts for two or three hundred of the most desperately hungry people he could find and then lead these throngs of ragged men, women, and children through the most crowded and Sabbath-breaking parts of his neighborhood to Christ Church, Blackfriars, for morning service. "It was," said the Revd Brown, "a sight not more interesting than most extraordinary."[57]

Several years earlier, Henry Mayhew, in his endorsement of the street orderly idea, expressed regret that its originator had been so "completely unacknowledged by the public" who, he added, "owe him a heavy debt of gratitude." What attracted Mayhew was the seeming practicality of Cochrane's solution to the problem of how to employ pauper labor productively without injury to the self-reliance of the worker or serious disruption of the free-market system.[58] From our perspective, his claim on our attention is the comprehensiveness of his street reform concept and the contrast it provides to the more restricted parameters of liberal reformism. Cochrane did not use metaphors of circulation or respiration; he never described the city as a growing, gasping organism, nor was he much interested in removing obstacles to free movement. His discourse had to do with fairness, justice, and community, rather than with locomotion. For him the city street was a setting for reform, not the object of it. It is true that he used fear about the miasmal gases the streets supposedly gave off to forward his program for employing pauper labor, but he was convinced that he had found the formula for keeping surfaces clean and sweet; therefore his mind never rested on that problem but raced ahead to the injustices and incompetence in the existing social structure. His shortlived but remarkable *Poor Man's Guardian* shows the range of that mind, as well as its naivety and eccentricity. He wished to abolish the Act of Settlement which restricted the right to receive welfare to one parish and would allow destitute people who, he reminded his readers, bore a heavy burden of indirect taxes, to apply for assistance anywhere in the kingdom. Instead of the existing anomalous system, he wanted one, uniform rate to pay for social welfare. Workhouses he would have turned into refuges for the aged, sick, and homeless and into labor exchanges where the unemployed could register their skills and employers could post their requirements. Works projects, organized along the lines of his street orderlies and using the device of the uniform to avoid stigma, would be there for any able-bodied workers who wished to volunteer for public service. London should have a real municipal government with sufficient power to provide public conveniences and amenities, to erect model housing, and to force landlords to bring their premises up to standard, that standard being, in his words, "a *Fit Social State*." If systematized and properly led, the city could, he believed, be the agency for promoting community and for assisting poor people in their already existing desire to climb the ladder of social improvement. He suggested that municipal authorities might be given the ownership and management of utilities, especially gas and water, and that they might use income from those services to finance this assistance.[59]

What began in a proposal to please Oxford Street merchants by giving them a wooden paving ended in a radical program, one that seems considerably less quixotic to us than it did to many of his contemporaries. They, including those who had sympathy for his causes, found his desire for recognition embarrassing, his motives suspect, his tactics outrageous, his style uncouth – and it is not difficult to understand why they should have done so. But tolerance and respect increase with historical distance. We can accept him now as an outstanding example, to use his own self-description, of that valuable and rare specimen, the "practical enthusiast."

8

RESCUING

The awakening of evangelical enthusiasm that Cochrane experienced in 1852 became an increasingly common occurrence in that decade and the following one. Up to that point, he, like other optimistic humanitarians of the early Victorian period, sought to remove the physical, social, and political impediments which prevented poor people of every description and religious persuasion from living happy and self-directed lives. He would free the disadvantaged in the burgeoning cities so that they might follow their natural inclinations to improve themselves. To this end he demonstrated and agitated. But toward the close of his life he seems to have abandoned utility for salvationism. By making this shift he provides us with a convenient bridge to another era of reform, one that led large numbers of men and, now on a significant scale, women into the streets of London to minister to the poor. The faith that sustained this new vanguard of reborn Protestants did not rest on the expectation that fallen humanity would choose the good if given a chance to do so but on the conviction that personal salvation obliged those who sensed it to bring the good news to all sinners who could be reached. As one evangelist remarked, "Why do we not gather where the fish are?"[1] Hence many missionaries of this second Evangelical Awakening[2] burned with zeal to obey Christ's command to "Go out quickly into the highways and hedges, and compel them to come in, that my house may be filled" (Luke XIV, 23).

In comparing the revival spirit of the eighteenth and early nineteenth centuries with this second one, Kathleen Heasman notes a widening of aim, from the older and narrower concentration on winning likely converts and then deepening the faith of those won, to a determination to reach people at the furthest remove from the congregation of the already saved. In this way evangelists would demonstrate their faith to the pagans and infidels of the city's meanest neighborhoods.[3] In this more outward phase many evangelical rescuers became an actual part of the life of the London streets rather than remaining occasional excursionists into the province of sin. Missionaries lived in shelters deliberately placed in the roughest areas, entered the city's stews to bring the message of redemption, and walked the dark streets to invite prostitutes to midnight tea and Christian sympathy. What they discovered opened their eyes to the extent of wretchedness that existed in the capital. In stages, they became active in providing shelters from the hazards of street life and then went beyond mere rescue into active and highly organized social work among the depraved and destitute in their own environments. So often and so energetically was this pattern repeated in the mid-Victorian period that Sir James Stephen could say, with good reason, "Ours is the age of societies."[4]

Illustrations abound. Society-building, the taking of the Christian message outside the walls of city churches and chapels, the establishment of settlement houses and shelters, programs for rehabilitating ex-convicts or prostitutes have their institutional histories, in-house biographies, and published reminiscences. Out of this accumulation we will focus upon one evangelical rescuer, John "Rob Roy" MacGregor, and two of the societies he established, the Shoe-Black Brigade and the Open Air Mission. MacGregor and his societies are particularly relevant to a study of street reform: both he and they embodied so purely the evangelical outlook and employed a "science" or "method" which in the 1850s already resembled the one worked out by Cochrane in the 1840s. Furthermore, these similarities in means can be conveniently contrasted with differences in ends. MacGregor did not form his societies for the purpose of shaming or pressuring civic or national authorities into providing decent housing, humane welfare agencies, or sanitary environments. He was neither an agitator nor a radical but an upholder of the *status quo*. His belief in "system" arose out of a wish to fulfill God's ordinances as effectively as possible and not from any expectation that it might be possible to build a "Fit Social State" here on earth.

To some extent at least the enthusiasm both Cochrane and MacGregor had for uniforms, brigades, drill, and rigid discipline can be explained by family tradition. Both were born into distinguished Scottish military families. In 1825 the 5-week-old John was carried by his mother and army major father aboard an East Indiaman, bound for the subcontinent. The ship caught fire in the Bay of Biscay and quickly sank with the loss of a hundred lives. Infant and parents were rescued. This was not, however, MacGregor's only dramatic baptism and rebirth. After a brief recuperation in Edinburgh, mother and child set out by sea for London, were shipwrecked, and then saved again. Moved by this apparent demonstration of divine purpose, Hannah More, a family friend, sent knitted boots and a poem:

Sweet babe *twice* rescued from the yawning grave,
The flames tremendous and the furious wave,
May a *third* better life thy spirit meet,
E'en Life Eternal at the Saviour's feet.[5]

This blessing turned out to be a prophecy, at least in the sense that the child felt a religious inclination seemingly from the cradle on. The family moved to Ireland in 1838 when the father was put in charge of the Irish Constabulary. John attended Trinity College and there determined to become a missionary. Devout though the Church of Scotland parents were, they objected to this zealous extravagance and persuaded the young man to go to Cambridge instead; there he exercised his taste for muscular Christianity by rowing and leading a Bible class at the Jesus Lane Sunday School. Not a complex person, he nevertheless had an impressive variety of interests. While still an undergraduate, he began writing the first of many pieces for *Punch* and articles for *The Mechanics' Magazine* on such subjects as the electrification of railways and the theory of prismatic colours. Journalism and books on adventure continued to occupy much of his time even after he took his degree, read for the Bar, and set himself up as a patent lawyer with chambers in the Inner Temple. Particularly popular with public school boys throughout the rest of the century were accounts he wrote of his adventures in a canoe and tiny sloop (both with names the same as his *nom-de-plume*, Rob Roy) on the rivers and waterways of Europe, Canada, and the Near East. During 1868–9, for example, he paddled and sailed his canoe from Alexandria down the Suez Canal to the Red Sea, ending in the Holy Land. Proceeds from accounts of this expedition, called *Rob Roy on the Jordan*, went to help fund one of the dozen or so causes he was deeply involved in, the Prevention and Reformatory School Society. This contribution he supplemented by performing over a number of years in public engagements where he would appear in Arab dress and act out some of the more perilous episodes in his tale.[6]

Boyish himself, he did much of his writing with male adolescents in mind, and, being spared the necessity of laboring hard at his legal profession, he was able to devote most of his working hours to rescuing youthful criminals, vagrants, and street waifs. This he began to do as soon as he moved to London from Cambridge in 1854. The Revd Baptist Noel introduced him to urban mission work. Soon after, while still reading for the law, he volunteered to teach in The Field Lane Ragged School in Clerkenwell, where the omnipresent Lord Shaftesbury, then Lord Ashley, was the honorary chairman. Recognizing the value of this new recruit, Shaftesbury almost immediately put him on the managing committee of the Ragged School Union, an organization aimed at co-ordinating the policies and management of the many voluntary schools created throughout the poorer areas of London to tame and Christianize the large number of homeless or neglected children (Shaftesbury's estimate was 30,000 or more) who spent their days in the streets and some of them, their nights sleeping in doorways or under carts and railway arches.[7]

It was this association with Shaftesbury that gave MacGregor his general position on juvenile problems. The great philanthropist took advantage of any opportunity to convey his message that street children were not "Arabs"; in other words, they were not isolated, shifting, patternless wanderers but instead formed a distinct group in society, distinct even from poor urban children in general. (He did not develop the concept of a subculture but came fairly close to doing so.) They had leaders, chains of authority, codes of conduct, and defined boundaries around territories or "lurks." They constituted, said Shaftesbury, "a numerous class, having habits, pursuits, feelings, customs, and interests of their own. . . ." A journalist in 1855 made much the same point: "Street boys, indeed, are a distinct species of the human family."[8] It followed then, that these street children required special treatment if they were to be punished in a constructive way for petty crimes, rehabilitated, or even detached from their self-perpetuating micro-society. Magistrates, teachers, prison wardens, or philanthropists who did not bear this in mind were doomed to fail in their work of correction and rescue. MacGregor certainly paid attention to this advice, as did, of course, Mary Carpenter, Rowland Hill, and their allies in the crusade for special laws and institutions for juvenile offenders. In an article MacGregor wrote in 1856 for *Leisure Hour* called "Ragamuffins: or, London Street Boys and What Can Be Made of Them," the beginning metaphor is of two currents of movement along the city's pavements, one flowing five or six feet from the surface and the other moving quite independently about two feet lower down, in a different direction, toward different objects, and making different sounds. The lower stratum, he wrote, was a "powerful, numerous, ubiquitous community, with most complicated rights and privileges, and jealously-guarded vested interests, as everyone soon finds out who tries to meddle with them, either to suppress or improve them."[9]

As was the case with so many other Victorians who took this theme, his disapproval of gutter ways was often combined with a certain amount of sentimental admiration for those to be found there. One commentator on the phenomenon in New York called the street waifs of that city "an army of happy barbarians."[10] MacGregor had too much direct experience with suffering to go that far; yet he did see that this community of street children had useful functions, one of them, the public deflating of displays of false dignity. The life had, he conceded, its charm for young people of adventurous dispositions. "Uncontrolled freedom" might be the source of danger from the perspective of that loftier stream where adults moved, but a compelling attraction to young people in the stream beneath. Any attempt to reach the lower stratum must take this difference in perspective into account: to place a street child in an ordinary school or to send a girl or boy off to the colonies without some special transitional preparation was to court disaster – a warning MacGregor sounded as a London school board member after the Forster's Act of 1870 advanced the process of forming a national system of elementary education.[11] Twenty years earlier this Shaftesburian message had appeared in a report of the Ragged School Union:

> We have, moreover, greatly abated the amount of juvenile delinquency and have cleansed the metropolis, not by pouring out from it the filth of our streets, but by passing these children through a cleansing and filtering process, before we poured them forth in a rich and fertilising stream on the colonies of our country.[12]

It is not surprising then that MacGregor's best-known project, the Shoe-Black Brigade, grew out of his experience as a teacher at the Field Lane Ragged School. Partly because of his efforts, the activities of that school expanded beyond providing rudimentary education and Christian training to sheltering some of the homeless among the pupils. Subsequently he was one of the most active in promoting the establishment of voluntary industrial and reformatory schools to which, after 1854, magistrates could choose to send convicted juveniles.[13] But he also became aware that placing delinquents in institutions and setting up refuges for some hundreds of waifs and strays were inadequate responses, given the dimension of the problem. So, like Cochrane, he sought some kind of "practical philanthropy,"[14] one that might utilize the dirty streets themselves and make street work part of a "cleansing and filtering process."

Edwin Hodder, in his eulogistic biography of MacGregor, tells the story of how, on a November evening in 1850, the 25-year-old Scot and three other Ragged School teachers – two of them fellow barristers from the Temple and Lincoln's Inn – walked arm in arm up Holborn Hill after a meeting called by Shaftesbury to consider how boys from the schools might be employed during the forthcoming Great Exhibition. Carrying on this subject as they walked, one of the group mentioned seeing shoeblacks in the streets of Paris and Rotterdam and suggested trying the experiment when the city would be filled with foreigners accustomed to the service. The response from the others was enthusiastic; each pledged 10s. on the spot, the estimated cost of a set of brushes and some sort of uniform. MacGregor immediately plunged himself into the task of forming a society and soliciting funds. Only Shaftesbury responded, but his gift of £5 was enough to launch the Ragged School Shoe-Black Society.[15]

The same idea had occurred to Cochrane three years earlier. After first securing promises of co-operation from the police, he sent a number of his uniformed orderlies out to polish shoes. The problem was, he noted, that London gentlemen seemed to be inhibited about exposing their dirty boots and trouser bottoms, unable to "withstand the public gaze," and the project was soon aborted.[16] Initially MacGregor met the same resistance, but tourists responded and the press gave a boost, especially after the Society marched the red-shirted brigade to the Crystal Palace for a celebration. In the first seven months the Shoe-Black Society recruited thirty-six boys, aged 12-15, from what MacGregor called "the criminal and destitute class."[17] At the year's end they had cleaned 102,000 boots and shoes and had each earned an average of 2s. 2½d. a day, a success that was marked by a tea-party at the Field Lane School with Lord Shaftesbury in the chair and Dr Southwood Smith, Edwin Chadwick, and William Macaulay distributing plum cake and prizes.[18]

Demand did not decrease with the closing of the Exhibition. In 1854 the Society formed two new brigades, each with its own territory and distinctive tunic-uniform, and by the 1890s there were ten, including one administered by the Society of St Vincent de Paul for Catholic boys, a large sector of waifdom not accommodated by the energetically Protestant founders of the original movement. Before he died in 1893, MacGregor spoke of his satisfaction at having provided the "means of polishing the understandings of a generation of Cockneys."[19]

This success made MacGregor a recognized expert on the subject of urban youth while still in his twenties. Concern about a rising rate of juvenile delinquency had caused authorities to welcome almost any suggestion about ways to deal with the problem. Thus, not more than a year after the shoeblack experiment was launched, we find him being questioned at length by a Select Committee on Criminal and Destitute Juveniles about his "method" and how it might be applied more generally. He assured the Committee-men that it could:

> The results should show that boys can be taken as nuisances from the streets and as criminals from the gaols, and be made useful servants to the public, able to earn an honest livelihood during their reformation, and finally become religious and respectable lads, or leave us as colonists.

This reformation could be "affected by the activity of voluntary agency, by kindness and constant attention, and above all by continuous discipline; that is, daily and hourly incentives to good conduct, and discouragement of bad."[20]

Crucially important to that discipline, he impressed upon his questioners, was the uniform with the numbered badge; it made inspection easy and encouraged the public to report misconduct. He put it this way in a piece on the shoeblack he published the same year: "His coat is so red that bad companions dare not meddle with him; and he is watched by many eyes."[21] Assigning a uniformed boy to a station has the further advantage, he added, of making him known to the police constable on that beat; thus the boy can be protected from non-uniformed competition. MacGregor told the Select Committee that the arrangement whereby the Police Commissioners would license bootblack agencies and approve stations had made acceptable to the authorities a street activity that had once been a source of aggravation.[22]

Perhaps even more important than these external controls were the internal ones which the uniform induced. Wearing it gave the boy a sense of belonging, an *esprit de corps*, which would act as a substitute for the street-youth community from which he was now separated. MacGregor would have been glad to second a pronouncement by Henry Drummond, in an address to Harvard University students in 1903. There is no point, said this Boys' Brigade organizer, in trying to use conventional inducements or techniques on a big city rough. What you do is put him in a hall, place a military cap on his head and a leather belt around his waist and shoulder and say, "Now, Private Hopkins, stand up." So long as you have him in uniform, Drummond advised, "you can order that boy about until he is black in the face."[23]

Obedience and a willingness to be ordered about against one's preferences – these were qualities MacGregor also valued. He praised the volunteer movement of the 1860s (and no one save Lord Elcho could have been a more dedicated Volunteer Officer) because of its power to teach former Chartists to value order and patriotism. But he would vehemently have denied that his ultimate aim was to control the young and restless males among the urban poor in the interest of Queen, country, empire, or even social peace; the promotion of these interests was merely a by-product. The real object of this disciplining, uniforming, and drilling was to create stalwart individuals, Protestant Christian soldiers ready to march as to war against "idleness, dissipation and vice." Thus the real victory was to be a personal and a moral one.[24] That victory could be won even in the city streets but only under a "proper agency," one that would insure that arrangements could be carried out "systematically"; otherwise, "the effort might become an evil instead of a blessing."[25]

His agency, in this case the Shoe-Black Brigade, leased an old house on Off Alley, near Charing Cross. Each boy was to assemble there early in the morning, scrubbed and in uniform, for prayers – usually led by MacGregor or by one of his barrister colleagues. Then the boys would march out, two by two, to stations assigned and regularly rotated by a resident superintendent. At six in the evening they would reassemble, check in their red tunics, numbered badges, and polishing equipment, and pay in the money they had received. Three times a week they would be expected to attend their respective Ragged Schools, and on Sunday they would report back for a bible class.[26] But the Brigade was not yet a total institution. At least initially most boys slept at home or wherever they could find shelter. But MacGregor had a low view of parental influence among the city poor and, of course, recognized that the task of "reformation" had little chance to work if boys retained some freedom to experience the enticements of unsupervised street life. Therefore the Society soon set up a dormitory in the attic at Off Alley, and in 1854 a new East London Brigade headquarters provided room and board for fifty shoeblacks. Other refuges were added in the 1860s.[27] For many boys, the Brigade became a home.

Incentives to good conduct were supplied by special insignia, prizes, but primarily, by promotion and demotion. MacGregor impressed the Commissioners with the importance he attached to these features of his system. Regularity, honesty, and industry would advance a boy to the top of three divisions, each division being assigned stations, graded according to the amount of income they could be expected to provide. Thus misconduct threatened a loss of income as well as status. Dishonesty or "restlessness or unwillingness to submit to discipline, which is extremely strict," meant dismissal. In the first year, MacGregor admitted, twenty-five had to be discharged. But he did not think this a high figure considering that the first batch came entirely from the Field Lane School and not from the whole Union and included twenty-seven who had been in prison and twenty-nine who had been abandoned by drunken, convict parents. He was proud of the fact that only twelve of the twenty-seven ex-convicts had to be discharged for incompetence and only four for misconduct.[28]

From the beginning, there were criticisms, even from inside the Ragged School Union, that however salutary this discipline might be, the work itself was degrading – kneeling all day at the feet of customers – and that it led nowhere. MacGregor replied that this method taught self-reliance, the first step in the ladder upward. The boy would recognize, even as he knelt, that what he was doing was not just some disguised form of begging, an awareness the Society reinforced by doing what it could to discourage the public from adding more to the penny price. Also, the lad would be aware, since the Society was self-supporting, that he was not a charitable ward. Dedicated work would bring him immediate benefits. He would receive 6d. a day, regardless of earnings, that amount then deducted from any surplus. Whatever surplus there was would be divided evenly: a third for the boy immediately, a third for his savings account (with safeguards against impulsive withdrawal or parental raiding), and a third to pay for the Society's expenses. Nothing was given entirely free; there was a nominal price for refreshments in the coffee room, for room, board, uniforms, and polishing equipment.[29] This way, it was hoped, close supervision and self-help could be reconciled, and boys could learn regularity from an institutional environment without being institutionalized and could be assisted without being pauperized.

Clearly, this was no stop-gap enterprise. MacGregor hoped to put all waifs and strays into uniformed service of one kind or another.[30] He was delighted when the Electric Telegraph Co. agreed to station black-trousered and red-jacketed members of the Brigade near their main outlets to carry messages and parcels.[31] A red-shirted "Broomer" Brigade was another of his projects. Broomers could be contracted to keep the pavement in front of shops and offices clean. It occurred to him that girls might be given a variety of outdoor, traditionally female tasks: "Brassers" might, again on contract, keep door plates gleaming; "Steppers," dressed in uniform frocks and bonnets, might be given pipe clay and pails of water to whiten the front steps of houses.[32] New York newsboys were organized; why could London's not be as well? Horse-holding, knife-sharpening, window-cleaning; the possibilities were almost limitless. Indeed, might it not be feasible to turn over the entire work of keeping the city clean to juveniles, organized under a "proper agency?"[33]

Experience did shrink these expectations somewhat. MacGregor had to concede that boys who were accustomed to the unconstrained life of the street had no training in delayed gratification and therefore made poor contract workers. The reward and the service must be nearly simultaneous if they were to be "constant and active in their labour."[34] He also reluctantly came to the conclusion that girls could not be protected from the evils of the street environment, even by his system. As he or a like-minded contributor to the *Reformatory and Refuge Journal* concluded in 1861: "With regard . . . to girls, I can conceive of no plan of organisation by which the dangers which must beset them in the streets could be averted."[35]

Thus expectations for large-scale rescue by means of systematized street work diminished in the 1860s even while the process of forming new brigades and constructing new refuges was expanding. A spokesman for the Reformatory and Refuge Union, which MacGregor founded, expressed resigned disappointment that, in spite of all the philanthropic activity that so characterized the age, the number of vagrant boys on the streets seemed not to have diminished and the rates for juvenile crime seemed not to have declined. Reflecting in 1866 on the quickening of social work activity during his youthful manhood, MacGregor made a distinction between his philanthropic aims and the reformism of the era just passed. The older radicalism looked to legislation; he and his fellow evangelicals of the newer generation aimed to reform "people and not politics, characters and not institutions, life and not laws."[36] It would be enough if only some individuals could be reached, improved, and saved.

Therefore his homilies were full of examples of how individual boys in his "Red Republic" had been socialized and given self-respect. He told of young scamps who had once lived by pinching vegetables from shops but were now "tugging away at timber in Canada," serving Her Majesty in the armed forces, or "pocketing dollars" in the States. He cited the case of a juvenile thief with a drunken mother and no father, who, after putting on the red shirt and working in the streets with his box and brushes, "obtained a situation as an in-door servant"; at last report he had "commenced family prayers in the kitchen" and was "giving every satisfaction." Then there was young Parker who, having come to the City Reds with a bullet still lodged in his neck from a burglary attempt, used the money accumulated in his savings account to buy a kit for Australia, where he now lived and prospered.[37] This was the way MacGregor and so many of his fellow evangelicals measured success. What effects these refuges, protected savings accounts, and institutionalized boy societies had on the family economies and the communal life of the urban poor was not a subject that interested him, even though he was aware that there were effects. He lacked Cochrane's concern for improving not just individual character but features of the urban political and social structure. Searching out boys in the greatest need of rescue, attracting these "buzzing bees" and seeing them "properly hived,"[38] improving their characters by exposing them to moral choices, and offering incentives for choosing honesty and hard work, providing by means of elementary schooling and character references chances to escape from the attractive yet deadly life of the streets – these were his preoccupations. In this emphasis on individual rescue he epitomized one characteristic of street reform shared by most mid-Victorian liberals.

Compulsory elementary education, the gradual replacement of the family economy by an individual wage system, state social insurance, widening opportunities for adolescent employment, advances in the decasualization of adult labor during the Great War, and the coming of the motor vehicle and its cleansing effect reduced the need and opportunities for such projects as MacGregor's, although the many-coloured shoeblack brigades remained conspicuous features of London street life in late Victorian and Edwardian times. At the turn of the century bootblacks still smiled from countless Christmas cards, postcards, cartoons, and "scraps," the caption usually reading "clean your boots, Sir?"[39] (See Plate 13.) But by the 1920s boy labor in the streets had lost its appeal to philanthropists. When in 1925 *The Shaftesbury Magazine* commemorated the one hundredth anniversary of MacGregor's birth, it noted that only one Brigade remained and it was made up of men 30 years old or more, most of them handicapped. "The whole of modern practice," the article said, "is against encouraging young lads to earn their livings on the streets." It did acknowledge, however, that the social and economic changes that had made MacGregor's system redundant had also reduced the supply of zeal and dedication – qualities MacGregor possessed in such abundance.[40]

This Victorian institution may have shriveled with the new century, but another of MacGregor's projects for using streets to save souls, the Open Air Mission, continues to this day. Like his Shoe-Black Society, it would use "system," this time applied to street preaching. He recalled how the idea occurred to him. Walking through Whitechapel on a Sunday afternoon in 1853, he noticed clumps of people gathered around lay preachers. At one gathering, he said, "a popish argument was going on. I joined in and argued for an hour with some good."[41] Much stimulated, he invited two experienced open-air preachers to meet with him at the Field Lane School, and together they formed the Mission. Its purpose was to give organization and regularity to what had been to that point spontaneous responses by individuals to Christ's call to go out into the streets and bring the poor into the fold.

Preaching in the open air, usually in fields, village greens, or commons, to those people who had chosen to be there had always, of course, been part of evangelism; what stirred the 23-year-old barrister's imagination was the notion of using the city street rather than some enclosure or protected space. Not that street speakers, on religious or other topics, were unknown before the mid-nineteenth century: Lord Shaftesbury spoke in the 1880s about how in his youth street preaching "was looked upon as the vilest thing imaginable; when it was offensive to the mind of the magistrate as to the mind of the mob." In those wilder days, he said, the sight of a street preacher provided a "dearly-loved opportunity for what is called cock-shy; dead cats, rotten eggs, and everything that came to hand being largely used for this purpose." Then he added, "What a change do we see now!"[42]

The change that Shaftesbury noted and that MacGregor contemplated in 1853 was from a spontaneous, often emotional and highly sectarian or eccentric, and mainly working-class phenomenon to one that was organized, controlled, non-sectarian, and attractive to respectables of all classes, but particularly to middle-class men "of education as well as piety,"[43] the kind of persons to be found teaching for the Ragged School Union. This new breed of evangelists would need unusual capabilities of self-control, ardor that was balanced with common sense, coolness in the face of "turbulent interference," absence of fanaticism – qualities lacking in the "poor and despised men"[44] who had been holding forth on curbs and street corners. It was MacGregor's insight that a society, devoted to training professional street preachers and supported by the eminent, including leaders of the Anglican Establishment, would be needed to bring this change about. Probably Gawin Kirkham, the second Secretary of the Open Air Mission, was not exaggerating much when he wrote: "To Mr. MacGregor's undying honour be it said, he discovered the great cause of open-air evangelism to be a soul without a body, and left it possessed of corporate existence."[45]

MacGregor's social position and his connection with the intelligentsia – he was on visiting terms with the Carlyles and the Dickenses – and with the military and police, as well as the philanthropic establishment, secured the active support for the Mission of, for example, Lords Radnor, Kinnaird, and Shaftesbury, the Duke of Manchester, S.M. Peto (the railway builder), Sir Edward Buxton, George Moore, Lady Olivia Sparrow, Laurence Oliphant, and, most important of all, the Commissioners of the Metropolitan Police, the Archbishop of Canterbury, and the Bishops of London and Winchester. An entry in the diary MacGregor kept in 1856 reads, "Archbishop Tait came to Covent Garden market in his robes with me, and spoke in the open air."[46] At an annual meeting of the Mission held in the Mansion House in 1884, Shaftesbury reflected that open-air services had become "perfectly normal." A movement which had been "discredited to the widest possible extent" was now celebrating its thirtieth birthday in the Lord Mayor's Palace.[47] The change of image was, he thought, almost complete.

The system worked out for the society derived from experience with the Ragged School Shoe-Black Society: carefully screen the applicants, instruct them in appropriate street behavior, teach them how to prepare services and how to speak, assign them to regular stations and inspect these stations, and finally, make sure that the police have advance notice of when and where a meeting will take place. To receive a red ribbon for his Bible, the emblem of full membership, a preacher would agree to perform during seasons of clement weather twice a day, seven days a week, at the appointed station, usually accompanied by apprentice preachers and other supporters. As in the case of the bootblacks, headquarters were near Charing Cross. Other stations tended to be located near street markets or just off major thoroughfares. Thus Brewer Street and the Brill in Somers Town, Cromer Street off Brunswick Square, the Seven Dials, Hollis Street, the Caledonian Road, Mile End Gate, and Tower Hill were places where frequenters came to expect regular hymn and prayer services.[48]

Regular members of the Mission, almost one thousand of them by the "Golden Age" of the 1880s, gathered together the first Monday in every month to compare experiences and to receive instruction. Their primer was MacGregor's widely circulated *Go Out Quickly*. It was the first of many in this genre,[49] all more or less with the same message: be prepared for a peculiar environment; what is appropriate inside may be inappropriate outside. "Word-spinning," for example, is generally to be avoided. It might be fashionable in the pulpit now, cautioned a Mission secretary, but do not try it at the Obelisk in Blackfriars Road. If you do, you will be likely to hear, "Go on, old buffer" or "Ain't he fine?" "My Eye!"; or some vulgar urchin will cry, "What a mouth for a tater."[50] Other dicta followed the same practical line: "Be brief; don't bawl"; follow Dr Guthrie's advice: "Prove, Paint, Persuade"; "Begin low, speak slow; / Aim higher, take fire." Be sparing with prayers and keep them short; never read long passages from the Scriptures; start with a hymn, and if you cannot arrange for a harmonium accompaniment, try a cornet. "Always imagine you have a fool in your audience, and talk to that fool." Even so, never seem to be patronizing. Prepare, but not to the point that you are unable to react spontaneously to noises, interruptions, or street events. Under no circumstances argue with a drunk or get into a doctrinal dispute. Have your helpers stand facing you and instruct them never to interfere with a disturber. If a policeman asks you to move on, comply; do not stand on your rights. Above all, the manuals urged, be interesting; remember that you have before you "a concourse of fortuitous atoms," that you must win their attention with "heart power" before you can direct their intellects.[51]

As one might expect, spokesmen for the Open Air Mission constantly assured themselves and the public that these methods were proving successful. *The Annual Report* for 1855 stated with pride that 71,970 people had listened that year to 1,405 services with an encouraging average of 51 a session. According to MacGregor, only one in ten services had been interrupted and only one in fifty had been disrupted.[52] Even so, those who ventured to preach the gospel in the streets needed all the discipline and support they could command. Non-believers were never the major problem; their attacks tended to be "systematic" and could be anticipated and answered with system. But in what MacGregor called "the very dens of Popery" it could be a different story. George Heath, who spent most of his adult life with the Mission, recalled how violent these confrontations could be in the 1850s. He said in those early days he was regularly followed and harassed by a gang of twenty Irish "Dock Rats" on his way to the station in the Mile End Road. Another regular, Godfrey Pike, remembered seeing an old woman climb down from her garret to throw a can of hot water on a preacher, shouting "Soup for Protestants."[53] At first the Mission countered by renting on Sundays a triangular open-air enclosure at King's Cross expressly as an arena for a controlled controversy with secularists and Catholics. Strongly as he cautioned against engaging in doctrinal dispute with other Protestants, MacGregor rejoiced in doing righteous battle with everyone else and made himself the centrepiece of these Sunday afternoons. A diary entry for November, 1858, reads, "At King's Cross found Mr. Calnon, the Papist opponent. We had the most pleasant, orderly, and useful controversy I ever recollect. Three turns each, that is, an hour and a half."[54] But this doctrinal athleticism was soon abandoned. Even though the entry to the triangle was wide, passers-by seemed reluctant to enter. So the Mission decided to concentrate its activities during the temperate months to the ecumenicism of the open road.

There they needed to be protected by the police. Four to eight constables were regularly assigned to such trouble spots as Tower Hill and the Seven Dials. Annual reports spoke of the excellent spirit of co-operation that the Police Commissioners were showing, especially Colonel Henderson, Sir Richard Mayne's successor. However the police records show, especially during Henderson's time, tension between a desire to assist the street missionaries in their work of pacification and the clearer duty to keep stationary crowds from blocking traffic, annoying residents, and attracting trouble-makers. As in the case of street prostitutes, pressure to act on one side of the question was quickly offset by pressure from the other. It was difficult to escape from this dilemma by appealing to the law – another similarity with street solicitation. The Highway Act of 1835 ordered police to remove any person "who shall wilfully obstruct the passage of any footway." A street preacher, it would seem, could hardly avoid doing just that. Like the hawker of umbrellas, he used every art to attract and hold in front of him the largest crowd possible, and the police seemed content in the early days of the Open Air Mission to apply the same policy to both: ignore the obstruction unless a traffic jam builds up or a resident complains. Since the Mission preachers gave advance notice and were trained in crowd control and restraint, there seem to have been few complaints. This situation began to change in the late 1850s and 1860s when visits by the American evangelists, Moody and Sankey, inspired hundreds of amateurs to go around, as a Police Superintendent put it, "holding forth in the streets."[55] Mayne and Henderson began to receive letters like one written by a Mr Emmerson of St John's Wood, who said that he and his family were being driven to distraction by the continual row outside his windows. The next Sunday the police observed and reported that four preachers in succession carried on from 6:30 in the evening until 10:00 and that the crowd had to be moved to one side to allow people returning home from Regent's Park to get through. Mayne asked for a legal opinion about what he should do in such cases since more and more thoroughfares were being similarly blocked. He was told that willful obstruction and refusal to move on were indictable offenses. If the police wanted to take action before Quarter Sessions they might get a conviction. But that alternative was hopelessly slow and cumbersome; summary jurisdiction was needed. Magistrates, however, were confused about whether the clauses of the Highway Act which provided such summary action for obstruction of a footway actually applied to London, and if they did, whether the preacher, in his own person, could be considered an obstruction since it was possible to argue it was his listeners and not he himself who were blocking the way.[56] Neither of these "nice questions" was quickly answered; in 1887 the Commissioner was still looking for clarification.[57]

With the formation of the Salvation Army in 1878 the dilemma for the police greatly intensified. MacGregor's concern had been to change the image of street preaching, to make it orderly and respectable; the followers of William Booth marched in processions through the streets, led by brass bands, shouting blood and fire. Not a middle-class movement, it was not greatly concerned with respectability. Also, it stirred violent opposition, some of it organized by what was called the Skeleton Army. A report from D Division on April 13, 1880, gives us a notion of how these marches appeared to those responsible for keeping streets open and orderly. Early in the afternoon of April 11, about twelve persons, led by their Captain, "Happy Eliza" Haynes (see Plate 15), set out from Omega Hall on the way to Edgware Place, singing as they went and followed by two hundred shouting and hooting youths. The procession stopped at Edgware Place to pray and sing a hymn, then returned to yet another meeting place in the Marylebone Theatre; by this time the train of juveniles had grown to three hundred and was growing noisier. A few hours later, the twelve began the same excursion again. Having been warned by a policeman at Edgware Place not to sing or halt on the return trip, they stuck to the centre of the roadway, dodging orange peels and clods of dirt. When a boisterous crowd blocked the way in front of the Theatre, four police constables helped the Salvationists to run this gauntlet. Inside, the police sergeant in charge informed Captain Haynes that nearly a hundred inhabitants of the neighborhood had signed a petition asking that something be done to suppress the marches, the trumpets and drums, the singing, the corner preaching, the continual uproar. She promised to leave the brass band behind next time, explaining that it was only used when coming into a new district. She would stop the halts for curb preaching and only sing through two streets along the way. But, she insisted, her group had a perfect right to march, to sing, and to expect police protection.[58] And in this, the Commissioner had to acknowledge, she was right. Marching and collecting crowds was not illegal. Colonel Henderson emphasized the point in a letter to an Open Air Missionary: if there was no actual obstruction and if there was no formal complaint, then police must not interfere.[59] Although there were times and places where everyone knew there would be trouble and "evil disposed persons" would be attracted, police were expressly forbidden to take preventative action. The Superintendent of D Division complained that Sundays had become times of stress. His men were fatigued from constantly accompanying Salvation Army marches and could not walk their beats. He asked whether it was right that one movement should so distort the use of his resources.[60] (See Plate 14.)

If solid citizens of the Edgware Road had come to regard street evangelism as an intolerable invasion of their privacy, then perhaps another shift had occurred in the current of street reform. The third quarter of the century had been characterized by a determination on the part of middle-class, and some aristocratic, evangelicals, to control confusion and disorder so that their agents could bring the message of redemption to what they believed to be the semi-pagan poor of the city and so that they might do battle at first hand with the forces of evil. After some initial resistance religious as well as secular authorities welcomed these rescuers as allies, even though the sophisticated might be embarrassed by so much "primitive" earnestness. After an interview with MacGregor in 1855, Bishop "Soapy-Sam" Wilberforce noted in his diary, "A curious specimen of earnest evangelical, Protestant man, very narrow and earnest, ready to burn a Tractarian or spend himself in preaching the Gospel to the poor."[61]

This guarded willingness on the part of members of the church leadership to work with rather than suppress open-air services developed just at the middle of the century. One Anglican clergyman received a reprimand from his superiors in 1848 for conducting an open-air ministry. Calling himself "A Country Parson," he replied to his Archdeacon in the form of an open letter. Withdrawal from the city would leave its streets to the "Chartist and infidel lecturer," he said. Turning inward, concentrating on building churches and freeing church pews, was no way to reach the "vast heathen residuum." He admitted that "Methodist extravagances and fury of enthusiasm" in an earlier day had proven "an explosive combustible" and had to be "put out of reach." But times had changed. To overcome the Chartists' near monopoly over the streets, members of the church must go there, not as an "irregular auxiliary force," but as a regular, licensed arm of the Bishop of London. Let ardent but sound clergy and laymen venture out, he urged, "on the notorious broadways of sin," to the very places where Chartist or "common street preachers" now harangue the volatile multitude. Recognize, he told the Archdeacon, that urban growth has made the parochial system ineffective; find a substitute, another way to reach the urban poor which will sustain or at least not destroy "clerical conformity and the force of Church Ordinances."[62]

This was the kind of plea to which MacGregor was responding. His "system" seemed to Tait and many other Church dignitaries in the 1850s and 1860s to be at least one of the ways. His method would control a tendency to religious extravagance; it would insure that preachers were sober and of sound doctrine and not, as the Revd Fredrick Briggs put it, "vain spouters – such as one encounters frequently on the London streets."[63] The control would come from a responsible committee: only by this means, MacGregor insisted, could the association between street preaching, political radicalism, and the "infusion of error" be broken.[64]

By the time that Captain Eliza Haynes was making her brave sorties on Edgware Road, organized, disciplined street evangelism had long since ceased to be an innovation. Had one visited, say, Islington Green on a Sunday afternoon in 1879, one would have discovered a traffic jam of proselytizers, most of them organized and trained in the special techniques of street preaching. The Open Air Mission would be there but so would the Christadelphians. Members of this sect would emerge from their meeting house nearby to join the knots of listeners and ask, complained a Mission preacher, "chapter and verse for everything you advance." Not far from his stand, on the corner by the statue of Sir John Myddleton, was the territory of "unbelievers," Jews and Gentiles fighting their battles of "negation and misinterpretation." If that were not competition enough, members of the Revd C.B. Sawdays's congregation would circulate among the listeners, attracting attention away by urging one and all to take part in the revival meeting under way in the Agricultural Hall around the corner. As the Mission agent observed, this scene was "not always edifying," especially since it was the police who often had to bring the curtain down.[65]

Similar scenes of zeal and competition could have been observed in many working-class districts that Sunday afternoon. Another veteran of the Open Air Mission, who served the station near the market in Somers Town, observed that in front of the Midland Railway arches, "error is as self-confident, and truth as bold as ever." A half-dozen groups could be found there, "preaching, expounding and exclaiming on almost any subject that can be named." One could, by moving a few steps away from the Mission station, hear in action Romanists, the Christian Evidence Society, Secularists, Humanitarians, Temperance

Advocates, Anti-vivisectionists (usually holding aloft gruesome diagrams), and floating over all, "the sweet voice of song" from a choir standing outside the Revd Z.B. Waffendale's Presbyterian Church.[66] The day when volunteers from among the educated middle-class could hope to dominate the open forum of the London streets was clearly over. Concern about the possibility of revolution had passed. There were alarms from time to time about outbreaks of hooliganism and garotting, and the Trafalgar Square riots of the mid-1880s frightened inhabitants of the West End, but, generally speaking, the streets became progressively safer after 1860.[67] The police, who once had welcomed organized street preachers as allies in a struggle to maintain order, began increasingly to regard them as, according to one of Sir Richard Mayne's legal advisors, "a great public nuisance."[68]

These shifts in the temper of reform argue against using a simple, unilinear model. At times and in some circumstances those interested in or charged with removing obstructions and facilitating movement were willing to tolerate or even to encourage the intrusion of missionaries, preachers, and uniformed workers onto footpaths and carriageways and were willing to accept the street furniture: the drinking fountains, urinals, pillars, posts, cabstand shelters, and watering troughs that were introduced into the streets in such profusion in the age of cheap cast iron.[69] At other times and in other circumstances this tolerance and willingness diminished. The point is that until the motor vehicle started to make street furniture hazardous and polishers and preachers anachronistic, all the types of street reform ran concurrently, now in tension, now in consonance.

9

BREATHING

An Irish essayist and poet, John Fisher Murray, in an article for an 1839 issue of *Blackwood's Edinburgh Magazine,* asked why it was that Paris had its leafy boulevards, Madrid its Prado, Rome its Corso, Vienna its Glacis, while the greatest city in the world had nothing remotely equivalent. He was not greatly impressed by the boast that London had more green areas, more public parks, and more planted squares than any of its rivals, for in the *"terra incognita"* of her East End, people lived "precariously from day to day, in low, unventilated, and densely populated neighbourhoods" without access to such open spaces.[1] His question was still germane at the end of the Edwardian period; to be sure, an impressive number of people's parks had been added (a large one in the East End), a great many disused burial grounds had been converted into neighborhood gardens, some West End squares had been opened to the public, and the commons around the margins of the city had been preserved. Yet the fact remained that no major street had been constructed or reconstructed to serve specifically as an urban amenity. Those who cared sufficiently about this lack of generosity toward the streets to remark about it publicly tended to blame the "time-is-money" preoccupation of the Londoner, the climate, vested interests, or, more likely, the absence of a civic authority with the will and the funds to impose some large plan. But there was another explanation. It was that many of those people who had a highly developed civic consciousness became preoccupied in finding alternatives to streets and, to serve their reform purposes, employed rhetoric which presumed the street to be a source, or *the* source, of urban ills.

The metaphor which compared parks and commons to "lungs" seemed to have made its appearance in the 1820s, and Murray used it in the title of his article. He was concerned that his readers, relieved as they were by the passing of a cholera epidemic, might become complacent and forget that "an undercurrent of pestilence" constantly "lurks" in great cities and that everyone, and not just the poor, suffered from the effects of "bad drainage, bad air, bad water, and bad smells."[2] In this sense, if in no other, London was, he thought, a single entity. The collective body, like the individual one, needed to draw fresh air into the lungs in order to purify the blood stream. The difficulty was that "the pulmonary organs" served only one part of the collective; in the part occupied by the poor majority, fresh air could not enter and bad air could not escape. He wanted his readers to consider that new waves of epidemic were constantly gathering and preparing to wash over the whole community, west as well as east. Therefore he advised Parliament, in whose hands the welfare of the city's collective body rested, to reflect before permitting the next joint-stock, "sack-em-up" company of speculative builders to ravage green places like Primrose Hill. No other authority could be counted on to protect what "instruments of public respiration" still remained, for aldermen, Lords of Manors, parish vestrymen "would enclose the sun of heaven itself, if they could let out its rays at so much a year." Moreover, responsible authorities should not content themselves with protecting the populace from depredations, they should act positively and build broad avenues from west to east, allowing fresh air, "the very first element of civilization," to reach places where it was most needed.[3]

Apparent here is the notion of the city as a breathing organism which inhales the poison it exhales. In a vague way, Murray, like many others during the middle part of the century, connected cholera with defective respiration and thus with the greatest killer of them all, tuberculosis – then more commonly called "consumption." Around that "insidious, implacable" invader grew, as Susan Sontag has demonstrated, a cluster of associations with debilitating characteristics, supposed by critics of urban life to be endemic to that particular environment – among them, excessive passion interspersed with lassitude and over-excitement, leading first to flushes and then to pallor.[4] Although, as Sontag points out, the tubercular bacillus (identified in 1882) can attack many parts of the body, the disease was, in the popular mind, specific to the lungs. The lungs, in turn, are constructed in such a way that connections between disease and clogged, polluted urban passageways came naturally and compellingly. Oxygen, needed to remove impurities from the blood, enters along two broad avenues, one to each lung. These passageways then subdivide into smaller and finer tubes, ending in clusters or *culs-de-sac* where contact between air and capillaries takes place and where the exchange of properties, purity for waste, happens. The very act of breathing in pure air is called "inspiration." Thus the metaphor could be adapted to diagnose not only the physical but the spiritual ills thought to be generated by congestion and to indicate what treatment might be most effective: clearing the passageways, broadening the avenues of inspiration and respiration, opening up sources of oxygen supply, and finding means to bring oxygen into the small enclosures where an exchange, purity for impurity, takes place.[5]

This metaphor was appealing to promoters of parks for the people, flower-growing, neighborhood gardens, window boxes, tree-planting, and open space preservation: it gave reformers a common language. Accordingly, their assumptions about the restorative qualities of nature, their diagnostic techniques, and their regimen of treatment were similar, particularly since enthusiasts for one of these causes tended to lend support to all the others. From the mid-1860s onward, many societies formed to preserve not only greenery and open spaces but also aesthetically valuable buildings, historic sites, and animal species. On their subscription lists, the same names tended to appear: Lord Mount-Temple, Lord and Lady Brabazon, Octavia Hill and her sisters, Henry Fawcett, James Bryce, John Stuart Mill, Charles Dilke, various members of the Buxton family, Robert Hunter, Samuel and Henrietta Barnett, Hardwick Rownsley, George John Shaw-Lefevre, and a handful of others, many of them liberals of "advanced" views, most of them influenced by Ruskin. Because there was so much linkage, there is a tendency to ignore divergences in aim and in method of analysis and to place these reformers, collectively, in the context of a romantic, arcadian reaction against the "industrial spirit," the fragmenting tendencies of urban living, and the seemingly inexorable invasion of bricks and mortar into the harmony of the surrounding countryside – where the "real" England lay open and vulnerable.[6]

It is true that in the right mood, probably all of these reformers would have subscribed to Emerson's dictum that "we need nature, and cities give the senses not room enough." Most of these conservationists and greenery promoters would, for example, have nodded agreement had they been present when Sir John Thwaites officially opened Finsbury Park in 1869 saying, in his speech, that 'People's Parks like this one . . . enable the working man to sustain that increased labour which is one of the great sources of national wealth.'"[7] Reformers in general would also have supported the contention of *The Builder* that filthy habits and "gross indecency and vice" originate in excessive density rather than in some inherent moral defect.[8] Most of these reformers had homes in the country or paid frequent visits there, and all believed that trees, grass, and flowers had therapeutic powers. They were convinced that workers would be better producers and more loyal citizens if they spent their leisure strolling in the park rather than idling on street corners. These values they held in common. They differed, however, in their attitudes toward the city environment. Some believed it to be intrinsically toxic and looked for antidotes; others looked to the modern (reformed) municipality as the best hope for the future progress of civilization and wanted parks and other open spaces to be part of the urban fabric, supplements to already existing attractions.

This chapter will examine this difference as it appears in the projects or recommendations of four reformers: George Godwin, who labored to convince the readers of his journal that crowded streets, dwellings, and workplaces, but not the city itself, were the causes of urban afflictions; Octavia Hill, who demonstrated, in her campaign to secure playgrounds for slum children, a moral and aesthetic revulsion against city life; Sir James Pennethorne, architect of an East End park who learned from those working people, whose tastes he sought to refine, that a park for the people needed to be a park by the people; and, finally, George John Shaw-Lefevre, who spent a remarkably long and active life trying to instill in Londoners a sense of public ownership and the civic pride that goes with it.

The premise on which the first of these reformers, George Godwin, built his reputation as a socially minded journalist appeared in succinct form in an address he gave in 1864 to a social science congress: "the breath of man is fatal to his fellows."[9] That conviction came from his experience as a Londoner. Born in Brompton in 1815, the son of a London architect, he spent much of his adulthood in direct contact with the city's exhalations, residing and working an easy walking distance from Holborn, Bloomsbury, Islington, and the City. He died in Kensington in 1888, when that region, a self-contained village in his youth, had become completely integrated into the metropolitan area. Although a practicing architect, he was best known for his contributions to the theory of art and architecture. *The Builder* became, under his editorship (1844–83), one of the most influential critical voices in these fields and a powerful advocate of social amelioration by means of architecture.[10]

Much of what he reported about the conditions of worker dwellings and streets came from first-hand experience. Few Victorians, Mayhew and Dickens included, knew London better or had a deeper sense of its horrors and glories. There was authority behind Godwin's persistent call for people to look beyond the immediate evils of epidemic, contaminated water, inadequate sewage disposal, excessive drinking, and increasing incidents of crime to what he believed to be the prime mover: overcrowding in homes, alleys, courts, streets, and workplaces. His argument was that without those reforms which were primarily the province of the architect, so long as poor people were crowded together and forced to breathe in what they and other poor people exhaled, no amount of sanitary engineering, medical intervention, policing, or philanthropic endeavor could produce lasting benefit. This piece, written for *The Builder*, boils with almost Carlylean indignation:

Our cooping up in dark and noisome tanks of tenements those of flesh and blood like ourselves – our undrained, unkennelled, black and hideous wynds, unfitted as receptacles for dogs, or vile beasts – these we cram thousands and hundreds of thousands of our fellow beings into, out of sight and out of way, and then boast of our western squares, and the one or two main arterial streets – while dense and solid blocks, and ramifications of thinly-drawn inferior veins of coagulated evil breedings lie around and flow inwards at every turn.[11]

A leading article, written several years later, cited Parliamentary committee reports to back up these generalizations: of 104 letter-press printers who had less than 500 cubic feet of air to breathe, 13 spit blood, 13 had habitual catarrh, and 18 had other related diseases. In Liverpool, where density in poor areas was four times higher than in equivalent London regions, death rates were significantly higher.[12] Why that should be so was the subject of an article, appearing in 1865: tubercles, little granular bodies deposited from the blood, could be found, even before they had a chance to reach the lungs, in the mucous membranes of the air tubes.[13] The physical damage this condition supposedly caused was only part of the price of overcrowding: moral damage was equally great. Where no privacy is possible, there can be no self-respect, and, without self-respect, individuals first feel discouraged, then reckless – gradual degeneration being the usual pattern from there.[14] An 1872 edition printed a poem called "Crowded Out" which contained these lines: "Men cannot thrive as rats do, in a sewer or a sink, / And from holes that are not homes arises the evil born of drink."[15] "Overcrowding," Godwin had explained a decade earlier, could be defined simply in terms of air quality. Given an adequate supply of pure air, propinquity was not physically or morally harmful. Where supplies of pure air were inadequate, all of the symptoms of overcrowding could be expected: debility, fever, premature death, impoverished widows and orphans, and widespread pauperism. The tragedy of the Black Hole of Calcutta had been, Godwin wrote, a dramatic demonstration of the effects of overcrowding but one that was easy to forget, since our senses quickly adjust to the "atmospheric ocean that surrounds us." Persons inside this atmosphere experience loss of muscular power, impaired appetite, insomnia, and generalized depression but may never make a connection between those symptoms and the quality of air they breathe.[16]

While Godwin repeated these warnings during the four decades of his editorship, he waited until the 1860s before turning his attention to the need not only for better ventilation but for multi-storied buildings to relieve crowding in central city areas, and for an extensive program of street-widening, to secure more open spaces, more lung capacity. He had already made the point that the streets offered slum dwellers more privacy than they could find indoors. This was, he believed, part of the chain linking overcrowding with moral decay; like most of his fellow urban reformers, he assumed that leisure spent in the unsettling, dirty, distracting streets could not be recreative and certainly could not be innocent. Responding to the increasing demand in the 1860s for recreational facilities, resulting from a shortening of work hours for many laborers and an increase in real incomes among the lower middle-class and the working-class elite, Godwin turned his attention to means for supplying London's poor with "innocent recreation": park construction, preservation of common lands, and provisions for gardening and flower displays.[17]

The astonishing success the Commons Preservation Society (formed in 1865) had in its court battles to save Hampstead Heath, Wimbledon Common, Epping Forest, Blackheath, and so many smaller open spaces owed much to support given by newspapers and journals, *The Builder* being a particularly valuable ally. When, for example, Hampstead Heath was threatened, Godwin wrote that "no greater calamity, of a physical character, can befall London than the covering of Hampstead Heath with buildings." Every pedestrian, he continued, would feel the evil effects if developers were allowed to convert this woodland "into a smoke-producing, deoxygenating crater, wafting a fresh canopy of foul vapour over the oppressed city."[18]

Warnings of this kind continued during the heat of the struggle to save the Heath, but, as a general rule, *The Builder* tended to qualify its support of preservationism and park construction, pointing out that large projects seldom reached those most in need. So long as, for example, 45 percent of families in Finsbury continued to live in one or two rooms, the provision of a few open spaces, to act as antidotes to the evils this overcrowding bred, would have no lasting effect; it followed that preservers, planters, and architects must work in tandem. So far, that co-ordination had not been attempted. A retrospective article appeared in 1874, noting the accomplishments of the previous thirty years: a "great chain of parks" had been forged to connect Nash's Regent's Park in the north to Pennethorne's Victoria Park in the east and his Battersea Park in the south to Kensington Gardens, Green Park, and St James's in the west. Outside that ring, a band of commons had been secured for city dwellers, making it possible for Londoners to breathe easier in every sense than they might have done even a decade earlier. But then the writer asked, were the daily lives of poor Londoners, as a consequence, much improved? He thought not. In the brick "wilderness" around the Seven Dials, the Ratcliffe Highway, or in such bucolic-sounding places as Hatton Garden or

BREATHING

Hughes' Fields, the only open spaces providing escape from the squalid rooms of the slums were airless courts and swarming streets. Children played midst the grime and noise of Clare Market within sight of the closed gates of little-used Lincoln's Inn Fields. Russell, Gordon, Bedford, Euston, Soho, and Red Lion Squares stood next to some of the worst rookeries, but were closed to the public and occupied mostly by gardeners. It was, he said, four miles in a straight line from Regent's Park to Victoria Park, but the path from one to the other led through a brick labyrinth. It was another four miles from Battersea Park to the market gardens of Peckham and then eight miles from Clapham Common to Finsbury Park: what lay between those islands of greenery was a modern Babylon, only without the hanging gardens.[19] The refrain sounded like the famous music-hall song:

> O it really is a very pretty garden,
> And Chingford to the eastward could be seen.
> With a ladder and some glasses,
> You could see to Hackney Marshes,
> If it wasn't for the 'ouses in between.

For Godwin, it was in these in-betweens where the real work of renewal should be concentrated.

One step, he suggested, might be to connect the existing large open spaces by means of a wide, circular boulevard. He would line it with trees and lay it out with flower beds and playgrounds, thus bringing beauty, fresh air, and "innocence" to the most stagnant recesses of the breathing city. He thought it might also be possible to bring the values of wild nature close to the centre by constructing a preserve in Fulham. There, nature might be allowed "a little latitude of expression" to "do her own work in her own lovely way." "Dame Nature" could be the "sole gardener"; trees could be left to look like trees and not, as on the Embankment, be turned into "upright sticks" with a "mophead of leaves at the top."[20]

Given Godwin's consistent efforts to confront his readers with the actual conditions of places where poor people slept, walked, and worked, his proposal does not seem escapist or anti-urban. No Englishman of the century had a keener appreciation for the spacial values of the built environment. He criticized new streets and their frontages with the eye of a connoisseur, constantly drawing attention to London's man-made treasures and felicities. His credo was "where art is dominant, nature is but subservient and ornamental, and *vice-versa*."[21] He insisted that places with strong architectural values like Trafalgar Square or the surroundings of the Houses of Parliament not be diminished in effect by what he called in 1874 "the present mania for 'grass plots' and 'bedding-out.'"[22] London should not be turned into a garden; not all of its streets and open spaces needed to become leafy bowers and glades. Instead, the aim should be to build and to preserve contrast and variety, to retain the excitement of artifice, and to heighten its effect with trees, lawns, and flowers. Above all he wished planners, conservationists, and builders of parks, tenements, workshops, and streets to measure their achievements by whether or not their projects increased the opportunity for the poor as well as the rich to breathe freely and to live interesting, productive, and healthy lives.

Had Octavia Hill, our second reformer, been a steady reader of *The Builder*, as no doubt she was, she would have agreed with most of what its editorialists recommended even though she would not have joined in their celebration of urban values. Her commitment to the task of bringing natural beauty, cleanliness, fresh air, and recreational spaces to slum doorsteps and interiors had a different premise. Like Godwin, she wanted neighborhood playgrounds and small green spaces, wished to grace the homes of the poor with flowers, and promoted efforts to make commons and parks accessible to all. Her object, however, was not simply to enhance the beauties and virtues of city life but to provide antidotes to "urbomorbis," to make the poison London exuded less toxic. For her, the great city was a wen and not a heart.

This difference in perspective derives, at least in part, from the fact that, unlike Godwin, Hill was not a Londoner. She was not attracted to the city but came to work and to care for its casualties. Born in 1838 into an atmosphere of high-mindedness (her mother headed the Christian Socialist Ladies Co-operative Guild and her maternal grandfather was Southwood Smith, the sanitary reformer), she spent much of her childhood in rural settings just outside of London's northern margin. In later years, she returned frequently in her memory to the sense of freedom she had once experienced near what she referred to as "the natural sources of simple pleasures": the meadow flowers near Finchley, the shady lanes of Epping, sunny afternoons at her grandfather's house in Highgate, with its view of Kenwood House and Hampstead Heath. It had been her childhood fantasy, she recalled, "to find a field so large that I could run in it forever." Her mother once said of her: "She can scarcely walk, she goes leaping as if she were a little kangaroo."[23] Although she began her London career while still an adolescent, she always retained the image of railways reaching out toward the country and transforming the fields and woods where she had once enjoyed those romps; her sense of being inexorably closed in was acute because intensely personal.[24]

One hears this nostalgia in nearly everything she wrote. Facing defeat in one of her first attempts to save the country from the city (in this instance, a plot of land in Swiss Cottage), she remembered having walked hand in hand with poor families from Marylebone over ground which led "like a green hilly peninsula or headland stretching out now into the sea of houses." As you ascend that hill, she wrote, you "climb out of London"; the headland "lifts you" until you can see "London hushed below you – even London hushed for you for a few minutes, so far it lies beneath."[25]

Wordsworthean sentiments of this kind led her to become an early recruit to the Commons Preservation Society and to become one of its most forceful workers. She was in the front lines of the battle to secure Hampstead Heath for the public and, that victory won, joined the Society's founder, Shaw-Lefevre, in a drive to convince municipal authorities and private benefactors to add more acres. She also poured her considerable energies into Henry Fawcett's campaign to extend the commons preservation movement to the entire country and, toward the end of her career, shifted more and more of her activities to the world outside the capital. With several others, she formed the National Trust, the agent for preserving country lands and estates.

For three decades, however, Hill was deeply involved with London and with the effort to provide better housing for London's poor. This career took a practical turn in 1864, when John Ruskin gave her money from an inheritance so that she might buy three slum houses in Marylebone and manage them according to the principles of "5 percent philanthropy," an experiment that expanded greatly in the years that followed and made her into a national figure. She always denied that anything like a "Hill Plan" had ever been invented, "at least one," she remarked, "that was any more complex than what a sensible young housekeeper" would employ when putting a home in order and starting a family. There was no method, she said, only gentleness, firmness, sympathy, and discipline, and there was only one, simple object: to assume the duty of a responsible parent and to guide her charges toward self-reliant autonomy.[26]

By no means insensitive to the crippling effects of physical poverty, she nevertheless traced the cause of the degeneration she saw around her, not directly to the cramped, airless, ugly slum courts, but to the effects of living so far from the visible evidence of God's providence. On one occasion she asked a group of middle-class co-workers to reflect on how different were their memories of childhood from those of poor Londoners. Your imaginations are stocked, she said, with images of country pursuits: "early wild flowers formed your delight, harmonies of music, bright dress or picture, open spaces where you could burst out and move freely," whereas most city-bred people could only draw upon images of denatured streets.[27] One listener, Henrietta Barnett, was impressed by this analysis of the process of degradation and, in an appeal to the Child's Country Holiday Fund, expanded on this theme. "There are," she said, "so few things so pathetic as the pleasure memories of the poor. You whose lives are over-crammed with interests cannot realize the 'thought barrenness' of an alley-bred child."[28] According to Hill and her followers, the city was the confined and artificial nursery of its own evils.

The remedy was the balm of green nature and "the healing gift of space." The first function of the Kyrle Society, which Octavia Hill, with her sister Miranda, founded, was to bring flowers to hospitals, workhouses, and homes, the object being to awaken poor people to the sights, sounds, and smells of nature. It was her conviction that it did no good to place slum dwellers, people accustomed to "monotonous lives punctuated with sprees," in antiseptic, model tenements and expect them to act like civilized human beings. A propensity to drunkenness, vulgar tastes, absence of any strong communal sense, and a "deeply-rooted habit of dirt," being the consequence of their alienation from nature, it followed, Hill maintained, that the first step in reclaiming the casualties of urban life was, by sympathetic guidance, to introduce them to the calming influences of nature, that "passionless reformer."[29]

Finding a substitute for the street was, therefore, a high priority in Hill's reform agenda. Because a child, brought up in the license of the street, learned as part of its "nature" to demand excitement and immediate gratification, what was needed was a controlled environment where that boy or girl might be taught to play. By "play" Hill meant an activity or a game which had rules and well-defined goals and developed disciplines necessary for group participation. In the walled-in playground she paid her Marylebone tenants to construct on the site of a refuse dump (a lesson in self-help), children could be taught these skills, free of contamination. There they would experience play for the first time, be led to give up the violent amusements they had learned on the streets, and experience the freedom that arises from self-control.[30]

What the objects of Octavia Hill's paternalistic benevolence thought about the recreational opportunities opened to them, how working-class mothers felt about sending small children, usually supervised by older siblings, out to play in the streets, what men and women wanted to do when they had time for an afternoon in Finsbury Park or a day on Hampstead Heath, were not questions Hill, confident as she was about what city dwellers should want and feel, thought needed asking. Indeed, only rarely in the volumes of testimony compiled by Victorian investigators of recreational facilities and requirements does one hear the views of the majority of users expressed. However, we do have one valuable piece of evidence: Victoria Park. As a writer of religious tracts noted in the 1890s, London's first "People's Park" became, even before its official opening in 1846, "a laboratory" for studying, on a grand scale, East London's tastes in leisure activities.[31]

Such, of course, was not the purpose of the park's sponsors. They intended it to be a lung, a restorative, a course of instruction in respectability, self-control, emulation, rationality, and family values, a counter-attraction to the allurements of streets and gin palaces, and a means of appeasing the discontent that had been finding expression in Chartism. But from the start the people of Hackney, Bethnal Green, Bow, and Stepney refused to accept the role of passive recipient and made demands. One reason they were able to get what they wanted with so little resistance was that the architect, Sir James Pennethorne, was a Regency figure and had what Sir John Summerson has called a Regency plan of "metropolitan improvements."[32] That means that his object was not to give the powerful another instrument of social control but to give the city an ornament, one that would transform and renew a blighted area.

Calling Pennethorne a Regency figure would have made his contemporaries smile, since circumstantial evidence suggested that James and his two brothers and two sisters may have been issue of a protracted liaison between their mother, Mary Anne Bradley, and the Prince Regent himself.[33] Mary Anne and her husband, John Nash, claimed that the children belonged to a relative, but this did not still the rumors. Whatever the circumstances, Nash treated James, if not as a son, at least as an heir to his professional enterprises. He involved him in the construction of Regent's Park and St James's Park and gave him responsibility for renovating Buckingham Palace and for building Park Village east of Albany Street (the "ancestor of all picturesque suburbia").[34] On retiring, Nash saw to it that his protégé inherited his position as architect to the Chief Commissioner of Woods and Forests, the body responsible for the development and management of Royal lands and properties. Thus, when Parliament took advantage of a windfall to authorize the East End park, the experienced Pennethorne took charge.

What he envisioned was no mere lung but a scheme for urban renewal on the same scale as the Regent Street and Park project. The new Victoria Park would be made to connect with Bethnal Green and Stepney by means of a broad, tree-lined boulevard, leading through a magnificent square of houses and bringing park-like values to blighted areas between the park and the river. The idea was to build handsome rows of terraced houses on the margins to attract the wealthy, thus improving property values and bringing in revenue to defray expenses and improve facilities. A winding drive through arrangements of hillocks and natural-seeming copses was to give the terraces an appropriate setting. As for the layout of the park itself, it would replicate the picturesque design favored by Nash.[35]

It should not be supposed that Pennethorne had no concern for the poor people in whose midst this green open space and boulevard would be placed. He hoped that renewal, achieved by the importation of a contingent from the wealthy middle class, would raise incomes and spirits generally, as well as provide models of decorum and respectability. But anxiety about the tastes and morals of the lower orders is seldom apparent in the reports and correspondence to be found in the Victoria Park Papers. Pennethorne seems to have assumed that at least where appreciation of the values of green open spaces was concerned, differences in cultural values among the classes were not irreconcilable; therefore, he was not offended when approached about making some changes by the residents of Hackney and Bethnal Green. When, for example, he was petitioned during the construction stage for provision of bathing facilities, he did resist at first, on the grounds that "respectable personages" would be constantly offended by the sight of naked men and boys, and suggested an ornamental water instead. Nevertheless, when pressed, he conceded to the wishes of the petitioners and did so with generosity. Men from nearby dye and tanning works received a bathing lake where, on their way home from work, they could wash themselves. Boys flocked to the bathing lake in huge numbers (girls had to be content with a large sand box). Lt Colonel J.J. Sexby, park supervisor for the Municipal Board of Works during the latter part of the century, recalled seeing some 25,000 naked males wading and swimming one summer morning in the 1890s, before 8:00 a.m.[36]

Long before that scene took place, it was obvious that the park would be, as Sexby described it, "a splendid playground for the East End," and not merely a decorous walk where rich residents might mingle without embarrassment with visitors from Mile End Road. For one thing, the expected immigrants from Belgravia never arrived. Therefore, Pennethorne saw no good reason to deny park users the opportunity to take part in the designing process. By the 1860s, the pattern had been established: working people would organize themselves and petition for cricket grounds, tennis courts, gymnasia, facilities for a model boat club or rowing club, an ornithological or horticultural society, or for summer band concerts, and, shortly after receiving the petitions, the authorities would comply (although they refused requests to accommodate football players until the 1880s). As the park's historian, Charles Poulsen, noted, the people of the East End not only took the government's gift to their hearts, they took it over.[37]

Thus Victoria Park was, from its formal opening in 1845, both a romantically curving and shaded public walk, offering relief to panting lungs and innocent pleasures to families dressed in their Sunday best and also a playground and entertainment centre (see Plate 16). The combination proved to be an enormous success from the start. On the first Good Friday after the gates opened, the appositely named Mr Mobbs and his force of uniformed park-keepers had a busy day screening out the drunk and disorderly from among the 25,000 visitors who poured in, but found the task well within their capacities.[38] Attendance grew steadily for the rest of the century. A census taken on a day in 1892 counted 303,515, making Victoria Park by far the most heavily patronized in the metropolitan area, with Pennethorne's Battersea Park, at 109,783, a distant second.[39]

A Chartist demonstration in 1848, described *con brio* by Sexby, showed how thoroughly and quickly Pennethorne's conception had turned into a different kind of people's park from what had been intended. Even after social tensions relaxed, there were signs that the space might indeed become what a group of petitioning householders in 1848 referred to as "an area for disseminating Democratical Infidel Principles."[40] Although speakers had been in the habit of holding forth on Sunday afternoons from the 1860s on, it was in the late Victorian and Edwardian periods that Victoria Park became London's main outdoor forum, or as some contemporaries put it, "forum and agin 'em."[41] Hyndman, Mann, Tillett, Morris, Shaw, and Burns spread the socialist gospel there under trees called the Six Sisters, secularists challenged evangelicals, and preachers from Anglican missions took on Roman Catholic theorists in fervent but apparently disciplined debate. Participants of all persuasions testified to the high level of the exchanges between audiences and speakers as well as between speakers themselves. Noting that performers needed to have done their homework, the Revd F. Winnington Ingram, a muscular Christian who could have stepped into a play by Shaw unrehearsed, remarked of the audiences: "they remind me of the ancient Athenians; they have a passion for outdoor discussion."[42] The analogy was apt; the place that had been intended by its sponsors to be a Hyde Park for the East End had become something more: a reconstruction in unusual circumstances of a public space in the traditional sense.

In turning Pennethorne's picturesque conception into a place for "rational recreation," but of a character considerably at odds with what most middle-class people meant by the term, the people who lived close by demonstrated their capacity to assert their own cultural values. Nevertheless, it would be stretching the point to claim that none of the objects of the reform movement were accomplished. Pennethorne was right to assume that workers would respond to a naturalistic layout of trees and grass and to ornamental flower displays. Everyone who knew the park before the Great War remarked on how popular was the carpet bedding, often associated with Victorian middle-class taste, but sometimes spoken of as a Cockney garden.[43] Those who enjoyed the floral spectacles of the virtuoso gardener, John Gibson, and walked with their families along the sylvan lanes were not the contemplatives and those who used the sporting grounds or practiced their wit in exchanges with the stump speakers were not the activists. The mistake so many reformers made was to make these kinds of classifications. Working-class park users did at times want to escape from the noise, confusion, and pollution of the street yet, at other times, sought in the park the same sociability, boisterousness, and stimulation that street life offered. Even that qualification about what working people wanted needs further qualification. Gender and age determined, at all social levels, what park users sought. This was the finding of a survey carried out by the Greater London Council in 1968. As might be expected, it showed that women with small children tended to travel only short distances and to those places equipped with playgrounds. Children old enough to be on their own preferred informal areas where they could play ball games, ride cycles, and watch birds and animals. Adolescent youths of both sexes looked for more sedentary activities, such as walking, sitting on the grass, meeting friends, although boys were willing to travel farther and liked larger spaces than did girls. Among adults, the attraction of quiet, the enjoyment of trees and flowers, increased with advancing years. For this group and, significantly, for everyone over the age of 15, the things most appreciated, and by a large margin, were scenery and general layout. As for frequency of use, that depended to a considerable extent not just on sex and age but on education and place in the employment hierarchies: people in the professions and skilled workers were more likely to visit a neighborhood open space on weekdays and a large park on weekends than the less skilled, less well-educated, or the retired or unemployed.[44]

Too many changes have taken place in the history of leisure and popular culture to assume that what is true about the behavior of people in the reign of Elizabeth II must be true about the subjects of Queen Victoria or Edward VII. Nevertheless, it is useful to keep this survey in mind when making statements about what leisure values "the people" or "the working class" once looked for in park, common, playground, or, for that matter, street, as the decades of the nineteenth and early twentieth centuries succeeded each other. Pennethorne's park was popular because it turned out to be more eclectic than he had wished or anticipated, a conclusion with which few Victorian campaigners for the preservation or construction of public open spaces would have been comfortable.

One of the most active of these campaigners was George John Shaw-

Lefevre (see Plate 17). Sweetness and light were part of his inheritance. His maternal grandfather, Ichabod Wright, translated Dante into English, and his father, Sir John George, was a linguist of extraordinary talent as well as an eminent civil servant. High and low politics, world events, discussions about legal reform, tales of travel, art, literature, a tradition of Whiggish tolerance, high-mindedness, and general culture surrounded his life for ninety-seven years, from his birth in London in 1832 to his death in 1929. Eton, Trinity College, Cambridge, the Inner Temple, a few years on the circuit, election to Parliament at age 31 as MP for Reading (his paternal grandfather's old seat), marriage to an earl's daughter, quick promotion to a series of undersecretaryships under Russell and Gladstone and a place in the 1868 cabinet, experience as First Commissioner of Works followed by promotion to the Local Government Board in Rosebery's cabinet, retirement from Parliament after the Liberal débâcle of 1895, only to be followed by an important new career at the London County Council, and then, in 1909, a peerage with the title Baron Eversley – the chart of his public life seemed to be one long, upward curve, an unfolding of some benevolently inclined family destiny. Yet, in his correspondence with Gladstone, there is a note of disappointment, of feeling left out, his unceasing labors in so many ministerial assignments and on so many commissions and committees not adequately acknowledged. Perhaps it was because, as a fellow Cobden Club member thought, he lacked personal magnetism and had about him "a certain self-absorption" that he never managed to rise much higher than the third rank among Liberal statesmen. Nevertheless, when measured by accomplishments, both as a parliamentarian and as the leader of a long, painstaking struggle to secure for public use the common lands within reach of Londoners, his claim on historical memory seems to be more substantial than many of his more famous associates. Anyone who has hiked through the coolness of Epping Forest in flaming August or smelled the earthy fragrance of Hampstead Heath on a blustery afternoon in March owes Shaw-Lefevre a moment of grateful thought.[45]

It was not just a coincidence that the year the struggle for commons preservation began in earnest, 1865, was the starting point for what the Liberal theorist A.V. Dicey named the era of "collectivism." The preservation movement clearly articulated the changes liberalism was undergoing, an evolutionary process which moved from a concentration on the need to remove obstacles in the way of the freedom of individuals to make contracts to an emphasis on communal welfare, the existence of social property in capital, and the need to improve the environmental conditions in which individual choice must be exercised. The trajectory of Shaw-Lefevre's half-century-long public career precisely traces that development. From his first struggle in the 1860s to preserve Wimbledon Common until his advocacy of a somewhat guarded version of "municipal" or "practical" socialism as a Progressive member of the London County Council forty years later, his concern to defend the public interest gradually shifted into a concern to implant a sense of public ownership in the consciousness of a democratic citizenry. He underwent this gradual change while remaining loyal to the Gladstonian agenda: home rule, tenant rights, and land reform for Ireland, retrenchment in military spending, arbitration as the way to settle international disputes, self-determination for the Balkan nations, parliamentary reform, and free trade. After the last, sad cabinet meeting before the Grand Old Man retired, Shaw-Lefevre sent Gladstone a note saying that since he had agreed with his policies perhaps more consistently than any other cabinet member, he would be feeling the loss of the party's leader the most keenly.[46] By that point, however, Shaw-Lefevre had advanced much further in the liberal progression than most of the Gladstonian rank and file. He had joined with John Stuart Mill and Robert Lowe in an early attempt to give married women control over their own property, introduced legislation to protect the rights of workers to combine, and had sponsored the Tramways Act of 1870, opening the way for public ownership of public transit, a move that greatly expanded municipal enterprise.

Although indefatigable to the point where he sometimes exasperated friends as well as foes in his pursuit of causes, a clue to the reason why his governmental appointments were always unglamorous, he was attractively undogmatic, claiming to be a thorough English pragmatist. This claim he substantiated in his highly successful strategy as head of the Commons Preservation Society (CPS). He recognized that the best chance to check enclosure in the Metropolitan region would be to proceed through the courts rather than try to push legislation through Parliament, where the interest of landed property would be tenaciously defended. The courts did prove to be far more flexible than Parliament. A historian at heart, he wrote the chronicle of the many remarkable legal victories he and the society's principal lawyer, Robert Hunter, won. The brilliantly executed campaign finally culminated in an 1876 law which insured that no more common land would be lost to the public.[47]

In the course of this struggle, CPS supporters developed, as a rationale for giving commons preservation a high priority in the reform agenda, the argument that city dwellers, living and working in artificial environments, needed unstructured open spaces, preserves of "native wildness." Robert Hunter described the commons as "untutored." Sidney Smith claimed that it was *élégance négligée* which made them especially attractive. There was, supposedly, a special balm in "unconscious loveliness" to soothe those who were forced to spend so much of their time in "reeking, noisome, fetid" dwellings, alleys, and streets.[48]

Rhetoric of this kind reminds us how freighted with value judgments were the phrases reformers, in particular, used to describe how people moved through different kinds of spaces. On the street, one tended to "walk briskly" if on the way to work or to "saunter listlessly," "loaf," or "idle" if one were young, male, of the lower orders, and at leisure. In the park, one "strolled" or "promenaded," guided by paths and conscious of the requirements of public decorum. On the commons, one might "roam" or "ramble" and do so "far and wide," "without hindrance or interruption."[49] It seemed to follow that, for those whose working lives were governed by routine and whose opportunities for spontaneous behavior were constantly being circumscribed, a day on the commons was the best possible therapy. As a resident of Epping pointed out in 1865, people could "run about" on the heath or forest without getting in each other's way, while in the "prim park," many of the restraints of daily life had to be observed.[50]

Canon Rownsley commented in the 1880s on what he perceived to be an awakening interest among "the intelligent class of artisans" to this way of enjoying the outdoors. This perception made him hopeful that enjoyment of "the country-walk and the field-side ramble" would nourish patriotism in Britain the way it had done in Germany. There, he pointed out, contact with the soil and the natural features of the countryside had become "not only a national need, but a racial one." Should Londoners, he said, be given similar opportunities, pride in common ownership could also be expected to grow and with it a renewed sense of commonality.[51]

Although it is doubtful that the commons preservation movement had such far-reaching effects, there can be no doubt that it, together with the drive to construct people's parks, represents the greatest and most enduring achievement of the nineteenth-century effort to provide poor people with "rational recreation."[52] However, this achievement acted to divert energy and attention away from efforts to improve the quality of the city streets as places to *be* in. It helps to explain why Cheapside never stood a chance of being turned into a Boulevard St Michel.[53] As John Fisher Murray had pointed out in 1839, apologists for London used the considerable extent of London's green spaces to avoid responsibility for bringing amenities to the doorsteps of ordinary citizens.

Some Victorians, Godwin and Pennethorne among them, did think it possible to design streets with an urban aesthetic in mind. As we have already seen, bold and imaginative proposals were put forward and, on occasion, seriously considered. A particularly fanciful idea for making the streets into green spaces was put forward in the late 1850s by a railway engineer named W.B. Adams. He suggested that the roofs of London terraced houses be planked and tarred, like a ship's deck, or be fitted with slates joined with cork and then planted with shrubs and flower gardens to give the city "aerial streets." They would be ideal places, he explained, for children to play and for housewives to hang out laundry. Enthusiasm kindling, he added: "Think of the wine parties, supper parties, and open-air dinners, that might take place with the upper crust of London restored to its proprietors!"[54]

Adams was not the only one to recognize that it might be better to bring greenery close to where people lived and worked than to set aside tracts of green space at a distance. More down-to-earth reformers like the prominent landscape gardeners Alexander Mackenzie and William Robinson wanted to concentrate efforts on seeing to it that trees be planted, wherever possible, along streets and that poor areas be provided with "small, simple squares."[55] As they were aware, the provision of parks and commons had done little or nothing to withdraw or to divert leisure activities from the streets except, perhaps, on special holidays.[56] A mother, living with a large brood in a two-room dwelling in Edwardian Stepney, was as likely as her early Victorian counterpart to send all but her youngest out into the street to play; young people were as likely to gather on a summer evening under the street lamp on the corner in Edwardian times as they were when Victoria came to the throne.[57] Octavia Hill was distressed that so few from slum areas ever went for a stroll on the Embankment or for a walk in the park; she attributed that neglect partly to shyness about appearing shabbily dressed in a public place and partly to having been brought up midst "the excitement of street tragedies."[58] That the theater of the street could ever be comic or that the influences of street life could ever be positive would not have crossed her mind, and the same might be said about most of the other street reformers: so much of the emotional appeal of their causes depended on awakening politicians and the philanthropically-minded to the physical and moral danger of leaving things as they were.

One contemporary who was critical of this negative attitude toward street culture was Alice Gomme, whose charmingly illustrated *Children's Singing Games* was published in 1894. She was a folklorist of distinction and a collaborator with her husband, Lawrence Gomme, in a campaign to direct antiquarians away from an exclusive concern with ancient times and far-away places and toward the customs, past and present, of their own British localities, London, of course, included. Not surprisingly, she was as disposed to find value in the street recreations she could observe as Octavia Hill was to overlook them. "When one considers," Alice Gomme wrote, "the conditions under which child-life exists in the courts of London . . . it is almost impossible to estimate too highly the influence these games have for good in town-bred populations" – something, she added, which "our reformers" might consider before expressing their "dismal forebodings."[59]

Although most of the reformers she was referring to believed that street construction and reconstruction were the essential factors in urban renewal, even those among them who were enthusiasts for building park-like streets tended to equate the terms "broad," "straight," or "regular" with the powers of light and health and "narrow," "confined," or "twisted" with the powers of darkness and illness. Planted streets were to be, to use William Robinson's words, "veins of salubrity."[60] He and those who shared his point of view wished their green highways to be instruments for slicing through the tangled byways of an older urban organization and culture, through a way of life, ironically, that many late twentieth-century cities are attempting, however superficially, to recreate or refurbish.

William Morris was not aiming directly at the Victorian "green party" when he attacked those reformers who would, if they could, "make streets into decent prison corridors, with people just trudging to and fro from work."[61] None of the four individuals who have been selected here were answerable on this indictment. Their god was not efficiency or some narrow version of utility. All of them were convinced that Londoners needed beauty and variety in their homes and surroundings as much as they needed cleanliness, order, and space. If London in our own time has paid little regard to the social, aesthetic, and environmental implications of road development, the chain of responsibility does not lead directly to their doors. Yet, in adopting the organic metaphor, in assuming that London was an ailing body, facing incipient apoplexy or respiratory failure, these cultivated and well-intentioned reformers must be included among those who, to quote Morris again, wished to clear "the streets of everything that may injure their delicate sensibilities." Morris, a reader of *The Builder*, a speaker in Pennethorne's Victoria Park, a close friend and admirer of Octavia Hill's, an associate of Shaw-Lefevre's in many causes, maintained that streets "filled with costermongers, organs, processions and lecturers of all kinds" were good streets and that attempts to beautify, purify, and ventilate often endangered everything which gave a city zest. Of our four characters, only Godwin might have appreciated Morris's point that what most reformers wished to clear away gave the city its "life-pulse." Even Godwin was prone to use, whenever convenient to the purpose at hand, rhetoric which associated the street with moral and physical sickness. There is irony in the conclusion that the people most concerned about preserving artifacts from the past and providing city dwellers with the healing balm of nature tended to fix on what they took to be the vices and to be largely indifferent to preserving and embellishing the virtues of street life.

10

INHABITING

On April 24, 1906, a few minutes before midnight, Police Constable Horace Page, on point duty in Regent Street, arrested a 25-year-old, fashionably dressed Frenchwoman who gave her name as Eva D'Angeley. He took her to the Marylebone Street Police Station and charged her, under the Vagrancy Act of 1824, with behaving in an indecent and riotous manner. By all accounts, the arrested woman seemed composed and went along quietly with Page, occasionally smiling at him and chattering in her native language. Questioned through an interpreter at the Station, she denied being a prostitute and claimed that she was a respectable married woman and had merely been waiting for her husband. An hour later a man, who gave his name as René D'Angeley, appeared and stood bail. He confirmed Eva's story, saying that he had been walking with her and a business associate, a dealer in bijouterie named Rubens, and had separated from her to see Rubens home. Eva was then released and told to appear to have her case heard the following morning.

When she stood before the magistrate, G.L. Denman, the next day, she requested time to present a character witness, her Marylebone landlord, Mr Gage. Denman granted a delay. This gave police time to interview Gage and Rubens. The landlord had nothing to say against either of his tenants; Rubens said he had known the couple in Paris, where they "bore a high character for respectability."[1] Thus, when the proceedings were resumed early in May, it was clear that it would not be a routine case. Unrattled by this knowledge, Constable Page stated his version of events crisply and firmly. He had observed Eva on numerous occasions, crossing and recrossing the street for the purpose of soliciting gentlemen. His partner on the beat confirmed that this was so and added that she had been unusually dexterous at escaping when he or Page tried to give her the required warning that, if she persisted, she faced arrest. On the night in question, however, Page managed to corner her and ask her what she was doing. Supposedly she said, "Me no speak English." Nevertheless Page, who had been at this kind of duty for three years, assumed that she was using a familiar tactic and proceeded to give the routine warning. He said that the accused listened, smiled, replied, "Oui, oui," and then immediately made her way across the street to accost a passer-by. At that point Page made the arrest.

Denman, as he explained later, was inclined to believe this version of what happened, particularly since the defendant made no attempt to contradict it. Nevertheless, Denman dismissed the case, even though Rubens had not honored his promise to appear. It was his practice, the magistrate said, to dismiss whenever a man came forward and testified to being the husband of an accused woman and to having been aware of her whereabouts. Since René had so affirmed, he released Eva, but not before giving her, through an interpreter, this advice:

> When she had been in London a little longer she would find out that no respectable married woman would walk and wait about Regent-street alone at that time of night. It was very unfortunate that it should be so, but it was notorious that many of those about the street at night were not of a respectable class. One could not shut one's eyes to that fact. The only thing the police could go by was whether persons had some real business there at that time of night. She would be very well advised not to go out alone in that sort of neighbourhood at night.[2]

Doubtless Denman and other magistrates had given many similar homilies without attracting any particular notice. But it became obvious that this occasion would be different when, several days later, René D'Angeley walked into the Marylebone Station, asked for Inspector MacKay, and, apologizing for the trouble he was about to cause, revealed that he had been approached by a solicitor acting for Dr Maurice Gerothwohl and his attorney, Sir George Lewis, and been persuaded to take further action, something, he confessed to MacKay, he had no real stomach for. This news set off alarm bells, for Lewis had a formidable reputation as a lawyer and a private investigator. His exposé of Richard Pigott as the forger of the letter used to discredit Parnell had won him a knighthood. In addition, he was a friend of Edward VII, a connection which had resulted in a baronetcy. Any case in which he was involved was certain to receive publicity. Police understood that he had approached D'Angeley as part of a strategy to clear the reputation of his client, Gerothwohl, a lecturer in French at Trinity College, Dublin, who had been arrested, along with a friend, on a drunk and disorderly charge. As in the D'Angeley case, Denman had ordered these defendants to be discharged without implication of innocence. It was obvious that Lewis was about to lead an attack on Denman as a first step in a campaign against police procedures.[3]

The attack came promptly. The *Daily Mail* called the advice Denman gave Eva "astonishing" and denounced police arrogance and corruption, using Constable Page's behavior as an example.[4] For the past several years public reaction had been building against attempts by the police to respond to pressures generated by the most recent of several purity crusades. Some Tory opponents of the new Liberal Government took up the cry against police corruption and indifference to civil liberties and badgered the Home Secretary, Herbert Gladstone, about the need for investigation. To reduce the heat, the Prime Minister, Campbell-Bannerman, agreed to the appointment of a Royal Commission to inquire into the behavior of the Metropolitan Police. Its findings were everything the police could have wished. Detectives shadowed René and Eva and followed them to Paris. A lead there took the investigation to Algiers where evidence showed that Eva, under the name of Clavel, had been a street walker in El Bar, a nearby town where René had met her. His real name was Soubiger. He had come to Algeria from London, got into trouble with the police, and, facing prosecution for carrying unlawful arms, fled with Eva back to London. There he seems to have lived off what Eva could earn at night on Regent Street. Satisfied that these were the facts, the Commission Report duly exonerated Constable Page and stated its opinion that the behavior of the police had been "discreet and correct."[5] There the D'Angeley affair ended.

But the issues raised by Denman's treatment of Eva and his parting remarks to her were to prove more enduring. What the magistrate had implied was, first, that he recognized and regretted the disparity between the ideal that all of His Majesty's subjects were free agents on the public thoroughfare and the reality that some were more equal than others. Second, by switching in his choice of object from "women" to "persons" when he came to speak of whom the police were monitoring on the night-time pavements, he showed his reluctance to acknowledge openly that it was a gender issue. Third, he indicated that men and women entered streets on different terms. Had Eva been unable to produce René (whom Denman must have suspected of being a pimp), and had René not accepted responsibility for Eva's actions, she would have been found guilty and punished. Fourth, Denman left hanging in the air the inference that any woman who refused to abide by conventions about respectable behavior should be held responsible for the consequences, no matter how innocent she might be of any immoral action or intent. Finally, it is clear from his surprised reaction to the furor his words caused that Denman believed he was simply saying what every Londoner knew to be true.

He should have been aware, however, that a magistrate is not always entitled to cite actual practice in order to justify a decision. Was

Denman invoking the double standard as the *de facto* law of the land? Other justices had already got into serious difficulties for seeming to do so. In 1887 Mr Justice Newton had stirred up a hornet's nest by dismissing Elizabeth Cass, arrested, like Eva, for disorderly soliciting on Regent Street. Newton said, on that occasion:

> If you are a respectable girl, as you say you are, do not walk Regent-street or stop gentlemen at 10 o'clock of a night. If you do you will be fined or sent to prison. Go away, and do not come here again.[6]

In response to this, the newspapers had made the same assertion as they were to do later about the potential danger to civil liberties such a doctrine posed, but the remedies they suggested on both occasions were mostly aimed at curbing the discretionary powers of the police in making arrests and the tendency of magistrates to assume guilt on the basis of police evidence alone. Rarely did these critics address the question of the double standard itself or ways to bring the actual experience of half the population into some kind of approximation to the ideal of free movement and equal access.

So much of the rhetoric of the time had to do with the notion that women's place was in the home that we are tempted to accept this as the explanation for why so much of the indignation aroused by the Cass, D'Angeley, and similar cases spent itself in talk. Warning women to avoid using the public streets except under male protection and with male permission can be interpreted as a way of reinforcing the doctrine that women's nature was best attuned to the privacy of domestic life. Restricting women's mobility in public could, therefore, serve to maintain the male power structure at a time when women were gaining control over their own property and demanding full citizenship and equal opportunity in the work place. From this perspective, Denman's warning to Eva can be understood as one example of the restrictive process. Women and men readers of the *Daily Mail* might agree that it was outrageous to give legal authority to the proposition that some citizens could not expect police protection if they chose to enter certain public spaces, yet those same readers would be likely to remember and to heed Denman's warning long after their indignation had passed. Anxiety about loss of reputation, as well as fear about the possibility of being touched, insulted, harassed, and sexually assaulted, inhibited women from claiming the rights they were acknowledged to possess and, it could be argued, restricted their entry into the public sphere.[7]

Venerable and useful though this concept of separate spheres has been, it has some disadvantages as a conceptual framework since it tends to neglect the variables of class, race, and ethnicity and to be a static rather than a dynamic model. Over the course of the nineteenth and early twentieth centuries, the experience of being in public and in private spaces was constantly being redefined, that redefinition being different for different groups of people.[8] A move to a leafy middle-class suburb meant that wives and daughters would enter the streets of the central city only occasionally to shop or to attend concerts, to go to the theater, or to participate, with some male escort, in special events. Victorian and Edwardian photographs of streets in the City confirm the impression that users of this financial sector were predominantly male. Women and girls may have been only a small current in the diurnal stream that flowed from City to suburb and back again, but they crowd the pictures taken of street markets, public parks, and working-class courts and pavements. Increasing family size and progressive overcrowding caused girls as well as boys to use the streets as extensions of the home and to go outside for social and, sometimes, sexual contacts. Also, the average Londoner of both sexes traveled far more often in 1910 than in 1810. Expanding work opportunities outside the home meant that women joined men in increasing numbers on the morning and evening pavements later in the nineteenth century.

To be in a public space is not necessarily to be a determinant of it. One specialist on urban geography thinks that women in our own time "live in public like a subject people."[9] It is possible, of course, to find places in nineteenth-century London where men entered at certain times on women's terms. A mid-Victorian gentleman intent on making his way through the Haymarket at night might well have felt more of an object than a subject. Also, girls and women could, on occasion, be assertive and aggressive. A local North London newspaper in 1869 was distressed to report that "for a long time past," young women had been in the habit of walking down Islington's Upper Street on Sunday evenings arm in arm and amusing themselves by forcing passers-by into the gutter.[10] On the other hand there can be no doubt about which way the balance of power usually tipped.

The distribution of power set rules of entry and behavior for every street, and in nineteenth-century Britain wealth commanded power and mediated constraints on women's mobility. On the carriageway men almost always held the reins but women who could order out the family carriage or afford a cab fare gave the directions. From the 1830s a clerk's wife or a skilled workman's daughter could avoid the unpleasantness of walking through filthy streets in long skirts, petticoats, and lightweight shoes by hailing an omnibus. Once on board, physical contact between strangers was impossible to avoid, and this sometimes proved embarrassing, especially when the crinoline became popular. But the conductor who took her pennies as she entered was responsible for the safety of his passengers and was expected to preserve a degree of decorum. What wealth and status could not provide a woman was freedom from the consciousness that she needed protection for her costume, her honor, and her body. Wealthy young women did not, as a rule, ride alone in private carriages or hired cabs. Cab-drivers were notorious for their bad tempers and language; also cabs were used sometimes by prostitutes and their clients and thus the taint and the taboo. Few upper-class women would ever have had the experience of entering an omnibus and those who used them were expected, until about 1890, to sit inside the cramped interior instead of enjoying freedom and entertainment on the knife-board bench above. Jane Carlyle's decision to take an omnibus on one occasion became for her a significant act of protest as well as an adventure which, because it was unconventional, quickened her blood. Suffering one day, as she so often did, from her famous husband's insensitive neglect, she decided to break a spell of illness and depression by riding unescorted to Regent Street where she had a mutton chop and a glass of bitter at Verrey's, the restaurant outside of which Constable Page many years later was to take hold of Eva D'Angeley's arm. Jane Carlyle found the experience of independent movement profoundly exhilarating, "and for the outrage to 'delicate feminism,' I am beyond all considerations at present."[11]

No better example of the fact that women and men shared public spaces in the nineteenth century but "inhabited" those spaces on different terms can be found than the daily shifts of social climate on Regent Street.[12] On a weekday afternoon fashionable ladies while shopping there would feel in command of the territory and, unless they paused too long in front of certain shop windows, could go about their business and pleasure without being brushed up against or otherwise insulted. But as soon as darkness fell, the human dynamics changed completely. During the day the social geography (or "shopography" as one wit put it) was defined by women with the means to command deference from male shopkeepers and policemen; at night, simply to enter the street unescorted by a man marked a woman either as "fair game" or "on the game."

The terms for street use changed over time from street to street. Everyone knew what the rules for Regent Street were; they had remained more or less constant from the time the street was constructed. However, had Elizabeth Cass decided on Coronation Night, 1887, to escape the confinement of the dressmaker's shop where she lived and worked and go for a stroll at night along High Holborn instead of the more distant Regent Street, she would probably never have had to go through her ordeal. The constable on point duty in Holborn probably would have noticed an attractive young woman walking alone. That famous street also once had, before the vice market moved westward, a notorious reputation. Therefore, the policeman would have kept an eye on her, but it is unlikely that he would immediately have jumped to conclusions when she paused in her walk and doubled back, as Cass seems to have done on Regent Street. Even so, Cass's status and purpose would have been determined on the basis of location, no matter which street she had been on, whereas typecasting of men would have included many more variables.

It would be legitimate to object that a concentration on gender can draw attention away from other factors like class, ethnicity, or institutional identity. Since riding was more prestigious than walking, the wealthy of both sexes tended to spend little of their time on the pavements. A late-night stroll from Parliament to home in Kensington or Mayfair or a brisk walk to and around clubland could be undertaken without loss of status, and it was permissible for matrons to walk alone in daylight along fashionable West End streets, although, until the easing of social restrictions in the Edwardian period, unmarried girls would have needed a chaperon. Two well-bred, mid-Victorian sisters, Emily and Ellen Hall, thought it best to disclose the fact that they had walked alone in London to the privacy of their diaries.[13]

Nevertheless, most London women had no servants to run errands for them or to chaperon their daughters. Progressively as one moved down the social ladder the pavement became the daily market, the workplace, the passageway between home and job, the main locus of weekend recreation, the place to meet friends and lovers. Necessity had to prevail over aspirations to higher status. Street workers, by definition, were disqualified from the status race, except, of course, within their own low rank, yet they too were bound by a multitude of conventions. Some tasks which were reserved for females, like flower-selling, and some where women predominated, like going from door to door to buy kitchen grease and dripping, followed traditional notions of women's work. For some reason, certain kinds of dirty jobs were done entirely by males and some were not. Girls and older women sometimes were crossing-sweeps, but scavengers were invariably men and boys. Flushermen were just that, but the revolting task of sorting out and picking over the huge rubbish tips at Lett's Wharf, just east of Waterloo Bridge, was left exclusively to women. Women cleaned and sold fish but men slaughtered animals and sold meat. As we have seen, shoeblacking was boy labor just as child-minding, largely a street occupation, was mostly done by girls. Begging or singing for reward was open to all, but women instrumentalists were confined, for the most part, to strings. When it came to who might sell what, the sorting mechanism often had to do with ethnic background as well as or instead of gender. Mayhew tells us that Jewish girls as well as boys were the ones who sold strawberries and old knives and scissors.[14] Gypsy women had a near monopoly on fortune-telling. From mid-century, ice cream vendors who were not Italian or apple sellers who were something other than Irish could expect to meet with considerable hostility. Olive Malvery, because she had a dark complexion and a slight East Indian accent, was accepted by street people and protected by them in a way that could not have happened had she not been perceived to be outside the normal class sorting process. Bible women could not have walked the dark streets to invite prostitutes to midnight tea and prayer had they not been protected by their special religious status. Malvery sometimes borrowed a Salvation Army uniform when she wanted to go to such pits of London as Green Arbour Court ("Ye Shades! What a place!") because she discovered that even in that area people would make way and smile.[15] Access to public streets and to the activities carried on there were full of all kinds of restrictions on just about everyone's free movement and free enterprise. Those who made the rules that governed the streets were usually men, and they tended to use this power to secure the best jobs and territories for themselves – but not always and not everywhere.

What keeps the generalization about men and women inhabiting streets on different terms from being too loose a concept is that women, across age and ethnic boundary lines, have always felt vulnerable to sexual assault or harassment when they enter and make their way through a street whether or not it is familiar territory. This is a consciousness that seems to have been a constant over the years, altering mainly in degree and, to a certain extent, in methods of coping.[16] It is a consciousness that men of whatever social level do not habitually carry around with them.

Surveyors for a 1989 BBC television documentary discovered that nine out of ten women in their sample were afraid to be out on the streets at night. Far fewer men admitted to feeling anxious even though they were, statistically, at far greater risk of being robbed or assaulted.[17] In a 1987 study of violence against women, the author, Anna Clark, begins: "All women know the paralysing fear of walking down a dark street at night, hearing mysterious footsteps clicking behind, wondering whether the night out was worth these moments of terror."[18] This fear has a long history. Early in the present century, a London journalist, Clarence Rook, recounted how his sister, Esther, came to his home late one evening by cab and in an agitated state. Having grown impatient with waiting for a bus, she had decided to walk down Oxford Street; and, when the crowds on the pavement thinned, became aware of being followed. Rook asked her if she had looked around and she replied, "Of *course* I didn't. But a girl can *tell* when anyone is following her." At this point a male friend of Rook's dropped by for a smoke and, after introductions, told of having, that night, observed a young woman, obviously frightened, walking quickly down Oxford Street. Wishing to help, he had hurried to catch up to offer his assistance and had almost reached her when she suddenly jumped into a cab and sped away. Rook's conclusion: men and women occupy the same pavements and sit side by side on trains and omnibuses, yet "the two sexes remain curiously apart."[19]

Whether this psychological distance would have been the same in late eighteenth-century or Regency London is open to discussion, particularly since the question can have no definite answer. When neighborhoods still contained a mixture of rich, poor, and in-between, a certain amount of contact between opposite sexes of different classes would have been unavoidable. It is, however, difficult to assess the quality of that contact or its effect on women's sense of vulnerability. Also, modulations in feelings about the display of sexuality in public must have had effects on the way men and women related to each other, although the formal rules governing civility, which regulated deportment and perhaps permitted a more relaxed mixing of the sexes, were not necessarily observed in the same way at all social levels.[20] Judging by the many warnings females of the time were treated to in the novels and advice manuals, a visit to London was full of peril; unmarried girls were cautioned that without male protection they were likely to be seduced or raped, regardless of the strategies they adopted.[21]

The introduction of gas street-lighting, safe forms of public transport, and the success of the New Police in gaining control of the streets probably reduced the actual risk to both men and women of being physically assaulted on the street, whether sexually or otherwise, this trend becoming clear in London sometime in the 1860s.[22] Statistics about the incident of rape and attempted rape in the Victorian period are not reliable; nevertheless, we can be reasonably sure that the chance of experiencing this kind of violence was then, as it is now, far higher off the street than on it.[23] It is certain that the decrease in the probabilities of being physically assaulted on the streets did not moderate the tone or amount of cautionary material women received and, presumably, absorbed. Indeed, the attention the popular press gave to lurid accounts of White Slave trafficking, to the disgusting details of the Jack the Ripper murders, and to descriptions of similar horrors, served to exaggerate and internalize fears among women who lived in large cities.[24] It is in the context of these fears that the reaction to Denman's warning to Eva D'Angeley needs to be placed.

There was another explanation for why streets remained danger zones for women even though the probability of being physically attacked was decreasing: sexual harassment, thought of as any unwanted and persistent intrusion, did not diminish during the nineteenth and early twentieth centuries and actually may have increased. Julia Clara Byrne, who made a living in the middle part of the century writing essays, complained that "quiet, modest young girls, steadily executing their little errands," constantly had to face the prospect of being "teased, followed, and bullied when they walk out unattended." She claimed that, in spite of the appearance in 1829 of the constable walking his beat, the streets had become, in her own memory, increasingly unpleasant for women and girls to venture into, especially after dark.[25] Mrs C.S. Peel, looking back to her London girlhood in the 1880s, recalled that she had once been allowed to go with her young cousin through Victoria Square and across Buckingham Palace Road to buy gloves at Gorings. "We felt," she wrote, "that anything might happen to us . . . the excitement was delicious." But when she was older and had managed to break into the male world of Fleet Street journalism, she found the daily journey to work considerably less entertaining:

> Although I was quietly dressed, and I hope looked what I was, a respectable young woman, there was scarcely a day when I, while waiting for an omnibus, was not accosted. I perfected myself in the art of staring blankly through the ill mannered persons who offered their undesired attentions.[26]

Few middle-class Edwardian women had better opportunity to perfect this art of self-protection than Olive Christian Malvery, whose entertainment, journalistic, and social rescue work took her to every corner of the metropolis. She developed a manner which kept unpleasant intrusions to a minimum, but, she said, she knew of many others who were not so skilled or fortunate. She gave an example of an encounter at a woman's club with the wife of a prominent barrister who told of having that afternoon been followed all the way along the Strand. As she walked from Charing Cross to Treloar's shop to look for carpets, her pursuer kept calling, "My Dear." Shaken though the woman was, Malvery reports, she could not bring herself to give the man in charge. "Women hate doing this sort of thing," Malvery said, and added that it was wrong to suppose that females could avoid harassment merely by going about their business in a quiet way; nothing, she said, could be farther from the truth. The kind of men who walk slowly by West End shops or wait outside workrooms in the East End require no signals or signs of encouragement before making their approaches.[27] Fear was, under these circumstances, prudence.

A detailed and graphic account of how girls learned to be "instinctively afraid" can be found in Virginia Woolf's *The Pargiters*, a "novel-essay" which eventually was published, shorn of the essay component, as *The Years*. In one passage in a fiction section of the original draft,

Rose, a 10-year-old girl whose family lives in a large house on Abercorn Terrace, a solid middle-class area between Ladbroke Grove and Bayswater, slips out of her house just at dusk to make a foray to a shop that was nearby, but deep "in hostile territory." On the way back she comes upon a man, leaning on a pillar box. "As she ran past him, he gibbered some nonsense at her, sucking his lips in and out and began to undo his clothes." This experience makes an indelible mark and causes her instinctively in the years ahead to call up this guilty image of "street love" when offered "other loves inside the drawing room." By contrast, Rose's brother, when he encounters a prostitute, suffers no trauma; indeed he feels as a consequence bonded with other males. Woolf points the moral: thus do women lose their liberty and limit their opportunities in the social and economic market place.[28]

Some men were also aware of this evil or were at least ready to admit that there was a problem and that it was serious and not simply in the natural order of things. Dr William Acton, whose main interest was in investigating and theorizing about prostitution, said that "any attractive woman, of whatever station, who walks unattended in London is subject to indelicate, and often indecent overtures."[29] As noted in an earlier chapter, Soloman Cohen, an official with a Jewish rescue agency, testified to a Parliamentary Committee in 1906 that girls were constantly being spoken to in the streets and sometimes asked a constable to walk with them through certain stretches.[30] Charles Vollhardt, one of the managers at Swan and Edgar, a well-known department store, gave his opinion to the same committee that harassment of women shoppers had been increasing steadily during his thirty years at the store, so much so that lady customers who paused to look in the store's windows ran a serious risk of being molested. Well-dressed "Gents" would brush up against them, raise their hats, and apologizing for making the physical contact, attempt to start a conversation by offering refreshments. Vollhardt recalled that several days previously the daughter of one of the store's directors had stumbled inside, half-fainting, after having been surrounded by three men and subjected to that kind of treatment. He said he discovered on this occasion that it was no good making complaints to the authorities, for there was little police could do unless the woman molested was willing to go to the station and press charges, "an ordeal," Vollhardt admitted, "which not one lady in ten thousand would face."[31]

As both the Cass and the D'Angeley cases make clear, the police were, usually inadvertently, part of the problem. By isolating certain night-time streets and regularizing prostitution there (formally under the Contagious Diseases Acts in some cities, and informally in London), they assisted in the process of professionalizing the prostitute and setting her off from the casual and seasonal purveyor of sex. That permitted men who found it amusing or ego-inflating to harass women to excuse their conduct by pointing out that a particular woman exhibited some sign associated with the profession: walking slowly, making eye contact, using cosmetics, smoking, dressing unconventionally, deviating in her path from the straight line. It does also seem likely that the police themselves were occasionally among the harassers, although to what extent cannot be determined. However, a considerable weight of evidence shows that the constable was far more often the protector. The fact that his legal powers to interfere when a man insulted or solicited a female pedestrian or exposed himself to her were severely circumscribed made it nearly impossible to make an arrest; however, his repertoire of informal methods of control was extensive.

How and why the law, the magistrate, the Home Office, and Scotland Yard did not give the constable clear direction and explicit powers cannot simply be explained by the fact that all these institutions were male and therefore inclined to support the male power structure, although that interpretation is not without weight. When officials from one or another of those bodies were questioned about why the man on the beat had no clear directives, there is a genuine-sounding note of perplexity in their answers and a tendency to take the position that law and law enforcement must tread lightly in areas where popular opinion and custom give no clear lead. Take, for example, the responses to this question of the Chief Magistrate of the Bow Street Police Court, Sir Albert de Rutzen, a man who in 1906 had been on the bench much of his long life. When asked by members of a Royal Commission if he had had much experience with cases where men molested women, he tried to recollect: perhaps in the last forty years one or two had come before him, but, as far as he could remember, these charges involved some form of physical assault and not merely touching or making an indecent remark or gesture. He admitted that he was not sure what he would do if a woman found the nerve to go to the station and bring charges under the Vagrancy Act of 1824 or the Police Act of 1839 because a man had spoken to her and had kept insisting that she take tea with him or something of that nature. He supposed he would grant a summons. In any case, he said, the matter was hypothetical since he had never had the occasion to decide what his policy might be. What advice had he for women so annoyed? Rutzen thought she might seek out a constable who could caution the man about behaving in a way that might lead to a breach of the peace; possibly this would act as a deterrent. As for ways that the law might be improved and the constable be given clearer directives, he was afraid he had nothing practical to suggest. The problem, he admitted, was serious. There was a real evil out there on the streets of London to which existing enforcement and judicial powers held out little remedy. On the other hand, he remarked, female reticence was a large part of the problem, and that was a social and moral phenomenon not easily accessible to the law.[32]

Sir Albert's point of view was by no means uncommon; other witnesses, called before this Commission, took much the same line. Sir Mackenzie Chalmers, top mandarin at the Home Office, thought any tightening of the legal definition of soliciting might conflict with working-class courting rituals. "Their manners," he informed his hearers, "are not quite the manners of other classes."[33] Emily Cook, who published an amusing sketch of London life in 1902, gave an illustration of the point Chalmers was, rather gingerly, trying to make. An earnest and politically active young woman friend had found herself next to a young artisan on top of an omnibus – in the Edwardian period, a popular trysting place; he spoke to her and finding him intelligent, she asked him what he thought about the Eight-Hours Bill, then before Parliament. He gave his views but accompanied them, to her consternation, with a series of nudges, "this being, I have reason to believe," Cook editorialized, "the first preliminary to courtship in his class." The young woman pretended not to notice until nudges became squeezes, the episode ending with a scramble down the iron staircase and a quick exit.[34] Chalmers and Cook probably wished their remarks to be taken as reminders of the need for middle-class people to respect differences in class cultures. Nevertheless, an anecdote of that sort, if served up in quantities, as it often was, did have the effect of discouraging attempts to secure for women of all social conditions freedom to inhabit the streets on something like an equal basis with men.

The Royal Commission Report, made public in 1908, cited the testimony of Chalmers, Rutzen, and others to support their recommendation that nothing be done. They took the position that laws against indecent intrusions were already on the books should women choose to use them; and if women almost never so chose, that was because, in their modesty, they had decided that the indignity of taking legal proceedings outweighed the indignity suffered in the offense. Therefore, this was an area into which the law should not boldly trespass. The Commissioners admitted that a double standard existed and recognized that it violated the dictum that law and law enforcement should be general and not particular, but they could see no remedy. "It is not the fault of the Police," they declared, "that unchastity on the part of the woman, as compared with unchastity by a man, is looked on with much more gravity in the former than in the latter case." Every British subject might be equal in theory before the criminal law but not necessarily before the bar of customary morality. Women, the Commissioners thought, subscribed to this double standard by being harder on their own sex than on the other. "It may be," they concluded, that this form of inequality is one of "the fundamental facts of human nature"; and if so, it would be futile to attempt "to put down unchastity by legislation."[35]

Women and men who found such complacency maddening sometimes took matters into their own hands, especially if they were involved in one of the late nineteenth and early twentieth-century social purity movements. Ellis Hopkins turned her considerable energies in the 1880s to what she believed to be the root cause of prostitution, rape, and harassment: men's impurity, lack of self-control, and willingness to treat women as objects to be exploited. Her White Cross Army and League and the National Vigilance Association which grew out of W.T. Stead's exposure of the international traffic in young girls joined in a widespread effort to construct shelters to keep homeless girls off the streets, but used activist tactics also. These societies pressed for the appointment of women police and the placement of women wardens at police stations and engaged in some sporadic attempts to expose the customers involved in street sex, especially individuals who preyed on innocent women.[36] William Coote, Secretary of the National Vigilance Association, whose zeal in sniffing out vice seemed narrow and excessive even to many of the purity movement enthusiasts, described one action, carried out by a sub-committee chaired by Millicent Fawcett, who later became the leader of the non-militant wing of the women's suffrage movement. On receiving a report about a 16-year-old servant girl who was being persistently harassed by a 60-year-old man, Fawcett's response was decidedly militant. Not discouraged by repeated rebuffs, the pursuer had sent the girl a letter, inviting her to luncheon and an afternoon at the Zoo. Under instructions, she arranged to meet him in front of the British Museum where Coote, Fawcett, and a number of others waited. When their prey arrived, they sprung the trap. Before a constable came to intervene the group seized the predator and pinned a sign on his back reading: "Dr. W—M—, of the Army and Navy Club. This scoundrel has been caught in the act of attempting to abduct an innocent girl." Coote noted proudly that the man promptly left the country; even so, he made no claim that such tactics had any lasting effect as a deterrent.[37] Insignificant in itself, this incident does capture some of the spirit of the women's movement at the end of the century and the willingness of its moral reforming wing to shift from a preoccupation with defense to the offensive. This movement and the Suffragette confrontations which were soon to follow must have had a tonic effect on women's spirits, acting to heighten awareness of how fear functioned to restrict liberty and opportunity. Nevertheless, this new mood probably did not discourage and may, indeed, have encouraged men who were disposed to attack and to annoy women whenever they entered public spaces.

It is easy to overlook the fact that retaliation, whether of this middle-class variety or carried out in those more informal ways of striking back which working-class women and girls developed in the give and take of the daily routine, was, like harassment, part of the pattern of street life. The image of the Victorian woman as a delicate flower or a "timid deer" has had its day. It was in the resources available for protection that the experiences of women of different social levels differed. The early Victorian illustrator, Thomas Shotter Boys, includes a pedestrian scene in his *London As It Is*, published in 1842. Present are a lady and her two children who are watched over by a nanny. At the rear of this small procession is a liveried servant carrying a long, heavy staff topped with a metal ball, not so much a weapon as a symbol of strength and authority.[38] For less grand matrons, female domestics had to serve, although employment of young women as protectors was not without its ironies. A woman essayist of the 1850s wrote:

> I have seen ladies, no longer either young or pretty, shocked at the idea of traversing a street's length at night, yet never hesitate at being "fetched" by some female servant, who was both young and pretty, and to whom the danger of the expedition . . . was by far the greater.[39] (See Plate 18.)

Those who could not buy protection of any sort needed to make arrangements with friends and family members. East End mothers, before sending an older daughter on an errand at night, would try to make sure that she took a little brother or sister with her. Harsh punishment for lateness was another form of protection, one which must have embittered the atmosphere of many working-class homes.

On the other hand, the high density of working-class areas and the many small shops and stalls such density creates meant that there were many eyes watching what happened on the pavements. Robert Roberts recalled how difficult it was for a young person in his part of Edwardian Salford to evade the scrutiny of the "Old Queens," whose eyes were constantly tracking the passing scene through their lace-curtained windows.[40] Jane Jacobs, in her *The Death and Life of Great American Cities*, makes the case that on streets where sidewalks are heavily used and lined with small shops, a sense of mutual responsibility can grow, especially if the commercial exchanges that go on are part of a web of "natural cross connections." In those circumstances, low-intensity contacts can take place and protective networks can form. Where many eyes are watching and identifying individuals as they pass, safety increases and apprehension diminishes.[41] Thus some of the drawbacks of inner-city living conditions could provide some compensations, although we should bear in mind that the interconnections

Jacobs speaks about depend upon more stability and commitment to neighborliness than the circumstances of many nineteenth-century slums allowed.

When the mix was right and a sense of neighborhood identity had a chance to develop, working-class girls seemed to respond as joyfully to the lure of the streets as did boys; indeed their response was often too exuberant for people who were interested in attracting them into the more "suitable" atmosphere of girls' clubs and societies. A publication in 1909 of the Federation of Working Girls' Clubs, called *In Peril in the City*, described midnight gatherings outside gin palaces where boys and girls danced and shouted "boisterous music hall choruses." It reported that Cockney girls "got up to kill," with trailing flounces, velvet dresses, flowing feathers, and sham jewelry, strolled arm in arm on Saturday and Sunday evenings, or paired off with "very young" men. No wonder, commented the writer, that these young people prefer the street to their crowded rooms.[42] Emily Cook also described these displays but found them amusing rather than disheartening. She liked the "fresh exuberance of spirits" of these noisy parades, the girls shouting out at passing adults: "You are a fine old corf-drop, you are!" or "Ere's a fine four penny lot!" or the favorite music hall catchline, "Where did you get that 'at?"[43]

Cook would have agreed with Walter Besant's observation: "The love which these young people have for the streets is wonderful, especially this is the case with girls."[44] That "street love" could sometimes be attractive is also the spirit of Ford Maddox [Ford] Hueffer's portrait of East End Monkey Walks: boys move together at first, straw headgear tilted; then one or two make eye contact with the featherhatted girls ahead; voices go higher, and "little shoves and nudges pass like waves in a field of corn." As the "kindly dusk falls," one youth after another slips free from his pack, until "little by little the knots dwindle away altogether." From place to place, said Hueffer, the ceremonials vary. In Westbourne Grove young shop assistants raise their bowlers and drawl, " 'How are you; Miss —?' for all the world as they do in Rotton Row." But manners are different in Mile End Road or Shepherd's Bush where a factory girl is likely to "slap likely youths violently on the back" and get a poke in the ribs in return, both sides in this courtship ritual "uttering obscenities positively astounding, without any obscene intention in the world." There in the grey city, all this life burgeoning – "London young and pagan."[45]

That such improbable stretches as the Mile End Road and Fleet Street could be made young and pagan, at least for a while, demonstrates how social groups define street spaces. On summer weekend evenings the groups shaping these physical environments were boys and girls together meeting and inhabiting public places on common terms. That so few safe and attractive spaces were created where the sexes of all ages could mingle easily and safely is testament to the myopia of reformers and street builders in the Victorian and Edwardian eras. They did give Victoria Park to the East End, and its users made it a true public place, but they built no successful promenades. Londoners during the half century before the 1914–18 War had to go to Paris to discover the delights of café-sitting where all could occupy neutral ground and choose for themselves how they would relate to the urban swirl around them. The recent conversion of Covent Garden and the development of pedestrian streets nearby, the advent of outside tables on Charlotte Street, and the spreading of that custom elsewhere have somewhat blurred the boundary lines between the different "social maps" men and women have drawn for themselves. In this respect, at least, London at the end of the twentieth century is richer than it was a hundred years earlier. It remains a matter of debate, however, whether or not these improvements and the other significant advances toward gender equality have done much to free women from those anxious moments when, at night, they hear the "mysterious" sound of footsteps gradually growing nearer.

11

PLANNING

Shortly before the beginning of Queen Victoria's sixty-four year reign and again at its end, reform energies were quickened by a sense that the city's growth was out of control. In both instances this perception and the responses it evoked preceded the arrival of revolutionary innovations in technology: first the steam railway that reached London not long after Coronation Day and then the petrol-driven motor vehicle, still something of a curiosity when the Queen died. In 1837 prophetic minds were aware that commuter trains would cause further distortions to a city, already aimlessly destroying its boundaries, unless public opinion and Parliament could be awakened to the need for action. In 1901 these same warnings were being sounded about the effect of electric trams and motor vehicles. Even the language reformers used was similar at either end of the Victorian period. Sir John Wolfe Barry, whose 1898 speech on London traffic has already been noticed, counselled planners to have "Greater London" and not merely "Urban London" in mind, considering that "an active circulation is kept up, as in the human body, from all parts to and from the central heart of the system."[1] In 1914 *The Times*, in a series of articles on "that monster of many problems – the traffic problem," described "the ceaseless flow" of the city's "life-blood" through the highway arteries and along its "net-work of veins," and spoke about various reform projects as though they were anatomical interventions, clinical decisions about whether to proceed by way of surgery or regulatory treatment.[2]

This medical discourse with its concern about congestion of the blood vessels gives coherence to the whole period of street reform over the span of at least a century. For example, while Wolfe Barry deplored the absence of a real municipal government and the "incurable *petitesse*" of the vestries, boards, and corporations left in charge of London's affairs, he nevertheless recommended bypass surgery, not treatment. He would leave the diseased parts alone and superimpose a wide, new artery to connect heart with extremities. He would design it in such a way that the need for police regulation and administrative supervision would be minimal: the design of the street could make sure that drivers kept in line and moved along safely and swiftly. Having devoted a brilliant career to building bridges (his part in constructing Tower Bridge won him a knighthood), docks, underground railways, and stations, he tended to think of London as a circulatory system: if radical intervention could get the blood flowing freely again, all would be well.

But for others at the turn of the century, the activities of the brain came to be almost as prominent in the organic metaphor as the heart. The creation of the London County Council (LCC) in 1888 caused many to rejoice at the thought that at last the capital of a great empire had become fully conscious and would be able, henceforth, not simply to respond reflexively, as the heart does, but to direct the forces acting upon it. The most enthusiastic planners were among the Progressive majority which dominated the Council until deposed by the more conservative Moderates in the 1907 election. Made up mostly of "advanced" Liberals and Fabians, Progressives constantly labored to break free of the constraints placed on the LCC's powers. Lord Salisbury had defined London as "an aggregate of municipalities." Progressives of all sorts took as their object the shaping of those aggregates into, as their charter stated, "a united Family for its Common good."[3] To achieve that goal for a county region which was already bursting its seams at the moment of its inception, they put their faith in the usefulness of a central nervous system and in a co-ordinated system of municipal transport, not designed specifically to relieve traffic blockages but to reach into each separate aggregate and weave them all together. The congestion which concerned them most was not on the streets but in the inner-city slums. John Benn, who headed the Highways Committee until 1904, was passionately committed to the construction of a network of tramlines because he believed that it would create one municipal entity. Like George Bernard Shaw, he looked forward to the day when laborers as well as bank managers could work in the city and raise their children in the country.[4] His confederate, John Burns, former tram driver, militant socialist, and in 1906 Liberal Cabinet Minister, took every occasion to deplore the ravaging of the remaining green areas on and beyond the edges of the county at the "dictates of squalid commercialism."[5]

Differences between the "holistic" approach favored by municipalists like Gomme, Burns, and Benn and the surgical procedure recommended by imaginative engineers like Wolfe Barry did not produce conflict between them; both groups agreed about the diagnosis and were optimistic about chances of recovery. It did mean, however, that priorities would not be the same. The municipalists wished to bring Londoners together; Wolfe Barry wished to improve their circulation.

His approach was to predict how accelerated growth in the future age of science and speed would affect the constantly spreading organism and then to provide it with arterial throughways so smooth and straight and wide that they could never become clogged. Gomme and his associates, on the other hand, were much more likely to ask questions about what ends speed and smooth internal circulation were supposed to serve. Wrote Gomme in 1897: "direct communication should be from somewhere to somewhere, and should take all matters into consideration."[6]

In the background of both reform approaches was a concern about the consequences of continuing to allow market forces to establish, fix, and undermine social and geographic boundaries. A series of violent demonstrations by the East End unemployed in 1886 and 1887 and the Dockers Strike in 1889 jolted the West End into awareness of how desperate and how dangerous housing and employment conditions for casual workers had become in the inner city. Expectations that the tramway expansion of the 1870s would draw clerks and better-off working people away from the crowded centre and leave room behind for casual laborers and their families were disappointed. Peckham, Camberwell, Wandsworth, Battersea, Fulham, and other lower-middle-class and working-class suburbs did expand but failed to create the expected housing vacuum in the slum areas.[7]

To complicate matters further, this extension of the horse tramway service and the introduction of working-class commuter fares proved to be a powerful engine for expediting movement in and out of the center. Recognizing how these developments were strengthening the case for municipal control, Salisbury's Tory ministry made what has been called a "pre-emptive strike":[8] in the County Councils Act it made the Metropolitan area, except for the City, a county with an elected government. Engineers responded to this rapid expansion with a paroxysm of rail-laying along extensions to the existing underground system, through the deep tubes, down the centres of streets, and over the newly constructed rights of way for cross-city trains. Electrification of the underground, the light railways, and the tramlines was begun around the turn of the century. Tube trains were, of course, electrified from the start. By 1903 most of these projects, as well as the construction of additional Thames bridges and the widening of others, had been completed. These feats accomplished, Balfour's Government agreed to appoint a Royal Commission to take stock of what effect all this activity was having on "locomotion" in the metropolis.[9]

During the two years the Committee interviewed witnesses, the public became conscious of what William Haywood in the 1860s and Wolfe Barry in the late 1890s tried to impress upon it: that building more and more underground and surface railway tracks had "largely increased the amount of traveling from one part to another of the central parts of London, adding greatly to the movement of those inhabiting the town itself."[10] Or, to use a crisper formulation, "facilities create traffic."[11] Between 1900 and 1925 the number of passenger journeys increased fifteenfold.[12] This conclusion, backed by a flood of statistics, the engineering mentality found easy to grasp but difficult to accept. In an editorial on the 1905 Report of the Royal Commission on Metropolitan Transport, *Engineering*, one of the two leading professional journals, commented on how various individuals in the past had tried to solve one of the most complicated of modern riddles: "how to move goods and people expeditiously from place to place." Robert Stevenson thought he had the answer in the railway locomotive; it would be a "disperser and distributor"; instead, the editorialist commented, railways led to further "aggregation." After that, Sir John Fowler proposed the underground railway as the solution, only to discover, while the system was still incomplete, that the greater the movement below the surface the greater were the numbers above. Streets had been widened and straightened to accommodate the build-up of cabs and horse omnibuses, and "still we were jostling each other off the pavements, or blocking the roads with cabs and carriages." So, the editorial continued, we now burrow even deeper, using Greathead's tunneling shield, and produce the tube, yet the streets grow more congested by the hour. Electric trams and motor buses have arrived, and, who knows, one day we may be able to fly from point to point; still, inevitably, the familiar tangle will again appear, for "the more that is done to unravel it the more involved it becomes." Nevertheless, not wanting to leave his readers too disheartened, the writer concluded by suggesting that perhaps improved telephone service might offer a way out, since that communication technology, unlike the others, might actually decrease the need to move about.[13]

Undaunted by the force of its own logic, the journal went on in subsequent issues to recommend building arterial throughways. Wolfe Barry himself took a leading part in this campaign to incorporate in the design of a highway system the fact that, for the first time in history, electrical and internal combustion engines were making it possible to travel on the streets at a rate faster than seven or eight miles per hour. Speed, Barry thought, might untie the knot; therefore, planners needed to devise a way to allow through traffic to move at the pace of the electric motor. He was convinced that his own plan (inspired in part, he acknowledged, by Haywood's proposal in 1867) supplied the key to how this might be done. Standardization and separation would be his principles. He would give Greater London a 120-foot-wide east–west limited access highway connecting Bayswater Road and Whitechapel and passing through or near Russell Square.

Lanes of east-bound traffic would be separated from west-bound by a sunken way for electric tramlines and another path for bicycles, either sunken or raised. Intersecting by means of bridges would be several smaller north–south streets, also uniformly fitted out with passages at different levels for tracks, bicycles, and horse-drawn vehicles. Great though the initial cost might be, the benefit, he maintained, would be far greater: families of modest income could move to the outer ring, access to trade and pleasure would become more convenient for everyone, and "the stress of life would be lightened."[14]

Noteworthy about this plan for an engineered utopia is that it marked a shift of interest back to the street as the critical factor in the urban communication system and at a time when the petrol motor vehicle was still undergoing its birth process. In 1897 Londoners were startled to see a four-wheeled cab which resembled all the others except in one respect, there was no horse. Two years later, the Motor Traction Company experimented with an "oil motor omnibus" service between Kennington and Oxford Circus. However, the petrol buses "vibrated abominably" and broke down frequently, while the battery-powered cabs, nicknamed "humming birds," needed frequent recharging and constant replacement of their India-rubber tires; so by 1900 both experiments had been abandoned.[15] As for the private motor car, Shaw-Lefevre's Locomotives on Highways Act (sponsored by a Tory Minister after the fall of the Liberal Government in 1895) withdrew the crippling restrictions and made its use possible. However, as late as 1905, the majority of experts (Wolfe Barry among them) who supported the Report of a Royal Commission on Traffic, released that year, gave their opinion that, at least for the foreseeable future, electric tramways and not motor buses would be the principal means of public transport on heavily traveled streets. That automobiles would ever fill the urban arteries, "like the red corpuscles in the blood,"[16] still seemed too remote a possibility to consider seriously, although Lord Balfour, as early as 1901, looked forward to the time when London would have "a system of radiating thoroughfares, confined to rapid (say, fifteen miles an hour or over) . . . auto-car propulsion."[17]

Wolfe Barry's vision of the modern throughway was constructed around the tram and the bicycle, but his principle of segregation according to speed could easily be applied to newer technology. For those who agreed with him that speed might accomplish what widening, straightening, and regulating had failed to do, the task ahead was to get horses and pedestrians out of the way. Also there was the possibility that "cross" traffic, which was bound to increase incrementally, could be kept out of local shopping and residential areas.[18] How that remedy was to effect a permanent cure advocates of circular ring roads, radial throughways, or cross-town bypasses did not, however, explain. The experience of the second half of the twentieth century shows that traffic is attracted to the fast motorways and that, since most of these vehicles are destined for some terminal spot within the city, the shopping streets will remain as congested by slow-moving vehicles and parked cars as before. An equilibrium does eventually evolve, but only at the point where commuters reach what Stephen Plowden calls "a tolerable level of congestion" (tolerable, that is, to the driver but not necessarily to society at large). His formula is: "If the capacity of the road network is not increased, the mileage performed will stabilise, and if the capacity is reduced, the mileage will be reduced correspondingly."[19] Even though early twentieth-century traffic engineers lacked experience of the effect of large volumes of motor bus and automobile traffic, they might have arrived at similar conclusions. Most experts were aware that express commuter trains and underground lines had not solved the problem of congestion, but it did not come easy to the engineering profession to conclude that large-scale engineering solutions could be, as often as not, self-defeating.

There was another difficulty with the arterial approach, one that reformers might have been expected to grasp: by accelerating lateral growth, by promoting "decentrism," fast and convenient motorways were bound to aggravate the condition they were supposed to cure. Especially in the period from the Boer War to 1914, engineers, like so many other Britons, were anxious about preserving London's position as the hub of empire, the centre of world trade and finance, and the symbol of the country's status as a first-rate power and civilization. They were aware of the possibility that unchecked expansion and development might eventually destroy the meaning of London altogether. Even so, they seemed to prefer that their right hand not be aware of what their left hand was doing.

Because the planners at Spring Gardens thought of transit as a means rather than as an end in itself, they avoided some of these difficulties, but they did have trouble reconciling their wish to relieve overcrowding by removing slum families to the suburbs with their desire to preserve some kind of geographical integrity, a "territorium," for the city. Some of them would have been willing to cut a swath east and west through the heart of the metropolis, but other more sober heads recognized that such projects would be hopelessly expensive, given the severe constraints placed on their capacity to raise financing and the indifference of Parliament. They might have done what Shaw-Lefevre and others suggested and worked out a skeleton plan for controlled growth; that way each small piece of the puzzle might, by increments, eventually have been fitted together. Asked in 1913 if there ever had been such a comprehensive scheme, Gomme, obviously rattled, said "Yes, there are schemes."[20] What he probably meant was that immediate prospects for enlarging the powers of the LCC and giving it the resources and administrative authority to co-ordinate plans for housing, street, and transportation development had been at least temporarily postponed by the defeat of the Progressives in the 1907 election and by the determination of the Moderate majority to put a cap on large-scale municipal enterprises.[21] On the other hand, there is no evidence that before 1907 the various elements within the Progressive coalition had ever worked out any practical resolution to the problem of how "dispersal" of population by means of some kind of municipal transit system could be reconciled with "the dream of a single London woven into one great municipal system."[22] Progressive municipalists wanted to retain the "concentrated big city" which steam technology had helped to create[23] and at the same time to put the working population on the move in electrified municipal tramcars. Those who responded to the rhetoric about making London into one "family" were not at all clear about who would be invited in and who left out. Was London to be a county, the administrative region defined by legislation in 1888, or was it to be Greater London? If the latter, how could even a more robust LCC act as the agency for implanting a sense of unity and commonality? Would a Greater London Council be the solution or would continued expansion make that body redundant also? How, in other words, could one grasp the ungraspable? To such questions as these, few municipal idealists had confident answers.

There was certainly no lack of discussion of these questions in the public forum. Some Edwardians deplored the rapid colonization of the countryside and blanched at the thought that a region a quarter of the size of Belgium was in the making, neither country nor city but a collection of scattered houses, workplaces, and shopping centers. But others welcomed the advent of such a post-urban world. H.G. Wells was one of them. He was delighted with the possibility that much of the south of England might eventually turn into a cluster of communities, "laced together" by motor vehicles and electrical communications, although he did admit that the transition process might be acutely uncomfortable. During that stage segregated arterial highways would indeed be built (at a decent interval after the Americans or Germans had led the way), but these super-highways would soon fill up and create "whirlpools of traffic" at every exit. He said that "any pensive Londoner" could observe this phenomenon at the intersection of Shaftesbury Avenue and Oxford Street, and "the wider the affluent arteries the more terrible the battle of traffic."[24] In time, however, the final stage "of a great development of centrifugal possibilities" would be reached. At that point London would have ceased to be a city in the conventional sense and have become a "great bazaar," serving one built-over region, stretching from the Highlands of Scotland southward. When that happened there would be no country and no city but instead, one huge, inhabited, artificial garden. Communication technology would then allow the residents of this "private *imperium*" to choose freely and frequently what style of life they wished. London would become merely one of those choices, to be resorted to whenever centrifugal man should wish to indulge in the "hot passion for the promenade."[25]

This was an extreme version of the "delocalization" solution to urban problems, a solution embraced by other Fabians and by such promoters of the Garden City concept as Raymond Unwin and Ebenezer Howard.[26] On the other hand, other late-Victorian and Edwardian visionaries refused to accept the premise that new communication technology must cause London to self-destruct, that the age of great cities was almost over. Lawrence Gomme was one of the most thoughtful and fervent of these. That "the future life of the people will be in cities" was the theme for all of the many secular sermons he preached.[27] The thought that the modern city was rediscovering its ancient role as the focus of identity and the carrier of civilization was his source of inspiration. Cities rather than nations or empires would, he believed, determine the future. It might even be, he wrote in 1914, that it was London's destiny to become "the capital city of the new world."[28]

This was more than merely high-flown rhetoric. What is interesting about Gomme's concept of the city was that it existed for him not so much as a place, fixed in time and space, but as a state of mind. Though born in London in 1853, he and his wife and children spent much of their time at a country house in Buckinghamshire where his father's family had its roots. Yet a more devoted Londoner than Lawrence Gomme it would be difficult to imagine. Immediately on finishing his education at the City of London School (H.H. Asquith was a schoolmate) he accepted a junior staff position at the Spring Gardens headquarters of the Metropolitan Board of Works and was still there, at a senior post, when the LCC was established in 1888. To the surprise of the newly elected Councillors, who expected nothing good out of the old regime, they found a nucleus of devoted staff who responded enthusiastically to the Progressive agenda.[29] The Council put Gomme in charge of preparing statistical and other evidence to present to parliamentary committees and then promoted him to the top administrative position, Clerk of the Council, in 1900. In 1911 he was knighted for these services. When he died in 1916, two years after his retirement, *The Times* obituary notice observed that "few men have had a more profound knowledge of the past and present greatness of London and few have done more to make London known to its people."[30]

What the notice writer was referring to was not just Gomme's career as a municipal administrator but as a historian and folklorist, although, in fact, all of his activities seem to have been of a piece; his approach to history was premised on his theories about prehistory, while his speeches and writings about all aspects of London's past gave direction to his efforts on behalf of a great variety of municipal enterprises. His public and domestic lives were equally intertwined since his wife, Alice Berthe Merck, was, as we have noted earlier, a prominent folklorist in her own right.

Gomme's interest in London's prehistory began after his connection with the Metropolitan Board of Works. At the age of 23 he collaborated with five others who shared his interest in making the collection of customs, rites, and myths more "scientific" to form the Folk-Lore Society.[31] What he and the others objected to was the unsystematic collecting of lore and the attempt to trace its antecedents to some generalized savage past, ignoring the fact that every cultural event has a "function" within a specific social structure and institutional framework specific to the original racial features of each ethnic group. Gomme believed that every custom, game, dance, superstition, law, or maxim that survived from the distant past originated in some actual event or everyday practice. Folklorists, he thought, were often so intent on relating what they found to some *mythos* that they do not bother with the "search for a *persona* or a *locus*."[32] The reward for undertaking that painstaking search from a fragmented, complex present to a preliterate, homogeneous, racially differentiated, distant past would be to discover the institutional antiquity of a culture. Consequently, he admonished his fellow searchers to begin at home. Londoners need not go to exotic places for their material since the long sequence of that city's past provided a clue to the peculiar meaning of the city's historical role in the life of the wider nation. The data, he pointed out, lay all about them, in sermons, maps, newspapers, legal records, criminal trials, old buildings, and the configuration, as well as the names, of so many of the streets. Speaking to a gathering of local government workers in 1913, he used old maps to show that Park Lane was developed along the end of the narrow acre strips of the ancient manor farm, which explains why that street had its peculiar zig-zag frontage.[33] For him, much of London had textual references of this kind; read with care, they would disclose the idea of the city as it evolved over the span of two empires. To put Londoners in touch with this living past would be to awaken a pride and sense of civic virtue the city had known under the Romans. This conviction explains why he admired William Morris, made friends with Charles Ashbee, and put endless labor into the project, sponsored by the LCC, to make a register of all buildings of historical or architectural interest in the city, especially those threatened with demolition.[34] In 1910 he published a list of outdoor memorials in the city which recalled historical events;

he also was partly responsible for persuading the LCC to fix plaques to the walls of buildings where famous Londoners had once lived. What the mindless pursuit of profit had rent asunder in the nineteenth century could, he thought, be put together by an awakening of pride in past glories. His constant theme was: London is not a collection of local loyalties, not a "province covered by houses," not a legal definition, not a circulatory system, and not a bazaar; it is an "idea," a way of life, a "method of civilization," a "monument to human progress."[35]

Gomme's conception of London as an idea disclosing itself and realizing itself through history[36] has obvious, though unspecified, origins in the idealist philosophy found in so much of the language of late Victorian and Edwardian New Liberalism. He believed the content of this idea to be a passion for civic virtue. It can be no accident that one of his seven sons, Arnold Wycombe Gomme, became a noted specialist on Thucydides,[37] the ancient historian who, through the voice of Pericles, praised Athens as the "school of Hellas." Any member of the large Gomme household would have been thoroughly instructed in the concept of the polis and the central part it once played in ancient Greece as an economic entity, a defined geographical place, and a communal organization in which "affairs are the affairs of all."[38] It was this ideal which Lawrence Gomme believed to be re-emerging in London after the lapse of centuries. In the new imperial relationship he believed was also evolving, London would again become "an institution *sui generis*," and its inhabitants would recover a Periclean sense of being a special people whose historical mission it was to become the school of Britain and her Empire, the model of what citizenship and civil life could be at their best, the example to their countrymen of how freeborn people can resist "tyrannical kings and bad citizens."[39] How this classical ideal could be applied to a sprawling city, with its millions living in separate class enclaves, he believed to be the greatest issue of the new century. Like his Progressive associates at Spring Gardens, he was impressed with how municipal governments in Birmingham and Glasgow were meeting that challenge and was unwilling to concede that the capital city was an anomaly. Unrestricted market forces had stretched the city out of shape, but that did not mean, he thought, that planning must forever be a futile exercise. Therefore, he rejected the Wellsian proposition that communication technology must inevitably shape the environment. It was his credo that great cities shape their own environments, develop their unique institutions and cultures, and create transportation systems to further those ends.

Gomme had been schooled in the art of the possible by a lifetime of behind the scenes struggles to expose inefficiencies and anomalies in the organization of the City Corporation and to defend LCC policies against attacks by Non-conformists who objected to paying rates for Anglican schools placed under county control. He was in a perpetual tug-of-war with vestries and borough councils who resisted street improvements and tramline extensions. Involved as he was with preparing LCC submissions and drafting legislation he had a more detailed knowledge than anyone else of the barriers the Salisbury ministry had placed in the way of municipal autonomy and of the tactics of ratepayer resistance organizations. Nevertheless, he shared with Fabians like Sidney Webb, socialists like John Burns, Progressivists like John Benn, a conviction that historical forces were tending toward collectivism and away from the *laissez-faire* state. Like so many liberals of the period, he sought a compromise between excessive interventionism and excessive individualism and thought he had found it in the utilitarianism of John Stuart Mill and in the "Municipal Idea." For a series of lectures on local government which he gave at the London School of Economics, he took Bentham's "great and simple words" as his theme: "The public good ought to be the object of the legislator; general utility ought to be the foundation of his reasonings."[40] Gomme recommended as an intermediate way Mill's application of that doctrine to the subject of natural monopolies. Starting with the assumption that individuals perform best in the ordinary business of life if left to their own devices, he would follow Mill's advice and limit governmental intervention to functions where, as in the case of clean water supply, the interest and judgement of consumers are insufficient to guarantee the goodness of an essential commodity or where, as in the case of education for children, a vital service cannot be performed adequately by uncontrolled private interests. Where such circumstances as these justify intervention, the prejudice should be in favor of local government, since it was apt to be the most directly responsive to public opinion and to constantly changing conditions. Nevertheless, this conception of what municipalities could legitimately undertake was highly elastic since, like Mill, he would include any enterprise that required a joint stock company form of organization, especially if that enterprise was necessary to maintain the general welfare. Here utility should be the guide. If the necessary service could not return a profit except at a cost which excluded the poorest members of the community, then the municipality had a responsibility to provide that service or at least to regulate it. He would also include in that category any service which might be supplementary to the exercise of some fundamental right – for example, a good system of public transport. The entire community benefited from having public transit, including members who never used it. To spare individuals who could afford to hire a private cab the pain of having to pay for a service they did not need, utility suggested that a municipal tramline require passengers to buy tickets and that it attempt to be self-supporting. Correspondingly, cab-riders should not object if income from tram fares were used to subsidize special low-cost tram tickets for less fortunate members of the community, since efficient means of moving about were necessary conditions for performing most communal functions. Guided by such principles, Gomme believed municipal services (usually referred to at the time as "municipal trading") might be extended without the lockstep of socialism or the waste and irresponsibility of uncontrolled free enterprise. It was time, he told his listeners, to jettison the term, "Municipal Socialism," or at least to tone down the "ignorant passion" that expression seemed always to stir up.[41]

Gomme's plea for calm and moderation came in 1897, at the time when resistance to LCC Progressivism was mounting and formal political battle lines had been drawn for a showdown between municipalization and the forces of free enterprise. How that struggle was carried out in the period before the Great War can be closely observed when, about 1905, the LCC's municipal tramways collided head-on with the privately-owned motor bus companies. By that time, the electrified tram had become not only a means of transportation but a symbol of the possibilities of municipal enterprise.

This connection between tramcars and civic-mindedness was first effectively made in Scotland, not London. Shortly after the city of Glasgow had taken over the running of the tramways in 1894, advocates of urban renewal, promoters of "national efficiency," and American Progressivists were making pilgrimages there to observe what they took to be an ideal industrial community in action. Most were impressed with how the transit authorities had managed at the same time to cut fares (one mile for ½d.) to the point where working people could afford to move to the suburbs and to improve the working conditions for tramway employees.[42] In addition, the tramcars seemed to run safely, on time, and at a profit. Supporters of civic planning and management took this success to be proof that a way had been found to control urban development without abandoning the free enterprise system. Because it so conspicuously served the general interest, the tramcar, splendidly embellished with the city's coat of arms, could be taken as a token of social harmony and class reconciliation.[43] At least this was the way "earnest Progressives" like Gomme[44] and more ideologically committed ones like John Benn, Sidney Webb,[45] and John Burns[46] understood the Glasgow experiment; they became convinced that it offered a way to "keep the municipal spirit alive"[47] and to revive "the old-time enthusiasm for a richer, fuller civic life."[48] Furthermore, it would be a practical way to convert London's congestion into an instrument of social reconstruction. Frederick Howe, an American supporter of municipal trading who wrote a book in 1907 about the lesson outsiders should draw from the Glasgow and London experience, said that the success of municipal enterprises should not be measured entirely by their financial record but also by their capacity to give ordinary citizens confidence that their city belonged to them. "Each day," Howe wrote, the trams "bring a sense of the city to the people."[49]

Parliament did not have such idealistic objects in mind when it passed legislation making municipal ownership of tramlines possible in 1870. Shaw-Lefevre explained that his Tramways Bill was simply intended to give the public more control over the tracks, already in the process of being laid down in their streets. Part of the control mechanism he introduced was a provision authorizing municipal authorities to construct tramways and to purchase, after twenty-one years, the stock of companies with leases to operate tramlines. It was not the intention of the bill that municipalities should undertake to manage their own operations.[50] Nevertheless, in less than twenty years they were beginning to do so, either because no private company was willing to meet the expense of the service required by the city or because private companies saw no reason to put up capital to convert from horse power to electricity, considering how short a time they might have to recover their investment. In turn, failure to make improvements provided ambitious municipalities with justification for becoming managers.[51] Leases began to expire in the 1890s; by 1905, about 60 percent of the nation's system was publicly owned and operated.

In 1892, after a bitter factional struggle, the LCC began acquiring, piece by piece, the various disconnected private tramline ventures which had penetrated into the inner suburbs from the north, south, and east but had been prevented by local authorities and the City Corporation from entering the central area.[52] This resistance, which continued in full force when the LCC labored to fit the pieces into a rational, cross-city pattern, came mainly from commercial interests and middle-class home-owners, who feared for their property values should the "cars," with their mainly working-class and lower-middle-class clientele, arrive on or near their doorsteps. John Burns, in particular, had caustic things to say about this anxiety to maintain the West End as "a close preserve for smart society" and how the "butterfly shopping class" (lower-middle-class women) preferred to ride on a bus rather than use a tram, "the workers' vehicle."[53] Improved carrying capacity, lower maintenance costs, and cheaper petrol in the 1920s allowed buses to match the lowest fares charged by trams and to pack in more passengers; but before that, women who chose not to enter the rush-hour scrum on the tram or be part of the press inside paid the slightly higher fare and took the bus. Thus, while the tram had thoroughly proletarian connotations from the beginning, the bus never found a secure place "in the order of things."[54]

The decision to change from horse power to electricity arrived on cue with the end of Victoria's reign (see Plate 19). It also nearly coincided with the arrival of a practical petrol-driven bus. When called to testify in 1903 and 1904 before the Royal Commission on Metropolitan Traffic, Gomme and most of the other witnesses were so intent on getting an endorsement for their tramway concept that they preferred to avert their eyes from the possibility that a rival was waiting in the wings. Commentators on the Commission's 1905 Report, however, were quick to point out that defect. John Pound, Director of the London General Omnibus Company, said that the introduction of a serviceable motor bus onto London streets was imminent; when this new technology appeared, it would render obsolete the "unwieldy and cumbersome tramcars," unless, of course, the LCC found ways to legislate it out of existence.[55] As it turned out development was even faster than Pound could have expected. In 1904 there were 31 self-propelled buses – steam, petrol, and electric; two years later there were 773, mostly petrol-driven. In 1908 three of the largest omnibus companies merged. In 1910 the first of the famous B-type, the "Old Bill," a double-decker seating thirty-four, was licensed. Between 1909 and 1913 numbers rose from 1,180 to 2,750.[56] The publicly-owned electric tram and its formidable rival, the privately-owned motor bus, now had the field of cheap transport to themselves. The horse omnibus, horse tram, and horse-drawn cab had all but disappeared. Horses were still needed to pull most of the commercial vans, small delivery carts, and the heavy coal, lumber, and brewery wagons, but the number of horses stabled in London had dropped from about half a million in 1905 to 110,000 in 1910.[57] (See Plate 20.)

The best source for learning about the contest between the two remaining forms of public surface transit and the doctrines they had each come to represent is the appendices of the Select Committee on Motor Traffic which Asquith appointed late in 1912. Ostensibly, the subject for its inquiry was a sharp increase in the number of accidents to pedestrians coincidental with the replacement of the horse. Between 1904 and 1908, when horse-pulled omnibuses and trams were fast disappearing, the proportion of accidents to population increased by 60 percent. At the beginning of that period there were 155 road deaths and 384 injuries and at the end, the death toll had risen to 537 and the number of injuries had doubled. Statistics showed that where traffic was heavy, buses killed more people than any other type of vehicle, while trams caused the highest number of injuries.[58] Taxis and private cars were already proving to be lethal on less crowded suburban streets where greater rates of speed were possible. Surprisingly, horse-drawn vehicles still headed the list as late as 1911 for both deaths and injuries.[59]

Serious though these findings were, there was a subtext underneath the discussion about the relative safety of various forms of transportation and about whether accidents were caused by fast-moving vehicles or by the carelessness of untrained pedestrians.[60] The safety issue, it was generally recognized by all interested parties, could be used to promote the merits of municipal socialism and to retard the ambitions of the private bus companies. The Liberal Government in power saw to it that most of the Select Committee members were sympathetic to the Progressive objective: to make a case for creating a Traffic Board, under LCC control, or at least sympathetic to its objectives.[61] Lawrence Gomme, John Burns, John Benn, Frederick Harrison, and their allies on the Committee, including Shirley Benn, Allen Baker (a Canadian businessman turned Progressive municipalist), and the Socialist, Will Thorne, wanted such a board to have the power and financial independence to assign heavily traveled routes, wherever possible, to the tramways, to close these routes to buses, and to use the bus system as a feeder to the trams, tubes, underground, and city railways. Responding to a question from a Committee member, Gomme stated the premise he believed any co-ordinating agency should adopt: "It seems to me a somewhat ridiculous position for a great city like London to be subject to the results of competition rather than the results of organisation."[62]

Tempers flared when the Committee members who were sympathetic to this point of view interviewed Sir Edward Henry, the Metropolitan Police Commissioner. Part of the Progressive agenda was to put London in charge of its own police force.[63] Integration, they believed, required that planners and enforcers be of the same mind. Henry, being aware that mines had been planted, tried to tread carefully, especially when he was asked if he thought it would be a good idea to give police the authority to keep certain types of vehicles to appointed lanes or to forbid them access to some routes. He answered that although the idea had obvious virtues, he would hate to put his men in the position of having to discipline the general public on the public street, where sentiment was so powerfully in favor of a high degree of individual freedom. When it was pointed out that the question had to do with buses and not pedestrians or private vehicles, he replied that the bus was "the poor man's vehicle." Was it fair, he asked, to forbid the use of a particular street to the poor man's conveyance while the rich man goes wherever he likes in his taxi?[64] Understandably, this question and this logic did not sit well with the questioners.

The Committee Report contained most of what Gomme and his

confederates at the Council wished to hear. The reaction of the motor interests was predictably indignant. The editorial writer for an engineering journal wrote that the behavior of the Committee was the strongest argument for an independent police force, one that could not be pressured by local politicians, especially those of Fabian persuasion. The dead weight of bureaucratic organization, he continued, particularly when applied to any new and developing technology, stifled innovation.[65] Besides, other motor interests argued, trams called for a much larger capital outlay than buses and were less flexible and therefore more obstructive to the flow of traffic. Trams were, they conceded, able to move larger volumes of traffic, but that would only be an asset, ironically, on those streets least able to accommodate two lines of tracks. Although it would have been difficult confidently to predict the outcome of this contest before the war, we, of course, know from our perspective which side eventually won. The last tramcar ran through the London streets in 1956, and long before that the double-decker bus had become the symbol of the British capital in the same way that the taxi had become the symbol of Paris. Eventually, in 1933, a Traffic Commission with powers to co-ordinate transportation facilities was finally set up, but the LCC only sent representatives and did not control it.

The dream of a harmonious urban entity brought to life by a rationally planned and organized system of publicly owned and managed transportation never did come true, although it continues to lie in the collective unconscious and occasionally surfaces. Since tram construction was a class issue, the hope that it might be a vehicle for class reconciliation was frustrated almost from the start.[66] This resistance and the great cost of subway construction in the dense city centre also help explain why the plan to knit, by means of street rails, the separate corporate interests and loyalties into one overriding interest and loyalty was never given a real trial. In retrospect, it does seem highly unlikely that any plan to facilitate travel could have contained the explosive centrifugal forces released by the era of mass automobile ownership.

A concerted effort of containment would have required agreement among reformers about ends. Instead, what planners, whether of the Gomme or Wolfe Barry variety, had in common was an indifference to the concept of the street as the Londoner's "only true Republic." Instead, there was a variety of aims. Benn, Webb, Burns, and Gomme wanted the LCC to become the citizen's "guardian angel,"[67] on the street and, it seemed, in almost every other public place. Wolfe Barry wanted streets engineered so that they would deny entry to some and direct the path of others. Bus operators and automobile lobbyists sponsored drives to teach pedestrians their place. Lord Montagu of

Beaulieu, who called himself the "leader of the Automobile party" in Parliament, and Sir John MacDonald, President of the Scottish Automobile Club, both wrote manuals instructing people who wished to cross streets that they must use their eyes, and not judge the nearness of oncoming vehicles by the clop of hoofs. They advised pedestrians that, when they did cross, they must proceed at a diagonal from the curb, facing traffic, and on reaching the center, make a right angle from there to the opposite side.[68]

Not everyone took kindly to all of this solicitude for their safety and general welfare; some were stirred to anger. Referring to the behavior of private motorists, G. Lowes Dickinson, a spokesman for the "New Liberalism," asked in 1906 why an entire nation needed to "groan under a public nuisance which increases every day until it has reached a malignity and magnitude altogether unprecedented." He thought it outrageous that street users should be exposed to material and moral danger "in order that a handful of rich men may indulge themselves freely in a particularly fatuous and ignoble sport." Is everything rapid progressive? Must every citizen who does not own a motor, he asked, "become a kind of outlaw on his own highway?"[69] The moral danger he was referring to was the loss of a sense of self-determination and the consequent loss of a sense of public responsibility; the material danger was more obvious and immediate. Testimony given in the 1913 Commission described how a bus driver, spotting tram customers waiting at the curb to board, would cut in between and fill his own vehicle instead or would harass unloading trams by passing on the inside, leaving "passengers no alternative but precipitous flight."[70]

People in such situations could, presumably, take comfort in the thought that the law still held them to be "virtually free agents." That they bravely continued to behave as though they were was a source of distress among law enforcers. As one police traffic specialist, Alker Tripp, pointed out, Londoners could not be treated as though they were, say, Berliners. It was a particularly onerous duty, he noted, with, one suspects, a mixture of ruefulness and pride, to be obliged to teach the disciplines required by motor traffic to "a people in which the sentiment of liberty is so ingrained and intolerance of authority so marked as is the case in this country."[71] A particular Edwardian gentleman who customarily crossed Fleet Street during morning rush hour while reading a copy of *The Times*, a cautionary figure to Lord Montagu, a celebrant of speed, might be regarded, instead, as a determined protector of a long and valuable tradition.

CONCLUSION

Between 1899 and 1905, years that marked the Progressive ascendancy at the London County Council, street reformers of the late Victorian and Edwardian era built a monument to their zeal and their aspirations, an avenue reaching for three-quarters of a mile from Holborn to the Strand.[1] Frederick Harrison took great pride in being, in 1891, the first to come forward with the proposal. He would cut a wide, straight path through what was usually referred to at the time as "congeries" of mean and squalid streets and alleyways in the slum areas around the old Clare Market; doing that would allow sunlight and the light of reason to enter and free the flow of traffic north from the Thames bridges. Harrison, the high priest of the positivist Religion of Humanity, rejoiced that an era of scientific management was dawning; its leaders would be sociologists who had "all their lives studied the Present and the Past with a view to transform them into the Future."[2] His colleagues, at Spring Gardens, including those who did not share his point of view, agreed that the project was needed. Pennethorne had drawn up plans in 1836 for a similar cross-town throughway, a proposal that the Metropolitan Board of Works had reconsidered in 1855 and the LCC in 1891, the majority concluding on these occasions that the reconstruction of so large and dense an area would be far too costly, considering that local government had few resources to draw on other than the hard-pressed ratepayer. There were others who objected to the clinical severity of the positivist aesthetic.[3] Was it not a part of the Metropolitan Ideal to bring beauty into the lives of people who had been robbed of it by the forces of unrestrained capitalist development? Did wide, straight lines express a truly democratic ideal? Was Harrison so intent on the future that he wished to obliterate all reminders of London's past?

Thanks largely to George John Shaw-Lefevre, who became Chairman of the Improvements Committee of the LCC in 1897, ways were found to secure the necessary financing and to work out compromise responses to these criticisms. When Parliament vetoed a request that the LCC be allowed to tap ground rents, that is, tax the owners of the land on which the rated buildings were constructed, Shaw-Lefevre saw another way out and got a majority on the Council to agree: he would condemn as much land along the rights of way as possible and lease it to governments and corporations interested in building along a grand avenue deliberately designed to convey prestige and power. Particularly if Parliament could be induced to guarantee loans on favorable terms, ratepayers might be spared all or most of the cost.[4] How a great "improvement" of this kind was to improve the daily lives of ordinary people who lived and worked in Holborn, the Seven Dials, and the region around Covent Garden, tended to be lost sight of or covered over by the assumption that any new housing arrangements the city could provide would have to be better than what already existed.

Shaw-Lefevre's resolution of the problem of how to give a straight, wide passageway aesthetic values was to build a crescent at the south end as a terminal feature so that the two symmetrical facades would have a *vista*; the crescent would also provide additional, and highly valuable, building land, thereby bringing in additional revenue. With all financial, social, and aesthetic obstacles seemingly overcome, the task began of purchasing property and clearing the right-of-way over some thirty-four acres, more than twice the space needed for the streets themselves. By the autumn of 1905 the works were deemed close enough to being finished and, on a bright day in October, King Edward VII came to give Kingsway and Aldwych their ceremonial opening. As usual on such occasions the event was loaded with symbolism, but because the project was conceived by a committee which encompassed a cluster of reform sentiments and priorities, the signifiers were necessarily mixed. Wanting to take advantage of the opportunity to display the LCC's many accomplishments, Shaw-Lefevre and his Improvements Committee invited 12,000 children from schools now under LCC control. Accordingly, the King's speech was written to include remarks about how the audience, like the streets, represented the future "of my Empire." On display was the magic of electricity, symbol of dynamic modernism and the energy behind the Metropolitan tramline that was being built in a shallow tunnel under the streets (see Plate 21). It powered the hoisting mechanism for drawing up the decorative gates across the broad avenue. C.M. Fitzmaurice, who took over from Alexander Binnie as chief engineer in 1901, had arranged with Chubb and Co., the famous locksmiths, to construct a pedestal, topped by an electric motor encased in a gilt ball. At the appropriate moment, this device, suspended on wires, would be lowered in front of where the King was to stand. He would then insert a golden key, closing the circuit, and up would go the gates. Everything went according to plan except that the King was so bemused that he forgot to declare the streets open. Also,

CONCLUSION

because the mechanism operated silently, only a few among the large gathering actually were aware of what was happening. How much more dignified and fitting it would have been, some thought, had there been the expected sounding of trumpets and ribbon cutting. The rest of the ceremony, however, proceeded on customary lines and to everyone's satisfaction. In his speech, the King expressed gratification that "superior accommodation" had been provided for 3,700 of his subjects who had been displaced by the construction and concluded by congratulating the city for having acquired this "perpetual memorial of the capacity and enterprise of your Council."[5]

Most editorials followed the lead given in a commemorative booklet Gomme had prepared for the occasion and welcomed this new north–south artery as the most important "improvement" since the opening of Regent Street in 1820. However, a leader writer in *The Builder* thought the comparison specious. For one thing, it ignored Haywood's much more challenging Holborn Viaduct; of greater importance, it ignored the sad fact that this latest addition to London's communication system was merely a "line of street improvement" carried out without any "complete and consistent design." By contrast, it had been Nash's great achievement to realize, from end to end of Regent Street, one "great architectural scheme."[6]

This criticism gradually achieved a near consensus, especially after the Conservative victory in the acrimonious 1907 municipal election campaign tended to tarnish almost everything that Progressivist zeal had accomplished. Disillusionment became more general when large investors took several years to respond to the offer of leaseholds, and much of Kingsway remained a naked swath. Sarcastic suggestions were frequently made about how this expensive "folly" might be put to use; one of these was to turn it into the world's largest municipal roller-skating rink.[7]

A decade of prosperity before the war did eventually attract government offices and large British, American, and Commonwealth corporations. By 1918 Kingsway was nearly filled out.[8] It had been Shaw-Lefevre's idea to have the distinguished architect, Norman Shaw, judge between eight invited contestants for an overall design. Perhaps that way, he thought, the speculative chaos which characterized the evolution of Shaftesbury Avenue and Charing Cross could be avoided.[9] Two thousand pounds in prize money was duly paid out, but nothing more was heard about the winning design; according to *The Builder*, "the less educated majority of the Council" out of "sheer commercial greed" had decided that any requirement obliging a builder to conform to some concept of "architectural dignity" would lower the leasehold values. The result was that every proposal was decided on an *ad hoc* basis, reflecting the changing political configurations and personalities of a committee of elected officials.

We would be mistaken, however, to assume that the Kingsway and Aldwych that evolved before 1914, and that have come down to us more or less intact, convey nothing sufficiently coherent to allow them to be read as a document in the history of Victorian and Edwardian street reform. For one thing, the overall design was the conscious choice of people who had the experience of half a century of street construction behind them, even though the concept they decided on was remarkable for its lack of originality. Like Pennethorne's New Oxford Street, it would be a rectilinear passageway whose visual values depended on Renaissance (or "Wrenaissance") perspective.[10] Also like that predecessor, its purpose would be to relieve traffic congestion at a particular bottleneck while acting, at the same time, as a form of slum clearance and social control. Ironically, however, there is no indication that any members of the LCC were thinking about how their north–south throughway might affect other urban arteries or that they envisioned it as one part of some comprehensive traffic plan. Over the whole Victorian era the need for a central planning agency had been a constant refrain; yet when London finally got one, and at a time when reformers were in an unusually strong position, the LCC constructed a new throughway with no more consideration of its effect on the whole urban organism than Pennethorne's Commissioners of Woods and Forests had given to the construction of New Oxford Street. That the LCC lacked sufficient powers to carry out systematic reconstruction, while not beside the point, fails to explain why visionaries had such restricted vision, or why they seemed to have learned so little over the course of seventy years.

One answer may be that many of them, John Burns and John Benn in particular, were far more interested in building a tramway system than a street or highway system; therefore, their eyes were fixed, not on the surface traffic Kingsway and Aldwych would bear, but on the tramline underneath. The obstacle in the way of a co-ordinated tramline network, as we have seen, was the expense and difficulty of carrying passengers through the central core. The American city of Boston, also with narrow streets and a dense central area, solved this problem by building shallow subways for tramcars, and New York was thinking of doing something similar. Benn got the LCC to send experts to America; when they gave the expected favorable report, Benn was able to get permission from Parliament to use the Holborn–Strand project as an experiment. Therefore a line, starting at the Angel in Islington, would connect with the Embankment by means of a subway under Kingsway and Aldwych. It opened for business early in 1906, using single-decked cars instead of the usual double-deckers, in order to save the cost of a deeper excavation. How an experiment which was to test the feasibility of joining all lines together in a network was to be carried out effectively by using cars designed for one link only was a contradiction noticed at the time. Neither as a solution to a specific congestion problem nor as one to a more systematic circulation problem was Kingsway a success. What is more, the reasons for this failure could have been predicted as easily by Haywood in the 1860s as by Wolfe Barry at the turn of the century.

A more fundamental contradiction was a lack of concern about the effects of the project on working-class communities. Given the genuine desire on the part of the Kingsway planners to make it possible for poor people to become healthier, better educated, and better able to enjoy the amenities of city life, it is surprising that their insensitivity to the consequences of breaking up neighborhoods was almost as great as any of their Victorian forerunners. Octavia Hill's experiments with rejuvenation rather than demolition had made little impression.

It has been noticed that Fabians, New Liberals, and other radicals shared with the existing establishment many similar social values and did what they could, as Chris Waters puts it, "to wed workers to a system of cultural preferences that was part of the dominant culture."[11] Some in the Progressive coalition had Charles Cochrane's belief in the innate goodness of most working-class people and assumed that if given an opportunity, they would choose to be clean, sober, moderate in their behavior, and high-minded in their tastes; but the prevailing attitude was that popular culture had been so debased by decades of brutal neglect that rescue and a thorough retraining would be required to prepare poor Londoners for the brighter future before them. One looks in vain for any sign of appreciation of the positive values of street and alley life. It was one of Shaw-Lefevre's proudest boasts, on the occasion of Kingsway's opening, that by acquiring so much slum property, his Committee was responsible for closing down fifty-one beerhouses and pubs and that the LCC had agreed to sacrifice revenue by stipulating that intoxicants could not be sold on the developed properties. The displaced families whom the Council moved to specially built housing in Millbank and on the site of Reid's Brewery in Clerkenwell would discover that their puritanical landlords expected them to be rational in their habits and choices of recreation.[12] Thus ironies abound. The defenders of the public interest against profit-hungry free enterprise agreed to a financing scheme which guaranteed that their streets would be given over to monopoly capitalism, and the poor Londoners these streets displaced were treated callously by elected officials who were determined to give them richer and fuller lives.

At least one journalist in 1905 wondered what Lawrence Gomme, the author of the commemorative booklet about the history of the project and its setting, must have thought about the finished product.[13] Would this "accomplished archaeologist," if released from the self-denying ordinance required by his position as Clerk of the Council, be likely to echo his pamphlet's rhetoric about how London acquired a monument to civic dignity, an architectural amenity worthy of comparison with Regent Street? How must he really have felt about so much demolition of ancient buildings, churches, and graveyards in an area of the city so rich in historic associations?[14] These questions should have troubled all preservationists on the Council – not a small or inconsequential group – but it was Gomme who had written so much and spoken so often about how the sense of being inheritors of a glorious past could give the citizens of a constantly expanding city a kindred feeling and knit them together into one family. His comment on past styles had demonstrated a fondness for the picturesque and a distaste for the excessively orderly and rational. On the other hand his sympathy with the Progressive agenda was so obvious that only the respect everyone felt for his dedication and erudition protected him from partisan attack.[15] Involved as he was in the struggle to protect and advance the Municipal Idea, he would not have wished his reservations to get in the way of one of that ideal's most significant victories.

It is fitting that Gomme, the historian, did what he could to preserve some record of the past by having photographers and artists hired to record the frontages of buildings about to be destroyed and to make detailed drawings of particularly interesting interior details. He also solved the controversy about what names would be most appropriate for streets intended to have clear symbolic meaning. Discussion on this issue lasted for over a year. Practical businessmen on the Council proposed "Connecticut Avenue," presumably because they believed this compliment to the United States might attract American investors and encourage the growing influx of American tourists, many of whom stayed in the grand hotels on or near the Strand. "Broadway" was another suggestion along the same lines. This was the one Max Beerbohm pretended to favor; he said he liked the modern, New York sound of it; being unhistorical, clinically descriptive, impersonal, and antiseptic, it perfectly bespoke the city London was, regrettably, in the process of becoming.[16] Concern about "Americanization" provoked all manner of patriotic feelings. The task of clearing the path for the streets began just as the Boer War broke out; while excavation and construction were underway, Britain signed a naval agreement with Japan, made the *Entente cordiale* with France, and began realigning her relationship with Russia. The completion date for the streets coincided with the quickening of the naval race with Germany. The apprehension

CONCLUSION

of impending conflict called, some believed, for an assertion of national pride and imperial dynamism but expressed in such a way that civic dignity might not be lost sight of. To satisfy all of these requirements was no simple matter. Gomme found a way by turning to ancient maps. They showed that the crescent street bordering the Strand was being constructed on the site, first occupied by a Roman encampment, of a Danish settlement called Aldwych. Maps also indicated that approximately along the line of the new avenue, a road had once connected Holborn with Theobalds, the palace of King James I. Therefore, one street, Kingsway, would pay compliment to the long continuity of throne and nation, while the other, Aldwych, would remind Londoners of the long continuity of their city. Needless to say, all factions in Council came together, gave a unanimous vote of agreement, and thanked Gomme for finding so judicious a solution.[17]

Even now, almost a century later, the strains of *Pomp and Circumstance* still linger along the entire length of that "boring" and unlovable corridor.[18] This connection with Edwardian imperialism gives Kingsway character; the street is not generic and meaningless. We are reminded of past glories and long extinguished aspirations. But one is not inclined to linger in order to savor this atmosphere; Kingsway is not and never was a place that attracted strollers or lovers or prostitutes, for that matter. Except where Aldwych meets the Strand, there is little that the eye rests on comfortably or for long. Ever-mindful of the need to give Londoners lungs, Shaw-Lefevre was able to secure £825 to plant a row of plane trees on both sides of the street, but for some reason they were a long time growing. Some highly unscientific testing discloses that it is the rare Londoner who can recollect today whether Kingsway has trees or not. Crossing the sixty-foot expanse of roadway is a particularly risky and unpleasant experience. The tunnel has long been boarded up; traffic at rush hours is dense, and the air is unpleasant to breathe. Waiting for a bus there seems interminable.

Such a litany of shortcomings compels the listener to wonder about reasons why. Was it a failure of imagination, a fault in conception, meagerness of financial resources, or should responsibility be extended more widely to the culture in general? As we have seen, there was a long tradition of criticism which identified the insularity of the English people as the determinant of the urban artifact. The English man and woman, the argument goes, valued interior spaces and lavished wealth and affection there. At the same time, class consciousness made close proximity in public distasteful. Thus London ladies and gentlemen could enjoy the gregariousness of Parisian street life because the mixture on the boulevards was foreign; at home they would have been part of the mixture and would have felt embarrassed and uncomfortable. A professor of architecture, Beresford Pite, was inclined to believe that it was this "absence of unity of feeling" which explained why, in his generation, the dreary best street designers could do was Shaftesbury Avenue, Charing Cross Road, and the newly-opened Kingsway.[19]

Compelling though generalizations about the "inward-looking quality of London"[20] may be, they suffer from the disadvantages inherent in all sweeping statements about national or civic character. Nevertheless, this is a more satisfactory explanation than the administrative and economic ones that have been offered. It was Sidney Webb's confident assertion that jerry-builders had been allowed to shape London because Parliament had refused to give municipal authorities the finances and power to plan and control.[21] But on this one occasion Parliament did give the LCC the opportunity to build something extensive and expressive of their urban ideal. Fabians and New Liberals, most of them ardent democrats and many of them experienced preservationists and green space advocates, did the planning for Kingsway and approved the design. It was true, of course, that they lacked the windfalls and special circumstances that allowed Regent Street, Holborn Viaduct, and the Embankment to be carried through on a generous scale, but it is obvious from the attitude they took toward the people and buildings they displaced that, even if Parliament had allowed them to tax the surplus profit of ground landlords, they would never have given London an attractive promenade or anything approximating a *grand boulevard*.

The builders of Kingsway would not have wanted the avenue they created to be shaped by the culture of the people whose lives they had disrupted or the character of the streets they had destroyed. They could see no redeeming value in narrow, run-down Wych Street with its cluster of sixteenth-century gabled houses and were positively delighted to obliterate picturesque Holywell Street, with its "narrow squalid cavalcade of books, many of them of a faintly scurrilous nature."[22] Down went the pubs, and down, with hardly a quaver, went Lyons Inn, the Opera Comique, and the Strand, Olympic, and Globe Theatres. Clinicians that they were, they could see little worth saving, even as references and reminders, in streets that many centuries of use had evolved. Instead they constructed a passageway that people would hurry through on their way to somewhere else, an artery in a "communicational node" instead of a vital public space within a great city.

Still, there are some signs, a century later, that the process of absorbing or recolonizing the work of this imperialist intruder may have begun. Some of the scar tissue has begun to fade, especially along the northern third of the street. Trees do indeed grow along the entire length. In the freshness of early June, starting south from Holborn tube station, one has a fleeting sense of being about to enter a leafy

CONCLUSION

bower. The way leads, keeping to the east side, through what was a decade or so ago barely the germ of a market: a display of newspapers and a small flower stall. Now, as far as Twyford Place, something only a little short of a full-fledged street market has grown up. Set back on Gate Street under an orange umbrella is an orderly display of fruit and vegetables. Tucked away behind a glittering array of costume jewelry and racks of cotton T-shirts and denim shorts is a tiny book stall. On the periphery are several places to sit outside and have a coffee or an ice-cream. Across the street, in front of the forbiddingly slick and shiny shop and office facings, hot baked potatoes in their jackets may be had, and it is possible to sit down and eat them while reading an *Evening Standard*, bought, a few steps away, from a tiny sparrow of a lady who has been at her post, just south of the corner of Parker Street, "since '43, when mother died, God rest her soul." Nearby, above the once-handsome porch of an Anglican church, built in 1910, an inscription invites the passer-by to "Enter Rest and Pray," although nothing human has entered through the rotting doors with their two large, flat Victorian-looking padlocks for many years. Street people sleep rough in the oval shelter before those doors amidst flattened lager cans, foraging pigeons, and assorted decaying matter. The spirit of Dickens, perhaps, has attached to the wall on one side a crude sign reading "Loaves and Fishes."

Thus Lawrence Gomme's faith in the ability of this ancient city to reassert its sense of self may not have been quite so fanciful as it seems. What is striking about the long effort to relieve congestion and control the teeming flux is the strength London seems to be able eventually to summon in order to recover from the injuries it has inflicted on itself in the name of reform, efficiency, rationality, sanitation, improvement, development, modernization, or some other term of explanation or justification.

It is by no means certain, however, that this reclaiming and healing process can continue into the next century. Only a few years after Kingsway was built, the petrol engine won a clear victory over electric propulsion and eventually gave anarchy and dehumanization a destructive force surpassing anything Victorians or Edwardians had to reckon with, even taking into account the wounds inflicted by the arrival of the steam railway. Neither did the social web during the nineteenth and early twentieth centuries have to withstand the rending effects of corporate and public bureaucracies capable of generating such massive regional "regeneration" schemes as Canary Wharf or the proposed King's Cross mega-project. The story of nineteenth-century reform contains a lesson Londoners, indeed urban dwellers everywhere, would do well to consider: that supposedly "blighted" street complexes contain people who have, over time, made their passageways into places. "Improvements" worthy of the name must be sensitive to those local cultures and incorporate what is healthy and attractive in them. Then, given London's remarkable recuperative powers, change might actually benefit those who live and work near "that mighty heart."

NOTES

INTRODUCTION

1 Ferdinand Braudel, *On History*, Chicago, 1980, p. 27.

1 IMAGINING

1 Samuel Osherson and L. A. Singham, "The Machine Metaphor in Medicine," in Elliot Mishler, *et al.* (eds), *Social Contexts of Health, Illness and Patient Care*, Cambridge, 1981, p. 218.
2 Robert Schofield, *Mechanism and Materialism*, Princeton, 1970, p. 54; Bryan Turner, *The Body and Society*, Oxford, 1984, pp. 77–80.
3 John O'Neill, *Five Bodies*, Ithaca, NY, 1985, p. 51.
4 Mary Douglas, *Purity and Danger*, London, 1966.
5 Earl of Halsbury, *The Laws of England*, London, 1911, vol. 16, pp. 16–21.
6 W. J. Loftie, *In and Out of London*, London, 1875, pp. 15, 23.
7 E. Cook and A. Wedderburn (eds), *The Works of John Ruskin*, London, 1907, vol. 19, p. 24.
8 Max Byrd, *London Transformed*, New Haven, Conn., 1978, pp. 14–15.
9 [A. Wynter], "How Our Millions Circulate," *Once a Week*, 1866, vol. 2, p. 234.
10 Laurence Sterne, *Tristram Shandy*, vol. 1, ed. Anderson, New York, 1980, p. 33; commented on in Byrd, *Transformed*, p. 5. See also Louis Landa, "London Observed: The Progress of a Simile," *Philological Quarterly*, 1975, vol. 54, pt. 1, pp. 275–88.
11 John Glynn, *London and Westminster Improved*, London, 1766, p. 16.
12 Frederick Cartwright, *A Social History of Medicine*, London, 1977, pp. 122–3.
13 William Buchan, *Domestic Medicine*, London, 1827, pp. 67–72, 111–14, 299–300.
14 Margaret Pelling, *Cholera, Fever and English Medicine*, Oxford, 1978, pp. 36–7.
15 H. J. Dyos, "Greater and Greater London," in D. Cannadine and D. Reeder (eds), *Exploring the Urban Past*, Cambridge, 1982, p. 40; Ken Young and Patricia Garside, *Metropolitan London*, London, 1982, pp. 4–21.
16 Alexander Welsh, *The City of Dickens*, Oxford, 1971, pp. 23, 37; Byrd, *Transformed*, pp. 142–51; O'Neill, *Bodies*, pp. 51, 68; Donald MacRae, "Body, as Social Metaphor," in J. Benthall and T. Polhemus (eds), *The Body as a Medium of Expression*, London, 1975; Barrie Greenbie, *Spaces: Dimensions of the Human Landscape*, New Haven, Conn., 1981, pp. 119–20; Graeme

Davison, "The City as a Natural System," in D. Fraser and A. Sutcliffe (eds), *The Pursuit of Urban History*, London, 1983, pp. 362–70.
17 Douglas, *Purity*, p. 4.
18 The geography of Regency London is described by William Connor Sydney, *The Early Days of the Nineteenth Century: 1800–1820*, London, 1898, esp. vol. 1 (of 2), pp. 112–26.
19 *Illustrated London News*, 31 October, 1846.
20 A. D. Morgan, "Some Forms of Undiagnosed Coronary Diseases in Nineteenth Century England," *Medical History*, 1968, vol. 12, pp. 344–58.
21 *Punch*, 1846, vol. 11, p. 114.
22 John Cantlie, *Degeneration Among Londoners*, London, 1885, p. 24.
23 Peter Brimblecomb, *The Big Smoke*, London, 1987, pp. 39–62.
24 Cantlie, *Degeneration*, p. 33; Isaac Burney Yeo, M. D., "On Change of Air," *Nineteenth Century*, London, 1889, vol. 26, pp. 194–207.
25 *Letters of Charles Lamb*, E. V. Lucas (ed.), London, 1935, vol. 1, pp. 241, 244.
26 Quoted in Joel Richmond, *Traffic Wardens*, Manchester, 1983, p. 129.
27 Isaiah Berlin, *Two Concepts of Liberty*, Oxford, 1958, pp. 7–16.
28 A theme of Richard Sennett's, *The Fall of Public Man*, New York, 1977.
29 J. G. Harding, "Walks in London," *The True Briton*, 1851, vol. 1, p. 6.
30 Susan Davis, *Parades and Power*, Philadelphia, 1986, pp. 13–14.
31 Harold Clunn, *The Face of London*, London, 1932, pp. 7–8.
32 H. G. Wells, *Anticipations*, London, 1905, p. 51.
33 F. M. Hueffer, *The Soul of Modern London*, London, 1905, pp. 8–9, 24, 159–62.
34 Clunn, *Face*, p. 8.
35 *Saturday Review*, 1866, vol. 21, p. 257.
36 H. J. Dyos, "Street Improvements in Regency and Early Victorian London," in Cannadine and Reeder (eds), *Exploring*, pp. 85–6.

2 STRAIGHTENING

1 *Guardian*, 14 May, 1990, p. 2.
2 *Punch*, 1846, vol. 11, p. 217.
3 ibid., 1845, vol. 9, p. 163.
4 John Wolfe Barry, *Address*, London, 1899, pp. 7, 12–13, 21.
5 ibid., pp. 16, 18–19.
6 Hansard, 1860, vol. 158, col. 745.
7 Arthur Cawston, *A Comprehensive Scheme For Street Improvement in London*, 1893, vol. 7, pp. 13, 27–8.
8 ibid., pp. 49–50.
9 George John Shaw-Lefevre, "London Street Improvements," *Contemporary Review*, 1899, vol. 75, pp. 203–17.
10 Donald Olsen, *The City as a Work of Art*, New Haven, Conn., 1986, pp. 29–34.
11 John Summerson, *The Life and Work of John Nash, Architect*, Cambridge, Mass., 1980, p. 132.
12 H. J. Dyos, "Urban Transformation," *International Review of Social History*, 1957, vol. 2, pp. 259–65; Henry Jephson, *The Sanitary Evolution of London*, London, 1907, p. 29; Sidney Smirke, *Suggestions for the Architectural Improvement of the Western Part of London*, London, 1834, p. 57.
13 T. C. Barker and M. Robbins, *A History of London Transport*, London, 1963, vol. 1, pp. 64–5.

NOTES

14 *Saturday Review*, 1867, vol. 24, p. 309.
15 ibid., 1866, vol. 21, p. 257.
16 *Times*, 29 April, 1867, p. 8; 15 August, 1867, p. 8.
17 Barker and Robbins, *London Transport*, vol. 1, p. 65; John Timbs, *Walks and Talks about London*, London, 1865, p. 290.
18 *Engineering*, 1869, vol. 8, p. 10; Harold Clunn, *The Face of London*, London, 1932, p. 72.
19 John Davis, *Reforming London*, Oxford, 1988, pp. 55–6.
20 David Owen, *The Government of Victorian London*, Cambridge, Mass., 1982, p. 241.
21 *Minutes and Proceedings of the Institution of Civil Engineers*, 1894, vol. 67, p. 376.
22 *Times*, 14 April, 1894, p. 7.
23 ibid., 25 October, 1849, p. 4; Royston Lambert, *Sir John Simon*, London, 1963, pp. 118, 134–6, 138–9, 186–90.
24 *Times*, 14 April, 1894, p. 7; *Dictionary of National Biography*, vol. 22 (suppl.); *Report of the Works Executed by the Commissioners of Sewers of the City of London During the Year 1851*, 1852, and ibid., 1852–3, 1854; Henry Tomkins, *Report Upon the Pavements in Use in the Metropolis*, London, 1872, p. 7; Charles Welch, *The History of the Worshipful Company of Paviors of the City of London*, London, 1932, p. 34, and his *Modern History of the City of London*, London, 1896, p. 403.
25 *Times*, 8 November, 1869, p. 8.
26 *Builder*, 24 April, 1869, p. 320.
27 William Hardman, *A Mid Victorian Pepys: Letters and Memoirs*, ed. S. M. Ellis, 1923, p. 234.
28 Clunn, *Face*, pp. 72–5.
29 *Builder*, 20 November, 1869, p. 930.
30 *Engineering*, 1869, vol. 8, p. 339.
31 ibid., pp. 421, 424.
32 *Proceedings of Civil Engineers*, 1894, vol. 67, p. 376.
33 William Haywood, *Traffic Improvements in the Public Ways of the City of London*, London, 1866, pp. 67–9, 79.
34 A. C. David, "Innovations in Street Architecture in Paris," *Architectural Record*, August 1908, vol. 24, p. 111
35 Haywood, *Traffic*, p. 67. For evidence that he not always practised what he preached see Owen, *Government*, p. 382, fn. 25.
36 *Times*, 31 July, 1868, p. 12.
37 Avner Offer, *Property and Politics*, Cambridge, 1981, pp. 171–2; Joseph Firth, *The Coal and Wine Dues*, London, 1886, pp. 3–12.
38 *Times*, 20 July, 1824, p. 2; Felix Barker and Ralph Hyde, *London as it Might Have Been*, London, 1982, pp. 82–6.
39 Hansard, 1825, vol. 12, col. 1029.
40 Barker and Hyde, *London*, pp. 136–40; George Chadwick, *The Works of Sir Joseph Paxton*, London, 1961, pp. 206–12.
41 Select Committee (S.C.) on Metropolitan Communications, 1854–1855, vol. 10, qs 716–17.
42 ibid., q. 711.
43 ibid., q. 814.
44 Violet Markham, *Paxton and the Bachelor Duke*, London, 1935, p. 278.
45 Hansard, 1862, vol. 167, col. 1473.
46 Paxton's name is only mentioned once in passing in David Owen's

comprehensive treatment of how the Embankment came to be constructed: *Government*, ch. 4.
47 S. C. on Turnpike Trusts, 1864, vol. 9, q. 2958.
48 Repr. in *Times*, 15 November, 1866, p. 10.
49 *Illustrated London News*, 1865, vol. 46, p. 601.
50 Thomas Holmes, *London's Underworld*, London, 1813, pp. 52–63, 230.
51 John Stokes, *In the Nineties*, Chicago, 1989, pp. 139–43. For a discussion of how the Embankment was treated in Edwardian drama, see Sheila Stowell, *A Stage of Their Own*, Manchester, 1991, pp. 139–43.
52 See C. Alexander, S. Ishikawa, and M. Dilerstein, *A Pattern Language*, New York, 1977, pp. 168–73.
53 Owen, *Government*, p. 96.
54 Harold Clunn, *London Rebuilt 1897–1927*, London, 1927, pp. 115–19.
55 George Sala, "Locomotion in London," *The Gentleman's Magazine*, January–June, 1874, vol. 12, p. 464.
56 Walter Creese, *The Search for Environment*, New Haven, Conn., 1966, p. 50.
57 Max Beerbohm, "The Naming of Streets," *Pall Mall Magazine*, 1902, vol. 26, p. 139.
58 Creese, *Search*, pp. 77–90.
59 "Which is the Most Interesting London Street?", *Strand Magazine*, 1907, vol. 34, pp. 314–22.

3 SMOOTHING AND REGULATING

1 Henry Gordon, *Some Aspects of Metropolitan Road and Rail Transit*, London, 1919, p. 62.
2 *Proceedings of the Institution of Civil Engineers*, 1886, vol. 87, pp. 456–7.
3 ibid., 1866–7, vol. 26, p. 106.
4 S. C. on London (City) Traffic Regulation Bill, 1866, vol. 12, qs 539–42; *Engineer*, 1 December, 1868, pp. 439–40.
5 *Engineer*, 1 December, 1868, pp. 439–40; *Builder*, 19 December, 1868, p. 926.
6 *Engineer*, 18 December, 1868, p. 467.
7 ibid., January–June, 1869, vol. 27, p. 66; *Times*, 9 December, 1868, p. 5; *Engineering*, July–December, 1868, vol. 6, p. 537.
8 ibid., p. 66; *Builder*, 9 January, 1869, p. 28.
9 *Engineer*, 22 January, 1869, vol. 27, p. 62.
10 H. Alkar Tripp, *Road Traffic and its Control*, Roadmakers' Library, London, 1938, vol. 7, p. 252; J. F. Moylan, *Scotland Yard and the Metropolitan Police*, London, 1929, p. 252.
11 John Hollingshead, *Today, Essays and Miscellanies*, London, 1865, vol. 1, p. 125; George Turnbull, "Pavements," in Walter Besant, *London in the 19th Century*, London, 1909, p. 341.
12 W. T. Jackman, *The Development of Transportation in Modern England*, New York, Kelly repr., 1970, pp. 232–3; Francis Sheppard, *Local Government in St. Marylebone, 1688–1835*, London, 1958, pp. 55–6.
13 William Haywood, *Traffic Improvements in the Public Ways of the City of London*, London, 1866, pp. 33–4, 39.
14 Edward Flower, *The Stones of London*, London, 1880, pp. 4–5.
15 Alan Stapleton, *London Alleys, Byways and Courts*, London, 1924, pp. 3–4.
16 Turnbull, "Pavements," p. 341; Hollingshead, *Today*, vol. 2, p. 125.
17 Earl of Halsbury, *The Laws of England*, London, 1911, vol. 16, pp. 16–21.
18 Sheppard, *Local Government*, pp. 131–200.

NOTES

19 Frederick Paget, *Report on the Economy of Road-Maintenance and Horse-Draught through Steam-Rolling*, London, 1870, pp. 4–5; P. Le Neve Foster, *Report on the Application of Science and Art: Street Paving and Street Cleansing of the Metropolis*, London, 1875, p. 3.
20 Paget, *Report*, p. 4.
21 ibid., p. 24.
22 Henry Tomkins, *Report upon the Pavements in Use in the Metropolis*, London, 1872, pp. 1–13.
23 William Haywood, *Report on the Accidents to Horses on Carriageway Pavements*, London, 1873, pp. 17–72.
24 See, for example, Henry Tomkins, *The Pavements of London*, London, 1874, pp. 3–16.
25 S. C. on Metropolitan Traffic, 1867, vol. 11, qs 309–11.
26 Sheppard, *Local Government*, pp. 193–200.
27 John Hollingshead, *Underground London*, London, 1862, p. 208; *Builder*, 6 October, 1860, p. 640.
28 *Engineer*, 15 October, 1869, vol. 28, p. 261.
29 Geoffrey Warren, *Vanishing Street Furniture*, Newton Abbot, 1978, pp. 10–11.
30 *Engineer*, July–December, 1868, vol. 26, p. 440.
31 *Times*, 14 February, 1867, p. 7.
32 ibid., 14 March, 1867, p. 9.
33 ibid., 29 April, 1867, p. 8.
34 Haywood, *Traffic*, p. 111.
35 *Times*, 29 April, 1867, p. 8.
36 See Fairman Ordish, "The History of London Traffic," in Appendix H, R. C. on London Traffic, 1906, vol. 4, pp. 887–96.
37 Metropolitan Pavement Act, 1817, 57 Geo. III, c. XXIX.
38 Metropolitan Police Act, 1839, 2 & 3 Vict., c. 47, pp. 291–2.
39 ibid.
40 Springett v. Ball, 1865; Halsbury, *Laws*, 1911, vol. 21, p. 416.
41 Tripp, *Road Traffic*, pp. 58–9, 100.
42 George Hooper, "Carriage Building and Street Traffic in England and France," *Journal of the Society of Arts*, 1890, vol. 38, p. 478; for another version see Robert Mahaffy and Gerald Dodson, *The Law Relating to Motor Cars*, London, 1910, pp. 141–2.
43 Halsbury, *Laws*, 1911, vol. 27, pp. 412–13; George Henry Oliphant, *The Law of Horses*, 6th edn, London, 1908, pp. 316, 342–3.
44 Charles Dickens, "The Dangers of the Streets," *All the Year Round*, 1866, vol. 15, p. 156.
45 John Moylan, *Scotland Yard and the Metropolitan Police*, London, 1929, pp. 242–3.
46 ibid.
47 Hollingshead, *Today*, vol. 2, p. 139.
48 Haywood, *Traffic*, p. 40.
49 Hollingshead, *Today*, pp. 146–7; S. C. on London (City) Traffic Regulation Bill, 1866, vol. 12, qs 7–262; S. C. (House of Lords) on Traffic Regulation (Metropolis) Bill, 1867, vol. 11, qs 6–245.
50 Public Records Office (PRO), Metropolitan Police Papers (MEPO), I, 47, 21 July, 1868.
51 Hansard, 1867, vol. 189, cols 1527–30.
52 ibid., 1867, vol. 190, cols 170–1.
53 Hooper, "Carriage," p. 479; Moylan, *Scotland Yard*, p. 246.

LONDON'S TEEMING STREETS 1830-1914

54 Hansard, 1873, vol. 216, cols 995–6.
55 Moylan, *Scotland Yard*, p. 247; S. C. on Motor Traffic, 1913, vol. 8, p. 4; *Guardian*, 25 October, 1990, p. 22.
56 Lawrence Gomme, *London in the Reign of Victoria 1837–1898*, London, 1898, p. 20.
57 R. C. on London Traffic, 1905, vol. 30, pp. 671–2, 633, 642–3.
58 F. M. L. Thompson, *Victorian England: The Horse-Drawn Society*, London, 1970, p. 12.

4 POLICING

1 S.C. on the Police of the Metropolis, 1834, vol. 16, pp. 4–6, 13.
2 S.C. on Cold Bath Fields, 1833, vol. 13, qs 4748–69, 4760–6.
3 Leon Radzinowicz, *A History of Criminal Law and its Administration from 1750*, London, 1968, vol. 4, pp. 180–3; Gavin Thurston, *The Clerkenwell Riot*, London, 1967.
4 S.C. on the Petitition of F. Young and Others, 1833, vol. 13, pp. 409–11.
5 ibid., p. 87.
6 ibid., qs 3917, 3919, 3893–5.
7 *Times*, 29 December, 1868, p. 6.
8 Harold Scott, *Scotland Yard*, London, 1954, p. 17.
9 G. Dilnot, *Scotland Yard*, London, 1929, p. 87.
10 Norman Gash, *Mr Secretary Peel*, London, 1961, pp. 498–9; *Times*, 29 December, 1868, p. 6; Geoffrey Cobb, *The First Detectives*, London, 1957, p. 12; Stanley Palmer, *Police and Protest in England and Ireland*, Cambridge, 1988, pp. 294–6; R. C. Mayne, *Four Years in British Columbia*, London, 1862.
11 Timothy Cavanagh, *Scotland Yard*, London, 1893, pp. 75, 77–9.
12 S.C. on the Police of the Metropolis, 1834, vol. 16, qs 106–8.
13 Henry Smith, *From Constable to Commissioner*, London, 1910, p. 194; William Ballentine, *Some Experiences of a Barrister's Life*, 6th edn, London, 1882, p. 275.
14 Wilber Miller, "Police Authority in London and New York," *Journal of Social History*, 1975, vol. 8, p. 92.
15 S.C. on the Petitition of F. Young and Others, 1833, vol. 13, qs 3997, 3999.
16 ibid., qs 4001–7.
17 Wilber Miller, *Cops and Bobbies*, Chicago, 1977, p. 180, fn. 16; Radzinowicz, *Criminal*, vol. 4, pp. 184–9.
18 Scott, *Scotland Yard*, p. 17.
19 David Goodway, *London Chartism*, Cambridge, 1982, p. 99.
20 S.C. on the Police of the Metropolis, 1834, vol. 16, q. 6282.
21 [A Working Man], *Scenes from My Life*, London, 1858, pp. 29–33.
22 ibid., pp. 30–3.
23 See Jerry White, *The Worst Street in North London*, London, 1986, pp. 114–15.
24 S.C. on the Police of the Metropolis, 1834, vol. 16, q. 6235; Radzinowicz, *Criminal*, vol. 4, pp. 174–5.
25 S.C. on the Police of the Metropolis, 1834, vol. 16, q. 4183; S.C. on the Sale of Beer, 1st Report, 1854–5, vol. 10, qs 1361, 1366.
26 Miller, *Cops*, pp. 32–44.
27 S.C. on the Police of the Metropolis, 1834, vol. 16, qs 154–5, 342.
28 ibid., q. 433.
29 S.C. on Cold Bath Fields, 1833, vol. 13, qs 668–9.
30 S.C. on the Police of the Metropolis, 1834, vol. 16, q. 433.

NOTES

31 V. A. C. Gatrell, "The Decline of Theft and Violence in Victorian and Edwardian England," in V. Gatrell, B. Lenman, and G. Parker (eds), *Crime and the Law: The Social History of Crime in Western Europe since 1500*, London, 1980, pp. 265–72; Philip Smith, *Policing Victorian London*, Westport, Conn., 1984, pp. 27–9.
32 Jennifer Davis, "The London Garotting Panic of 1862," in Gatrell, Lenman and Parker (eds), *Crime and the Law*, p. 199.
33 ibid., pp. 190–213.
34 R.C. on Penal Servitude, 1863, vol. 21, qs 1580–3.
35 Peter Bartrip, "Public Opinion and Law Enforcement," in Victor Bailey (ed.), *Policing and Punishment in Nineteenth Century Britain*, London, 1981, pp. 166–73.
36 Davis, "Garotting," pp. 191–9, 204–9.
37 R. C. on Penal Servitude, 1863, vol. 21, qs 1686, 1715, 1763, 1766, 1778.
38 See, for example, *Times*, 5 June, 1867, p. 12; 6 November, 1868, p. 6; 1 December, 1868, p. 6; Gareth Stedman Jones, *Outcast London*, Harmondsworth, 1976, pp. 241–3.

5 ENJOYING

1 M. H. Dziewicki, "In Praise of London Fog," *The Nineteenth Century*, 1889, vol. 26, pp. 1047–1055.
2 Thomas Burke, *The Streets of London*, London, 1940, pp. 136, 138.
3 Of the many works on rational recreation see especially: Peter Bailey, *Leisure and Class in Victorian England*, London, 1987 ed; Hugh Cunningham, *Leisure in the Industrial Revolution*, London, 1980; Helen Meller, *Leisure and the Changing City*, London, 1976; Gareth Stedman Jones, "Working-Class Culture and Working-Class Politics in London, 1870–1900," *Journal of Social History*, 1974, vol. 7, pp. 460–507.
4 Place Papers, BM Add. MSS 27825, f. 147.
5 Julien Franklyn, *The Cockney*, London, 1953, pp. 158–9.
6 Robert Roberts, *The Classic Slum*, Manchester, 1971, p. 32.
7 H. Taine, *Notes on England*, London, 1872, p. 9.
8 Ford Maddox Hueffer, *The Soul of Modern London*, London, 1905, pp. 139–41; Clarence Rook, *London Sidelights*, London, 1908, pp. 32–41, and George Sims, "London Sweet-Hearts," in G. Sims (ed.), *Living London*, London, 1901, vol. 2, pp. 14–19, describe these rituals in detail.
9 See, for example, Ralph Nevill, *The Gay Victorians*, London, 1930, pp. 1–2; Alfred R. Bennett, *London and Londoners in the Eighteen-Fifties and Sixties*, London, 1924, pp. 1, 345–64; Norman Douglas, *London Street Games*, London, 1916, pp. 119–20.
10 M. J. Daunton, *House and Home in the Victorian City*, London, 1983, p. 13.
11 A. Patterson, *Across the Bridges*, 2nd edn, London, 1912, p. 71.
12 A. Freeman, *Boy Life and Labour*, Birmingham, 1914, p. 152.
13 Reprinted in W. S. Jevons, *Methods of Social Reform*, New York, Kelly repr. of 1883 edn, 1965, p. 4.
14 ibid., pp. 4–9, 20–4.
15 H. R. Haweis, *Music and Morals*, London, 1871.
16 Quoted in Chris Waters, *British Socialists and the Politics of Popular Culture*, Stanford, Calif., 1990, pp. 98–9.
17 J. Ruskin, *The Queen of the Air*, London, 1905, p. 69.
18 ibid., p. 68.

19 ibid., p. 194; *Fors Clavigera*, in *The Complete Works of John Ruskin*, New York, 1875, pp. 208–9.
20 E. D. Mackerness, *A Social History of English Music*, London, 1964, pp. 154–69.
21 Dorothy Stein, *Ada: A Life and Legacy*, Cambridge, Mass., 1985, pp. 115–18.
22 H. Martineau, *Autobiography*, 3rd edn, London, 1877, pp. 354–5.
23 Philip and Emily Morrison (eds), *Charles Babbage and His Calculating Engines*, New York, 1961, p. xiii. Other works on Babbage and his interests are Anthony Hyman, *Charles Babbage: Pioneer of the Computer*, Oxford, 1982; Maboth Moseley, *Irascible Genius: A Life of Charles Babbage, Inventor*, London, 1964; as well as Charles Babbage, *Passages from the Life of a Philosopher*, London, 1864, and sections of his son, Major General Henry Babbage's, *Memoirs and Correspondence*, London, 1915.
24 C. Babbage, *On the Economy of Machinery and Manufacture*, London, 1832.
25 ibid., p. 8.
26 Karl Marx, *Capital*, tr. S. Moore and E. Aveling, London, 1887, p. 338; discussed in Hyman, *Pioneer*, pp. 117–21.
27 Babbage, *Passages*, pp. 243–4.
28 Hyman, *Pioneer*, pp. 103–4.
29 Babbage, *Passages*, p. 337.
30 Dickens's position was ambivalent: see his "Street Minstrelsy," *Household Words*, London, 1859, vol. 19, pp. 577–80.
31 *Saturday Review*, 1864, vol. 17, p. 649.
32 Michael Bass, *Street Music in the Metropolis*, London, 1864, pp. 2–5.
33 Babbage Papers, BM Add. MSS 37, 197, ff. 448, 451, 463–5, 467–8, 484.
34 ibid., 37, 198, f. 91.
35 ibid.
36 ibid., f. 95.
37 Hansard, 17 July, 1863, vol. 172, cols 972–3.
38 ibid., cols 974, 977.
39 ibid., 1864, vol. 174, cols 2117, 1531–2; 1864, vol. 176, col. 682.
40 ibid., 1864, vol. 174, col. 1531.
41 Babbage Papers, BM Add. MSS 37, 199, ff. 444.
42 Babbage, *Passages*, pp. 354–5.
43 J. F. Cooper, *England*, London, 1837, vol. 1, pp. 142–4.
44 *St James's Magazine*, 1865, vol. 13, p. 190.
45 Henry Mayhew, *London Labour and the London Poor*, New York, 1968, Dover repr. of 1861 edn, vol. 3, pp. 175–6.
46 Cunningham, *Leisure*.
47 S. M. Ellis (ed.), *A Mid-Victorian Pepys, Letters and Memoirs of William Hardman*, London, 1923, p. 264.
48 Quoted in Bass, *Street Music*, p. 92.
49 Babbage Papers, BM Add. MSS 37, 198, ff. 460.

6 WORKING

1 John Hogg, *London As It Is*, London, 1837, pp. 218–21.
2 Gertrude Himmelfarb, "The Culture of Poverty," in H. J. Dyos and M. Wolff (eds), *The Victorian City*, London, 1973, vol. 2, pp. 707–36.
3 Richard Maxwell, "Henry Mayhew," *Journal of British Studies*, London, 1978, vol. 17, pp. 87–102.

NOTES

4 P. Stallybrass and A. White, *The Politics and Poetics of Transgression*, London, 1986, p. 128.
5 John Thomson and Adolphe Smith, *Street-Life in London*, Harenberg edn, Dortmund, 1981, p. 85.
6 Olive Malvery, *The Soul Market*, London, 1906, p. 308. Another young woman, Mary Higgs, had the same idea at about the same time; see her *Glimpses into the Abyss*, London, 1906.
7 Olive Malvery, *Thirteen Nights*, London, 1908, p. 3.
8 Malvery, *Soul Market*, p. 237.
9 ibid., pp. 15–16.
10 ibid., pp. 135–45.
11 ibid., pp. 228, 148–9.
12 Described in Charles Montague, *Sixty Years in Waifdom*, London, 1904, pp. 94–95.
13 Charles Booth, *Life and Labour of the People of London*, New York, Kelly repr., 1969, vol. 1, pp. 57–8, delineates much more precisely the various strata.
14 Malvery, *Soul Market*, p. 135.
15 Olive Malvery, "The Heart of Things," *Pearson's Magazine*, 1905, vol. 19, p. 150.
16 Lynn Lees, "The Pattern of Lower-Class Life: Irish Slum Communities in Nineteenth-Century London," in S. Thernstrom and R. Sennett (eds), *Nineteenth-Century Cities*, New Haven, Conn., 1969, pp. 368–9.
17 Henry Blake, a Battersea costermonger and former President of the Costermongers' Association of Great Britain and Ireland, in testimony before the Royal Commission on Alien Immigration, 1903, vol. 9, qs 7686–714.
18 Lloyd Gartner, *The Jewish Immigrant in England, 1870–1914*, 2nd edn, London, 1970, p. 61; J. H. Stallard, *London Pauperism Amongst Jews and Christians*, London, 1867, pp. 8–9, 150–2.
19 ibid., qs 7903–49, 9567.
20 H. Mayhew, *London Labour and the London Poor*, London, 1861, vol. 1, pp. 58–60.
21 See, for example, a memorandum from Scotland Yard on treatment of costermongers, PRO, MEPO 2/199/10037 (*c.* 1884).
22 David Alexander, *Retailing in England During the Industrial Revolution*, London, 1983, pp. 68–71, 76.
23 S. M. Ellis (ed.), *A Mid-Victorian Pepys, Letters and Memoirs of Sir William Hardman*, London, 1930 edn, p. 284.
24 John Benson, *The Penny Capitalists*, Dublin, 1983, pp. 99–104; Francis Sheppard, *London 1808–1870: The Infernal Wen*, London, 1971, pp. 354–5. W. Hamish Fraser, *The Coming of the Mass Market, 1850–1914*, London, 1981, p. 100, thinks the decline of street selling began earlier.
25 Alexander, *Retailing*, pp. 62–3.
26 G. Dodd, *The Food of London*, London, 1856, pp. 1–2, 393–4, 515–16; Booth, *Life and Labour*, vol. 1, p. 53, calls street dealers "the most open and palpable servants of the people."
27 Quoted in Edward Bristow, *Vice and Vigilance*, London, 1977, p. 154.
28 S.C. on Theatrical Licenses and Regulations, 1866, vol. 16, qs 969–1210.
29 Quoted in Benjamin Scott, *State of Iniquity*, New York, 1968 repr. of the 1894 edn, pp. 30–1.
30 Judith Walkowitz, *Prostitution and Victorian Society*, Cambridge, 1980, pp. 24–8.
31 Abraham Flexner, *Prostitution in Europe*, New York, 1914, pp. 118–19.

32 ibid., pp. 299-300.
33 A retired City Commissioner of Police did state in 1906 that constables were constantly offered bribes by prostitutes: *Daily Mail*, 16 May, 1906, p. 5; see also William Ballentine, *Some Experiences of a Barrister's Life*, 6th edn, London, 1882, pp. 275-8.
34 Bernard Cohen, *Deviant Street Networks*, Lexington, Mass., 1980, pp. 1-6, 149-51, 173-5.
35 S.C. on Police Duties, 1908, vol. 50, pp. 91-3; vol. 51, qs 40278, 40508-9; Arthur Brinkman, *Notes on Rescue Work*, London, 1908, pp. 93-4; Mary Steer, *Opals From Sand*, London, 1912, pp. 23-4; Walkowitz, *Prostitution*, pp. 27-8, shows that prostitution in Liverpool became a self-regulating industry in which the police played a part.
36 Xavier Mayne [Edward Stevenson], *The Intersexes*, Rome, private printing, 1908, p. 100.
37 Randolph Trumback, "London's Sodomites," *Journal of Social History*, 1977, vol. 11, pp. 1-33; [Anon], *Yokel's Preceptor*, London, 1855, p. 6; [Jack Saul], *The Sins of the Cities of the Plain*, London, 1881, vol. 1, pp. 7-8; Jeffrey Weeks, *Coming Out*, London, 1977, p. 37; J. R. Ackerley, *My Father and Myself*, London, 1968, pp. 135-6.
38 Jeffrey Weeks, "Inverts, Perverts, and Mary-Annes," *Journal of Homosexuality*, 1980, vol. 6, pp. 118-19.
39 British Parliamentary Papers, Report of the Metropolitan Police Commissioner, 1908, vol. 51, p. 842.
40 ibid., 1914, vol. 54, p. 215; 1914-16, vol. 32, p. 153.
41 Weeks, *Coming Out*, pp. 39-41.
42 R. C. on the Duties of the Metropolitan Police, 1908, vol. 51, qs 40347, 40360-1.
43 ibid.
44 ibid., qs 47541-3.
45 ibid., q. 47659.
46 ibid., qs 40429, 40432, 40438, 40443-51; Robert Storch, "Police Control of Street Prostitution in Victorian London," in David Bayley (ed.), *Police and Society*, Beverly Hills, Calif., 1977, p. 50.
47 See list of regulations, MEPO 2/199/100379, 6 December, 1884.
48 MEPO 2, 48, 18 February, 1859.
49 ibid., 2 July, 1859.
50 Paul Harrison, *Inside the Inner City*, Harmondsworth, 1983, p. 367.
51 Carolyn Steedman, *Policing the Victorian Community*, London, 1984, p. 143.

7 CLEANING

1 57 George III, c. 29, pp. 323-4.
2 F. M. L. Thompson, *Victorian England: The Horse-Drawn Society*, Inaugural Lecture, 22 October, 1970, Bedford College, University of London, p. 12.
3 Henry Mayhew, *London Labour and the London Poor*, London, 1968, Dover repr. of 1861 edn, vol. 2, p. 194.
4 Thompson, *Victorian England*, pp. 14.
5 Francis Sheppard, *London 1808-1870: The Infernal Wen*, London, 1971, pp. 121-2: W. J. Gordon, *The Horse-World of London*, Religious Tract Society, London, 1893, p. 113.
6 Mayhew, *London Labour*, vol. 2, p. 195.

NOTES

7 Mayhew, *London Labour*, pp. 187–8; *Lancet*, 1865, vol. 1, p. 265; S.C. (House of Lords) on Traffic Regulations (Metropolis) Bill, 1867, vol. 11, q. 776.
8 William Haywood, *Report on the Accidents to Horses on Carriageway Pavements*, London, 1873, p. 32.
9 Gordon, *Horse-World*, pp. 183–9; P. J. Waller, *Town City and Nation*, Oxford, 1983, p. 52.
10 *Times*, 5 January, 1867, p. 7. A frost and a thaw two years earlier were the subjects of two full-page engravings in *The Illustrated London News*, 1865, vol. 46, pp. 84, 184.
11 W. Gordon, "The Cleansing of London," *Leisure Hour*, vol. 35, p. 602.
12 Thompson, *Victorian England*, p. 10.
13 *Times*, 2 July, 1847, p. 8. See also J. Winter, "The 'Agitator of the Metropolis': Charles Cochrane and Early-Victorian Street Reform," *London Journal*, 1989, vol. 14, pp. 29–42.
14 [Charles Cochrane], *Journal of a Tour made by Senor Juan de Vega through Great Britain and Ireland*, London, 1830, 2 vols.
15 ibid., vol. 2, p. 398.
16 G. Lloyd Hodges, *Narrative of the Expedition to Portugal in 1832*, London, 1833, vol. 2, p. 193; Charles Napier, *An Account of the War in Portugal between Dom Pedro and Dom Miguel*, London, 1836, vol. 1, pp. 94–5.
17 Marylebone Vestry Minutes, entries for 18 December, 1841, p. 54; 1 January, 1842, pp. 71–2; 8 January, 1842, pp. 77–8; 26 February, 1842, p. 166.
18 He made these points on many occasions but explained them most fully in National Philanthropic Association (NPA), *Report of Progress*, London, 1853, pp. 5–6.
19 Mayhew, *London Labour*, vol. 2, p. 258.
20 Commented on in Mayhew, *London Labour*, vol. 2, p. 6.
21 Joseph Whitworth, *Patent Street-Sweeping Machine*, London, 1845, pp. 3–7.
22 J. Whitworth, *On the Advantages and Economy of the Street-Sweeping Machine*, London, 1847, pp. 13–16.
23 ibid., p. 28.
24 NPA, *Report*, 1849, p. 102.
25 [C. Cochrane], *How to Improve the Homes of the People!*, London, 1849, p. 14; NPA, *Report*, 1849, pp. 130–1, 137–40; 1853, pp. 6–7. A line in the chorus of a broadsheet song, called "Street Orderly", read "Now don't make game of me as you pass."
26 NPA, *Sanatory Progress*, London, 1859, pp. 88–9; *Times*, 4 July, 1845, p. 6.
27 NPA, *Report*, 1849, p. 149; 1853, p. 5.
28 *Lancet*, 1849, vol. 1, p. 192; *Times*, 1 December, 1848, p. 3.
29 *Morning Advertiser*, 2 August, 1846.
30 NPA, *Report*, 1849, pp. 151–2; 1853, pp. 13–19; Mayhew, *London Labour*, vol. 2, pp. 259, 271–5; *Times*, 27 February, 1852, p. 4.
31 C. H. Rolph, *London Particulars*, London, 1980, pp. 162–3; see also J. C. Daws, *Report on the Investigation into the Public Cleansing Service*, London, 1929, pp. 60–5.
32 *Lancet*, 1865, vol. 1, p. 265.
33 [Cochrane], *Homes of the People*, pp. 9–12; NPA, *Report*, 1849, pp. 112.
34 NPA, *Sanatory*, pp. 83–7.
35 *Twenty-Third Annual Report of the Ladies' Sanitary Association*, April, 1881, pp. 12–14.
36 J. Stevenson, *Latrine Accommodation for Women in the Metropolis*, London, 1879, pp. 4–20.

37 W. Woodward, "The Sanitation and Reconstruction of Central London," in William Westgarth (ed.), *Essays in the Street Re-Alignment, Reconstruction, and Sanitation of London*, London, 1886, pp. 79–80.
38 Kathleen Tillotson (ed.), *The Letters of Charles Dickens*, Oxford, 1977, vol. 4, p. 528.
39 *The Poor Man's Guardian*, 18 December, 1847, p. 52; Health of London Association (HLA), *Report*, London, 1847, p. viii.
40 HLA, *Report*, 1847, pp. vii–68.
41 *Morning Chronicle*, 11 June, 1847, p. 7.
42 *Times*, 6 January, 1847, p. 5; 6 February, 1847, p. 7; *Sun*, 16 February, 1847, pp. 1, 4; 18 February, 1847, p. 2; *Morning Chronicle*, 16 February, 1847, p. 7; 2 March, 1847, p. 6; 24 February, 1847, p. 2; 1 March, 1847, p. 3.
43 A Westminster Elector [C. Cochrane], *An Address to the Business-Like Men of Westminster, with a Review of Juan de Vega*, London, 1847, pp. 8–20; *Times*, 2 July, 1847, p. 8; 29 July, 1847, p. 2.
44 *Times*, 30 July, 1847, p. 2; 31 July, 1847, p. 2.
45 F. C. Mather, *Chartism and Society*, London, 1980, p. 231; D. Goodway, *London Chartism*, Cambridge, 1982, pp. 111–14; J. T. Ward, *Chartism*, London, 1973, pp. 199–200; *Times*, 7 March, 1848, p. 8; 8 March, 1848, p. 6; 10 March, 1848, p. 4; 11 March, 1848, p. 8.
46 *Punch*, 1849, vol. 16, p. 102.
47 ibid., 1848, vol. 14, pp. 111–16, 138, 176, 186, 188, 191.
48 *Morning Chronicle*, 1 March, 1847, p. 4.
49 *Times*, 5 July, 1849, p. 5.
50 NPA, *Report*, 1849, pp. 114–30.
51 *Poor Man's Guardian*, 11 December, 1847, pp. 45–7; *Times*, 20 October, 1846, p. 5; 16 December, 1846, p. 4; *Morning Chronicle*, 16 December, 1846.
52 *Poor Man's Guardian*, 18 December, 1847, pp. 54–5; *Observer*, 12 December, 1847.
53 *Times*, 27 July, 1852, p. 6.
54 ibid., 29 July, 1852, p. 4.
55 [C. Cochrane], *My Connection with the Sabbath Movement in France in 1853–1854*, London, 1854, p. 47.
56 ibid., pp. 3–24.
57 J. Brown, "No Work in the Grave," *The Pulpit*, 1855, vol. 68, p. 19.
58 Mayhew, *London Labour*, vol. 2, pp. 257–9.
59 *Poor Man's Guardian*, 6 November, 1847, p. 4; [C. Cochrane], *Speech of Charles Cochrane Esq. at a Public Meeting in Favour of the Employment of the Poor*, London, 1848, p. 8; [Cochrane], *Homes of the People*, pp. 9–12; NPA, *Report*, 1849, p. 112.

8 RESCUING

1 Earnest Jealous, *On the Beaten Track*, London, n.d., p. 11.
2 Commentators on mid-Victorian evangelicalism draw attention to 1859 as the point when a second awakening reached British shores from America. But MacGregor and many like him were experienced street evangelists and resident rescue workers well before that date.
3 Kathleen Heasman, *Evangelicals in Action*, London, 1962, pp. 25–8.
4 Ian Bradley, *The Call to Seriousness*, New York, 1976, pp. 119–21, 135.
5 Edwin Hodder, *John MacGregor*, London, 1894, pp. 1–2, 25.
6 ibid., pp. 277–303.

NOTES

7 ibid., pp. 53–6; E. Hodder, *The Life and Work of the Seventh Earl of Shaftesbury, K.G.*, London, 1886, vol. 2, pp. 341–2, 225.
8 Hansard's Parliamentary Debates, 6 June, 1848, vol. 99, cols. 430–1. See also The Riverside Visitor, *The Great Army of the London Poor*, London, 1875, pp. 177–8, for a similar analysis. A London Pedestrian, "Street-Boys: The Contemplative Man's Irritation," *Sharpe's London Magazine*, vol. 7, 185, p. 340.
9 *Leisure Hour*, 1866, vol. 15, p. 455.
10 Helen Campbell, T. Knox, and T. Byrnes, *Darkness and Daylight*, Hartford, Conn., 1900, p. 112.
11 Hodder, *MacGregor*, pp. 381–2; Heasman, *Evangelicals*, pp. 84–5.
12 Hodder, *Shaftesbury*, vol. 2, p. 114. G. Holden Pike, *The Romance of the Streets*, London, 1872, p. 7, praised the Union for "cleansing the stream of London life at the fountain-head."
13 See, for example, articles signed by "Rob Roy" in *The Reformatory and Refuge Journal*, 1861, pp. 2–4, 104–8; 1863, pp. 1–2; 1865, pp. 10–11; 1866, pp. 101, 178.
14 Riverside Visitor, *Great Army*, p. 277.
15 Hodder, *MacGregor*, pp. 78–80.
16 *Poor Man's Guardian*, 6 November, 1847, p. 7.
17 S.C. on Criminal and Destitute Juveniles, 1852, vol. 7, q. 3445. Experience quickly showed that 16 and 17-year-olds were troublesome and the age limit was lowered; ibid., q. 3452.
18 J. MacGregor, "Shoe-Blacks and Broomers," *Ragged School Union Magazine*, 1851, vol. 3, pp. 267–8, republished as a pamphlet, *Shoe-Blacks and Broomers*, 1852, London.
19 Hodder, *MacGregor*, p. 88; P. Cunnington and C. Lucas, *Charity Costumes*, 1978, pp. 207–10.
20 S.C. on Criminal and Destitute Juveniles, 1852, vol. 7, q. 3457.
21 MacGregor, *Shoe-Blacks*, p. 8.
22 PRO, MEPO, 1/63, Mayne's letter to the Shoeblack Society, 8 May, 1868.
23 *Reformatory and Refuge Journal*, 1862, p. 106; Henry Drummond, *Our Boys*, London, 1904, pp. 6–7.
24 Hodder, *MacGregor*, pp. 239–40.
25 *Ragged School Union Magazine*, 1851, vol. 3, pp. 68–9.
26 S.C. on Criminal and Destitute Juveniles, 1852, vol. 7, q. 3465.
27 Charles Montague, *Sixty Years in Waifdom*, London, 1904, pp. 196–202.
28 S.C. on Criminal and Destitute Juveniles, 1852, vol. 7, qs. 3466, 3511.
29 ibid., q. 3557.
30 Hodder, *MacGregor*, p. 91.
31 S.C. on Criminal and Destitute Juveniles, 1852, vol. 7, q. 3495.
32 MacGregor, *Shoe-Blacks*, p. 91.
33 S.C. on Criminal and Destitute Juveniles, 1852, vol. 7, q. 3495.
34 ibid., q. 3490.
35 *Reformatory and Refuge Journal*, 1861, p. 108.
36 ibid., 1866, p. 101.
37 S.C. on Criminal and Destitute Juveniles, 1852, vol. 7, q. 3516.
38 MacGregor, *Shoe-Blacks*, pp. 6–7; "Ragamuffins," *Leisure Hour*, vol. 15, p. 457.
39 To be seen at the Bodleian Library, Oxford, in the John Johnson Collection under "Shoeblack."
40 *Shaftesbury Magazine*, 1925, vol. 77, 1925, p. 4.

41 Hodder, *MacGregor*, p. 146.
42 G. Holden Pike, *Beneath the Blue Sky*, London, 1888, p. 287.
43 The Open Air Mission (OAM) Occasional Papers, 1855, *Second Annual Report*, p. 4.
44 ibid., *Tenth Annual Report*, 1863, p. 7.
45 Frank Cockrem, *Gawin Kirkham*, London, 1894, p. 47.
46 Pike, *Blue Sky*, p. 274.
47 ibid., p. 287.
48 OAM, *Third Annual Report*, 1856, p. 7.
49 J. MacGregor, *Go Out Quickly*, London, 1855. Another early entry in the field was the Revd William Taylor, *Seven Years' Street Preaching in San Francisco, California*, New York, 1856, which attracted considerable attention in Britain.
50 Gawin Kirkham, *The Open-Air Preacher's Handbook*, 2nd edn, London, 1890, p. 113–15.
51 ibid.; Pike, *Blue Sky*, pp. 38–67; Evangelical Lay Preachers' Association, *The Lay Preacher's Guide*, (c. 1896), p. 113; MacGregor, *Go Out*, p. 5.
52 ibid., p. 3.
53 Pike, *Blue Sky*, pp. 283–6, 275.
54 Hodder, *MacGregor*, p. 160.
55 PRO, MEPO, 2/168, E. Division Report, 30 June, 1875.
56 ibid., Report of J. Mansfield, 10 May, 1867; G. Ellis to Mayne, 27 May, 1867; Opinion of Ellis and Ellis, 10 June, 1868; E. Division Report, 30 June, 1875.
57 *Daily Chronicle*, 7 March, 1887.
58 PRO, MEPO, 2/168.
59 ibid., E. Burton to Henderson, 3 August, 1880.
60 ibid., 6 June, 1884.
61 Hodder, *MacGregor*, pp. 197–8.
62 A Country Parson, *Authorized Street Preaching Proposed as a Remedy for Our Social Evils*, London, 1848, pp. 8, 11–18.
63 The Revd Fredrick Briggs, *Chequer Alley*, London, 1866, p. 22.
64 John MacGregor, *Open Air Preaching*, London, 1854, p. 3.
65 OAM, *Twenty-Sixth Annual Report*, 1879, pp. 26–8.
66 ibid., p. 28.
67 G. Stedman Jones, *Outcast London*, Harmondsworth, 1976, ch. 16; Victor Bailey, "Salvation Army Riots, the 'Skeleton Army' and Legal Authority in the Provincial Town," in A.P. Donajgrodski, (ed.), *Social Control in 19th Century Britain*, Totowa, NJ, 1977, p. 232.
68 PRO, MEPO, 2/168, G. Ellis to Mayne, 27 May, 1867.
69 Geoffrey Warren, *Vanishing Street Furniture*, Newton Abbot, 1978, pp. 10–11.

9 BREATHING

1 *Blackwood's Edinburgh Magazine*, 1839, vol. 46, pp. 213, 226.
2 ibid., p. 212.
3 ibid., pp. 212–27.
4 Susan Sontag, *Illness as Metaphor*, New York, 1978, pp. 5–26.
5 See *Lancet*, 1865, vol. 2, p. 151.
6 See, for example, Martin Wiener, *English Culture and the Decline of the Industrial Spirit*, Cambridge, 1981, pp. 41–72; P.D. Lowe, "Values and Institutions in the History of British Nature Conservation," in A. Warren

NOTES

and F. B. Goldsmith (eds), *Conservation in Perspective*, London, 1983, pp. 335–9; Avener Offer, *Property and Politics 1870–1914*, Cambridge, 1981, pp. 329–402; Martin Gaskell, "Gardens for the Working Class: Victorian Practical Pleasures," *Victorian Studies*, 1980, vol. 23, pp. 479–501.
7 *Times*, 9 August, 1869, p. 5.
8 *Builder*, 8 February, 1845, p. 62.
9 *Labourer's Friend*, 1 October, 1864, p. 63.
10 Robert Thorne, "George Godwin and Architectural Journalism," *History Today*, 1987, vol. 37, pp. 11–12; Ruth Richardson, "George Godwin of *The Builder*," *Visual Resources*, 1989, vol. 6, pp. 121–140.
11 *Builder*, 25 February, 1843, p. 33.
12 ibid., 20 March, 1847, p. 139.
13 ibid., 18 March, 1865, p. 193.
14 ibid., 28 October, 1848, p. 523.
15 ibid., 24 February, 1872, p. 151.
16 ibid., 14 June, 1862, p. 423; *Lancet*, 1865, vol. 2, pp. 94–5.
17 See Peter Bailey, *Leisure and Class in Victorian England*, London, Methuen edn, 1987; Hugh Cunningham, *Leisure in the Industrial Revolution*, London, 1980; Helen Meller, *Leisure and the Changing City, 1870–1914*, London, 1976.
18 *Builder*, 29 December, 1866, p. 950–1.
19 ibid., 14 March, 1874, p. 211; 11 April, 1874, p. 305.
20 ibid.
21 ibid., 17 October, 1874, p. 866.
22 ibid.
23 Enid Moberly Bell, *Octavia Hill*, London, 1942, p. 5.
24 Gillian Darley, *Octavia Hill*, 1990, pp. 172–6.
25 Octavia Hill, *Homes of the London Poor*, Cross repr, 1970, p. 93.
26 Anthony Wohl, *The Eternal Slum*, Montreal, 1977, pp. 177–99, gives a critical examination of her career as a housing reformer. For her labors on behalf of Commons Preservation, see Bell, *Hill*, pp. 141–55, 220–39; Gaskell, "Gardens," pp. 491–5; W. T. Hill, *Octavia Hill*, London, 1956, pp. 98–108, 125–47.
27 Octavia Hill, "Colour, Space, and Music of the People," *The Nineteenth Century*, 1884, vol. 15, p. 741.
28 Samuel and Henrietta Barnett, *Toward Social Reform*, London, 1909, pp. 329–30.
29 See Gaskell, "Gardens," pp. 479–501; Hill, *Homes*, p. 30; Henrietta Barnett, *Canon Barnett*, London, 1919, vol. 1, p. 141.
30 In *Homes*, pp. 28–9, Hill gives an entertaining account of how the playground was first received.
31 [H.W.], "Sunday in East London," *The Sunday at Home*, 1895, p. 791.
32 John Summerson, *Georgian London*, London, 1945, pp. 160–73, 272–3; Albert Fein, "Victoria Park: Its Origins and History," *East End Papers*, 1962, vol. 5, pp. 73–7.
33 John Summerson, *John Nash*, Newton Abbot, 1973, pp. 56–9.
34 Summerson, *Georgian London*, p. 168.
35 Charles Poulsen, *Victoria Park*, London, 1976, pp. 25–38; G. F. Chadwick, *The Park and the Town*, London, 1966, pp. 121–5.
36 Victoria Park Papers (GLC History Library), vol. 2, 17 January, 1845; 24 April, 1845; 19 May, 1846; 3 October, 1846; vol. 3, 21 June, 1847; J. J. Sexby, *The Municipal Parks, Gardens, and Spaces of London*, London, 1898, pp. 555–6.
37 Poulsen, *Victoria Park*, pp. 39, 44–57, 63–72.

38 *Illustrated London News*, 2 May, 1846, p. 285.
39 Poulsen, *Victoria Park*, p. 104.
40 Victoria Park Papers, vol. 3, 23 June, 1848.
41 Poulsen, *Victoria Park*, p. 96.
42 Quoted in [H.W.], "Sunday", p. 793.
43 See opening of Act I of G. B. Shaw's *Candida*, Brentano edn, New York, 1905, pp. 3–4.
44 Greater London Council, *Surveys of the Use of Open Spaces*, London, 1968, vol. 1, pp. 5–73.
45 *Dictionary of National Biography 1922–1930*, London, 1937, pp. 765–6; *Times*, 20 April, 1928, p. 11.
46 British Museum, Add. MSS, 444153, p. 311.
47 G. J. Lefevre, *English Commons and Forests*, London, 1894; G. J. Lefevre, *Commons, Forests and Footpaths*, London, 1910.
48 Hansard, 1864, vol. 176, col. 509; Robert Hunter's essay in Henry Peek (ed.), *Six Essays in Commons Preservation*, London, 1867, p. 363; Sidney Smith, *A Glance at the Commons and Open Spaces Near London*, London, 1867, pp. 4–5.
49 See, for example, John Maidlow, "The Law of Commons and Open Spaces," in Peek (ed.), *Essays*, p. 2.
50 Joseph Marshall's testimony before the S.C. on Open Spaces, 1865, vol. 8, qs 5424–5.
51 H. D. Rownsley, "Footpath Preservation," *The Contemporary Review*, 1886, vol. 50, pp. 384–5; see also Octavia Hill, *Speech of Miss Octavia Hill at a Meeting for Securing West Wickham Common*, n.d., p. 1.
52 J. M. Golby and A. W. Purdue, *The Civilization of the Crowd*, London, 1984, p. 103; Cunningham, *Leisure*, p. 94.
53 A. MacKenzie, *The Parks, Open Spaces and Thoroughfares of London*, London, 1869, p. 4.
54 W. B. Adams, *Once a Week*, London, 1859, vol. 1, pp. 519–22.
55 MacKenzie, *Parks*, pp. 3, 16–20; W. Robinson, *Gleanings from French Gardens*, London, 1869, pp. 75–6, 94–102, and his *Parks, Promenades and Gardens of Paris*, London, 1869, pp. xx–xxi, 59, 112–17.
56 Meller, *Leisure*, pp. 118–19; Cunningham, *Leisure*, takes as his theme the collision between reformers' wish to use leisure to promote social amelioration and the steady appropriation of leisure activities by the middle class.
57 Robert Roberts, *The Classic Slum*, Manchester, 1971, pp. 123, 126–9.
58 Hill, *Homes*, p. 92.
59 A. Gomme, *Children's Singing Games*, London, 1894, p. 10.
60 Robinson, *Parks*, p. 115.
61 H. L. Malchow, "Public Gardens and Social Action in Late Victorian London," *Victorian Studies*, 1985, vol. 29, p. 123.

10 INHABITING

1 *Times*, 2 May, 1906, p. 3.
2 ibid.
3 *Dictionary of National Biography*, Suppl. 1901–11, pp. 460–1; R.C. on the Duties of the Metropolitan Police, 1908, vol. 50, p. 216.
4 *Daily Mail*, 12 May, 1906, p. 5.
5 R.C. on the Duties of the Metropolitan Police, 1908, vol. 50, pp. 128, 217–21, qs 3841, 3845–8; *Times*, 1 August, 1906, p. 4.

NOTES

6 *Times*, 12 July, 1887, p. 11.
7 See Linda Kerber, "Separate Spheres, Female Worlds, Women's Place: The Rhetoric of Women's History," *Journal of American History*, 1988, vol. 75, pp. 9–39.
8 Lidia Sciama, "The Problem of Privacy in Mediterranean Anthropology," in Shirley Ardener (ed.), *Women and Space*, London, 1981, pp. 89–111.
9 Marshall Colman, *Continuous Excursions*, London, 1982, pp. 115–16.
10 *The North Londoner*, 1 May, 1869, p. 202.
11 James Anthony Froude (ed.), *Letters and Memorials of Jane Welsh Carlyle*, New York, 1883, vol. 1, pp. 422–33.
12 The phrase is used by Kerber, "Separate Spheres," p. 36, in commenting on a book by Christine Stansell, *City of Women: Sex and Class in New York, 1789–1860*, New York, 1986.
13 O. A. Sherrard, *Two Victorian Girls*, London, 1960, p. 228. Ellen also noted that she had thought it best not to mention to a girlfriend that she had been for a ride in an omnibus.
14 Henry Mayhew, *London Labour and the London Poor*, New York, Dover repr., 1968, vol. 2, p. 124.
15 Olive Christian Malvery, *The Soul Market*, London, 1906, p. 238.
16 Shirley Ardener, "Ground Rules and Social Maps for Women," in Ardener (ed.), *Women and Space*, pp. 28–9.
17 *Guardian*, 13 June, 1989, p. 17.
18 Anna Clark, *Women's Silence, Men's Violence*, London, 1987, p. 1.
19 Clarence Rook, *London Side-Lights*, London, 1908, pp. 290–7.
20 Roy Porter, "Mixed Feelings: The Enlightenment and Sexuality in 18th Century Britain," in Paul-Gabriel Boucé (ed.), *Sexuality in Eighteenth Century Britain*, Manchester, 1982, pp. 9–21.
21 John Price, "Patterns of Sexual Behaviour in Some 18th Century Novels," in Boucé (ed.), *Sexuality*, pp. 161–3.
22 V. A. C. Gatrell, "The Decline of Theft and Violence in Victorian and Edwardian England," in V. Gatrell, B. Lenman, and G. Parker (eds), *Crime and the Law: The Social History of Crime in Western Europe since 1500*, London, 1980; V. Gatrell and T. B. Hadden, "Criminal Statistics and Their Interpretation," in E. A. Wrigley (ed.) *Nineteenth Century Society*, Cambridge, 1972; David Jones, *Crime, Protest, Community and Police in Nineteenth-Century Britain*, London, 1982, pp. 117–21.
23 Clark, *Women's Silence*, pp. 15–16; Ruth Hall, *Ask Any Woman*, Bristol, 1985, pp. 32–59; Stephanie Riger and Margaret Gordon, "The Fear of Rape: A Study in Social Control," *Journal of Social Issues*, 1981, vol. 37, pp. 71–91.
24 Judith Walkowitz, "Jack the Ripper and the Myth of Male Violence," *Feminist Studies*, 1982, vol. 8, pp. 542–69.
25 J. C. Byrne, *Undercurrents Overlooked*, London, 1860, vol. 1, pp. 19–20.
26 C. S. Peel, *Life's Enchanted Cup*, London, 1933, pp. 54–5, 95, 106.
27 Olive Malvery [Mrs Archibald Mackirdy] and W. N. Willis, *The White Slave Market*, London, 1912, pp. 203–7.
28 Virginia Woolf, *The Pargiters*, ed. M. Leaska, New York, 1977, pp. 36–43; Susan Squier, "The Politics of City Space in *The Years*: Street Love, Pillar Boxes and Bridges," in Jane Marcus (ed.), *New Feminist Essays on Virginia Woolf*, London, 1981, pp. 216–37.
29 W. Acton, *Prostitution: Considered in its Moral, Social and Sanitary Aspects*, London, 1857, p. 117.
30 R.C. on the Duties of the Metropolitan Police, 1908, vol. 51, qs 40422–4.

31 ibid., qs 45882, 45891, 45894, 45898.
32 ibid., qs 44205–16.
33 ibid., q. 47655.
34 E. Cook, *Highways and Byways in London*, London, 1902, p. 422.
35 R. C. on the Duties of the Metropolitan Police, 1908, vol. 50, pp. 128, 135.
36 Edward Bristow, *Vice and Vigilance*, Dublin, 1977, pp. 94–173; Sheila Jeffreys, *The Spinster and Her Enemies: Feminism and Sexuality 1880–1930*, London, 1985, pp. 6–85; Kathleen Heasman, *Evangelicals in Action*, London, 1962, pp. 158–67.
37 William Coote, *The Romance of Philanthropy*, London, 1916, pp. 39–40.
38 T. S. Boys, *London As It Is*, London, 1842.
39 Diana Mulock, *A Woman's Thoughts About Women*, London, 1858, p. 33.
40 R. Roberts, *The Classic Slum*, Manchester, 1971, pp. 25–8.
41 J. Jacobs, *The Death and Life of Great American Cities*, New York, 1961, p. 3.
42 Federation of Working Girls' Clubs, *In Peril In The City*, London, 1909, pp. 15, 26, 35–8.
43 Cook, *Highways*, p. 436.
44 Walter Besant, *As We Are and What We May Be*, London, 1903.
45 F. M. Hueffer, *The Soul of Modern London*, London, 1905, pp. 139–41.

11 PLANNING

1 J. Wolfe Barry, *Address*, London, 1899, p. 3.
2 *Times*, 15 April, 1914, p. 6.
3 Alfred Gardiner, *John Benn and the Progressive Movement*, London, 1925, p. 514.
4 G. B. Shaw, *The Common Sense of Municipal Trading*, London, 1904, p. 63.
5 *Times*, 26 November, 1913, p. 6.
6 G. L. Gomme, *London in the Reign of Victoria 1837–1898*, London, 1898, p. 166.
7 Gareth Stedman Jones, *Outcast London*, Harmondsworth, 1976, pp. 207–14.
8 Robert Gray, *A History of London*, London, 1978, p. 293.
9 Arthur Beavan, *Tube, Train, Tram and Car*, London, 1903, pp. 112–14.
10 Barry, *Address*, p. 5.
11 Frank Pick, "The Organization of Transport," *Journal of the Royal Society of Arts*, 1936, vol. 84, p. 217.
12 Christopher Brunner, *The Problem of Motor Transport*, London, 1928, p. 9.
13 *Engineering*, 1905, vol. 80, p. 85.
14 Barry, *Address*, pp. 25–9.
15 Henry C. Moore, *Omnibuses and Cabs*, London, 1902, pp. 119–21, 269–73.
16 R.C. on London Traffic, 1905, vol. 30, pp. 587–99; *The Car*, 1903, vol. 1, p. 3.
17 Beavan, *Tube*, pp. 228–9.
18 J. F. Reynolds, *General Notes on the London Traffic Problem*, London, 1904, pp. 1–13; George Swinton, "London Congestion and Cross-Traffic," *The Nineteenth Century and After*, 1903, vol. 53, pp. 821–33.
19 S. Plowden, *Towns Against Traffic*, London, 1972, p. 15; see also C. D. Buchanan, *Mixed Blessings: The Motor in Britain*, London, 1958, pp. 88–92.
20 S.C. on Motor Traffic, 1913, vol. 8, q. 5016.
21 Gwilym Gibbon and Reginald Ball, *History of the London County Council, 1889–1939*, London, 1939, pp. 100–5; Elizabeth Baker and P. J. Noel Baker, *J. Allen Baker*, London, 1927, pp. 112–15; Alfred Gardiner, *John Benn and the*

NOTES

Progressive Movement, London, 1925, pp. 339–43, 421–3; John Davis, "The Progressive Council, 1889–1907," in Andrew Saint (ed.), *Politics and the People of London*, London, 1989, pp. 27–48; Harold Perkin, *The Rise of Professional Society*, London, 1989, pp. 137–48; Ken Young, *Local Politics and the Rise of Party*, Leicester, 1975, pp. 85–98.

22 Gardiner, *Benn*, pp. 478–9.
23 Hans Blumenfeld, "Transportation in the Modern Metropolis," in Larry Bourne (ed.), *The Internal Structure of the City*, Toronto, 1971, pp. 231-2.
24 H. G. Wells, *Anticipations of the Reaction of Mechanical and Scientific Progress upon Human Life and Thought*, New York, 1902, p. 28.
25 ibid., pp. 6–8, 18–71.
26 Patricia Garside, "West End, East End: London, 1890–1940," in Anthony Sutcliffe (ed.), *Metropolis 1890–1940*, London, 1984, pp. 241-2.
27 Quoted in Derek Fraser, "The Edwardian City," in Donald Read (ed.), *Edwardian England*, London, 1982, p. 58.
28 G. L. Gomme, *London*, London, 1914, pp. 349–50.
29 Saint (ed.), *Politics and the People of London*, pp. 23–4.
30 *Times*, 25 February, 1916, p. 5.
31 Richard Dorson, *The British Folklorist*, London, 1968, p. 202.
32 G. L. Gomme, "Opening address to the Folk-Lore Society for the Session 1891–1892," *Folk-Lore*, London, 1892, pp. 1–23; *Folklore as an Historical Science*, London, 1908, pp. xv, 2–11, 338–65.
33 *Times*, 4 December, 1913, p. 11.
34 See Gomme's preface to C. R. Ashbee (ed.), *LCC, Survey of London*, London, 1900, pp. iii-v.
35 G. L. Gomme, *London in the Reign of Victoria, 1837–1898*, pp. v-vi, 1–2, 38, 217; *The Making of London*, Oxford, 1912, pp. 237–48; *The Governance of London*, London, 1907, pp. 403–7; *The London County Council*, London, 1888, pp. iii-iv; *London*, pp. 347–50; *Return of Outdoor Memorials in London*, London, 1910, p. 7.
36 Gomme, *Reign of Victoria*, pp. v-vi; *Governance*, pp. 403–6.
37 H. D. F. Kitto, "Arnold Wycombe Gomme," *Proceedings of the British Academy*, 1959, vol. 45, pp. 335–44.
38 H. D. F. Kitto, *The Greeks*, Harmondsworth, 1968, pp. 69–71.
39 A refrain in nearly all of his work but stated succinctly before the London Society at the time of his retirement as Clerk to the LCC: *Times*, 9 April, 1914, p. 6.
40 G. L. Gomme, *Lectures on the Principles of Local Government*, London, 1897, p. 134.
41 ibid., pp. 137–223.
42 See, for example, a book by the editor of *The Junior Liberal Review*, Frederick Dolman, *Municipalities At Work*, London, 1895, pp. 65–8.
43 This is a digest of points made by Bernard Aspinall, "Glasgow Trams and American Politics, 1894–1914," *Scottish Historical Review*, 1977, vol. 56, pp. 64–84.
44 S.C. on Motor Traffic, 1913, vol. 8, q. 5045.
45 S. Webb, *Socialism in England*, London, 1890, pp. 108–10.
46 John Burns, *Municipal Socialism*, London, 1902, p. 5.
47 Testimony of John Benn, S.C. on Municipal Trading, 1900, vol. 7, q. 4129.
48 Burns, *Municipal Socialism*, p. 14.
49 F. Howe, *The British City*, London, 1907, pp. 82–99.

50 Hansard, 1870, vol. 199, cols 1080–5; T. C. Barker and M. Robbins, *A History of London Transport*, London, 1963, vol. 1, pp. 178–97.
51 John McKay, *Tramways and Trolleys*, Princeton, 1976, pp. 168–91; Malcom Falcus, "The Development of Municipal Trading in the 19th Century," *Business History*, 1977, vol. 19, pp. 153–155.
52 Beavan, *Tube*, p. 129; Gardiner, *Benn*, p. 217.
53 Gardiner, *Benn*, p. 245; Henry Gordon, *Some Aspects of Metropolitan Road and Rail Transit*, London, 1919, p. 62.
54 John Hibbs, *The History of British Bus Services*, Newton Abbot, 1968, p. 11.
55 R.C. on London Traffic, 1906, vol. 3, p. 569.
56 S.C. on Motor Traffic, 1913, vol. 8, p. 18.
57 *Engineering*, 1910, vol. 90, p. 749; 1914, vol. 97, p. 88.
58 S.C. on Motor Traffic, 1913, vol. 8, pp. 4–6.
59 R. P. Hearne, "The Perils of the Pedestrian," *The Strand Magazine*, 1912, vol. 44, p. 390.
60 Thoughtfully discussed in one of a series of articles on London traffic in *Times*, 14 April, 1914, p. 6.
61 *Engineering*, 1913, vol. 96, p. 259.
62 Quoted in *Engineering*, 1913, vol. 96, p. 259. See also the Report of the S.C. on Motor Traffic, 1913, vol. 8, pp. 38–43.
63 See the debate between H. Evans, "The London County Council and the Police," and James Stuart, "The Metropolitan Police," in *Contemporary Review*, 1889, vol. 55, pp. 445–61, 622–36.
64 S.C. on Motor Traffic, 1913, vol. 8, qs 3053–6, 3240.
65 *Engineering*, 1913, vol. 96, p. 259.
66 Gavin Weightman and Steve Humphries, *The Making of Modern London*, London, 1983, pp. 116–122.
67 J. Benn's phrase as reported in *Surveyor*, 14 October, 1904, p. 469.
68 S.C. on Motor Traffic, 1913, vol. 8, p. 12, qs 8957, 8960–1, 8970–80; R. P. Hearne, "The Perils of the Pedestrian," *The Strand Magazine*, 1912, vol. 44, 390–6.
69 G. L. Dickinson, "The Motor Tyranny," *The Independent Review*, 1906, vol. 11, pp. 15–22.
70 S. C. on Motor Traffic, 1913, vol. 8, p. 27.
71 H. A. Tripp, *Road Traffic and its Control*, London, 1938, vol. 7 of the Roadmakers' Library, pp. 58, 69–74, 101.

CONCLUSION

1 John Benn called it "the Symbol of the Progressive era"; quoted in Alfred Gardiner, *John Benn and the Progressive Movement*, 1925, p. 485.
2 Quoted in Royden Harrison, *Before the Socialists*, London, 1965, p. 268.
3 See the comment of M. Beachcroft in Paul Waterhouse, "Some Observations on the Report of the Royal Commission on London Traffic," *Journal of the Royal Institute of British Architects*, 1906, vol. 13, p. 387.
4 G. J. Shaw-Lefevre, "London Street Improvements," *The Contemporary Review*, 1899, vol. 75, pp. 203–13; *Times*, 14 October, 1905, p. 7.
5 *Times*, 19 October, 1905, p. 10; *Engineering*, 20 October, 1905, vol. 80, p. 527.
6 *Builder*, 21 October, 1905, vol. 89, pp. 409–10.
7 Harold Clunn, *London Rebuilt 1897–1927*, London, 1927, p. 62.
8 Harold Clunn, *The Face of London*, London, 1932, pp. 98–104.
9 *Times*, 23 February, 1899, p. 11.

NOTES

10 Percy Johnson-Marshall, *Rebuilding Cities*, Edinburgh, 1966, p. 19.
11 Chris Waters, *British Socialists and the Politics of Popular Culture*, Stanford, Calif., 1990, p. 145.
12 *Surveyor*, 1 April, 1904, pp. 423–4.
13 *Builder*, 21 October, 1905, vol. 89, p. 410.
14 According to Clunn, *Rebuilt*, p. 61, the buildings destroyed would have filled Hyde Park.
15 Only Col Rotton, a Moderate stalwart, raised the question of bias when Gomme's promotion to the Clerkship was debated: *Times*, 31 October, 1900, p. 10.
16 Max Beerbohm, "The Naming of Streets," *The Pall Mall Magazine*, 1902, vol. 26, p. 144.
17 London County Council, *Opening of Kingsway and Aldwych By His Majesty the King, Accompanied by Her Majesty the Queen*, London, 1905, p. 20; *Times*, 11 February, 1903, p. 10.
18 Benny Green, *The Streets of London*, London, 1983, p. 69, calls Kingsway "one of the most boring streets in Central London." Donald Olsen, "Victorian London: Specialization, Segregation, and Privacy," *Victorian Studies*, 1974, vol. 17, p. 265, writes, "it is not for Kingsway or the Senate House or the Post Office Tower that we love London."
19 See the discussion following an address by Paul Waterhouse, "Some Observations on the Report of the Royal Commission on London Traffic," *Journal of the Royal Institute of British Architects*, 1906, vol. 13, p. 420.
20 Donald Olsen, *The City as a Work of Art*, New Haven, Conn., 1986, p. 189.
21 ibid., pp 424–5.
22 Green, *Streets*, p. 67.

BIBLIOGRAPHY

CONTEMPORARY SOURCES

Manuscripts

Babbage Papers, British Library
Gladstone Papers, British Library
Place Papers, British Library
Victoria Park Papers, GLC History Library

Official papers and government publications

Parliamentary papers and reports

Hansard, Parliamentary Debates
Select Committee (S.C.) on Cold Bath Fields (1833), 13.
S.C. on the Petition of F. Young and Others (1833), 13.
S.C. on the Police of the Metropolis (1834), 16.
S.C. on Criminal and Destitute Juveniles (1852), 7.
S.C. on Metropolitan Communications (1854-5), 10.
S.C. on the Sale of Beer (1854-5), 1st Report, 10.
Royal Commission (R.C.) on Penal Servitude (1863), 21.
S.C. on Turnpike Trusts (1864), 9.
S.C. on Open Spaces (1865), 8.
S.C. on London (City) Traffic Regulation Bill (1866), 12.
S.C. on Theatrical Licenses and Regulations (1866), 16.
S.C. (House of Lords) on Traffic Regulation (Metropolis) Bill (1867), 11.
S.C. on Municipal Trading (1900), 7.
R.C. on Alien Immigration (1903), 9.
R.C. on London Traffic (1905), 30 (1906), 4.
R.C. on the Duties of the Metropolitan Police (1908), 50, 51.
S.C. on Motor Traffic (1913), 8.
Report of the Metropolitan Police Commissioner (1908), 51.
Report of the Metropolitan Police Commissioner (1914), 54.

BIBLIOGRAPHY

Unpublished government papers: central and local

Metropolitan Police Papers, Public Record Office
Parish of St Marylebone, Vestry Minutes

Printed materials

Books and pamphlets

Acton, W. (1857) *Prostitution: Considered in its Moral, Social and Sanitary Aspects*, London.
[Anon.] (1855) *Yokel's Preceptor*, London.
Ashbee, C.R. (1900) *LCC, Survey of London*, London.
Babbage, C. (1832) *On the Economy of Machinery and Manufacture*, London.
—— (1864) *Passages in the Life of a Philosopher*, London.
Babbage, H. (1915) *Memoirs and Correspondence*, London.
Ballentine, W. (1882) *Some Experiences of a Barrister's Life*, London.
Barnett, H. (1919) *Canon Barnett*, London.
Barnett, S. and H. (1909) *Toward Social Reform*, London.
Barry, J.W. (1899) *Address*, London.
Bass, M. (1864) *Street Music in the Metropolis*, London.
Beavan, A. (1903) *Tube, Train, Tram and Car*, London.
Besant, W. (1903) *As We Are and What We May Be*, London.
Booth, C. (1969) *Life and Labour of the People of London*, New York, Kelly reprint of 1902 edn, 5 vols.
Boys, T.S. (1842) *London As It Is*, London.
Briggs, F. (1866) *Chequer Alley*, London.
Brinkman, A. (1908) *Notes on Rescue Work*, London.
Buchan, W. (1827) *Domestic Medicine*, London.
Burns, J. (1902) *Municipal Socialism*, London.
Byrne, J.C. (1860) *Undercurrents Overlooked*, 2 vols, London.
Campbell, H., Knox, T., and Byrnes, T. (1900) *Darkness at Daylight*, Hartford, Conn.
Cantlie, J. (1885) *Degeneration Among Londoners*, London.
Cavanagh, T. (1893) *Scotland Yard*, London.
Cawston, A. (1893) *A Comprehensive Scheme For Street Improvement in London*, London, 7.
[Cochrane, C.] (1830) *Journal of a Tour made by Senor Juan de Vega through Great Britain and Ireland*, London, 2 vols.
—— (1847) *An Address to the Business-Like Men of Westminster, with a Review of Juan de Vega*, London.
—— (1848) *Speech of Charles Cochrane Esq. at a Public Meeting in Favour of the Employment of the Poor*, London.
—— (1849) *How to Improve the Homes of the People!*, London.
—— (1854) *My Connection With the Sabbath Movement in France in 1853–1854*, London.
Cockrem, F. (1894) *Gawin Kirkham*, London.
Cook, E. and Wedderburn, A. (eds) (1907) *The Works of John Ruskin*, London.
Cook, E. (1902) *Highways and Byways in London*, London.
Cooper, J.F. (1837) *England*, London, 2 vols.
Coote, W. (1916) *The Romance of Philanthropy*, London.

Country Parson (1848) *Authorized Street Preaching Proposed as a Remedy for Our Social Evils*, London.
Dilnot, G. (1929) *Scotland Yard*, London.
Dodd, G. (1856) *The Food of London*, London.
Dolman, F. (1895) *Municipalities At Work*, London.
Doré, A. and Jerrold, W.B. (1872) *London: A Pilgrimage*, London.
Douglas, N. (1916) *London Street Games*, London.
Drummond, H. (1904) *Our Boys*, London.
Edwards, P. (1898) *The History of London Street Improvements*, London.
Evangelical Lay Preachers' Association (c. 1896) *The Lay Preacher's Guide*, London.
Federation of Working Girls' Clubs (1909) *In Peril In The City*, London.
Firth, J. (1886) *The Coal and Wine Dues*, London.
Flexner, A. (1914) *Prostitution in Europe*, New York.
Flower, E. (1880) *The Stones of London*, London.
Foster, L-N. (1875) *Report on the Application of Science and Art: Street Paving and Street Cleansing of the Metropolis*, London.
Freeman, A. (1914) *Boy Life and Labour*, Birmingham.
Froude, J.A. (ed.) (1883) *Letters and Memorials of Jane Welsh Carlyle*, New York, 2 vols.
Glynn, J. (1766) *London and Westminster Improved*, London.
Godwin, G. (1854) *London Shadows*, London.
—— (1859) *Town Swamps and Social Bridges*, London.
Gomme, A. (1894) *Children's Singing Games*, London.
Gomme, G. L. (1888) *The London County Council*, London.
—— (1897) *Lectures on the Principles of Local Government*, London.
—— (1898) *London in the Reign of Victoria, 1837–1898*, London.
—— (1907) *The Governance of London*, London.
—— (1908) *Folklore as an Historical Science*, London.
—— (1910) *Return of Outdoor Memorials in London*, London.
—— (1912) *The Making of London*, Oxford.
—— (1914) *London*, London.
Gordon, H. (1919) *Some Aspects of Metropolitan Road and Rail Transit*, London.
Gordon, W.J. (1890) *How London Lives*, London.
—— (1893) *The Horse-World of London*, London.
Halsbury, Earl of (1911) *The Laws of England*, London, 16, 21, 27.
Hardman, W. (1923) *A Mid Victorian Pepys: Letters and Memoirs*, ed. S.M. Ellis, London.
Haweis, H.R. (1871) *Music and Morals*, London.
Haywood, W. (1866) *Traffic Improvements in the Public Ways of the City of London*, London.
—— (1873) *Report on the Accidents to Horses on Carriageway Pavements*, London.
Health of London Association (1847) *Report*, London.
Higgs M. (1906) *Glimpses Into the Abyss*, London.
Hill, O. (n.d.) *Speech of Miss Octavia Hill at a Meeting for Securing West Wickham Common*.
—— (1970) *Homes of the London Poor*, Cross reprint, London.
Hodder, E. (1886) *The Life and Work of the Seventh Earl of Shaftesbury, K. G.*, 2 vols, London.
—— (1894) *John MacGregor*, London.
Hodges, G.L. (1833) *Narrative of the Expedition to Portugal in 1832*, 2 vols, London.

BIBLIOGRAPHY

Hogg, J. (1837) *London As It Is*, London.
Hollingshead, J. (1862) *Underground London*, London.
—— (1865) *Today, Essays and Miscellanies*, London, 1.
Holmes, T. (1813) *London's Underworld*, London.
Howe, F. (1907) *The British City*, London.
Hueffer [Ford], F.M. (1905) *The Soul of Modern London*, London.
Jephson, H. (1907) *The Sanitary Evolution of London*, London.
Jevons, W.S. (1965) *Methods of Social Reform*, Kelly reprint of 1883 edn, New York.
Johnston, J. (1885) *Parks and Playgrounds for the People*, London.
Kirkham, G. (1890) *The Open-Air Preacher's Handbook*, 2nd edn.
Ladies' Sanitary Association (1881) *Twenty-third Annual Report*, London.
Lamb, C. (1935) *Letters of Charles Lamb*, ed. E.V. Lucas, London.
Loftie, W.J. (1875) *In and Out of London*, London.
London County Council (1905) *Opening of Kingsway and Aldwych by His Majesty the King, Accompanied by Her Majesty the Queen*, London.
London Playing Fields Committee (1891) *First Annual Report*, London.
MacGregor, J. (1854) *Open Air Preaching*, London.
—— (1852) *Shoe-Blacks and Broomers*, London.
—— (1855) *Go Out Quickly*, London.
MacKenzie, A. (1869) *The Parks, Open Spaces and Thoroughfares of London*, London.
Mahaffy, R. and Dodson, G. (1910) *The Law Relating to Motor Cars*, London.
Malvery, O.C. [Mackirdy] (1906) *The Soul Market*, London.
—— (1908) *Thirteen Nights*, London.
—— and Willis, W.N. (1912) *The White Slave Market*, London.
Martineau, H. (1877) *Autobiography*, London.
Marx, K. (1887) *Capital*, tr. S. Moore and E. Aveling, London.
Mayhew, H. (1968) *London Labour and the London Poor*, 4 vols, London, Dover reprint of 1861 edn.
Mayne, R.C. (1862) *Four Years in British Columbia*, London.
Mayne, X. [E. Stevenson] (1908), *The Intersexes*, Rome.
Montague, C. (1904) *Sixty Years in Waifdom*, London.
Moore, H.C. (1902) *Omnibuses and Cabs*, London.
Mulock, D. (1858) *A Woman's Thoughts About Women*, London.
Napier, C. (1836) *An Account of the War in Portugal between Dom Pedro and Dom Miguel*, London, 2 vols.
National Philanthropic Association (1849, 1853) *Reports*, London.
National Philanthropic Association (1859) *Sanatory Progress*, London.
Oliphant, G.H. (1908) *The Law of Horses*, London.
Open Air Mission (1855) *Occasional Papers, 2nd Annual Report*, London.
Paget, F. (1870) *Report on the Economy of Road-Maintenance and Horse-Draught through Steam-Rolling*, London.
Patterson, A. (1912) *Across the Bridges*, London.
Peek, H. (ed.) (1867) *Six Essays in Commons Preservation*, London.
Peel, C.S. (1933) *Life's Enchanted Cup*, London.
Pike, G.H. (1872) *The Romance of the Streets*, London.
—— (1888) *Beneath the Blue Sky*, London.
Proceedings of the Institution of Civil Engineers, vol. 26 (1866), vol. 87 (1886).
Raumer, F. von (1836) *England in 1835*, London, 3 vols.
Reynolds, J.F. (1904) *General Notes on the London Traffic Problem*, London.
Riverside Visitor (1875) *The Great Army of the London Poor*, London.

Robinson, W. (1869) *Gleanings from French Gardens*, London.
—— (1869) *Parks, Promenades and Gardens of Paris*, London.
Rook, C. (1908) *London Side-Lights*, London.
Ruskin, J. (1875) *Fors Clavigera*, in *The Complete Works of John Ruskin*, New York.
—— (1905) *The Queen of the Air*, London.
[Saul,J.] (1881) *The Sins of the Cities of the Plain*, London, 2 vols.
Scott, B. (1894) *State of Iniquity*, New York, repr. 1968.
Sexby, J.J. (1898) *The Municipal Parks, Gardens, and Spaces of London*, London.
Shaw, G.B. (1904) *The Common Sense of Municipal Trading*, London.
—— (1905) *Candida*, Brentano edn, New York.
Shaw-Lefevre, G.J. [Lord Eversley] (1894) *English Commons and Forests*, London.
—— (1910) *Commons, Forests and Footpaths*, London.
Sims, G. (ed.) (1901) *Living London*, London, 2 vols.
Smirke, S. (1834) *Suggestions for the Architectural Improvement of the Western Part of London*, London.
Smith, H. (1910) *From Constable to Commissioner*, London.
Smith, S. (1867) *A Glance at the Commons and Open Spaces Near London*, London.
Stallard, J.H. (1867) *London Pauperism Amongst Jews and Christians*, London.
Steer, M. (1912) *Opals from Sand*, London.
Sterne, L. (1980) *Tristram Shandy*, ed. Anderson, New York, 2 vols.
Stevenson, J. (1879) *Latrine Accommodation for Women in the Metropolis*, London.
Sydney, W.C. (1898) *The Early Days of the Nineteenth Century: 1800–1820*, London, 2 vols.
Taine, H. (1872) *Notes on England*, London.
Taylor, W. (1856) *Seven Years' Street Preaching in San Francisco, California*, New York.
Thomson, J. and Smith, A. (1981) *Street-Life in London*, Harenberg edn, Dortmund.
Timbs, J. (1865) *Walks and Talks about London*, London.
Tomkins, H. (1872) *Report upon the Pavements in Use in the Metropolis*, London.
—— (1874) *The Pavements of London*, London.
Webb, S. (1890) *Socialism in England*, London.
Welch, C. (1896) *Modern History of the City of London*, London.
Wells, H.G. (1902) *Anticipations of the Reaction of Mechanical and Scientific Progress upon Human Life and Thought*, New York.
Westgarth, W. (1886) *Essays in the Street Re-Alignment, Reconstruction, and Sanitation of London*, London.
Whitworth, J. (1845) *The Patent Street-Sweeping Machine*, London.
—— (1847) *On the Advantages and Economy of the Street-Sweeping Machine*, London.
[A Working Man] (1858) *Scenes from My Life*, London.

Newspapers and periodicals

Architectural Record
Blackwood's Edinburgh Magazine
The Builder
The Car
Contemporary Review
Daily Chronicle
Daily Mail
The Engineer

BIBLIOGRAPHY

Engineering
Folk-Lore
Gentleman's Magazine
Household Words
Illustrated London News
The Independent Review
Journal of the Society of Arts
Lancet
Morning Advertiser
Morning Chronicle
Minutes and Proceedings of the Institution of Civil Engineers
Nineteenth Century [and After]
The North Londoner
Once a Week
Pall Mall Magazine
The Pulpit
Observer
Pearson's Magazine
Poor Man's Guardian
Punch
Quarterly Review
Ragged School Union Magazine
Reformatory and Refuge Journal
St James's Magazine
Saturday Review
The Shaftesbury Magazine
Sharpe's London Magazine
The Strand Magazine
Sunday at Home
The Surveyor
The Times
The True Briton

Articles from books and periodicals

Barry, J.W. (1898–9) "The Streets of London," *Journal of the Society of Arts*, 47, 1–21.
Beerbohm, M. (1902) "The Naming of Streets," *Pall Mall Magazine*, 26, 139–44.
Brown, J. (1855) "No Work in the Grave," *The Pulpit*, 68, 19.
David, A.C. (1908) "Innovations in Street Architecture in Paris," *Architectural Record*, 24, 109–28.
Dickens, C. (1859) "Street Minstrelsy," *Household Words*, 19, 577–80.
—— (1866) "The Dangers of the Streets," *All the Year Round*, 15, 154–7.
Dickinson, G.L. (1906) "The Motor Tyranny," *The Independent Review*, 11, 15–22.
Dziewicki, M.H. (1889) "In Praise of London Fog," *The Nineteenth Century*, 26, 1047–55.
Evans, H. (1889) "The London County Council and the Police," *The Contemporary Review*, 55, 445–61.
Gordon, W. (1889) "The Cleansing of London," *Leisure Hour*, 35, 601–4, 676–80.
[H.W.] (1895) "Sunday in East London," *The Sunday at Home*.
Harding, J.G. (1851) "Walks in London," *The True Briton*, 1, 6.

Hearne, R.P. (1912) "The Perils of the Pedestrian," *The Strand Magazine*, 44, 390–6.
Hill, O. (1884) "Colour, Space, and Music of the People," *The Nineteenth Century*, 15, 741–52.
—— (1888) "More Air for London," *Quarterly Review*, 23, 181–8.
Hooper, G. (1890) "Carriage Building and Street Traffic in England and France," *Journal of the Society of Arts*, 38, 460–84.
London Pedestrian, (1855) "Street-Boys: The Contemplative Man's Irritation," *Sharpe's London Magazine*, 7, 339–42.
Low, S. (1902) "The Tangle of London Locomotion," *The Nineteenth Century*, 52, 922–40.
MacGregor, J. (1851) "Shoe-Blacks and Broomers," *Ragged School Union Magazine*, 3, 267–70.
—— (1866) "Ragamuffins," *Leisure Hour*, 15, 455–60.
Maidlow, J. (1867) "The Law of Commons and Open Spaces," in H. Peek (ed.), *Six Essays in Commons Preservation*, London.
Malvery, O.C. (1904–5) "The Heart of Things," *Pearson's Magazine*, 18, 466–76, and 580–9; 19, 40–9, 149–57, 354–65, and 594–602; 20, 100–7, and 205–9.
[Murray, J.F.] (1839) "The Lungs of London," *Blackwood's Edinburgh Magazine*, 46, 212–27.
Rownsley, H.D. (1886) "Footpath Preservation," *The Contemporary Review*, 50, 373–86.
Sala, G. (1874) "Locomotion in London," *The Gentleman's Magazine*, 12, 453–65.
Shaw-Lefevre, G.J. [Lord Eversley] (1899) "London Street Improvements," *Contemporary Review*, 75, 203–17.
Sims, G. (1901) "London Sweet-Hearts," in G. Sims (ed.), *Living London*, London, 2.
Stuart, J. (1889) "The Metropolitan Police," *The Contemporary Review*, 55, 622–36.
Swinton, G. (1903) "London Congestion and Cross-Traffic," *The Nineteenth Century and After*, 53, 821–33.
Turnbull, G. (1909) "Pavements," in W. Besant, *London in the 19th Century*, London.
Waterhouse, P. (1906) "Some Observations on the Report of the Royal Commission on London Traffic," *Journal of the Royal Institute of British Architects*, 13, 373–428.
Woodward, W. (1886) "The Sanitation and Reconstruction of Central London," in W. Westgarth (ed.), *Essays on the Street Re-Alignment, Reconstruction, and Sanitation of London*, London.
[Wynter, A.] (1866) "How our Millions Circulate," *Once a Week*, 2, 234.
Yeo, I.B. (1889) "On Charge of Air," *Nineteenth Century*, 26, 194–207.

SECONDARY SOURCES

Printed materials

Books and pamphlets

Ackerley, J.R. (1968) *My Father and Myself*, London.
Alexander, C., Ishikawa, S., and Dilerstein, M. (1977) *A Pattern Language*, New York.
Alexander, D. (1983) *Retailing in England During the Industrial Revolution*, London.

BIBLIOGRAPHY

Ardener, S. (ed.) (1981) *Women and Space*, London.
Baker, E. and Baker, P.J.N. (1927) *J. Allen Baker*, London.
Bailey, P. (1987) *Leisure and Class in Victorian England*, London.
Bailey, V. (ed.) (1981) *Policing and Punishment in Nineteenth Century Britain*, London.
Barker, F. and Hyde, R. (1982) *London as it Might Have Been*, London.
Barker, T.C. and Robbins, M. (1963) *A History of London Transport*, 2 vols, London.
Bayley, D. (ed.) (1977) *Police and Society*, Beverly Hills, Calif.
Bell, E.M. (1942) *Octavia Hill*, London.
Bennett, A.R. (1924) *London and Londoners in the Eighteen-Fifties and Sixties*, London.
Benson, J. (1983) *The Penny Capitalists*, Dublin.
Benthall, J. and Polhemus, T. (eds.) (1975) *The Body as a Medium of Expression*, London.
Berlin, I. (1958) *Two Concepts of Liberty*, Oxford.
Boucé, P-G. (ed.) (1982) *Sexuality in Eighteenth Century Britain*, Manchester.
Bourne, L. (ed.) (1971) *The Internal Structure of the City*, Toronto.
Bradley, I. (1976) *The Call to Seriousness*, New York.
Briggs, A. (1968) *Victorian Cities*, Harmondsworth.
Brimblecomb, P. (1987) *The Big Smoke*, London.
Bristow, E. (1977) *Vice and Vigilance*, Dublin.
Brunner, C. (1928) *The Problem of Motor Transport*, London.
Buchanan, C.D. (1958) *Mixed Blessings: The Motor in Britain*, London.
Burke, T. (1940) *The Streets of London*, London.
Byrd, M. (1978) *London Transformed*, New Haven, Conn.
Cannadine, D. and Reeder, D. (eds) (1982) *Exploring the Urban Past*, Cambridge.
Cartwright, F. (1977) *A Social History of Medicine*, London.
Chadwick, G. (1961) *The Works of Sir Joseph Paxton*, London.
—— (1966) *The Park and the Town*, London.
Clark, A. (1987) *Women's Silence, Men's Violence*, London.
Clunn, H. (1927) *London Rebuilt 1897–1927*, London.
—— (1932) *The Face of London*, London.
Cobb, G. (1957) *The First Detectives*, London.
Cohen, B. (1980) *Deviant Street Networks*, Lexington, Mass.
Colman, M. (1982) *Continuous Excursions*, London.
Creese, W. (1966) *The Search For Environment*, New Haven, Conn.
Cunningham, H. (1980) *Leisure in the Industrial Revolution*, London.
Cunnington, P. and Lucas, C. (1978) *Charity Costumes*, London.
Darley, G. (1990) *Octavia Hill*, London.
Daunton, M.J. (1983) *House and Home in the Victorian City*, London.
Davis, J. (1988) *Reforming London*, Oxford.
Davis, S. (1986) *Parades and Power*, Philadelphia.
Daws, J.C. (1929) *Report on the Investigation into the Public Cleansing Service*, London.
Donajgrodski, A.P. (ed.) (1977) *Social Control in 19th Century Britain*, Totowa, NJ.
Dorson, R. (1968) *The British Folklorist*, London.
Douglas, M. (1966) *Purity and Danger*, London.
Dyos, H.J. and Wolff, M. (eds) (1973) *The Victorian City*, 2 vols, London.
Ellis, S.M. (ed.) (1923) *A Mid-Victorian Pepys, Letters and Memoirs of William Hardman*, London.

Fairbank, J. (1974) *William and Catherine Booth: God's Soldiers*, London.
Franklyn, J. (1953) *The Cockney*, London.
Fraser, D. and Sutcliffe, A. (eds) (1983) *The Pursuit of Urban History*, London.
Fraser, W.H. (1981) *The Coming of the Mass Market, 1850–1914*, London.
Freedon, M. (1978) *The New Liberalism*, London.
Gardiner, A. (1925) *John Benn and the Progressive Movement*, London.
Gartner, L. (1970) *The Jewish Immigrant in England, 1870–1914*, London.
Gash, N. (1961) *Mr Secretary Peel*, London.
Gatrell, V., Lenman, B., and Parker, G. (eds) (1980) *Crime and the Law: The Social History of Crime in Western Europe since 1500*, London.
Gibbon, G. and Bell, R. (1939) *History of the London County Council 1889–1939*, London.
Golby, J.M. and Purdue, A.W. (1984) *The Civilization of the Crowd*, London.
Goodway, D. (1982) *London Chartism*, Cambridge.
Gray, R. (1978) *A History of London*, London.
Greater London Council (1968) *Surveys of the Use of Open Spaces*, 1, London.
Green, B. (1983) *The Streets of London*, London.
Greenbie, B. (1981) *Spaces: Dimensions of the Human Landscape*, New Haven, Conn.
Hall, R. (1985) *Ask Any Woman*, Bristol.
Harrison, P. (1983) *Inside the Inner City*, Harmondsworth.
Harrison, R. (1965) *Before the Socialists*, London.
Heasman, K. (1962) *Evangelicals in Action*, London.
Hibbs, J. (1968) *The History of British Bus Services*, Newton Abbot.
Hill, W.T. (1956) *Octavia Hill*, London.
Hyman, A. (1982) *Charles Babbage: Pioneer of the Computer*, Oxford.
Jackman, W.T. (1970) *The Development of Transportation in Modern England*, New York.
Jacobs, J. (1961) *The Death and Life of Great American Cities*, New York.
Jealous, E. (n.d.) *On the Beaten Track*, London.
Jeffreys, S. (1985) *The Spinster and Her Enemies: Feminism and Sexuality 1880–1930*, London.
Johnson-Marshall, P. (1966) *Rebuilding Cities*, Edinburgh.
Jones, D. (1982) *Crime, Protest, Community and Police in Nineteenth-Century Britain*, London.
Jones, G.S. (1976) *Outcast London*, Harmondsworth.
Kitto, H.D.F. (1968) *The Greeks*, Harmondsworth.
Lambert, R. (1963) *Sir John Simon*, London.
McKay, J. (1976) *Tramways and Trolleys*, Princeton.
Mackerness, E.D. (1964) *A Social History of English Music*, London.
Marcus, J. (ed.) (1981) *New Feminist Essays on Virginia Woolf*, London.
Markam, V. (1935) *Paxton and the Bachelor Duke*, London.
Mather, F.C. (1980) *Chartism and Society*, London.
Meller, H. (1976) *Leisure and the Changing City, 1870–1914*, London.
Miller, W. (1977) *Cops and Bobbies*, Chicago.
Mishler, Elliot, et al. (eds) (1981) *Social Contexts of Health, Illness and Patient Care*, Cambridge.
Morrison, P. and E. (eds) (1961) *Charles Babbage and His Calculating Engines*, New York.
Moseley, M. (1964) *Irascible Genius: A Life of Charles Babbage, Inventor*, London.
Moylan, J.F. (1929) *Scotland Yard and the Metropolitan Police*, London.
Nevill, R. (1930) *The Gay Victorians*, London.

BIBLIOGRAPHY

Offer, A. (1981) *Property and Politics 1870–1914*, Cambridge.
Olsen, D. (1986) *The City as a Work of Art*, New Haven, Conn.
O'Neill, J. (1985) *Five Bodies*, Ithaca, New York.
Owen, D. (1982) *The Government of Victorian London*, Cambridge, Mass.
Palmer, S.H. (1988) *Police and Protest in England and Ireland*, Cambridge.
Pelling, M. (1978) *Cholera, Fever and English Medicine*, Oxford.
Perkin, H. (1976) *The Age of the Automobile*, London.
—— (1989) *The Rise of Professional Society*, London.
Plowden, S. (1972) *Towns Against Traffic*, London.
Poulsen, C. (1976) *Victoria Park*, London.
Radzinowicz, L. (1948–68) *A History of Criminal Law and its Administration from 1750*, London, 4 vols.
Read, D. (ed.) (1982) *Edwardian England*, London.
Richmond, J. (1983) *Traffic Wardens*, Manchester.
Roberts, R. (1971) *The Classic Slum*, Manchester.
Rolph, C.H. (1980) *London Particulars*, London.
Saint, A. (ed.) (1989) *Politics and the People of London*, London.
Schofield, R. (1970) *Mechanism and Materialism*, Princeton.
Scott, H. (1954) *Scotland Yard*, London.
Sennett, R. (1977) *The Fall of Public Man*, New York.
Sheppard, F. (1958) *Local Government in St. Marylebone, 1688–1835*, London.
—— (1971) *London 1808–1870: The Infernal Wen*, London.
Sherrard, O.A. (1960) *Two Victorian Girls*, London.
Smith, P. (1984) *Policing Victorian London*, Westport, Conn.
Sontag, S. (1978) *Illness as Metaphor*, New York.
Stallybrass, P. and White, A. (1986) *The Politics and Poetics of Transgression*, London.
Stansell, C. (1986) *City of Women: Sex and Class in New York, 1789–1860*, New York.
Stapleton, A. (1924) *London Alleys, Byways and Courts*, London.
Steedman, C. (1984) *Policing the Victorian Community*, London.
Stein, D. (1985) *Ada: A Life and Legacy*, Cambridge, Mass.
Stokes, J. (1989) *In the Nineties*, Chicago.
Stowell, S. (1991) *A Stage of Their Own*, Manchester.
Summerson, J. (1945) *Georgian London*, London.
—— (1973) *John Nash*, Newton Abbot.
—— (1980) *The Life and Work of John Nash, Architect*, Cambridge, Mass.
Sutcliffe, A. (ed.) (1984) *Metropolis 1890–1940*, London.
Thernstrom, S. and Sennett, R. (eds) (1969) *Nineteenth-Century Cities*, New Haven, Conn.
Thompson, F.M.L. (1970) *Victorian England: The Horse-Drawn Society*, London.
—— (1974) *Hampstead: Building a Borough*, London.
Thurston, G. (1967) *The Clerkenwell Riot*, London.
Tillotson, K. (ed.) (1977) *The Letters of Charles Dickens*, Oxford, 4.
Tripp, H.A. (1938) *Road Traffic and its Control*, London, 7.
Turner, B. (1984) *The Body and Society*, Oxford.
Walkowitz, J. (1980) *Prostitution and Victorian Society*, Cambridge.
Waller, P.J. (1983) *Town City and Nation*, Oxford.
Ward, J.T. (1973) *Chartism*, London.
Warren, A. and Goldsmith, F.R. (eds) (1983) *Conservation in Perspective*, London.
Warren, G. (1978) *Vanishing Street Furniture*, Newton Abbot.

Waters, C. (1990) *British Socialists and the Politics of Popular Culture*, Stanford, Calif.
Weeks, J. (1977) *Coming Out*, London.
Weightman, G. and Humphries, S. (1983) *The Making of Modern London*, London.
Welch, C. (1932) *A History of the Worshipful Company of Paviors of the City of London*, London.
Welsh, A. (1971) *The City of Dickens*, Oxford.
White, J. (1986) *The Worst Street in North London*, London.
Wiener, M. (1981) *English Culture and the Decline of the Industrial Spirit*, Cambridge.
Wohl, A. (1977) *The Eternal Slum*, Montreal.
Woolf, V. (1977) *The Pargiters*, ed. M. Leaska, New York.
Wrigley, E.A. (ed.) (1972) *Nineteenth Century Society*, Cambridge.
Young, K. (1975) *Local Politics and the Rise of Party*, Leicester.
Young, K. and Garside, P. (1982) *Metropolitan London*, London.

Articles from books and periodicals

Ardner, S. (1981) "Ground Rules and Social Maps for Women," in S. Ardener (ed.), *Women and Space*, London.
Aspinall, B. (1977) "Glasgow Trams and American Politics, 1894–1914," *Scottish Historical Review*, 56, 64–84.
Bailey, V. (1977) "Salvation Army Riots, the 'Skeleton Army' and Legal Authority in the Provincial Town," in A.P. Donajgrodski (ed.), *Social Control in 19th Century Britain*, Totowa, NJ.
Bartrip, P. (1981) "Public Opinion and Law Enforcement," in V. Bailey (ed.), *Policing and Punishment in Nineteenth Century Britain*, London.
Blumenfeld, H. (1971) "Transportation in the Modern Metropolis," in L. Bourne (ed.), *The Internal Structure of the City*, Toronto.
Davis, J. (1980) "The London Garotting Panic of 1862," in V. Gatrell, B. Lenman, and G. Parker (eds), *Crime and the Law*, London.
—— (1989) "The Progressive Council, 1889–1907," in A. Saint (ed.) *Politics and the People of London*, London.
Davison, G. (1983) "The City as a Natural System," in D. Fraser and A. Sutcliffe (eds), *The Pursuit of Urban History*, London.
Dyos, H. J. (1982) "Great and Greater London," in D. Cannadine and D. Reeder (eds), *Exploring the Urban Past*, Cambridge.
—— (1957) "Urban Transformation," *International Review of Social History*, 2, 259–65.
Falcus, M. (1977) "The Development of Municipal Trading in the 19th Century," *Business History*, 19, 134–61.
Fein, A. (1962) "Victoria Park: Its Origins and History," *East End Papers*, 5, 73–90.
Fraser, D. (1982) "The Edwardian City," in D. Read (ed.), *Edwardian England*, London.
Garside, P. (1984) "West End, East End: London, 1890–1940," in A. Sutcliffe (ed.) *Metropolis 1890–1940*, London.
Gaskell, M. (1980) "Gardens for the Working Class: Victorian Practical Pleasures," *Victorian Studies*, 23, 479–501.
Gatrell, V.A.C and Hadden, T.B. (1972) "Criminal Statistics and Their Interpretation," in E.A. Wrigley (ed.), *Nineteenth Century Society*, Cambridge.

BIBLIOGRAPHY

Gatrell, V.A.C. (1980) "The Decline of Theft and Violence in Victorian and Edwardian England," in V. Gatrell, B. Lenman, and G. Parker (eds), *Crime and the Law*, London.

Himmelfarb, G. (1973) "The Culture of Poverty," in H.J. Dyos and M. Wolff (eds), *The Victorian City*, London, 2 vols.

Jones, D. (1983) "The New Police, Crime and People in England and Wales, 1829–1888," *Transactions of the Royal Historical Society*, 33, 151–68.

Jones, G.S. (1974) "Working-Class Culture and Working-Class Politics in London, 1870–1900," *Journal of Social History*, 7, 460–507.

Kerber, L. (1988) "Separate Spheres, Female Worlds, Women's Place: The Rhetoric of Women's History," *Journal of American History*, 75, 3–39.

Kitto, H.D.F. (1959) "Arnold Wycomb Gomme," *Proceedings of the British Academy*, 45, 335–44.

Landa, L. (1975) "London Observed: The Progress of a Simile," *Philological Quarterly*, 54, pt 1, 275–88.

Lees, L. (1969) "The Pattern of Lower-Class Life: Irish Slum Communities in Nineteenth-Century London," in S. Thernstrom and R. Sennett (eds), *Nineteenth-Century Cities*, New Haven, Conn.

Lowe, P.D. (1983) "Values and Institutions in the History of British Nature Conservation," in A. Warren and F.B. Goldsmith (eds), *Conservation in Perspective*, London.

MacRae, D. (1975) "Body as Social Metaphor," in J. Benthall and T. Polhemus (eds), *The Body as a Medium of Expression*, London.

Malchow, H.L. (1985) "Public Gardens and Social Action in Late Victorian London," *Victorian Studies*, 29, 97–124.

Maxwell, R. (1978) "Henry Mayhew," *Journal of British Studies*, 17, 87–105.

Miller, W. (1975) "Police Authority in London and New York," *Journal of Social History*, 8, 81–101.

Morgan, A.D. (1968) "Some Forms of Undiagnosed Coronary Diseases in Nineteenth Century England," *Medical History*, 12, 344–58.

Olsen, D. (1974) "Victorian London: Specialization, Segregation, and Privacy," *Victorian Studies*, 17, 265–78.

Osherson, S. and Singham, L.A. (1981) "The Machine Metaphor in Medicine," in E. Mishler, et al. (eds), *Social Contexts of Health, Illness and Patient Care*, Cambridge.

Pick, F. (1936) "The Organization of Transport," *Journal of the Royal Society of Arts*, 84, 207–21.

Porter, R. (1982) "Mixed Feelings: the Enlightenment and Sexuality in 18th Century Britain," in P-G. Boucé (ed.), *Sexuality in Eighteenth Century Britain*, Manchester.

Price, J. (1982) "Patterns of Sexual Behaviour in Some 18th Century Novels," in P-G. Boucé (ed.), *Sexuality in Eighteenth Century Britain*, Manchester.

Ranlett, J. (1982) " 'Checking Nature's Desecration': Late Victorian Environmental Organization," *Victorian Studies*, 26, 197–222.

Richardson, R. (1989) "George Godwin of *The Builder*," *Visual Resources*, 6, 121–40.

Riger, S. and Gordon, M. (1981) "The Fear of Rape: A Study in Social Control," *Journal of Social Issues*, 37, 71–91.

Rosenzweig, R. (1984) "The Parks and the People," *Journal of Social History*, 18, 289–95.

Sciama, L. (1981) "The Problem of Privacy in Mediterranean Anthropology," in S. Ardener (ed.), *Women and Space*, London.

Squier, S. (1981) "The Politics of City Space in *The Years*," in J. Marcus (ed.), *New Feminist Essays on Virginia Woolf*, London.

Stansell, C. (1982) "Women, Children, and the Uses of the Streets," *Feminist Studies*, 8, 309–35.

Storch, R. (1977) "Police Control of Street Prostitution in Victorian London," in D. Bayley (ed.), *Police and Society*, Beverly Hills, Calif.

Swaan, A. de (1981) "The Politics of Agoraphobia," *Theory and Society*, 10, 359–85.

Thorne, R. (1987) "George Godwin and Architectural Journalism," *History Today*, 37, 11–17.

Trumback, R. (1977) "London's Sodomites," *Journal of Social History*, 11, 1–33.

Walkowitz, J. (1982) "Jack the Ripper and the Myth of Male Violence," *Feminist Studies*, 8, 542–69.

Weeks, J. (1980) "Inverts, Perverts, and Mary-Annes," *Journal of Homosexuality*, 6, 113–34.

Winter, J. (1989) " 'The Agitator of the Metropolis': Charles Cochrane and Early-Victorian Street Reform," *London Journal*, 14, 29–42.

INDEX

Abercorn Terrace 182–3
Acton 67
Acton, William 183
Adams, Jane 105
Adams, W. B. 169
Agricultural Hall (Islington) 151
Aitchison, George 23
Albany Street 163
Albany Street barracks 113; *see also* prostitution, male
Albert, Prince 28
Alcheler, Jack (despatcher of horses) 119
Aldgate 115
Aldwych *see* Kingsway
Alexandria 137
Algeria 175
Alhambra Theatre (music hall) 68, 113
Alma-Tadema, Lawrence 33
Americanization 32, 65, 212
Ames, Percy 33
Angel, the (Islington) 210
Ashbee, Charles 198
Ashley, A. A. Cooper, Lord *see* Shaftesbury, Lord
Asquith, H. H. 197, 203
Astronomical Society 72; *see also* Babbage, C.
Australia 63, 144
Ayrton, Acton Smee 76

Bank, the 22, 125
Babbage, Charles, analytical and difference engine of 71–2; founds scientific societies 72; and Lucasion Chair of Mathematics (Cambridge) 71; and noise pollution 72–9 ; writes *On the Economy of Machinery and Manufacture* 72–3; opposed by merchants 77; on recycling urban detritus 123; and technocracy 72–3
Baker, Allen 204
Balfour, Arthur James 192, 194
Band of Hope 104
Barber, Harrison Ltd (despatcher of horses) 119
Barker, F., *London as it Might Have Been* 30
Barnardo, Thomas 104
Barnett, Henrietta 155, 161
Barnett, Samuel 155
Barry, John Wolfe 16–17, 25–6, 33; conception of street 205; and electric tramways 18; for restrictions on street use 18, 193–4; wants arterial throughways 190–5
Bass, Michael 75–6
Battersea 105, 192
Battersea Park *see* parks
Bayswater 5, 183, 193
Bazalgette, Joseph 14, 21, 40; builds Embankment 27, 29–30; *see also* Embankment
Bedford, Duke of 128
Bedford Square 159
Beerbohm, Max 32, 212
beggars 73
Belgravia 74, 164
Bellini, Vincenzo 77
Benn, John 191, 200–1, 204–5, 210; *see also* London Municipal Government, Progressives
Benn, Shirley 204
Bentham, Jeremy 200
Berlin 20, 74, 115, 206

INDEX

Berlin, Isaiah, *Two Concepts of Liberty* 9–10
Besant, Walter 77, 188
Bethnal Green 58, 70, 163–4
bicycles 40, 194
Binnie, Alexander 208
Birmingham 123
Bishopsgate 115
Blackfriars 113
Blackfriars Bridge 19, 23–4, 29
Blackheath 158
Black Hole of Calcutta *see* Godwin, George
Bloomsbury 124
Board of Works 29
Bond Street 33
Boer War 195, 212
Booth, Charles 77
Booth, William 149
Borough Road 43
Boston, Mass. 210
Boulogne 132–3
Bow 163
Boys' Brigade 141
Boys, Thomas Shotter 187
Brabazon, Lady (Meath) 155
Brabazon, Lord (Meath) 155
Bradley, Mary Anne 163
brass bands 8, 70, 75, 78
Brassers *see* MacGregor, J.
Brewer Street 146
Briggs, Fredrick 151
Bright, John 102
Brighton Line 34–5
Brill, the (Somers Town) 146
British Association for the Advancement of Science *see* Babbage, C.
British Columbia *see* Mayne, Richard (Admiral)
Brompton 5
Broomer Brigade *see* MacGregor, J.
Brougham, Henry 54
Broughton (Magistrate) 74–5
Brown, James 60
Brown, Joseph 133
Brunel, Isambard Kingdom 72
Brunswick Square 147
Brussels 66
Bryce, James 155
Buccleugh, Duke of 29, 128
Buchan, William, *Domestic Medicine* 3–4, 7
Buckingham, James Silk 128
Buckingham Palace 163
Buckingham Palace Road 182
Builder 24, 155–8, 160, 171, 209
burial grounds, conversion into gardens 153
Burke, Thomas 65, 77
Burns, John 34, 165, 191, 200–2, 204–5, 210; *see also* London Municipal Government, Progressives
bus *see* public transport
Buxton, Edward 146; *see also* Commons Preservation Society
Buxton family 155
Byrne, Julia Clara 182
Byron, Alfred, Lord 72

cab *see* public transport
Cabell, Benjamin Bond 128
Caledonian Market *see* markets
Caledonian Road 147
Campbell-Bannerman, Henry 175
Camberwell 192
Cambridge 137, 167
Camden 5
Canada 33, 137, 144, 204
Canary Warf 215
Cannon Street 5, 19, 23
Cantlie, John, and "urbomorbis" 7
Carlyle, Jane 146, 178
Carlyle, Thomas 73–4, 146, 156, 178
Carpenter, Mary 138
carriageway *see* street
Carvick, Georgiana 53
Carrier Street 130
Cass, Elizabeth 176, 178–9, 183
Cavanagh, Timothy 54–5
Cavendish Square 63
Cawston, Arthur 17–18, 33
Chadwick, Edwin 123, 125–6, 131, 140
Chalmers, Mackenzie 185
Chamberlain, Joseph 17
Champs Elysées 20
Chancery Lane 7
Chandos Street 122
Charing Cross 141, 146, 182
Charing Cross Road 13, 31, 209, 214
Charles Street 124
Charlotte Court 46–7
Charlotte Street 189
Chartism 56–7, 129–30, 141, 150–1, 163, 165

INDEX

Cheapside 19, 22, 33, 41, 119, 125, 169
Chicago 105
Child's Country Holiday Fund 161
cholera 4, 21, 118, 125, 128, 130, 153–4
Christadelphians 151
Christian Evidence Society 151
Christian Socialist Ladies Co-operative Guild 160
choral societies 70
Chubb and Company (locksmiths) 208–9
Church Lane 124, 130
Church of Scotland 137
City of London 5, 23, 128, 192; Corporation 19, 22–4, 47, 122, 199; Commissioners of Sewers 23, 120, 125; Police 6, 43, 47–8
City of London School 197; see also Gomme, G. L.
Clapham Common 159
Clare Market see markets; slum clearance
Clark, Anna 180
Clavel see D'Angeley, E.
Clerkenwell 73, 137, 211
Clunn, Harold 13–14, 24, 31
Cobbett, William 2, 52
Cobden Club 167
Cochrane, Basil 120
Cochrane, Charles 120–35 ; as agitator 120, 125, 127–32; baths and public toilets 126–7, 130; belief in innate goodness 121, 211; candidate for Westminster 129; connects dirt and contagion 120, 125–6; dies (1855) 133; as Don Juan de Vega 121, 129; his "Fit Social State" 134, 136, 144; founds National Philanthropic Association 125–6; and Health of London Association 126, 128; his *Journal of a Tour* 121; method of 125, 136; and the *Poor Man's Guardian* (and Society) 128, 130–1, 133; practical philanthropy of 133–4; recycling waste 122; reform objectives 123, 136; at St Marylebone vestry 121–2, 124; at siege of Oporto 121; and shoe-blacks 140; his soup kitchens 127, 129; street cleaning as training 123–4, 140; technology, use of 122; Trafalgar Square riot (1848) 129–30; and wooden paving 121; see also

National Philanthropic Association; street cleaning; Street Orderly Brigades
Cochrane, Thomas see Dundonald, 10th Earl of
Cockburn, Alexander 43–4
Cohen, Soloman 115, 183; see also Jewish Association for Protection of Girls and Women
Cold Bath Fields 50–1, 55, 60
Collins, William Wilkie 73–4
Cole, Henry 123
commons 153, 158, 167 ; Hampstead Heath 158, 160–2, 167; Wimbledon 158, 168
Commons Preservation Society 158, 160; rationale of 168–9; support from press 158; see also Shaw-Lefevre, George John (Lord Eversley)
commuting 13–14, 117, 177, 194
consumption see tuberculosis
Contagious Diseases Acts 111–12, 183
Cook, Emily 77, 185, 188
Cooper, James Fenimore 48, 77
Coote, William 115, 186; see also National Vigilance Association
Cornhill 26, 125
costermongers see street commerce; Metropolitan Police
Country Parson, A 150–1
Covent Garden see markets
Cowper, William Francis 29
Cromer Street 146–7
Cromwell, Oliver 9
Crystal Palace Exhibition (Great Exhibition, 1851) 19, 28–9, 45–6, 139–40
curb see street
Curwen, John see Tonic Solfa Method

D'Angeley (Cavel), Eva 173–6, 178, 181, 183
D'Angeley (Soubiger), René 173–5
Daily Express 104
Daily Mail 175–6
Darwin, Charles 72
Darwin, Erasmus 72
Daunton, M. J. 68
Davis, Jennifer 62–3
Davis, Susan 11
decentrism (delocalization) 195–7
Denman, G. L. 173–6, 181

INDEX

density *see* urban
Derby, Earl of 27, 57, 79
Devonshire, Duke of 128
Dicey, A. V. 167
Dickens, Charles 8, 45, 73–4, 123, 128, 146, 215
Dickinson, G. Lowes 206
Dilke, Charles 155
Dilnot, George 53
Disraeli, Benjamin 109
Dockers' Strike (1889) 192
Dodd, George, *The Food of London* 110
Dom Pedro, and the siege of Oporto 121
Douglas, Mary 4
Drummond, Henry 141
drunks 59, 101
Drury Lane 19
Dundonald, 10th Earl of 120–1, 129; *see also* Cochrane, Charles
Durham, Bishop of 128
Dziewicki, Michael 65, 77

Eaton Square 76
Edgware Place 149
Edgware Road 4, 77, 150–1
Edward VII 166, 174, 208
Elcho, Lord (Earl of Wemyss) 141
Electric Telegraph Company 142
Elephant and Castle 16
Ellis, Havelock 111
Elizabeth II 166
Embankment 15, 21–2, 26, 210, 214; Cleopatra's Needle on 30; construction of 28–9; destitute on 30; shortcomings as promenade 29–31; trees on 159; *see also* Bazalgette, Joseph; Paxton, Charles
Emerson, Ralph Waldo 155
Empire Music Hall 113
Endell Street 127
Engineer 36
Engineering 193, 205
Entente Cordiale 212
Epping Forest 23, 158, 160, 167, 169
Euston Square 159
Euston Station 5
evangelical awakening 135, 146
Evelyn, John, *Fumifugium* 7
Evening Standard 215
Eversley, Lord *see* Shaw-Lefevre, G. J.

Fabian Society 68–9, 191, 197, 200, 211, 214
Farr, William 119, 126
Farringdon Street 23–4
Fawcett, Henry 155, 161
Fawcett, Millicent 186
Federation of Working Girls' Clubs 188
Fermoy, Lord 76
Finchley 160
Finsbury 158
Finsbury Park *see* parks
Field Lane Ragged School 137, 139–40, 142, 145; *see also* MacGregor, John; Salisbury, Lord
Fielden, John 128
Fitzmaurice, C. M. 208
Fleet River 24
Fleet Street 7–8, 16, 19, 22, 26–7, 32, 36, 41, 68, 182, 188, 206
Flexner, Abraham 112
Folk-Lore Society 198; *see also* Gomme, Alice; Gomme, G. L.
footpath (footway, pavement, sidewalk), *see* street
Ford, Ford Maddox *see* Hueffer, Ford Maddox
Forster's (Education) Act (1870) 139
Fourier, Charles 72
Fowler, John 193
Freeman, Arnold 69
Fulham 192
Fulham Road 105
furious driving 43, 46

Gallon, Tom 33
Garden City Movement 197
Garrick Street 40
garotting: Act (1863) 62; panic 61–3
Gate Street 215
Gavin, Hector 125–6, 128
Gay, John 37
Gentleman's Committee of the Jewish Association for the Protection of Girls and Women 115
George IV 21, 27, 163
Gerothwohl, Maurice 174
Gibson, John 166
Gissing, George 77
Gladstone, Herbert 175
Gladstone, William 26, 35, 47, 68, 76, 167–8
Glasgow 129, 201–2

254

INDEX

Globe Theatre 214
Glover, Sarah Ann *see* Tonic Solfa method
Glynn, John 3, 22
Godwin, George 155–6, 160; appreciation for urban values 159–60, 169, 171; on Black Hole of Calcutta 157; edits *Builder* 156–8; on effects of urban density 156–9; on rational recreation 158–9; on social amelioration through architecture 157–8; suggests circular boulevard 159
Gomme, Alice Berthe Merck 198; writes *Children's Singing Games* 170; on street children 170–1
Gomme, Arnold W. 199
Gomme, G. L. 32–3, 191–2, 205, 211–12, 215; background of 197; favors organization over competition 199, 204; and Folk-Lore Society 198; as historian 197–9, 212; and Kingsway opening 209; follower of J. S. Mill 200–1; naming Kingsway and Aldwych 213; on traffic police 48; wants transit co-ordination 195–6, 204–5
Gordon Square 159
Grafton, Duke of 128
Gray's Inn 116
Gray's Inn Lane 116
Gray's Inn Road 127
Great Exhibition *see* Crystal Palace Exhibition
Great George Street 35
Great Stink of 1858 26–7
Great Tichbourne Street 105
Great War *see* World Wars, 1914–18
Great Windmill Street 124
Greater London Council *see* London municipal government
Green Arbour Court 180
Green Park *see* parks
Gregson, William 54
griddlers (glee singers) 78
Grosvenor, Lord Robert 128
Guardian 16, 31
Gulf Islands (British Columbia) *see* Mayne, Richard (Admiral)
gutter *see* street

Hackney 5, 159, 163–4
Hackney Road 63

Hall, Ellen and Emily 179
Hamilton, James 132
Hammersmith 120
Hampstead Heath *see* commons; *see also* Commons Preservation Society
Hanover Square 124
harassment of women *see* women
Hardman, William 24, 78
Hardy, Gathorne 109–10
Hare, Augustus 77
Harrison, Frederic 204, 207; *see also* positivism
Harvard University 141
Harvey, Daniel Whittle 6
Harvey, William 1
Hatton Garden 22, 25, 158
Haussmann, Georges-Eugene, Baron 14, 17, 28
Haweis, Hugh Reginald 70
Haymarket, as prostitution centre 115
Haynes, Eliza 149–51 *see also* Salvation Army
Haywood, William 16–7, 21–6, 33–4, 192–3, 209, 211; and accidents to horses 119; collects traffic statistics 21, 46; on London litter 119; promotes asphalt paving 23, 39; for regulation of streets 42; sanitary reforms of 47, 119, 126; on street orderly system 122, 125; lays sub-surface pipes 40; *see also* Holborn Viaduct
Heasman, Kathleen 135
Health of London Association *see* Cochrane, C.
Health of Towns Association 128
Heath, George 147–8
Henderson, Edmund (Metropolitan Police Commissioner) 48, 55–6, 111–12, 148, 150
Henry, Edward 204
Herschel, John 71
Herschel, William 71
Highgate 160
High Holborn *see* Holborn
Hill, Miranda 155, 162
Hill, Octavia 155–6, 170–1; anti-urban bias of 160–2; background of 160; as housing reformer 161–2, 211; and National Trust 161; on need for natural beauty 160–2; and open space preservation 160–1; teaches children to play 162

INDEX

Hill, Rowland 138
Himmelfarb, Gertrude 101–2
Hobbes, Thomas 10
Hodder, Edwin 139
Holborn 5, 19, 22, 178–9, 207–8, 213–14; Board of Works 116–17
Holborn Valley 22, 27, 139
Holborn Viaduct 22–6, 31, 40, 209, 214; *see also* Haywood, W.
Hollingshead, John 40, 45–7, 61
Hollis Street 147
Holloway 47
Holmes, Thomas 30, 77
Holy Land 137
Holywell Street 66, 214
Home Office 22, 35, 43, 47, 50–3, 56–7, 63, 76–7, 109, 113, 115, 129, 175, 185
Hopkins, Ellis, White Cross Army and White Cross League 186
Hopkins, Tighe 33
horses 7, 37, 39, 43, 45, 47, 118–19, 194, 203; accidents to 38, 119; population 118–19, 203
Howard Association *see* Holmes, Thomas
Howard, Ebenezar 197
Howe, Frederick 201–2
Hoxton Hall (Hackney High Road) 105
Hueffer (Ford), Ford Maddox 14, 77, 188
Hughes' Fields 159
Humbolt, Alexander 72
Hunt, Henry 52
Hunt, William Holman 73–4
Hunter, Robert 155, 168; *see also* Commons Preservation Society
Hyde Park *see* parks
Hyde Park riot (1866) 57
Hyde, Ralph, *London as it Might Have Been* 30
Hyndman, H. M. 165

Ilford 24
Illustrated London News 5, 13
India 104
Ingram, F. Winnington 165
Institution of Civil Engineers 34
Ireland 52, 54, 137, 168
Ireton, Henry 9
Irish constabulary 54
Irish potato famine 107

Islington 5, 151, 177, 210

Jack the Ripper 181
Jacobs, Jane 187–8
James I 213
Jennings, George 127
Jesus Lane Sunday School 137
Jevons, William Stanley 69–70
Johnson, Dr S. 2–3
Jones, Ernest 130
juvenile delinquency 139–40, 143–4

Kelly, Fitzroy 128
Kennington 194
Kensington 179
Kensington Gardens 158
Kensington Palace 21
Kenwood House 160
King's Cross 110, 148, 215
Kingsway 13, 207–8, 210, 213–15; construction of 209; criticism of 209, 211–13; opening ceremony 208–9, 21; *see also* Gomme, G. L.; Shaw-Lefevre, G. J.
Kinnaird, Lord 146
Kirkham, Gawin 146
Knight, John Peake 34–5, 41, 48
Knightsbridge 5
Kyrle Society 162

Labouchere Amendment 114
Ladbroke Grove 183
Ladies' Sanitary Association 127
laissez-faire: police policy of 49, 63–4, 74–7, 111; *see also* Metropolitan Police
Lamb, Charles 8
Lambeth Road 105
Lancet 128
Laplace, Pierre Simon 72
Lawrence, Alderman 47
Leicester Square 126–7
leisure *see* recreation
Leisure Hour 138
Lett's Wharf 179
Levellers 9
Lewis, George 174
Leybourn, George 71
liberalism 18, 191, 199, 200, 206, 211, 214; and street reform 10–12, 15, 17, 32, 40–1, 79, 144, 167
Liberal party 31, 167–8, 175, 191, 194, 204

INDEX

Lincoln's Inn 139
Lincoln's Inn Fields 159
Loftie, W. J. 2
London: definition of 4–5, 14, 19, 33, 154, 191, 195–7, 199
London, Bishop of 146, 151
London Bridge 19, 46
London, City of see City of London
London General Omnibus Company see public transport
London, Lord Mayor of 24, 27, 47, 128
London municipal government 14–15, 20; Greater London Council 196; London County Council 18, 167–8, 192, 195–6, 198, 202–5, 207–11, 21; Metropolitan Board of Works 14, 26, 31, 120, 197, 207; Metropolitan Commissioners of Sewers 130; Moderates 191, 196, 209; Progressives 168, 191, 196–7, 199, 201, 204, 207, 209, 211–12; see also municipal
London School of Economics 200
London Wall 25
Lord's Day Observance Society 133
Lovelace, Ada 72
Lowe, Robert 168
Ludgate Circus 22
Ludgate Hill 22, 41
Lushington, Charles 129
Lyons Inn 214

MacAdam, John Loudon 36; see also paving
Macaulay, William 140
MacDonald, John 206
MacGregor, John (Rob Roy) 150; adventures as "Rob Roy" 137; advice for street preachers 145–6; background of 136–7; his Brassers 143; Broomer Brigade 143; changes image of street preachers 145–6; on education for street children 137–9, 144; forms Shoe-Black Brigade (and Society) 136, 139–42, 145–6; 143–4; founds Open Air Mission 136, 145–6; and juvenile delinquency 139–41, 143–4; on nature of street children 138–9; and practical philanthropy 139, 144; and Prevention and Reformatory School Society 137; starts Reformatory and Refuge Union (and *Journal*); his Steppers 143; supports volunteer movement 141; system for shoe-blacks 136, 140–6; system for street preaching 145–7, 151; and uniforms 141–3; writes *Go Out Quickly* 147; writes *Rob Roy on the Jordan* 137
MacKay, Inspector 174
McKenna, Reginald 114
Mackenzie, Alexander 170
MacKirdy, Archibald 105
Madrid 153
Maguire, John Francis 76
Malvery (MacKirdy), Olive Christian 180, 182; background of 104–5; as costermonger 105–7; on costermonger culture 105–7; outlook of 107; writes *The Soul Market* 103–4
Manchester 123
Manchester, Duke of 146
Manchester Square 72, 77
Mann, Tom 165
Manners, Lord John 27, 128
Mansion House 16, 146
markets 177, 215; Caledonian 101, 106, 119; Clare 159, 207; Covent Garden 40, 105, 110, 127, 146, 189, 208; New Cut 105, 113; Petticoat Lane 68; Smithfield 23, 58, 101
Marrable, Frederick 24
Martineau, Harriet 72
Marx, Karl, and the *lumpenproletariat* 102; and Charles Babbage 73
Marylebone 5, 121, 131–2, 161–2
Marylebone Theatre 149
Matson, Catherine 113
Maxwell, Richard, comments on Mayhew 102; see also Mayhew, H.
Mayfair 22, 179
Mayhew, Henry 67, 78, 118, 179–80; author of "The Wandering Minstrel" 121; on costermongers 101–3, 106, 107–8: criticism of 101–2; on recycling urban detritus 123; supports Street Orderly Brigades 122–3, 133; as urban sociologist 101–2
Mayne, Edward 53
Mayne, Richard, Commissioner of the Metropolitan Police 13, 35–6, 43, 45–8, 51–64; background of 53–4; before R.C. on Penal

Servitude (1863) 62–3; before S.C. on Cold Bath Fields (1833) 51–2; before S.C. on Metropolitan Police (1834) 56, 58, 60–1; before S.C. on Metropolitan Traffic (1866) 46–7; before S.C. on Petition of F. Young (1833) 51–2; belief in a criminal class 61–4; his community relations policy 46–8, 55, 57, 59; concern about public relations 46–8, 55, 57, 59; personality of 54–5; and plainclothes police 55–6; policy on prostitution 111–12; policy on street preaching 146, 148–9, 152; and street music 74–7; on street workers 108–9, 117
Mayne, Richard (Admiral) 54
Mayne, Robert 54
Melbourne, Lord 50–2, 57
Mechanics Magazine 137
Metropolitan Police 5, 11–12, 41–3, 50–64, 141, 148–50, 181; authority over 52–3, 56–7, 204; charges of corruption against 55, 112–15; and community relations 48, 50, 57–60; as constabulary 52–4, 60; and costermongers 59, 108–9; crime prevention policy of 53–4, 57; formation of 50–3; guidelines 52–3; and male prostitutes 113–14; misbehavior of 50–2, 54–5, 59; as part of street culture 11, 59–60, 115–17; regulation of prostitution 111–15, 173–4, 178–9; regulation of traffic 42–9, 204; riot tactics of 57; and R.C. on Police Duties (1908) 112–13, 175, 183–4 ; uniforms for 55–6; working-class attitude towards 55–60; *see also* Rowan, C.; Mayne, R.; Peel, R.; S.C. on Metropolitan Police (1834)
miasmal theory of contagion 125–6, 133, 153–4
Midland Railway 34, 151
Mile End Gate 147
Mile End Road 148, 164, 188
Mill, John Stuart 73–4, 155, 168, 200; *see also* Gomme, G. L.
Millais, John 73–4
Millbank 211
Moderates *see* London municipal government
monkey walks 68, 188

Montagu, John, Lord Montagu of Beaulieu 9, 205–6
Monument Yard 110
Moody, Dwight L. 148
Moore, George 146
More, Hannah 136–7
Morning Chronicle 101
Morris, William 165, 171, 198
Mount-Temple, Lord 155
Motor Traction Company 194
motor vehicles 9, 68, 190, 194–6, 205–6: effect on cleanliness of streets 120, 144
municipal: idea 17, 168, 191–2, 196, 198–200, 205, 207, 212–14; reform 17; socialism *see* socialism; trading (enterprise) 168, 196, 201–2
Murray, John Fisher 153–4, 169
music hall 68, 71, 116
Myddleton, John 151

Naples 77
Napoleon, Louis 132–3
Nash, John 28; designs Regent Street and Park 18, 20–1, 30, 209; and J. Pennethorne 163–4
national efficiency 21, 110, 201
National Philanthropic Association *see* Cochrane, C.
National Trust 161
National Union of the Working Classes 50–2
National Vigilance Association 115, 186
Navarino, battle of 121
Nevskii Prospekt 29
Newgate Street 22, 25
New Cut *see* markets
New Oxford Street 19, 21–2, 210
New Road 5
New York 20, 138, 143, 210, 212
Newton, Justice 176
Noel, Baptist 137
Normanby, Lord 128
Northumberland Avenue 68
Notting Hill 67
Nottingham 34

Observer 132
Off Alley 141–2
Olympic Theatre 214
Omega Hall 149
Oliphant, Laurence 146

INDEX

Once a Week 29
Open Air Mission 145–8, 150; and the police 147–50; terms of membership 146
open space: as antidote or supplement to urban life 155–6, 158, 168–9; organic metaphors and 153–5; preservation of 155, 166–9; *see also* Commons Preservation Society; preservationism
Opera Comique 214
Owen, David 23, 31
Oxford Circus 113, 124
Oxford Street 19, 77, 121–2, 124, 180–1, 196

Paddington 113, 127
Page, Horace 173, 175, 178
Palace Yard 35
Pall Mall 61
Pall Mall Magazine 32
Palmerston, Lord 22, 27, 29, 31, 118; defines dirt 118
Paris 14, 17, 19–20, 26, 45, 47–8, 66, 111, 129, 133, 139, 175, 189, 205, 213
Park, Justice 54
Parker Street 215
Park Lane 41, 198
Park Village 165
parks 153, 155–6, 158, 165–6, 169–70, 177; Battersea 158–9, 165; Finsbury 155, 159, 162; Green 158; Hyde 45; people's 66, 153, 155–6, plate 16; Regent's 19, 149, 158–9, 163; St James's 113, 158, 163; Victoria 153, 156, 158–9, 162–6, 171, 189
Parliament 16, 19, 26–7, 29, 35, 43, 51, 75, 77, 154, 159, 163, 167–8, 179, 185, 190, 202, 208, 210, 214
Parnell, Charles S. 174
Patterson, Alexander 68
paving 34, 38; asphalt 23, 37–9; granite sets 23, 36–8; Guernsey pebbles 37; macadam 36–8, 120–1, 131; parish responsibilities for 38–9; as politics 36; Purbeck blocks 37; wood block 23, 38–9, 121–2
Paxton, Joseph 22, 31, 33; his Crystal Palace 27, 30; death of 29; promotes Embankment 28–9; suggests Great Victoria Way 28
Peacock, George 71

Pearson, Arthur 104
Peckham 159, 192
pedestrian(s) 36–7, 100–1, 158, 194, 203–6; crossings 44; rights of 11, 44; wheeled traffic and 11
Peel, Mrs. C. S. 182
Peel, Robert 42, 50, 52–4, 56, 58, 60
Pennethorne, James 18–19, 156, 163, 169, 207; background of 163; builds New Oxford Street 19, 21, 210; on culture and class 164–6; designs Battersea Park 165; and Embankment 29; and Victoria Park 163–6, 171; *see also* parks; Nash, J.
penny gaffs 111
people's parks *see* parks
Peto, Morton 17, 146
Petticoat Lane *see* markets
Piccadilly 33, 113, 115
Pigott, Richard 174
Pike, Godfrey 148
Pilkington, Hugh 61–2
pimps *see* prostitution
Pite, Beresford 213–14
Place, Francis 66–7
plethora concept 4, 6
Plowden, Stephen 195
Police Act (1839) 42–5, 74, 108; and costermongers 43, 108; and prostitution 184; and musicians 74; *see also* street legislation; Metropolitan Police
pollution, air 7–8, 153–4, 157–8
Poor Man's Guardian see Cochrane, C.
Poor Man's Guardian Society *see* Cochrane, C.
Popay, William 51–2, 55; *see also* National Union of the Working Classes; S.C. on Young Petition (1833)
popular culture 66–75, 164–6
pornography 66–7
Portland Place 120
Portman Square 131
positivism 207; *see also* Harrison, F.
Post Office 5, 40
Poulsen, Charles 164
Poultry, the 19
Pound, John 203
preservationism 32, 155, 158, 212; *see also* Commons Preservation Society; Shaw-Lefevre, G.

Prevention and Reformatory School Society *see* MacGregor, J.
Primrose Hill 154
Prince Regent *see* George IV
prostitution 10, 101, 110, 178, 213; alleged decline of 115; definition of 113–14; institutionalization of 111–13; male 113–15; pimps and 111, 114; police and 59, 111–13, 173–4, 183–4; White Slave Traffic 104, 181, 186; *see also* Contagious Diseases Acts
public transport 4, 13, 22, 39, 181, 200–1; cabs and cabbies 48–9, 55, 59, 178, 193–4, 200–1, 203–4; commuter trains 192–3, 195, 204; horse 39–41, 43–4, 192–3; London General Omnibus Co. 41, 203; LCC and 195–6, 199, 201–5; motor 193–4, 201–6; omnibus (bus) 16, 20, 49, 68, 177–8, 185, 204; railway 14, 190, 215; tramway 15, 191, 200–4 (horse 41, 202; electric 190, 192–4, 196, 201–2, 205–6; under Kingsway 208, 210–11, 213); underground 192–3, 195; tube 192, 204
Puget Sound 54
Punch 16, 130, 137
purity crusaders 12, 186
Putney debates 9

Queen Victoria Street 16, 22

Radnor, Lord 146
Ragged School Union 137, 139, 142, 146
Ragged schools 137–8; *see also* Shaftesbury, Lord
Randall (gardener) 20
Ranelagh Gardens 69
Ratcliffe Highway 33, 158
Reading 167
recreation 20, 65–79, 158, 162–3, 165–6, 168–9
Red Lion Square 159
Reformatory and Refuge Union (and *Journal*) *see* MacGregor, J.
Regent (Regent's) Street 12, 18–19, 48, 55, 68, 124, 163, 173, 175, 178–9, 209, 212, 214
Regent (Regent's) Park *see* parks
Rennie, John 27
Reynolds, George 130

Ringstrasse 14, 20
Roberts, Robert 67, 77, 187
Robinson, William 170
Rolph, C. H. 125
Rome 153
Rook, Clarence 77, 180–1
Roosevelt, Theodore 105
Rosebery, Lord 167
Rossini, Gioachino Antonio 77–8
Rotton Row 188
Rotterdam 139
Rowan, Charles, Metropolitan Police Commissioner 12, 43, 51, 53, 55, 60, 64, 146
Rownsley, Hardwick 155, 169
Royal College of Music 104
R.C. on Alien Immigration (1903) 107
R.C. on Metropolitan Traffic (1905) *see* traffic
R.C. on Penal Servitude (1863) 62
R.C. on Police Duties (1908) *see* Metropolitan Police
Royal Exchange 125
Royal Society of Literature 33
Rue de la Paix 26
rules of the road *see* traffic
Ruskin, John 155; music as moral instruction 70; and Octavia Hill 161
Russell, Lord John 128, 167
Russell Square 159, 193
Rutland, Duchess of 27
Rutzen, Albert de 184–5

Saffron Hill 74
St Giles *see* slum clearance
St James's, parish of 35, 125–6
St Martin-in-the-Fields 124
St Marylebone *see* Marylebone
St Mary-le-Bow 120
St Pancras, parish of 124
St Paul's Cathedral 21
St Paul's Church 127
St Paul's Churchyard 5
Sala, George Augustus 31, 33
Salford 67
Salisbury, Lord 191–2, 200
Salvation Army 105, 149
Sankey, Ira 148
Saturday Review 14, 20, 74
Sawdays, C. B. 151
Scotland Yard *see* Metropolitan Police
Scottish Automobile Club 206
Seine 20

INDEX

Select Committees: on Cold Bath Fields (1833) *see* Cold Bath Fields; on Criminal and Destitute Juveniles (1852) 140–2; on London (City) Traffic Regulation Bill (1866) 35, 46–7; on Metropolitan Communications (1855) 28; on Metropolitan Police (1834) 50, 56; on Motor Traffic (1913) *see* traffic; on Young Petition (1833) 50–1
semaphore *see* traffic, signal
separate spheres *see* women
Settlement, Act of 133
Seven Dials 147–8, 158, 208
Sexby, J. J. 164–5
Shaftesbury Avenue 13, 31, 196, 209, 214
Shaftesbury, Lord (Ashley) 128, 137–8; and Field Lane Ragged School 137–8; and Shoe-Black Brigades 139–40; and street children 138–9; on street preaching 145–6
Shaftesbury Magazine 145
Shaw, Albert 17
Shaw, George Bernard 165, 191
Shaw, Norman 209
Shaw-Lefevre, George John (Lord Eversley) 34, 155, 171; background of 166–7; and civic pride 156; and commons preservation 161, 166–8; and Kingsway, Aldwych 207–9, 211, 213; as Liberal politician 167–8; his Locomotives on Highways Bill 194; on municipal enterprise 168; his new liberalism 18, 168–9; his Tramways Bill 168, 202; and women's rights 16; *see also* Commons Preservation Society; Kingsway; municipal trading
Shaw-Lefevre, John George 167
Shelley, John 76
Shepherd's Bush 188
Shoe-Black Brigades *see* MacGregor, J.
shoe-blacks 59, 140, 145
Simon, John 23
Skeleton Army 149
slum clearance 19, 192, 195; in Clare market 207, 210–11; in St Giles rookery 5, 19, 131
Smirke, Sidney 19
Smith, Adolphe 102
Smith, Henry 55
Smith, Sidney 168–9

Smith, Southwood 140, 160
Smithfield market *see* markets
Snow Hill 22, 25
socialism 168, 201, 204; *see also* municipal
social purity movement 112, 186
Society of Arts 16
Society of St Vincent de Paul 140
Soho Square 159
Sontag, Susan 154
soup kitchen 127
South Eastern Railway 35
South Kensington museums 123
Southwark 54, 101
Sparrow, Olivia 146
Spring Gardens, (home of Metropolitan Board of Works, London County Council) *see* London, municipal government
Stallybrass, Peter 102
Stanley, Lord *see* Derby, Earl of
Statistical Society of London 72
Stead, W. T. 186
Stephen, James 136
Stepney 5, 58, 163, 170
Steppers *see* MacGregor, J.
Sterne, Laurence 3
Stevenson, James 127
Stevenson, Robert 193
Strand, the 16, 19, 22, 26–7, 32–3, 68, 207, 212–13
Strand Magazine 32
street: accidents 48–9, 203–4; animals on 46–7, 58, 61, 67, 101; arterial highways 8, 17, 25, 194–6, 207; attraction of to children 138–9, 170; camber of 37; carriageway 100, 119; concepts of "good" 15, 32–3; control of 12–13, 42, 108; culture of 8–9, 11, 65–70, 77–9, 170–1, 214; curb 39, 49, 100–1; dangers in 45–9; definitions of 1–2, 11, 100, 171; differentiation between parts of 37, 100–1; effect on character 68–70, 139, 170; equality in 10–12, 108; freedom of 9–10, 41–2, 44–5, 48, 50, 79, 175; furniture 40, 152; as green space 169–71; gutter 100–1; life 8–9, 14, 58, 65–8, 77, 135–6, 144–5, 171–2; as a locale 11–12, 14, 20, 42, 68, 78–9, 100, 109, 169, 171, 177, 213–16; movement in 20, 39, 79, 169, 176–8; refuges in 39; repairs

261

to 39–40, 49; social meanings of 11–12, 100–1; as source of urban ills 8, 153, 160–2, 170–2; structure of 12; terms of use of 11–12, 43–4, 177–8, 187, 189; verge 100; *see also* other listings under street and individual streets by name
street cleaning 23, 118–34; animals' wastes in 118–19, 121–2; responsibility for 42, 120, 125; and snow removal 119–20; and thaw 119; *see also* Cochrane, C.; Street Orderly Brigades
street commerce 8–9, 10, 59, 100–10, 116–17, 179; and the distribution system 110; increase in amount of 109; *see also* Himmelfarb, G; Maxwell, R.; Mayhew, H.; Malvery, O.; Metropolitan Police
street legislation 42, 100; Highways Act (1835) 42, 148–9; Michael Angelo Taylor's Act (1817) 42, 118; Police Act (1839) *see* Police Act (1839); Metropolitan Streets Act (1867) 45–7, 107–9; Tramways Act (1870) 168
street lighting 11, 65, 181
street music 8, 65, 67–71, 106, 179; Italian and German performers of 73–9; and noise pollution 71; and social harmony 69–71, 78; *see also* Babbage, C.; Bass, M.; popular culture; recreation
Street Orderly Brigades 126; in Boulogne 132–3; foundation of 122, 124; as police auxiliaries 122, 124; projects 124–5; removing stigma from 123–4; resistance from local authorities 124–5; *see also* Cochrane, C; Mayhew, H.
street preaching 145–52; *see also* MacGregor, J.; Metropolitan Police; Mayne, R.,Commissioner of Metropolitan Police
Suez Canal 137
Suffragettes *see* women
Summerson, John 163
Sun 129
Swiss Cottage 160

Taine, Hippolyte 67–8
Tait, Archibald, Archbishop of Canterbury 146, 151

taxi *see* public transport, cab
Telford, Thomas 36
Temple Bar 16, 22
Temple, the 139
Tennyson, Alfred 73–4
Thames 2, 23, 26–9, 65, 192, 207
Thames Embankment *see* Embankment
Theobalds 213
Thompson, F. M. L. 118
Thomson, John: claims photography is objective 103; on recycling urban detritus 103, 123; treats street worker as nomad 102, 107
Thorne, Will 204
Thucydides 199
Thwaites, John 155
Tillett, Ben 165
Times 20, 26, 41–2, 128, 130–2, 190, 197, 206
Tite, William 27
Tivoli gardens 69
toilets, public 126–7
Tonic Solfa method 70
Tottenham Court Road 77
Tower Bridge 191
Tower Hamlets 76
Tower Hill 147
Trafalgar Square 159; riots: (1848) 129–30; (1886, 1887) 152, 192
traffic 6, 29, 31, 33, 48–9, 193; Acts 43, 45–7, 148–9; blockages 16, 19, 21, 26, 39–41, 46, 190–1, 193, 195–6; Board 204; Branch 44, 48; Commission 205; cross 194; effect on economy 16, 19; patterns of 13, 19, 195; Royal Commission on Metropolitan Traffic (1905,1906) 192–4, 203; rules of 42, 44–5, 48; signals 35–6, 41, 48; Select Committee on Motor Traffic (1913) 203–6
tramway *see* public transport
Tramways Act (1870) 168
Trench, Fredrick William 27
Tripp, Alker 44, 206
tube *see* public transport
tuberculosis 3, 8, 154, 157
Twyford Place 215
typhus 118

underground railway *see* public transport

INDEX

Unwin, Raymond 197
Upper Street 177
urban: central nervous system metaphor 191; circulatory and respiratory metaphors 3–8, 10, 13–15, 21, 40, 125, 153–5, 158, 163, 171, 190–1, 196; density 66, 156–8, 171, 177, 187–8; expansion of 2, 4–6, 13–14, 180–1; as metropolis 4–5, 42; patterns of movement 18
utilitarianism 4, 17

vagabonds 10, 101, 114
Vagrancy Acts: (1824) 113–14, 173, 184; (1898) 114
Vauxhall 69
Venice 77
Verdi, Giuseppe 78
Vere Street 124
verge *see* street
Verrey's Restaurant 178
Victoria Park *see* parks
Victoria, Queen 3, 5, 13, 24, 37, 65, 144, 166, 170, 190, 203
Victoria Square 182
Vienna 20, 24, 153
Vigilance Society *see* National Vigilance Association
Vollhardt, Charles 183
Volunteers 63, 141

Waffendale, Z. B. 152
Walter, John 128
Wakley, Thomas 128
Wandsworth 119, 192
Warren, Charles 112
Waterloo Bridge 179
Waters, Chris 211
Webb, Sidney 200–1, 205, 214
Wellington, Duke of 54, 71
Wells, H. G. 14, 196–7, 199
Westbourne Grove 188
Westminster 129
Westminster Abbey 124

Westminster Bridge 29, 35
White, Allen 102
Whitechapel 19, 58, 145, 193; High Street 25
White Cross Army *see* Hopkins, Ellis
White Cross League *see* Hopkins, Ellis
White Slave Traffic *see* prostitution
Whitehall 33, 35, 54, 56
Whitworth, Joseph 123
Wilberforce, Samuel 150
Wilde, Oscar 114
Willson, Beckles 33
Wimbledon Common *see* commons
Winchester, Bishop of 146
women 126–7; attraction of street for girls 188–9; and class 177–9, 187; double standard for 175–6, 186–7, 189; and ethnicity 176, 179; harassment of 176, 178, 180–7; location as determinant of status 179; and mobility 101, 126–7, 177, 179–89; police and 186; provision of public toilets for 126–7; in separate spheres 176–7; sexual assaults on 176, 181, 186; and street employment 143, 179; suffrage 114, 186
Women's Temperance Union of America and Canada 105
Woods and Forests, Commissioners of 31, 163, 210
Woodward, William 127
Woolf, Virginia 182–3
'Working Man, A' 58, 60, 67
Works, First Commissioner of 167
World Wars: (1914–18) 13, 78, 109, 112, 144, 165, 189, 201; (1939–45) 117
Wren, Christopher 28, 210
Wright, Ichabod 167
Wyatt, Matthew and Thomas 27
Wych Street 66, 214

York, Duke of 27

Made in United States
North Haven, CT
15 November 2024